YESTERDAY, TODAY & TOMORROW:
MEETING THE CHALLENGE OF OUR MULTICULTURAL AMERICA & BEYOND

by PAUL D. CHRISTIANSEN, Ph.D.
& MICHELLE YOUNG

Yesterday, Today & Tomorrow:
Meeting the Challenge of Our Multicultural America & Beyond

By Paul D. Christiansen, Ph.D. & Michelle Young

Copyright 1996 by Paul D. Christiansen & Michelle Young

Published by Caddo Gap Press
  3145 Geary Boulevard, Suite 275
  San Francisco, California 94118

ISBN 1-880192-18-7

Price $29.95

Library of Congress Cataloging-in-Publication Data

Christiansen, Paul D., 1941-
    Yesterday, today, and tomorrow : meeting the challenge of our
  multicultural America and beyond / by Paul D. Christiansen and
  Michelle Young.
      p.   cm.
    Includes index.
    ISBN 1-880192-18-7 (alk. paper)
    1. Pluralism (Social sciences)--United States.
  2. Multiculturalism--United States.   I. Young, Michelle.
  II. Title.
  HM276.C519   1996
  305.8'00973--dc20   96-30359
                                                               CIP

CONTENTS

Dedicated
to the People of the World,
Their Cultures,
and the Great Mosaic

PREFACE

Paul D. Christiansen and Michelle Young have taken a bold step in using strategies for their readers that embrace major categories of diversity and cultural understandings. As one reads this book, multiple perspectives unfold which, under normal circumstances, would not be part of the reader's world of understanding diverse cultures. As such, it is one of the few books which attempt to do this without a specific audience (corporate audience, academic audience) in mind. The volume, then, is one that could be consumed by the general public and makes a major contribution of our understanding of all peoples.

First, they recognize and employ the autobiographical channel. It has long been known that autobiographical statements are the most powerful means through which cognition and affective perspectives are communicated. The use in this book of biographical excerpts is extensive yet each is short enough to capture the essence of an individual's identity and world view. Christiansen and Young begin with their own diverse semi-biographies emerging from Binghamton, New York, and Albert Lea, Minnesota. Geography is always part of the biographical framework and, knowing the power of geography, allows the reader to understand how these authors have grasped that significance. The reader becomes embraced by the experiences shared in these biographical statements, which point to the need for universal concepts of humanity.

Second, Christiansen and Young embrace philosophical elements that allow us to discover how an individual develops a belief system about life and how, as an adult, one chooses to function with all people—and especially with people unlike one's self. This philosophical base, in my judgment, becomes the foundation of all readings in diversity. After identifying one's philosophical base, it is much easier to understand the other behaviors, ideas, or suggestions emerging from that individual.

Among the most significant ideas included here are an understanding that cross-cultural communication is essential to a multicultural society, but yet that cross-cultural is not always the same as cross-racial. Prejudice and discrimination are separate entities, but physiological differences (beginning with skin color and hair texture) determine the extent to which one feels victimized by difference from others. This book provides multiple excerpts that allow one to comprehend the power of such distinction. While we recognize that the United States, as a whole, has never adopted or published a "policy on race," it has always functioned on individual (and sometimes geographic) concepts of racial difference, together with the economic and political meanings attached thereto. This volume helps one to understand that the quest for a universal concept of humanity in a multicultural, diverse world is inherently tied to economics, biography, politics, and public images.

The essence of Christiansen and Young's volume indicates that the acknowledgment of **difference** means that subsequent actions will reflect one's level of acknowledgment. There can be unity through diversification, which can lead to the betterment of humanity. America can continually be celebrated because no other country (or continent) deliberately professes to embrace diversity. The bonding of cultures can occur, according to these authors, through nationalism. Once this is embraced, then the music, the dance, the literature, the storytelling, and all the other features of one's humanity can be shared without being negatively evaluated. These authors also help the reader to know that "suspicion of difference" may be a common emotional reaction, but does not have to result in prejudice and discrimination.

The mind is our most powerful tool. Therefore, images are

critical to our understanding of each other. From the movies, to museums, to school curricula, Christiansen and Young have forged a broader concept of the role of the images which shape so much of our thinking. The inclusion of perspectives from numerous profiles, cultures, and experiences provides the reader with the significance of history, the power of color, the perspectives of people of color, and the extent to which military, economic, government, and media decision-making are all involved in transforming America into a universe of compatible humanity. Their writings force us to examine the extent to which our own human qualities are nonviolently developed and/or exposed. America needs such reading at this time.

Depending on the strength of character of each of us, we are all capable of performing acts of hostility. However, the extent to which we distance ourselves from perspectives which motivate prejudice, hostility, and discrimination will determine the extent to which we become part of the problem or part of the solution.

Christiansen and Young indicate, at one point, that we are all either part of the solution or part of the problem—that there is no other place to stand and no fence on which to straddle.

This volume forces one to interact with where one stands and, ultimately, to decide if that position is one which helps to meet the challenge of a multicultural America—and to attempt to go **beyond**. Indeed, this volume is a major contribution to the current concerns about diversity in a society such as ours.

—*James B. Boyer, Professor*
Curriculum & American Ethnic Studies
Kansas State University
and
Former Executive Director
National Association for Multicultural Education

FOREWORD

No two people could be farther apart in backgrounds and beliefs than the two of us. Coming from different areas of the United States, contrasting religious and ethnic backgrounds, and dissimilar traditions and customs, today we live on the same street on opposite ends of the community where we met. One of us lives one-half block east of a major thoroughfare, on the south side of the street; the other lives one-half block west of a major thoroughfare, on the north side of the street.

Our friendship grew out of our common interest in multiculturalism and our need to address discrimination and prejudice. We believe harmony can be achieved through an understanding and appreciation of our diversities.

We met because of this mutual interest. He was a multicultural specialist for a local school district. She frequently writes for multicultural magazines. But even this common belief and friendship hasn't always assured smooth sailing between us. Each of us have wanted to break through prejudice-based barriers, but our approaches have been as opposite as our backgrounds.

Yet, both of us agree in education-based methods for long-term multicultural growth. Education holds the key to understanding and cooperation and has inspired our decision to write this book. We hope you will learn about the diversities and common bonds among our world cultures in these pages, especially as these cultures interact within the borders of the United States of America, feeling a union with each through the most significant bond of all—our humanity.

ACKNOWLEDGMENTS

Our heartfelt thanks to the many, many people who helped us with willing ears, caring hearts, information, criticism, **time**, and vulnerable emotions. From the very beginning of this project, Cathy Fowler believed in us as a team, even when we questioned whether the concept and our combined efforts could be successful. As both friend and editor, Luella Nielsen was always there to guide, criticize, fine-tune, and praise. There were many folks who need to remain anonymous, yet they spoke with both heart and soul, revealing aspects of their own lives, their native lands, and their individual cultures.

Most important to the development of this book and to us as people who love all of the peoples of the world, these anonymous individuals simply trusted us. Dr. James B. Boyer encouraged us with this project and, in the process of his developing the preface for the book, reviewed the finished product with cover-to-cover delight.

Behind the scenes, there remain a wealth of people whose names and stories aren't included in our written efforts, yet they helped in those minute but significant ways that have allowed us to enrich the pages: Ruthanne Arredondo, for instance, a Spanish teacher at Tempe High School in Arizona, who gave us insights into the southwestern celebrations of *Cinco de Maio* and less well-known festivities; Keith Kaminski, of the Metropolitan Detroit Convention & Visitors Bureau, guided us through the marvelous maze of Michigan's people, places, and pleasures; the staff at the Australian Embassy in Los Angeles, who displayed their support of this project by sending us page after page of little-known information about the indigenous peoples of the land down under.

Were we to list every person who helped us to write this book, our list would probably span several pages. With that thought in mind—especially when we recall similar dangers we encountered in Chapter 6, The Africans—we believe the point of these acknowledgments might be lost. To every person who helped—even those who felt their assistance wasn't noteworthy—we thank you for your help. To every person, including all of the world's peoples, we thank you for being you.

ABOUT THE AUTHORS

Paul D. Christiansen

By contemporary educational standards, Dr. Paul D. Christiansen's poor vision—damaged perhaps after a bout with the measles—would have led to his identification as an at-risk student in elementary school. Testing revealed his severely limited vision in first grade, which resulted in difficulty in acquiring good reading skills. In many ways, in overcoming his own barriers, Christiansen has become more sensitive to those faced by others.

As a public school district multicultural specialist from 1989 to 1994, he conceived and supervised the development of *Unity Through Diversity: Multicultural Perspectives for Educators and Community*, a 133-page book which subsequently drew interest from school districts and businesses nationwide.

Christiansen's more than thirty years of professional, multi-culturally-related expertise includes developing, implementing, and evaluating more than fifty educational programs, conducting more than eighty-five courses, workshops, inservice programs, seminars, and conferences, and serving as a consultant to more than eighty superintendents and assistant superintendents and more than forty agencies and companies nationwide.

A former university instructor, Christiansen has also made presentations to more than sixteen boards of education, has served on more than thirty-five local, state, and national committees, and has been an officer in more than twenty professional and community organizations. He has also been the author of several articles, booklets, slide/tape presentations, computer programs, and a variety of books for a Saudi Arabian oil company. A member of the Chautauqua Literary and Scientific Society centennial graduating class, Christiansen's post doctoral university studies were taken at the University of Akron, Kent State University, Tufts University, the University of Phoenix, the University of Ottawa, and Arizona State University.

Thanks to some very special teachers who encouraged him during his early college years and his faith in Jesus Christ, Christiansen became committed to making a difference for others. Despite his many academic achievements, Christiansen believes the encouragement he, in turn, has given others has been his most valuable accomplishment.

Michelle Petitte Young

Michelle Petitte Young has written for multicultural publications since 1988. But multiculturalism influenced her life long before her appearance in *Journey, Visions* and *Career Focus,* three Communications Publishing Group Magazines.

The daughter of an Italian shoemaker and a Russian Jewish concert pianist, Young's St. Patrick's Day birth led her father to declare her, perhaps prophetically, his "Little League of Nations." At home, the Easter bunny and traditional Italian Christmas eve seven-course fish dinners held the same importance as Passover seders and Chanuka celebrations.

By the age of nine, she developed and wrote two versions of *"An Imaginary Musical Tour of Israel"* which she performed for Jewish and non-Jewish organizations and a wide variety of community service groups through much of upstate New York.

At sixteen, Young lived with the Oglala Sioux Indians in Pine Ridge, South Dakota, leading—upon her return home—to her first newspaper column and slide show presentations about life on the reservation.

Young's experience as assistant manager of the Binghamton Symphony Orchestra required extensive media contact and frequent television, radio, and newspaper interviews. She was directly responsible for raising attendance at an outdoor concert of the *1812 Overture* from an anticipated crowd of 3,000 to an actual audience of 25,000.

Young's magazine writing credits include *Phoenix, Seventeen, Police, Dental Economics, Racquet* and over 125 other publications along with a featured monthly column in Dell's *Horoscope*. In 1993 she was editor-in-chief of *Dry Heat USA*, a magazine billed as "the first coed, bilingual, multicultural" publication for teens and young adults. She also served as editor of *Champion*, a newsletter for parents of gifted children, for three years. Young was also editor of *Unity Through Diversity...*, mentioned in Christiansen's biography. Many of her works are housed in a multicultural library which was developed by Christiansen.

During the 1991-92 school year, the Tempe-Union High School District school board adopted Young's proposal for creating community and high school student councils to ease multicultural and racial tensions and gave the proposal a number two position in a fourteen-point, five-year strategic plan.

Born and raised in Binghamton, New York, Young currently lives in Tempe, Arizona, with her Hong Kong-born husband Kwong and their four sons.

INTRODUCTION

Remember when you were a child, and your mother offered you a new food to taste? Perhaps you, like so many of us, exclaimed, "No, I hate that stuff!" And you clamped your mouth shut in your stubborn fear of something new and strange. Similarly, many of us reacted in the same way with some of our parents' friends, burying our faces in our mother's skirts in hopes that the stranger would be gone when we looked again.

Xenophobia isn't synonymous with our childhood years, although we'd often like to pretend that's the case. We're too old to continue hiding from new people, and our fragile egos frequently impel us to act in contrary ways to our intentions. Rather than facing our fears of unknown situations and people, we—like Montressor in Poe's "The Cask of Amontillado"—allow ourselves to imagine insults that may never have happened.

Yesterday, Today & Tomorrow represents our combined effort to create an unthreatening, informal, and intimate forum in which you, the reader, can meet some of the people from several of the world's cultures. Two years of planning and development, research, and writing have been poured into the pages of this labor of love. But how can we ask you to meet these people and learn about their joy and anger, courageous moments, and fears unless we allow you to know us—first Paul Christiansen, then Michelle Young—better? The late Indira Gandhi once said, "You cannot shake hands with a clenched fist." We hope this book will be at least the symbolic beginning of many handshakes for you.

Paul Christiansen

When I think about my geographical place of birth, Albert Lea, Minnesota, then a community with a population of approximately 12,000, I entertain thoughts of coming from a typical American small town in the upper Midwest.

My family and childhood experiences were heavily Scandinavian-based and, more specifically, that of a strong Danish heritage. My paternal grandfather was born in Faaborg, Denmark, my paternal grandmother in a cave in northcentral Iowa. My maternal grandfather was born on a farm near Albert Lea, my maternal grandmother in Roskilde, Denmark.

Most of my early experiences took place within the extended family of my maternal grandparents and the Danish Lutheran Church (UELC). My home was located in an elementary school attendance area that included children from Native American, Mexican, Chinese, and Syrian backgrounds. Even though there were very few in number, I had friends from each of these groups. Not until I reflected on my childhood did I realize I had friends from various minority groups however.

I didn't think about my differences from these groups in negative terms, rather I must have been interested because we had a mutual acceptance and respect for one another and because I was able to expand my experiences as somewhat of an adventurer.

The only experience I had with African American families, however, was with one family. The father, a pleasant person who, in some ways, reminded me of Rochester on the *Jack Benny Show*, worked at a grocery store and made home deliveries. His name was Easter. *The Amos and Andy Show*, first popular on radio, was on television in the 1950s. Thanks to those performances of Rochester and Amos and Andy, I don't recall having negative feelings about African Americans. But I didn't have real personal experiences with African Americans, especially children, until I was about twenty years old.

But determining the degree to which early experiences have an impact on children can be difficult. Research has demonstrated the extreme importance of early childhood in our acquiring attitudes and feelings about people, work, responsibility, reward, punishment, and so on.

My parents, especially my mother, seemed to be accepting of people in general. However I can recall statements my father made of a direct and indirect nature. He'd warn that we needed to be careful about eating at Chinese restaurants for several reasons, including that they liked to eat dogs. We had to be careful about going uptown on Saturday nights during the summer because migrant Mexicans were in town. More subtle statements about the Chippewa Native American tribal dwelling places in Northern Minnesota went something like, "See those shacks over there? That's where the Indians live."

I don't want to be critical of my father, however, because I don't believe his motive was to put others down just for the sake of a putdown. Even more negative statements were made about other Scandinavian groups like the Norwegians and Swedes.

But my parents gave me positive attitudes, too, by their concern for helping others regardless of their cultural backgrounds. One family comes to mind very strongly. In fact, to this day, I still am richly blessed to visit them when I'm in Minnesota. They have an extremely interesting but stressful story to tell about living in Latvia, experiencing the Nazis in the Second World War, and the Russian takeover of their homeland after the War.

I was drawn to school at what I knew to be the only Danish college in the United States. People from over twenty states and several countries attended Dana, a liberal arts college about thirty miles north of Omaha, Nebraska. Living and learning with such a variety of individuals and cultures, I began to realize that mine was not the only background which could be considered American. A Californian of German heritage came to visit my home during a

Thanksgiving recess, and he commented about our food. Several dishes and their preparation methods were foreign to him. His observations surprised me, and I continued to examine myself in relation to other Americans.

In my junior year, I had an opportunity to take Minority Relations, an elective course. This course laid a foundation for my Ph.D. dissertation some thirteen years later.

Since childhood, perhaps because of the difficulties I had encountered as a student, I wanted to become a teacher. I received my first opportunity to teach in a metropolitan school district. Riverview School was located in an African American neighborhood, and about 90 percent of the students—including my fifth graders—were African Americans.

Teaching at Riverview offered many challenges. The teachers—treated like children and required to ask the principal's permission to use the restroom, a point today's teachers may find inconceivable—had to send a student to the principal's office with a note requesting permission. Yet with over nine hundred students at Riverview, sending a student to the office could absorb a great deal of time!

Soon after, I realized that sections of the curriculum were difficult to use. Developed out of a central district office, the curriculum had been prepared for white middle class students. I tried to adapt the curriculum to the students; but this approach was met with disfavor from district supervisors who believed that every fifth grade class in the entire school district should be on the same page on the same day. My assigned supervisors were white and, on one occasion, one told me, "when they start acting like us, we will treat them like us."

How sad to think that children from different socioeconomic backgrounds and cultures might have to acquire more wealth and change their culture before they could gain respect. Motivated to share these and my other experiences at Riverview, I wrote *A Dilemma in the Classroom: Riverview School A Typical American School?* so future children wouldn't suffer because of socioeconomic and cultural differences.

My M.S. and Ph.D. degrees led me to teaching opportunities in a variety of socioeconomic and cultural settings from third grade to graduate school, where I worked with and learned about people from many cultures. Becoming culturally literate doesn't require one to learn everything about every culture. A common bond can be established, using basic principles. People are people. If one demonstrates a sincere desire to understand others' ways and appreciates others for who they are, mutual respect can be achieved.

Michelle Young

When I think of my hometown, Binghamton, New York, ambivalent feelings rush forth. Many close friends still live there, and I miss them, just as I miss crisp autumn mornings, the transformation of summer green hills into rich autumnal blazing glory, and thick, often deep, white winter snows that bring seasonal peace to the Susquehanna Valley of that upstate New York community I left in 1986.

Norman Rockwell would have loved the county's Fourth of July fireworks display. Far from the sensational shows produced by major cities across the nation, ours was a splendid but modest spray of color in the night skies. On every national holiday, just like Rockwell's paintings, proud patriots flew Old Glory from homes on quiet, tree-lined residential streets, and more than a few of us lined Main and Court Streets to watch the Memorial Day and Columbus Day parades pass by our cheering voices and hand-held waving flags.

"Red," the friendly cop on the corner of Main and Front Streets, greeted everyone with a pleasant word or two. And every kid in town knew Walt Morrissey, the poultry shop owner who'd have plenty of live chicks, ducks, and bunnies for us, come Easter time.

Binghamton, one of the Triple Cities, and the even smaller cities surrounding its boundaries had its share of potluck church suppers, firehouse pancake breakfasts, clambakes, turkey raffles, and typical American barbecues with hot dogs and apple pie. But while we enjoyed hot dogs and apple pie at barbecues, Italian *spiedies*, sausage, peppers and onions, Polish *kielbasa,* and other wonderful ethnic dishes found their way to the picnic table.

Amiable relations extended from ethnic group to ethnic group, and as long as everyone remembered their neighborhood's and family's imaginary boundary lines, people mingled with and enjoyed their association with those of other ethnic backgrounds. Mozart, Schubert, Schiller, Goethe, Beethoven, and Handel Streets, all on Binghamton's West Side, helped to delineate the German and Austrian parts of town. Perhaps had Slovak names been less difficult for folks to pronounce, streets in the First Ward might have ended in "ova," rather than being named after trees—Maple, Oak, Elm, and so on. But warm relations did not bridge the gaps in understanding between cultures.

My grandmother, a Russian-born Jewish milliner, tried to understand differences between cultures when my mother was still a child, but perhaps Grandma tried too hard. Liberated seventy-five years before her time, Grandma hired ladies from different ethnic backgrounds to work in her shop. After determining a customer's cultural heritage, Grandma sent out an employee who seemed to fit the ethnic bill. Sadly, Grandma learned her lesson after a Czechoslovakian lady returned to the workroom, fuming because Grandma had sent her to speak with a Yugoslavian.

While some sections of town still retain an almost exclusive ethnic influence, cultural boundaries aren't quite as noticeable today, thanks to companies like Endicott-Johnson. Endicott-Johnson Shoe Corporation (E-J) and Gotham Shoes had both successfully carved their niches into the area by the early 1920s and shared their growth with Binghamton and its sister communities. After the Depression, for instance, E-J built homes for employees in an innovative, perhaps unprecedented show of gratitude for loyalty. These well-built E-J homes, no longer company-connected, drew people away from their ethnic base within the community and into an urban multicultural stew. Today, E-J employees and non-E-J people from every culture live in E-J homes.

As individual neighborhood boundary lines relaxed and people began associating with each other on a day-to-day basis, the quiet segregation of cultures evolved into an undercurrent of hostility, although still quiet, one that only occasionally boiled over into a physical or verbal display. Possibly no different than people from any other section of the country, Binghamtonians with less multicultural tolerance usually held prejudice to disdainful looks or overlooking opportunities for specific cultures or socioeconomic brackets.

The city's heartbeat, individually and as one of the Triple Cities, lies in the economy itself. Although Binghamton and its sister cities represented home to shoe manufacturers, Triple Cities-based major corporations also affected the tone of the area. Thousands of area residents found jobs as IBM, Savin, Singer-Link, Ansco, and General Electric moved operations to Broome County, generating an upswing economy for a while.

But changes at Ansco in the 1960s served as ominous economic warnings to the area, precluding industry cutbacks at General Electric and Singer-Link that proved no better. While none of the three actually closed their offices, certainly the economic tone was negatively affected and perhaps influenced IBM, during the 1970s, to move thousands of Endicott-based employees to Charlotte, North Carolina. After Savin's Johnson City plant closed in the 1980s, Binghamton's economic climate grew even worse. From what I've heard since we left, the area is still reeling from the effects.

The declining economy spurred multicultural tensions into a more open atmosphere. Although I remember crying when I was in kindergarten because my best friend accused me of killing God, and I recall a boy in a wheelchair throwing stones at me at ten because I was a Jew, my experiences with prejudice were so few and far between—or perhaps I was simply that innocent—that I truly didn't become aware of those differences that bred hostilities between people until I reached my teens. I knew the Italians and Irish in town had argued over whose church would merge with whose, but that was no different than the sibling rivalry my brother Jerry and I had then.

I learned quite a bit more about tolerance of other cultures after my mother—a wise and beautiful lady to whom I'm indebted for a rich education that extended far past the limits of my formal schooling—sent me to live with the Oglala Sioux Indians in Pine Ridge, South Dakota, one summer. My experience enriched my narrow world perspective and allowed me to grow while I fell in love with these wonderful Native Americans.

By my teens, I realized that prejudice, not analogous with any particular group of people, knows no age limits. At eighteen, I was living in New York City and was refused an apartment I had already paid to move into and had begun painting, because the landlady, an elderly woman, found out I was a Jew. And after I returned home, where I met my Hong Kong-born husband, I discovered just how insidious prejudice can be.

7

After we moved from a neighborhood where a next door neighbor tried daily to run my husband down as he walked the dog, we found we'd moved next door to a man who thought he was cute for saying he wouldn't borrow sugar from us, that he could borrow rice. Finally, a month before we left Binghamton, my husband lost his job for what witnesses later told us was blatant on-the-job prejudice. My husband had always told me I couldn't fight bigots because I merely gave them more reason to hate. Perhaps I learned the hardest lesson of my life when I realized he was right.

Since our move to Arizona, I've also learned that bigots, coming in all shapes, sizes, professional levels, and ethnic backgrounds, have become sophisticated in their ignorant approach to living in this multicultural world. Living in Arizona hasn't been much easier when it comes to bigotry. Here, multicultural prejudice frequently assumes a mask of socioeconomic prejudice. But prejudice is prejudice, no matter how people try to disguise it, and we no longer live in tiny neighborhoods with individual ethnic boundaries. Living in harmony with the world's wide variety of cultures demands our intercultural tolerance and understanding.

PART I

MOSAIC

Chapter 1

MULTICULTURAL STEW

Analogous to the threads of a magnificent, priceless tapestry, each of our lives intertwine with others, creating bonds with people we've never met and probably will never meet. The tapestry's beauty and value lies in transforming individual threads by weaving them, color by color, into multi-hued splendor. Were we to weave a monochromatic tapestry, its beauty would have to be defined in the weave itself, using many varieties of stitches.

The United States has always represented many of the world's cultures. Like other nations, the Union's astounding population boom has been both external—the result of continuous immigration—and internal. Although the melting pot concept has shifted to a multicultural one—emphasizing the need to respect all people regardless of their cultural backgrounds—Americanization is still taking place and enabling people to be Americans without feeling they have to discard certain aspects of their respective cultures. Even while retaining such differences, we can still share common bonds of being Americans.

By 1992, within the United States alone, 103 ethnic groups comprised the total population of the nation, doubling the numbers of ethnic groups spread from New York City to Los Angeles, from

Seattle to Miami, from Boston to San Diego in the early 1980s. Perhaps these changes frighten many people who have lived within the country's earlier cultural boundaries, because an abundance of misconceptions about the word **multicultural** linger today in the conversations of even the most intelligent and well-educated people.

Modern technological advances are propelling us into a global age in which the world is attaining new political and economic configurations. With rapid telecommunications and transportation, achieving unity is even more essential. But we need to differentiate between unity and unification, developing a keen understanding of their meanings and approaches.

By developing an awareness of and an acceptance for our common bonds of interdependence in our own and other societies, we encourage our own unity-conducive internal changes of attitude, based on respectful interaction and cooperation, resulting in our building a strong foundation for positive relationships. In comparison, force and other external stimuli, the integral units of achieving and maintaining unification, produce tentative unions that often dissolve with like amounts of force, as in the 1992 dissolution of Yugoslavian-Soviet bonds.

In *Megatrends 2000*, John Naisbitt and Patricia Aburdene discuss the concept of global homogenization amidst our maintaining traditional ethnic roots. It is possible to experience nationalism and still retain one's ethnic pride. Yet opponents of multiculturalism say this renewed focus on ethnic groups will merely serve to point out more people looking for sympathy and money to ease the pain from years of prejudice-based denial.

But without exception, every culture has suffered injustice as well as triumphs. We cannot erase history, nor should we. The pain and the joy provide us with a common bond, our humanness. Recognizing and accepting this natural factor in our relationships with any one culture or person, we can move in a positive direction toward our common goal of respecting, cherishing, and developing the unique qualities within each culture or individual.

We call this chapter "Multicultural Stew" because the stories in this section are from or about people whose ethnic backgrounds comprise more than one culture. Whether we call it stew, *ragout*, *cioppino*, or any other melange of vegetables and meat, the message is the same. Being human gives us no right to try making a form of

12

puree from the cultures. Neither tasty nor aesthetically appealing as puree, we proudly move into an appreciation of our ethnic diversity, its joys, and its pain.

Debora Britz
Brazilian and Jewish Cultures
Newspaper Reporter

Life has been treating me reasonably well, I thought as I savored my second tomato juice and struggled to tear open a tiny packet of unsalted peanuts. I was on a Delta airplane—where else can you enjoy this combination?—coming back from a five-day vacation in Acapulco, Mexico.

"Ladies and gentlemen, we'll be landing at Los Angeles International Airport in 17 minutes. Please return to your seats," said a flight attendant as my Italian-born companion returned from the plane's smoking section.

From my window, I could see that L.A. looked like the same old L.A.—mid-September hazy sunshine, puzzling bumper-to-bumper freeways, and intimidating skyscrapers sticking out of the ground. Still, the city had become my adopted home since August 1988, when I left Rio de Janiero for a University of Southern California master's degree, and I was safely back home. Or at least I thought so.

"US Citizens Only," read one of the signs for passport control. Franco and I turned away. A second read, "All Other Nationalities." It sounded like Numero Uno's "Pizza, Pasta, and More," where all foreigners belong to "More."

"*Andiamo di qua,*" said Franco, who pointed to counter number four with its shorter line. He explained to an immigration officer that he was entering the country as a tourist, while I attached my precious I-20 form to my Brazilian passport. This established my legal right to get in and out of United States an unlimited number of times, provided I carried a student visa.

I presented my documents confidently. The same officer now shook her head and told me she would have to call her superior. I was baffled. How could that bored-looking woman find anything suspicious about me, a young white (but happily tanned) female sporting a trendy black-and-white outfit? I speculated she might want to know why I also had a two-year-old Cuban visa. At this point, Franco—who was confirming his return ticket to Italy—thought I had gone to the restroom.

The officer's "superior" was a middle-aged woman whose name I'd rather leave out for the obvious reason that I don't want to mess with the FBI, CIA, or DEA. But because she reminded me of my least favorite aunt, Bertha, that's what I'll call her.

At first, Bertha talked to me in Spanish, which upset me deeply. Most people seem unaware my native tongue is Portuguese, even though Brazil is the largest country in South America, with 140 million people. Regardless of her ignorance, Bertha clearly thought she had nailed an illegal alien risking life and freedom to pursue the American dream.

In the meantime, the other passengers were openly staring at me as if I had a bomb hidden in my purse. I envisioned reporters crowding me up with microphones and such headlines as "Terrorist Tries to Blow Up LAX," "24-Year-Old Goes to Death Row," "Top Journalist Deported." I like this last one!

After asking me a few questions regarding my status in the United States, Bertha began to search my suitcase. "Brazilian girls always have a lot of beachwear," she sarcastically said, pulling out a yellow bikini. Then she went through my just-developed photographs, making remarks on "how beautiful Acapulco must be." She also tasted a milky medicine that I use for heartburn. She looked completely disappointed. "It does wonders," I told Bertha vengefully.

Not satisfied, Bertha took me to a tiny gray room where she and a co-worker taught me new meanings of the word "humiliation." Yes, Bertha searched me. "Turn to the wall, hands up, legs apart, don't move," she ordered. "Pants down now." She seemed an authentic SWAT series character.

Bertha had picked the wrong person. But I give her some credit because she probably reasoned that a smart drug trafficker might disguise as a young graduate. What concerned me is that the real kingpins continue to cross the US border net, while innocent Latin Americans become the target of intense discrimination, footing the bill for a worldwide plague.

Border-crossing-Berthas and bigots like her can be found anywhere in the nation. And perhaps their barbs would hurt even more, were it not for the wide variety of ethnic magazines published in the United States today. By highlighting specific ethnic role models as sources of inspiration for thousands of young people, these magazines serve as resource guides while combating racism directed against their particular groups.

The Fall 1991 issue of *Visions*, for Native Americans, carried the following profile on Sergio Maldonado. In April 1992, President George Bush appointed Maldonado to the National Advisory Council on Indian Education for a three-year term.

Sergio Maldonado
Arapaho and Mexican Cultures
Educator

If you asked Sergio Maldonado what he does for a living, he'd tell you he's Indian Education Supervisor and Chemical Abuse Prevention Coordinator for Tempe, Arizona, School District 3. For such an important title, you might expect his office perhaps filled with framed degrees—and the space to be important looking, too. But his small, otherwise simply furnished office displays childlike drawings and thank you notes on the walls, a desk piled high with paperwork, a few unfancy chairs, and books, books, and more books.

Children, education, and the words of Chief Joseph—"All men were made by the same Great Spirit.... All people should have equal rights"—fill a large portion of Sergio's world.

When he was still in college, he took a child development class. One day, his teacher asked each of the students to tell about their childhood in one or two descriptive words.

"Everybody was giving these flowery verses of what childhood was like, and I was just listening. All of a sudden, she directed her attention to me, and all eyes were upon me, I guess, because I was the only Native American in the class.

"'Mr. Maldonado,' she said, 'what was yours like?' And I immediately responded by saying 'short.' Everybody chuckled, thinking that I was trying to be humorous. Then it dawned on them that that's what it was like," says Sergio.

Because he grew up with his mother's Arapaho culture, Sergio always leaned toward and learned Arapaho ways from his grandparents. When Sergio, his two brothers, and two sisters were young children, the Maldonados traveled from their home in Tucson, Arizona, to Wind River Reservation in Wyoming, where his maternal grandparents still lived.

"I spent a good part of my life back home. I always longed for June to come around," says Sergio. "I knew I'd have three months with my grandparents, and that's all I wanted. Every summer that was my escape back to reality. Life in Tucson wasn't what I envisioned, and I didn't like it."

Sergio moved to Wind River when he finished high school in 1972. For the next three years, he learned farming and ranching from his grandparents. But Sergio realized "life wasn't there either. It was a good place to be, but I decided it was time to settle down and get serious about school.

"I needed complete structure," says Sergio, in order to avoid the alcohol and substance abuse he had seen. All he had to do was look around. "At 19 and 20, it was already dawning on me that there was more to life than just that. Schooling was probably going to be my best avenue for attaining a satisfactory life."

But Sergio had become more in tune with Arapaho ways too, and that explained his need to find a balance. He entered Arapaho Sun Dance ways, "putting things again in a better light, organizing my life, realizing that time is short.

"If we're aware via the Spirit that there are significant emotional and significant spiritual events, we seize those and use those for betterment of ourselves...so we can be of greater service in the eyes of the Grandfather," says Sergio. "That's not to say I've reached that balance, because it's an all-consuming, ongoing process. We make mistakes. We cannot continue to flog ourselves like most of us do. You own up to it. You make reparation, and you press on. The fool in the individual is when you repeat the same mistake. I choose not to repeat it. Therefore you adjust for it and press on."

Maturing helped Sergio to mellow the anger he once felt toward prejudice. Today, he has learned to blend Arapaho ways into his non-American Indian world. He pulls his long hair into a bushy ponytail, dons a white shirt, and suspenders, wears a turquoise post in each ear, and attempts to achieve balance in his life by being forced to assume a greater role in correcting and adjusting misconceptions about American Indians.

"I've learned to do it not so much in a hasty or hostile fashion as I would have as a young man back home with my grandparents, but in a diplomatic, educationally-related fashion. Diplomacy can get you a whole lot further.

"The non-Indian culture never had an inkling of what the Indian culture is all about. Therefore, they branded it as false, uncivilized. In the 1960s, Native Americans were not receiving an education that was adequate in a comparative level to the non-Indians off the reservation. It had to be adjusted," he says.

"My grandfather, concerned I would become involved in a greater degree than watching and listening and observing with the American Indian movement, made a very good point.

"We were fixing a fence. I was leaning on a shovel and digging a hole, and he was just leaning on his shovel, watching me.

"And he said to me, 'You know, Sergio, them Aimers,' as they were called, 'good people. They know what they want to do. I don't agree with them. They forget one thing.'

"I said, 'Yeah? What's that?' in between digging with the post-hole digger.

"'They want to live traditional, and that's fine. But we live in today's world.'

"And I said, 'So what's your point?'

"He says, 'They forget that them teepees were damn cold.'"

Years later, Sergio understood what his grandfather had meant. Indians had become accustomed to the contemporary niceties of everyday life, too.

"As you look at life in the contemporary world," says Sergio, "you see how far people have removed themselves from that basic spiritual tie with Grandfather. Everything is now material. Everybody is so consumed by having possessions. When you die, you go to your Maker in your birthday suit. The material means nothing. It's how you view everybody else."

Advising young people to "be thankful for what we have," he says Native Americans need to associate with people who have common interests, success-oriented people who recognize the need for books, for education, who recognize, "You're Arapaho? That's good!"

He warns people to avoid cliques where fast-growing negativity breeds more negativity, and to maintain a relationship with those people who have your best interests at heart—your family and your friends. Become as intellectual and just as legal as the non-Indians, he says. That's all part of the transitions he says we all experience.

When asked who may have influenced his life the most, he mentions his grandparents, his mother who always stressed reading good books and associating with good people, his father who taught him about work, Chief Joseph, Crazy Horse, and his Sun Dance grandfather who has taught him about leading a humble, spiritual life.

"How much I have to grow just to be at a level of spiritual concern and strength that he has," he says.

Sergio Maldonado has blended his life in the non-Indian world with the traditional ways of the Arapaho people. "We remember what's happened to everybody in the past, all the leaders. But we continue to press on. We've always been survivors. I think I will continue to be that way too."

Whether or not we choose to accept our particular individual ethnic heritage, that ethnic cultural background represents a significant factor in our self-perceptions. Jewish and Italian cultures have significantly influenced Michelle Young's life. She was only four years old when her father, "Polly," died; yet he instilled Italian pride in her.

Bruno's

Michelle Young
Italian and Jewish Cultures

She visited Bruno's every Sunday with her father. As they opened the door, the tinkling bell announced their arrival, and the heavenly familiar smells of aged provolone and Romano cheese, garlic, salamis, and pepperoni hanging from the pipes over the meat and deli cases welcomed them.

"*Buon giorno*, Polly!" Bruno, in his blood-stained apron, looked up from the last of Mrs. Fiato's meat order. When he was done, he returned the homemade sausage to the case, wiped his hands on his apron, and handed Polly's daughter a piece of nougat candy.

Polly looked at the Italian olives, Greek olives, cheese, and cold cuts in the deli case at the right of the counter. "Bruno, one pound each of the olives, *grazie*."

The little girl scuffed her feet on the freshly washed black and white linoleum, wrinkled her nose, and wandered to the back of the store to gaze at the meat case's contents. Her father joined her there, and they decided which meats to purchase together.

Returning to the large brass register at the front of the store, Polly paid for the order as his daughter sang along to the Italian music playing on the old brown radio on the shelf behind the counter.

"See you next week, Bruno."

"*Ciao*."

As they walked out, she glanced at her father and asked, "Can I help with the meatballs today, Papa?"

"Of course, *cara mia*," came the reply, "of course!"

◎ ◎ ◎

The legacy of my Italian roots seems inextricably tied to my childhood on Pine Street, where my family and I lived until I was seven years old. I can still see the dark green shingles on the building's exterior, the layout of the rooms, the linoleum and the wallpaper. I vaguely recall the placement of certain pieces of furniture, yet as many times as I've passed that apartment building since we left Pine Street, I can't remember whether there were three floors or four.

Although we lived in the Italian section of town, the family-like composition of our-close-knit neighborhood brought many cultures together. My Aunt Nellie and her family—Uncle Pete, their seven daughters and two sons—lived within walking distance from the walk-up apartment we called home. Mrs. O'Brien, a wonderful lady with a thick Irish brogue who often baby-sat for me, lived in our building, as did the Feldmans, a family with a wealth of ethnic backgrounds. One of the two families introduced me to peanut butter and jelly sandwiches and the *Howdy Doody Show.*

The MacDonalds owned the large house across the street, and the Monfortes lived in the building next door. Perhaps the lady across the street—she may have been from Eastern Europe—wore earplugs to muffle the sounds of my screams as she brought my curly chestnut locks under control.

I remember admiring beautiful white dresses and suits on the kids at the Black church on Easter morning. I don't remember when I noticed these kids had a different skin color than mine.

The neighborhood wasn't steeped in wealth, but we lived in unity and eagerly shared the richness of our individual cultures with our neighbors. Folks knew my mother was the organist at Temple Concord, and we children were being raised in the Jewish faith; yet no one raised their eyebrows when the rabbi stopped in for a visit.

But then no one was surprised to see my father put up the Christmas tree either—not even the rabbi. And other than when the nuns from the Catholic Church's catechism lessons came to visit my mother, asking why my oldest brother Jim hadn't come back to Wednesday's religious school break—Jim had secretly attended to avoid school until he discovered the nuns expected him to learn too—eyebrows were rarely raised at cultural differences in the neighborhood. We were accepted for who we were as people, and I felt at peace with myself and my roots.

But three years after my father died, Jim had joined the Marines and left home. Our family structure had changed, and my mother—who hadn't learned to drive yet—felt our economic situation would improve if we lived with my grandparents on the other side of town. We left Pine Street and entered a new world of assimilated Americans.

I didn't understand this different environment on Binghamton's West Side. On the surface, people were friendly. The inherent closeness of the Italian neighborhood was missing, although people from many lands lived on Beethoven Street, just as we had on Pine Street. But there was a distance, an air of aloofness that seemed to separate us from our neighbors in this new section of town.

Everyone, while they had their own cultures, seemed more blended, like homogenized Americans, as compared to the distinct cosmopolitan spicing of the world at large. As young as I was, I knew I had no interest in becoming what

I saw as a mush-like blend of one dominant culture. I wanted to be an individual who could be appreciated for what I might add to the world around me. Here, I felt alone, isolated, and I wanted to go back to my home on Pine Street.

As I grew older, my search for contentment in what I saw as a strange and cold environment seemed unending. The more I hunted for that internal peace I associated with Pine Street, the more I felt like a foreign body waiting to be plucked from someone's eye.

Classmates questioned my theological beliefs and said I couldn't be Jewish because I didn't have a "big schnoz." My grandmother kept a kosher kitchen, and she failed to appreciate my brothers' and my love of *kielbasa*, pepperoni, and Italian sausage. I missed watching television as we feasted on lasagna and other Italian delights at Danny Celeste's Tavern on Sundays; we couldn't walk to Celeste's anymore. On the other hand, Grandma's matzo ball soup tasted like another side of heaven, and I wasn't ready to give that up either.

My frustration lingered until 1983 when I married my husband Kwong. On our wedding day, we chose to make the ceremony a celebration of our ethnic backgrounds. Married in a Japanese garden under a hand-painted Chinese bamboo umbrella—our vision of the Jewish wedding *chupa*—Kwong broke the traditional Jewish wedding glass. We held our reception at the Sons of Italy Hall where we enjoyed traditional Italian rigatoni and meatballs in addition to the ethnic dishes brought by each of our guests to represent their own cultural backgrounds.

I have my own Pine Street at home today. Our four sons—beautiful Dondi-like youngsters with slightly almond-shaped, large Italian eyes—and our family enjoy the best of our roots. At Chanuka, we share *latkes* at home and at school. The boys bring red envelopes to share with classmates on Chinese New Year, just as we do at home. We have a Christmas tree, and a Charles Dickens Christmas village rests comfortably under the tree.

This is the world I know and love best, and I'm at peace on Pine Street again.

Not all children in the world are blessed with warm family roots and traditions. Some children are no worse for the wear from their experiences; others suffer beyond belief. The following appeared in *Visions*, Spring 1990.

David Terrazas
Apache and Mexican Cultures
Policeman

At nine years old, David Terrazas was filled with a lifetime of bad memories. In 1971, he was a far cry from his alcoholic mother, an Apache; his imprisoned father, a Mexican; the abusive foster parents; and the day he saw his older brother killed by a train.

Today, the 29-year-old policeman on the San Carlos Indian Reservation credits Bill Goldman, who was a counselor for troubled children at the residential home in Tucson, Arizona, and his own positive memories of that home with turning his life around.

"I remember a lot of the stuff he told me, and that led to my being able to think for myself," he says. His well-defined dark eyes glow warmly as he speaks of those happier times at the home.

Bike riding, go carting, ice skating, roller skating, sports, and arts and crafts supplanted those foster home days of flyswatter-forced naps while other foster children in the same home played outdoors, broken promises for toys, segregated bathrooms, and beatings by hand or handy items.

He doesn't remember being raised or cared for by his mother until he was about three years old, followed by a rapid succession of foster homes within two years.

Occasionally David was placed in more pleasant surroundings, but then problems cropped up, and it was time to move on again.

His life in foster placement became a constant roll from bad to good then back to bad again. The children's home became the first consistently positive environment he'd ever experienced, but David was released from the children's home after three years.

Offered a choice of a group transitional home or another high-supervision environment with the opportunity to work with horses and dogs, David chose the latter.

But this new environment was neither supervised nor structured, and David found himself involved in drugs, drinking, and smoking.

"Everything was innocent at the children's home. I felt like I was protected," he says. "All of a sudden a lot of this stuff had been open to me."

Everybody on the reservation has a sad story to tell, says David, and his problems continued to mount even after his marriage.

Homeless, jobless, and on welfare, David began to realize, "I was going to end up hurting somebody and there would be nothing I could use as a defense to get out of it." He knew he had to change, and proving himself would be a slow process.

21

Even after he became a police officer, life for David Terrazas remained tough.

"I've been in accidents. I've been accused of police brutality. I've even had arrest warrants issued for me while I've been on duty," says this man who seems so happy and peace-loving today.

The combination of his feeling unloved, unwanted, and prejudiced against could have given rise to his violent childhood anger, but David seems to have put his past behind him and has stopped feeling sorry for himself.

"You have to hold an image that you are a responsible person, that you control your own life, that you control yourself on the job," he says of his career in law enforcement. "You have to make the right decisions."

Within the last three years, David was promoted to supervisor of his shift. He'll proudly tell you about his education, how he achieved his G.E.D. after dropping out of school in the first half of 10th grade. He'll tell you about his state certification as a police officer through the State of Arizona and his certification as a Bureau of Indian Affairs police officer. In the past four years he's even received college credit for studies through Central Arizona College.

"Life could have been a whole lot different," he says, "but I'm thankful it wasn't. I still give a lot of credit to the children's home. No matter what environment you were raised in, it's all up to you whether you want to change it or not. Everybody has freedom to change their own life."

David Terrazas knows. He has changed his life, and in the process, he's made this a better world in which to live.

No matter our age, ethnic roots, or the environment in which we were raised, each of us has an opportunity to make this a better world for all.

On Halloween in 1992, 16-year-old Jorge Mora of Pueblo, Colorado, dressed as his mother's patron saint, St. Joseph, and gave the first of his annual Halloween parties for 60 members of Dream Weavers, a Pueblo-based organization similar to Make-A-Wish Foundation. Each member of the organization has some degree of terminal illness.

On his own, Jorge received donations from businesses and organizations for the party's games, prizes, pizza, and soda. Jorge, too, is a member of Dream Weavers.

Articles about Jorge's personal efforts to improve the world appeared in *Vista* in April 1993, *First Opportunity, Direct Aim* and *College Preview*. In the summer of 1993, Jorge Mora participated in World Youth Day in Denver. There, he met and received communion from the pope. Once again, he received media attention after Jorge ran to the pope and received a hug.

Jorge Mora
Mexican and Cuban Cultures
Student

Brain tumors are nasty business. Football great Lyle Alzado of the Los Angeles Raiders developed one, an ironic fatal result of steroids he took to enhance his booming career. But being faced with death comes even harder when you're 15-year-old Jorge Mora who has always been passionate about football and even more passionate about staying number one in his class.

"Jorge has a brain tumor."

The words rang through his parents' minds.

No small job of fumbling for the ball on the field before Jorge or one of his high school junior varsity football teammates got it and started running that last ten yards to score a touchdown. This time the opposing team was Medulloblastoma, an aggressive cancerous tumor. Jorge needed this touchdown to save his life.

Less than four months before the doctors gave Jorge and his parents those bone-chilling words, Jorge had celebrated his birthday and had been accepted as an eager participant in Arizona State University's Center for Academic Precocity (ASU/CAP). Identified as a gifted student at home in Pueblo, Colorado, he looked forward to his first time in a summer school and the challenges at Arizona State University (ASU).

"If I took grade level subjects (at home, through his first year in high school), the classes were a bore," he said.

At the ASU/CAP program, Jorge made a wealth of friends, gifted students like him, who felt the same desire to achieve. Stimulated by the ASU/CAP program's course work and perhaps excited by competition with his newly found friends, he finished the summer session with an A in intermediate algebra and trigonometry pre-calculus studies and a B in vocabulary development. The non-graded school survival workshop taught him to achieve his goals by focusing on his hopes for the future. He knew his time had been well invested.

But in October 1991, Jorge discovered his future might be much more limited than most boys his age even dream of considering, and he was angry. As a sophomore at South High School, he had the world at his feet and had become involved in many extracurricular activities, including swimming and—of course—football, all while maintaining his number one standing in his class of 305.

"I found out (about the brain tumor) while I was in the hospital," said Jorge. "They were pretty honest about it. I knew I couldn't do without surgery. It was either do or die."

From Parkview Hospital in Pueblo, he went to Denver Children's Hospital for the surgery. Relatives from all over the Southwest brought baseball caps when they came to visit, a gesture that eventually helped him forget his anger and refuse to give up.

But Jorge was impatient. Developing a positive attitude and determination to fight, he discovered, isn't an overnight kind of achievement—not when someone has told you tomorrow might not be there for you.

Heartbroken for her son, Gloria Mora kept a journal into which she poured her pain and frustration. Refusing to let Jorge know how desperately she wished she could kiss and make it better, she put a cheery smile on her face and the roar of the crowd at the football game in her visits with him.

After Jorge's first surgery, Gloria wrote, "Jorge woke up at 3:00 a.m., asking me for his homework. I got up and brought his books to him. He said, 'What's the use?' This was the only time he ever sounded defeated." The next day, she wrote, "I got mad at him. He smiled. He hadn't seen this side of me for a long time. It felt good to see him smile."

Encouraged by Jorge's progress, the doctors gave him a surgical implant at the end of October and allowed him to return to school two hours a day. Before his return to school on November 11, he met the LA Raiders and attended a game. But he quickly tired and left after the first half.

Radiation treatments started on November 21, compounding his fatigue with queasiness. The doctors prescribed medication for the nausea, but he developed an allergic reaction to the medication. In less than a month after his first surgery, Jorge lost 20 pounds.

Still, he focused on his studies, eager to absorb as much of his school world as possible. If he planned a quiet return to his classes, his younger sister Maria had other ideas. The school's public address system announced his return, and Maria, a frosh, kept tabs on his day through students and teachers.

As embarrassing as Maria's plan was, people were worried that perhaps he returned to school too soon. Certainly Jorge was reassured by his sister's overprotective attitude.

When he began losing his hair, a normal but embarrassing side effect of radiation therapy, he appreciated the baseball caps from his relatives even more for their ability to mask his hair loss.

At school, still unsteady, he walked very slowly. When he fell asleep from exhaustion, no one woke him; his teachers understood—just as they did when he got sick and left classes without permission. Forced to drop chemistry because his arm and hand shook so much, he concentrated on his other subjects, refusing to miss school.

He wrote so slowly, Jorge's teachers worried that he'd become self-conscious. Had his teachers asked him to, he would have removed his Dodgers baseball cap although he sat at a desk in front of the room. Doggedly determined, he persisted, going to school two hours a day. Three homework problems, once 15-minute tasks, became two-hour projects. Often needing extra class time to finish his work, he neither asked for nor received extra chances.

Geometry, once simple and logical, became a chore. Time and again, he asked questions when his sister helped with tutoring. His head hurt, and his weakened right hand trembled so much that he needed to write with two hands.

Medical personnel poked his arms for blood tests weekly to watch his blood cell count. Jorge grew more determined to beat this setback as the days passed. Back in Pueblo's Parkview Hospital after leaving Denver Children's Hospital, he threw himself into his studies, refusing to allow himself the privilege, luxury or time for self-pity and anger.

After Christmas, Jorge's doctors allowed him to swim and to attend school four hours a day. He loves football more than swimming, but football, he knew, was out of the question.

"You can't play if your head is fragile," he says, pausing some between words. His voice falters, another normal reaction to radiation. Although the treatments have temporarily slowed his speech and thought processes, he writes with one hand again. A warm and lively teenager, his voice dances with a smile now.

Back in school full time, Jorge says he's taken more hold of his life. "Life is too short," he says.

For Mother's Day, 1992, he bought a set of 20-pound weights for Gloria. In spite of his still weakened condition, he lugged his gift to his mother the entire three-fourths of a mile home. Gloria never expected him to run again, yet he's learned to walk, talk, run, and drive a car—all within the space of a year! But then, he's also jumping rope, lifting weights, bike riding, and playing tennis.

In October 1992, Jorge, now 16, took a date to homecoming—special enough for any other teen. To Jorge, perhaps homecoming represents life itself. He still has a long way to go, but this is the football game of his life. He's chosen to go for the touchdown.

When we consider the concept of culturalization, we need to think about our attitudes, beliefs, and the ways in which we approach new experiences, customs, and traditions. In general, our similarities and differences have probably been present since history was first recorded.

We cannot broadly classify people by race. Doing so serves little purpose other than for anthropological and genetic research. Instead, we need to understand and respect others more positively—regardless of their national origins, languages spoken, skin pigmentation, religious beliefs, and so on—by using words like *race, ethnic, culture,* and *heritage* with sensitivity. When we remember the ethnic and cultural ingredients in relationships between people, we begin to understand others as members of the human race rather than as prehistoric to modern sources of experimentation and study.

Ethnicity and *culture* are somewhat interchangeable terms. Ethnicity can be defined as the relationship of races or people according to their customs and tradition. Culture is the combination of all social interactions, including arts, beliefs, institutions, and all other human endeavors and concepts found within a community or population.

Isolation has always played a major role in cultural transmission between generations. The degree to which isolation affects that transmission varies, however, according to any particular culture and its location. Let's examine how the isolation factor works.

The Amish, for instance, chose to isolate themselves in what we now call the United States. Technological changes occurred in the areas surrounding the Amish settlements; however the Amish people have chosen to use some, but not all of these changes.

In contrast to the Amish way of life, Native Americans were isolated by external influences. Technological changes occurring in the areas around what were then called Indian reservations, frequently resulted in generational conflicts. Where one generation may have welcomed these changes, the other may have felt threatened by factors over which they had no control.

Similarly, a variety of natural boundaries—rivers, seas, oceans, forests, deserts, and mountains—served as instruments of isolation between groups of people, societies, and communities. But climatic changes—drought, flooding, lack of resources, population growth, and human curiosity about the unknown—led to an instinctual search for more.

What was beyond the next hill, the next body of water contributed to an urge to explore. People moved in groups or sent scouting parties to determine whether needs and wants could be met elsewhere. As these groups of people encountered other groups and saw their accomplishments or available resources, like children wanting the same play toys or treats possessed by other children, the incoming groups became eager to accomplish similar feats and obtain these new resources. In this way, the concept of trade became an accepted form of interaction between the two groups.

But trade wasn't always possible. Often one group was unable or unwilling to trade, forcing the other group to look elsewhere, forget about the trade itself, or take the desired item through aggressive or subversive means. As trade and conflict arose between groups, cross-cultural experiences conducive to the process of culturalization took place.

At first, limited forms of transportation restricted the number of inevitable but subtle changes occurring. But as technology developed, the interactions between communities or cultures increased, producing bicultural and multicultural communities. Still taking place today, culturalization has led to internal changes within groups or communities, thereby creating new cultures.

But cross-cultural experiences were influenced in several ways. Environmental factors affected the impact of these encounters between people in varying degrees, just as they have often affected the interactions of animals, plants, and mineral resources. Wars, territorial invasions or occupation, exploration, discovery, colonization, foreign aid, and so on often led to one group of people or one culture dominating.

Today, the world appears to be getting smaller. Natural boundaries no longer pose barriers from or to change. The development of rapid transportation and communication has extended the degree to which one group of people's activities affect another group. As a result, we need to look at opportunities and problems from a multicultural interdependent perspective. Without a clear understanding of where we've been in the past and where we are today, developing and achieving the means of establishing visionary goals for the future will be extremely difficult.

Whether we choose to identify ourselves as parts of a collective body of people or as separate individuals, we need to recognize our common needs, interests, desires, and other bonds as members of the human race. As individuals, families, communities, and nations, we need to understand and appreciate who and what we are—regardless of others' spoken or unspoken beliefs about us.

By building on our common foundation as world citizens and members of the human race, we will be able to develop more than a simple tolerance for others. We will have cultivated an understanding and appreciation for others regardless of their cultural differences from our own.

Failure to foster understanding and appreciation for others leaves us open to developing mistrust, stereotypes, and dislike for others, promoting covetous and envious attitudes for that which others have acquired or accomplished through their own means, thereby creating a fertile breeding ground in which power-hungry, self-interested forces lay blame for whatever on people of other racial, ethnic, cultural, or religious groups.

Throughout history and into the early 1990s, negative forces have polarized people, allowing misunderstandings to escalate into lies, hatred, discrimination, persecution, and atrocities. Adolf Hitler's Nazi hostilities prior to and during World War II resulted in the mass extermination of the handicapped, homosexuals, Russians, Poles, Jews, and other non-Aryan people. Similarly Ukrainians and Armenians experienced Josef Stalin's hard-line Russian Communist Bolshevik assaults. In the late 1970s, in what was then Cambodia, later the Khmer Republic, and now the People's Republic of Kampuchea, the Pol Pot regime eliminated over two million Khmer citizens of all ages.

The early 1990s saw Iraqi President Saddam Hussein's government attack the Kurds, a group of people who are considered to be descendants of the Medes from the Persian Empire. In the former states of Yugoslavia, a surface appearance of innocence has masked the macabre definition of the *ethnic cleansing* that took place, resulting in cold-blooded murder—genocide.

28

Although the conflict in Northern Ireland between the Protestants and Catholics had resulted in the loss of many lives, by 1992 the situation appeared to be self-contained, rather than escalating to that which one might call extermination levels. But a fine line bridges the differences between continued fighting and decimation of people, and only time will tell the results of Northern Ireland's problems.

Certainly many other examples of prejudice and hatred exist in the world, even in what we call the United States, but not all bigotry has been as blatant as some of the examples mentioned here. The more subtle forms, coated with ignorance, good intentions, or excuses, may be more accurately described in one observer's phrase, *finessed racism*.

People in every region of the world need to begin viewing multiculturalism as a positive process regardless of cultural and religious differences. We can and need to live together in an environment where understanding of and appreciation for others can take place.

What, then, are our common bonds?

Because of our spiritual bonds, regardless of our individual religious indoctrination, and because of our physical bonds for the same basic elements of sustaining life, we desperately need to understand and accept the concept of interdependence. At times, circumstances make the concepts of dependence and independence appropriate, important, and essential. However, when we deal with or relate to other people, we need to function in a spirit of interdependence, encouraging the spirit of cooperation, concern, respect, and sacrifice between us.

We all need the components of physical life—air, water, food, and shelter—just as we need an environment in which safety, security, and purpose are tantamount to our mental and spiritual well-being. But major differences and ideas frequently occur concerning the best methods for achieving a safe, secure environment which results in the provision of meaningful purpose for each member of society. In essence, the major motivating factor of this book lies here.

Today, we live in a world which appears to be polarized, within and among nations. This disparity will need to be resolved. Yet simultaneously, individuals seem to be more interested in their heritage and cultural roots. How can we live in the United States, as we know it today, as well as throughout the world, and lead productive, creative, cooperative, and respectful lives while these two diametrically-opposed concepts—homogeneity and individualization—are unresolved? We will demonstrate how two such opposing concepts can work together; that is, how individuality can grow and develop within an interdependent society or in the world as our collective body.

Multiculturalism needs to be established by developing unity through diversity. The phrase **unity through diversity** appears to involve two opposing ideas, because we've been led to believe that unification is the only way to accomplish unity. However, the terms unification and unity actually oppose each other. Let's look at these two terms in relation to cultural diversity and multiculturalism.

Unification can be compared to whalebone bodices of the 19th century because both require forcing bodies into uniform standards to achieve conformity. Like those inhibiting, air-constricting bodices of the 1800s, the concept behind the expressions *melting pot* and *funnel* require an active move away from individual diversity toward one rigidly created goal.

Unification has become outmoded, just as the whalebone bodices and even the girdles of the 20th century did. Why? Because we can only force conformation of bodies into whalebone bodices, 20th century girdles, or pre-determined concepts of excellence for just so long. Eventually something will pop out—at one end or another.

Undoubtedly, the ladies of the 19th century rebelled against squeezing their 24-inch—more or less—waists into 13-inch tourniquet-like contraptions. After all, how many of those wasp waists stayed that wasp-like after they'd been through the rigors of childbirth? Certainly many women abandoned 20th century girdles for similar reasons!

Similarly, unification could be compared to why a marriage won't work when a spouse attempts to remake a partner—or why leopards will never become tigers. You simply can't fake it for long. Sooner or later, something has to give, and it usually will.

We saw the dissolution of Yugoslavian-Soviet ties in 1992, illustrating this very principle. Unification stems from the outside, moving from diversity to uniformity, focusing on external stimuli to achieve and maintain by force. Not only does the essential principle of unification absorb a lot of effort in the process of achieving those preconceived ideals, but, frankly, consistent use of force requires an inordinate amount of energy.

Unity, on the other hand, asks nothing more than acceptance of individuality. As we move from uniformity to diversity, we experience internal attitudinal changes that result in our learning to accept others and, eventually, in others' acceptance of us. By changing our own thinking first from a model of unification to a model of unity, we begin to achieve respect, cooperation, economic opportunity, and so on.

Parallel to the tapestry described in the beginning of this chapter, each of us has a clay tile to add to the mosaic. Each tile plays an integral part in the making of the mosaic. If one tile disappears, the beauty of the mosaic is flawed by the obvious gap.

We need to have unity, and unity can be achieved through diversity, in turn creating the mosaic of our world. Our differences provide for creativity and richness in life. If each of us begins or continues to think in terms of unity through diversity, we can put this concept into action so each of us, old and young alike, will participate in the gifts our lives and our world have to offer.

Each of us has that right.

Chapter 2

THE AMERICANS

If you were asked to describe America, would you mention the trees and rocky coastline of Maine, the paved streets on Boston's former cowpaths, and the hustle and bustle of New York? Would you remember Washington, DC's cherry blossoms and North Carolina's tobacco fields, or Iowa's cornfields? Or would Alaska's fresh winter frontier, Seattle's Pacific mists, and the Celluloid corporations in Sequoia-laden California paint a more likely picture for you?

In contrast to present-day images of America, the name's roots go back to Amerigo Vespucci's discovery of Central and South America. A German cartographer from the 1500s, crediting Vespucci with the discovery of the New World, named the entire region—from the northern tip of North America to the southernmost point of South America—"America."

The colonial founders of the United States, neither intending arrogance nor disrespect for other inhabitants of the region, simplified the nation's formal name and created a psychological and geographical boundary still in use today. Thomas Jefferson, Thomas Paine, Michel-Guillaume-Jean de Crevecoeur—later known as J. Hector St. John—and countless others wrote about America in pre-

and post-Revolutionary essays.

De Crevecoeur's *Letters from an American Farmer,* published in 1782, described late 18th century life in the United States. "What is an American," his third "letter" written in essay form like the other eleven, defined an "American" as a hard-working and courageous member of the new country's population, whose descendants would someday serve as catalysts for great changes in the world.

But these builders of the nation encouraged imagination and innovation, praising new achievements and visionary philosophers, establishing the New World as a global fountainhead of progress. Men like Noah Webster and Benjamin Franklin set the stage for stable growth.

And their descendants did serve as prominent catalysts of world growth, producing legends like John F. Kennedy, Sally Ride, Martin Luther King, Jr., Rosa Parks, Ralph Bunche, Jonas Salk, and a host of others. Yet the New World inspired much more than even colonial dreamers thought possible.

The hopes and dreams of 18th century philosophers became the reality of the 19th, 20th and 21st centuries, inspiring far-reaching global change. Unconcerned with ethnic or national boundaries and unrestrained by imposed limits of their own imaginations, visionary leaders like Albert Schweitzer, Sun Yat-sen, Gandhi, Dr. Tom Dooley, Mother Theresa, and Guglielmo Marconi influenced world change far from the shores of the New World, inspired by one common goal—the betterment of humanity.

To us, America is Toronto's sculpted tulip gardens, Ottawa's changing of the guard; snowy peaks, emerald forests, and mountain lakes in the Rockies. America is Independence Hall in Philadelphia, St. Louis' Mississippi riverboats and cobblestone midtown streets, jazz in New Orleans, Costa Rica's fertile plateau, Southern Chile's spectacular coastline, Brazil's majestic Amazon, coral reefs on the Cuban coasts. Rich in culture and beauty, creativity and history, America is the New World.

"The Americans" celebrates all people from North America, through Central America, the Caribbean Islands, and the nations of South America with that same goal—the betterment of humanity—in mind.

In October 1992, several major port cities along the United States' coastlines planned a gala quincentennial celebration of Columbus' arrival on American soil. The celebration's enormous accompanying publicity virtually overshadowed another major event sponsored by Indian Women in Progress, an old organization dedicated to preserving Native American culture.

Acting as catalysts for what apparently was the only Native American Quincentennial Celebration in the nation, Indian Women in Progress celebrated 500 years of Indian heritage.

On October 10 of that year, Indian Women in Progress hosted a quincentennial Indian buffet in the Turquoise Room at Scottsdale Community College in Arizona. People from many ethnic backgrounds and all walks of life attended the dinner, sharing authentic Native American dishes and taking part in various Indian traditions described by members of several tribes.

The organization honored Harry Mitchell, a former high school history teacher and Mayor of Tempe, Arizona, who gave the following speech that night. His personal family heritage is rooted in Scotland, but his words plant him firmly on American soil.

Harry Mitchell
Scottish Culture
Educator and City Mayor

Last night at dinner I was talking with my wife about the remarks I would make today and she motioned to my shirt. My wife and I, and my shirt, were all having spaghetti for dinner.

Now most people think of spaghetti as Italian cuisine. But the pasta for spaghetti originated from the Orient and was brought to Europe by Marco Polo.

The tomatoes for spaghetti sauce are a gift from Native Americans. Before Columbus, Italians never had tomatoes to put on their spaghetti.

Many of the spices in the sauce originally came from India.

My wife, who cooked the meal; her family originated [in] Czechoslovakia.

My family originated [in] Scotland.

Even though many consider spaghetti an Italian dish, I disagree: It is an American dish. My evidence? You can buy spaghetti in cans...that proves it's American.

But what really makes it American? The tomatoes are native of this land but the other ingredients are not.

What makes anything or anyone American? Well, the essence of America is not where our ingredients or our people come from...although that is important. The essence of America is what we believe. The essence of America is our value system. The essence of America is what we think, [what] we feel, and even what we eat.

It is important to know history. It is important to know about our Native American heritage. It is important to recognize the role Columbus played in our country's founding.

But more important, is that we believe in the same values, that we band together for a common good.

We have a history comprised of many different ingredients. And our history shows that like a good meal, these ingredients work the best when they all work together.

I would like to read you a quote from the book *A Cherokee Feast of Days* by Joyce Sequichie Hifler.

What is striking about this quote is the value system that is expressed. It is an ethic that forms the basis of our country's very existence. It is a belief that was talked about long before Columbus set foot on this continent.

I quote: "When the season begins to change, nature gives us a new view of creation—a creation in which we are not alien. We were never an afterthought. This was prepared for us the same way we provide everything a newborn needs before it arrives. Our seasons can be renewed as well.

"But it is our decision, because we have freedom of choice.

"We are not programmed by nature. The Great Spirit gave us life and the wisdom to maintain it—and to enjoy it as well."

Some of you may recognize the sentiments expressed in this quotation. They are: life, liberty, and the pursuit of happiness.

This is the value system expressed by a Native American, by leaders of the French and English enlightenment, by Thomas Jefferson, by Martin Luther King, Jr.

This value system came from many different places, but we have all embraced them as our own. And that is what we celebrate today.

36

When we asked one woman to write her experience, she immediately responded, "Impossible! My family ancestry includes John Quincy Adams. In fact, one of my ancestors came over to the colonies in 1637, another married a native. How much more American do you want me?"

Anonymous
English and Scottish Cultures
New York State Farm Wife

My sister and I are among a diminishing group of families who can trace roots back to pre-DAR [Daughters of the American Revolution] on both sides of the family. The Boston Commons was a grazing pasture when my family owned land near where the downtown store of Jordan Marsh now stands.

I spent my childhood in New England, my teen years in upstate New York. At that time, during the late 1950s, I had no idea what cultural differences were, much less what prejudice was. But as I reflect back to those years ending what I call the Victorian era, a time in which I was fortunate enough to have been raised, my lack of opinions about cultural differences and prejudices can be attributed to the times.

Where you lived represented yours and your family's friends' status. As a child, my friends consisted of a close group of family friends. My horizons during my teen years expanded beyond family, and my group of friends grew.

We had a few blacks in my high school. One was even a cheerleader with me. She was good! But the biggest prejudice at that time was "Don't even look at Elvis" and "Avoid the motorcycle gang with black leather jackets!" Being a bit of a rebel, I finally fulfilled a 20-year wish to ride one of those forbidden motorcycles in 1982.

During my adulthood, working and raising two sons challenged my early protected lifestyle to the fullest. Since I was old enough to walk, I was drilled with good manners: be polite, use this fork to eat that with, keep your elbows off the table, don't slurp, children are to be seen not heard, stand up, don't slouch, watch your tongue, respect your elders...using first names was one of the biggest hurdles I had to overcome. Everyone was Mr. and Mrs. It wasn't until I realized I was insulting people that it became easy to use first names.

From my perspective, I'm impressed that first-generation European Americans—my only source of close observation—are raised as hard, honest workers in comparison to the second generation who lose the European ways and become Americanized, losing some of the emphasis of the actual immigration.

Two of my most favorite people immigrated to the United States many years ago. My Dutch friend became a naturalized citizen of Canada and immigrated to the United States, where she became a naturalized citizen too, in the 1960s. Her experiences and hardships give me a better appreciation of my birthright.

Upon her arrival in Canada, she was housed in a shack behind a barn on a farm where she and her husband both worked to earn enough money to enter the United States. They worked very hard for very long hours before being able to continue their immigration into the United States. He had to have a job in the United States before being allowed to immigrate. She eventually became the treasurer of a small company, where she still works today.

My mother-in-law came to the United States in the early 1930s in an even still harder immigration than my friend from Holland experienced. Farm hands were allowed to work here in the 1930s, and my father-in-law, who was college-educated in agriculture, worked as a farm hand while his wife remained in Switzerland. At that time, the United States had strict immigration regulations.

My mother-in-law talks about having her hands examined for calluses, her proof that she worked on a farm. But they also needed to have jobs in this country and, in 1931, $8,000 in a bank account!

They borrowed the money from family in Switzerland, and they paid it back. Together, they owned a dairy on a rented farm until the late 1950s, when they were able to buy a small house and my father-in-law found a job working in a tire recapping shop where he worked well into his 70s. To this day, my mother-in-law maintains a work-oriented schedule, rising early, cleaning, cooking, and taking care of herself in her home. She's 85 now.

Some Europeans immigrated to the United States for economic reasons, often from usually quiet and peace-loving nations. Still others came to escape constant turmoil in their homelands.

Throughout history, key areas of the world have developed reputations for being hot spots of political unrest. Often located where several countries cluster together, political upheaval in one country seems to create inflammatory chain reactions in surrounding countries.

For many years, Latin America has held a reputation for being one of these political hotbeds. A volcanic-charged atmosphere during the mid- to late-1940s and into the mid-1950s in several of these countries resulted in Juan Peron's Argentine dictatorship in 1946, the eruption of a decade of tensions in Colombia that left over 200,000 dead from 1948 to 1958, and Fidel Castro's 1959 seizure of power in Cuba.

Following the 1961 United States-supported Bay of Pigs invasion of Cuba and the 1962 Cuban missile crisis, the area settled into relative quiet for another five years. But the effects of political tension continue to touch citizens of these nations long after the smoke has cleared.

Hispanic Magazine's editor and publisher, Alfredo Estrada, was just two years old when his family left Cuba. They left, not surprisingly, "for political reasons" in 1961. Although he, of course, can't recall the details from personal experience, his story is as rich as his Cuban culture.

Alfredo Estrada
Cuban Culture
Editor and Publisher

Following their departure from Cuba in 1961, Alfredo Estrada and his family lived in Spain for three years.

"When I moved from Spain to the United States, I didn't speak a word of English. But within a couple of months, I spoke as well as anyone," he says. Perhaps because the family had left their home country for political reasons, he says the Cuban experience was "very different. I never felt a conflict between my Cuban culture and American assimilation. For me, it was always a very positive thing.

"I was extremely proud of my Cuban heritage. I never felt like a minority, growing up. I was the only Hispanic in my class, but I was proud of the difference and was never discriminated against."

Cherishing that difference, he prided himself on being the only kid in his surroundings who would speak Spanish, his language at home with his parents. And for Alfredo Estrada, cherishing that difference may well have been the reason why he typically took guava and cheese to school for lunch.

"It's difficult to generalize in saying it's the same for everybody," he says, pointing out that many Cubans had similar experiences.

Where he was raised in the United States didn't appear to have an influence on his perception of the country. The family lived in Michigan and Texas, in Greenwich, Connecticut, where he attended high school. In Massachusetts, he attended Harvard, and eventually he earned his law degree at the University of Texas at Austin.

"When I went back to Cuba as a journalist in 1991, I realized I wasn't Cuban in the sense of being a Cuban citizen anymore," he says. "I'm very American, but there's a tie there. Growing up, my identity was Cuban. Any ties to Hispanic culture were through Cuba versus Mexico or Puerto Rico.

"Being Hispanic became a political and demographic issue. The 1970 census first used it. The need to be identified made sense of being a minority.

"Before, people identified with specific cultures. Now, it's inclusive with a broader cultural context. From the non-minority point of view, the concern about minorities and the benefits they receive for being minority, I wouldn't discount that. The benefits range from being on the cabinet and Supreme Court to scholarships and so on.

"The idea of being Hispanic is diverse and includes political and economic agendas as well as cultural. Clearly, there are a number of ways to approach it. You can view it from the feel-sorry-about-me perspective—the negative—or from the viewpoint of empowering people, moving up the ranks in corporate America—the positive."

He was the only Spanish-speaking person in his early schooling, but he never thought about his heritage when he became attracted to the opposite sex. "I married a non-Hispanic."

In contrast to Alfredo Estrada's experience, Luis Nuñez discovered the influence his surroundings played on life in the United States.

Luis Nuñez
Dominican Culture
Blue Collar Worker and Student

In my neighborhood, everyone spoke Spanish, so it wasn't really bad.

Adjusting to life in upstate New York was different because the Hispanic population wasn't as readily accessible. I found myself adjusting to upstate New York more than I did in New York City. The hardest thing, perhaps, might have been the cold. We didn't have to wear coats and hats in the Dominican Republic. Just tee shirts and shorts. It's 80 to 85 degrees, year round.

In the City, you had few adjustments because most of your friends were Spanish. The English language I picked up. I didn't find it that hard.

When I was in school, I worked full time. But trying to get a decent job was difficult, although I think you make your opportunities. You take advantage of what's there. I've tried. It hasn't come through yet.

Yet how we choose to integrate our cultural heritage depends at least partially on our immediate surroundings. If we have no connection to our ethnic roots on a day-to-day basis, we may separate ourselves from those ties.

On the other hand, if concrete bonds have been created, we may respond to our instincts for roots through a variety of means. Where one person will regularly use ethnic dishes or rely on other cultural traditions, another will find fulfillment in ethnic arts.

Artisan Charles Carrillo turned to devotional arts. "He's Cherishing the Old Ways," written by Penny Morris, appeared in *Career Focus* Magazine in 1991, and *New Mexico* Magazine carried a subsequent article by Morris, highlighting another of the old arts created by Carrillo's wife and children in July 1992.

Charles Carrillo
Mexican Culture
Santos Maker

"Cherish the old ways. Believe in the values of your parents and grandparents because they will come full circle in your life," says Charles Carrillo, an award-winning Santos maker.

Charles, a soft-spoken, intense man, is living proof of New Mexico's long history, a richly interwoven blending of [Mexican, Native American] and [European] cultures.

[In 1981], while he was working at the University of New Mexico as an archaeologist, Charles started researching and making hand-carved devotional items. He had no idea he'd ever be ready to quit his full-time job at the University.

"You have to realize Hispanics are conservative and don't easily give up hard-earned benefits like insurance and retirement," says the master Santero. He smiles, recalling the difficult decision he faced in giving up modern day ideas of security and happiness.

His family, culture, and religion have been a major force in influencing his life and his decision to give up the benefits of working for others.

His father, a school administrator with the Albuquerque Public School system, impressed Charles at an early age with the value of education.

"Every summer my father would take my twin brother and me to the country to work in the fields. Father wanted to show us our connectedness with the land, where our roots were. Our heritage." He chuckles and adds, "He wanted to show us if we didn't want to be laborers, get an education."

His father was the first in the family to get an education, Charles says. "Ph.D. Right up the ladder as high as he could go. It was a struggle coming from a poor Mexican background, but he understood the value of an education. Father always said, 'Education will not open the door, but it will show you where the door is. You have to open it.'"

Charles learned his father's lessons well. He, too, is just finishing his Ph.D. in anthropology. But he also learned the lessons of his culture.

"My mother valued the simple things in life. She sewed all of our clothes, and we didn't know what store-bought bread was," he says. "My grandmother was poor. What we call salt poor. But she had a rich culture and language. She also had the richness where it counts—in her heart."

Debbie, his wife, laughs as she talks. "Oh yes," she says. "We have a TV and a microwave. But we also have the traditional clay pots."

Charles believes food preparation and cooking are a vital part of one's heritage. "The smell of the traditional foods cooking in the kitchen recalls beautiful memories of my grandmother," he says.

Charles, Debbie, Estrellita, 10, and Roan, 6, their two children, spend little time watching TV or using the microwave. When the family is not busy with art shows, like the one Charles recently attended at the Taylor Museum where he was overseeing the accuracy of the Penitente Santos display, and sharing the love of their culture with others, everyone scours the countryside for products necessary to do his art form.

"We make the varnish from the pitch of the piñon tree," says Debbie. "All the pigments come from certain rocks and flowers. We need to find the flowers when they are at their peak to get the bright hues needed for the Santos."

Both Charles and Debbie feel their lifestyle has a positive effect on their children.

"Estrellita went to her first show when she was three months old. Consequently, she grew up with it and is not shy. She is able to talk to people anywhere, anytime." Even Roan, says Debbie, went to his kindergarten class and demonstrated how his dad uses gypsum to prepare the wood for painting. Both parents feel the children are learning how to deal with all types of people. Unafraid of asking questions, the children are being steeped in the richness of their culture.

"They will be the ones to carry on tradition," says Charles of his children. "We are living the lifestyle and values of the Hispanic people. If they carry that on, what more is there to be proud of?"

When asked about his most exciting moment in the art world, he recalled a time [in 1988] when he was chosen from hundreds of New Mexican artists to make a Retablo, a flat religious image for King Carlos and Queen Sophie of Spain. Then he said, "No, my most exciting moment—the one that touched my heart, my soul, and wrenched my gut—was at a regular art show. I had a small Retablo of the Santo Niño on display. An elderly Hispanic man kept going past it, touching it, making the sign of the cross and kissing it. Suddenly I got up and presented it to him. 'Here. It is yours,' I said. He was so happy, he cried. Imagine that. A grown, proud man crying. If my own people cannot buy my Santos, then I am not a Santero. I am just an artist. If I take it away from the people I make it for, I'd better pack my bags and leave."

But not all who attend art shows understand the ways of the Santeros. Charles knew prejudice existed. His father, Charles had seen, had felt its ugly head rear up in the field of education. At the recent Spanish Market Art show in Santa Fe, Charles, too, felt the bite.

A well-dressed lady stopped in front of him at the show, asking, "Where are all those Indians?"

Charles shrugged and didn't answer. A friend with the lady said this was a Mexican folk art show from people up in the hills.

The lady frowned and said, "Oh. People with no education." She turned to Charles and pronounced the words carefully. "Have...you...ever...been...to...school?"

"Only...as...far...as...a...Ph.D.," he replied.

"Discrimination hurts," says Charles, "and I never accept it or say I'll learn to live with it." He never reacts violently to prejudice; but he lets the person know it doesn't please him. "If you let it get the best of you, they win," he tells young people.

Charles Carrillo is a gentle man with a burning passion, the passion of mixing the best of the old and the new. His love of family and tradition, his strong abiding faith and pride in his culture make him a man one long remembers and admires.

Regardless of our individual heritage, surroundings, or other identifying characteristics, each of us looks for ways in which we can live peacefully in today's world. Mimi McBride was an elementary school librarian at the time the following article appeared in the spring 1992 issue of *Visions* Magazine. She has since begun her own business, moving more deeply into making her life a full translation of that which being an American Indian means to her. The article has been modified slightly because the name of the school is no longer relevant to the story.

Mimi McBride
Dakota Sioux Culture
Businesswoman and Former School Librarian

Forget those stereotypes of strict, gray-haired, bespectacled librarians with fingers glued to pursed lips saying "Shhh!" A beautiful, smiling librarian, Mimi McBride, greets eager young readers with encouraging words to believe in themselves.

"The hardest thing I've had to develop was self-confidence and self-concept. I've had the worst time believing in myself. It was kind of ingrained into me, not to be overbearing and loud," says Mimi, a Dakota Sioux from the Fort Totten Reservation in Devil's Lake, North Dakota. "I still have to work on it, but I'm stronger now than I've ever been in my whole life. It's taken years of experience, work, a lot of talking to myself and believing in being proud of who I am and what I am."

But lack of self-confidence and self-concept may be the reasons behind her becoming a librarian, Indian educator, artist, and musical entertainer.

Still small when she and her family moved away from the reservation, Mimi entered the multicultural world of Montana's public schools.

"I retained some of my language and learned about our culture from strong traditional relatives like my mother and my Aunt Rita. But we had to get into the mainstream whether we wanted to or not," Mimi says, adding that her adjustment to the mainstream world was hard because she, like other minority kids, felt different and unequal to her peers.

"It's important for kids to feel equal," she says, stressing the need for teachers "to realize where kids are coming from and to be aware of and know how to deal with the differences in the ways they're raised." Teachers, she says, need to make children proud of what and who they are, where they come from, and to understand it.

No one knocked down or built up her self-esteem in public school. Teachers just didn't say anything. Recalling how people mistreated her when she began junior high school, Mimi says, "I really didn't care until I was at the end of junior high."

Describing at least part of her youth as being "rather rowdy," she remembers one teacher who embarrassed her in front of other students and took her to the principal, who said, "I've heard about you."

But an aunt, who was crowned Miss Indian America in 1955, inspired Mimi to start caring enough about herself to want "to do something different. I went through a change.

"She was a good role model for me because she was so beautiful," says Mimi who also credits an older sister and her mother with being role models.

"My mother went through a very hard life. She didn't have her own shoes. She went through a time when Indians would go into restaurants where they wouldn't be served. I think that's why she pushed us," Mimi says, noting her emotions torn between feeling hurt by her mother and understanding her mother's need to push Mimi and the rest of the family to get an education.

"Without her, I wouldn't have gone into music. I would have never known I had anything," says Mimi. "She really pushed me in school. At the end of junior high, I decided I'd try to do better, started getting into art and got some art awards."

That taste of success in art led Mimi to enter high school longing to balance some knowledge of her own cultural music with knowledge of classical strains. In her senior year, she applied for a music scholarship. Although she'd tried for opportunities, "I'd never quite make it," she says. "We just don't feel the confidence, and that's what kills it."

Determined to believe in herself, she told herself "'I'm just as good as anybody else. I can do just as well.' I went in there and did it, and they gave me a scholarship which was, for me, a real accomplishment."

Mimi entered the University of Montana on a small scholarship, majoring in music and vocal performance. A soprano, she stayed there for two years. Then an uncle who worked in Arizona State University's Indian Affairs office discovered an ASU program in library science and invited Mimi and her sister to visit.

She entered the ASU Educational Technology Department's Library Training Institute for American Indians and graduated with a bachelor of arts degree in elementary education with minors in music and library science.

"I was really happy about it," she says. "I've always believed that elementary education is the most important time for kids to learn and to start believing in themselves."

After Mimi began working as a teacher of library usage on the Salt River Indian Reservation, Dr. John Tippecannic, Director of ASU's Center for Indian Education, visited and invited her to enter the master's degree program in Indian Education. She seized the opportunity. But two years into the program, Mimi jumped at still another opportunity, took a six-month leave of absence, and went to the National Indian Education Association (NIEA) in Minneapolis to reclassify the Project MEDIA Library's Native American evaluations of books, films, filmstrips, and so on, according to the Library of Congress system. After training Joyce Yellowhammer to continue the job, Mimi left to finish her master's degree in library science and education.

Mimi's professional life really picked up after that. At ASU she trained teachers to develop cultural curriculum materials. Next, she became an information specialist at the National Indian Training and Research Center. While there, she began singing contemporary music professionally with an all-Indian group. At their first performance—the National Indian Education Association Conference in Albuquerque, New Mexico—she met ASU's vice president of academic affairs who opened doors for a project Mimi herself had developed.

From presentations to key ASU administrators and Native American faculty members to endorsements by the NIEA, American Indian Library Association, and the National Education Association, Mimi's project became a dream come true—all the way to funding and a permanent endowment for the National Indian Education Clearinghouse in 1987! Since renamed the Labriola National American Indian Data Center, the project is now under the auspices of ASU Libraries.

"I really care about American Indian education because I had such a hard time," says Mimi who emphasizes a need for using positive approaches in education. All kids, she says, "need to be respected for their diverse backgrounds; they should be proud of what they are."

Proud of her own background, she works to eliminate historical discrepancies, misconceptions, and stereotypes—not only those associated with the Sioux cultures, but with all Native Americans. In recent classes, she highlighted Billy Mills' Olympic achievements, saying, "He's done really well, although he had a lot of trouble adjusting."

We need "to think of things in a positive way," she says. Concerned with our perceptions about other cultures, she's been working with students, teaching multicultural ways of celebrating holidays and respecting our differences. "It's easy for kids in the mainstream to lose their identity and [relationship to] the cultural things of life," she says. "Kids should be proud of what they are."

And with Mimi McBride around, making positive changes and making kids proud of their heritage might just become another attainable dream!

If a conflict arises between the environment in which we were raised and our ethnic perceptions, the conflict may act as a positive influence in our determination to succeed.

"I was at a conference once, and somebody talked about IBM—International Business Machines. I was the next speaker and said, 'Where I come from, IBM doesn't mean IBM. It means Itty Bitty Mexican,'" said Dr. Agustin Orci, a superintendent of schools in San Antonio, Texas.

"Almost a year later, somebody caught me in the hall and said, 'You don't remember me, but I heard you speak at such and such a place. I remember that comment you made about Itty Bitty Mexican. You must be very sure of yourself to get up before 500 people and say that. You must have a lot of confidence in yourself.' I never thought of it that way. Call me an Itty Bitty Mexican. Who cares? To me, it was fun...not an ethnic joke. An ethnic joke is different. This is kind of like making fun that I'm short."

The catalyst for introducing multicultural education to Tempe, Arizona, Elementary Schools, Orci earned the honor of being named 1992 Superintendent of the Year in the large school districts category at the annual joint conference of the Arizona School Administrators and School Boards Association. If a phrase could epitomize Orci, the subject of the following article appearing in *Career Focus* in spring 1992, his would read, "independent, but not reckless leadership."

Agustin A. Orci
Mexican Culture
Superintendent of Schools

When his younger sister died from polio, Dr. Agustin Orci's parents sent him to live with his grandparents in Douglas, Arizona, a small mining community on the border. Attending public school in America scared him because he couldn't speak English. Students speaking Spanish were often spanked.

Most of the other students were "Anglos" when he started school. Dr. Orci, now superintendent of Tempe, Arizona, Elementary School District 3, was too young to remember why the situation changed, but suddenly his fourth grade classroom enjoyed many cultures from which lifelong friendships between Hispanics, Blacks and "Anglos" developed.

Perhaps multicultural memories of school friends led Mexico-born Dr. Orci to realize in adulthood, "It's not what your blood tells you you are, it's what you think you are." Those in authority discriminated against him, as did peers who ridiculed his good grades, but he never allowed others' negative attitudes to bother him.

"My biggest fear was to grow up and be stuck in the mines or in the copper smelter. I worked in the smelter during the summer," says Dr. Orci. "Most of the people who worked in the town were in some way dependent on the company store. I knew that wasn't for me. I saw the ticket out of there as a diploma."

Today, a hard hat sits on a credenza behind his impressive looking desk in his spacious office. Not a reminder of when he worked as a hod carrier toting bricks to the brick mason, the hard hat is a memento of the new administration building now housing his office.

"I've always believed you could do more through the inside than you can through the outside," he says, recalling his early days as a school official who protested to a school board about those spankings for speaking your native tongue.

During the late 1970s, Dr. Orci, then a Clark County, Nevada, School District assistant superintendent, went to the Dean of the College of Education at [the University of Nevada] Las Vegas.

"I really would like to do some teaching," he said.

"Great!" said the Dean. "Would you want to teach a course in multicultural education?"

A new phrase for Dr. Orci, he replied, "Gee, I don't know anything about multicultural education."

"Well, you can read, can't you?" the Dean asked, and Dr. Orci thought, is that supposed to qualify me? Still he agreed to teach the course.

Combining his own background with extensive reading, he developed and eventually taught several multicultural education courses, picking up the interest "simply because I accidentally fell into it."

Today he conducts multicultural education workshops, [stressing] communications and leadership, in Tempe, still finding his accidental discovery interesting. He's also been instrumental in developing a department of multicultural education and bringing a specialist into the job.

"I love to talk to people about multicultural education, changing demographics, how change is going to affect everyone, how society is changing, and we have to adapt to it," says Dr. Orci.

Growing up in neither poverty nor wealth, Dr. Orci's family didn't own a car or a television. But back then, few families owned cars, and there simply was no TV in Douglas.

Not missing what he never had, Dr. Orci's love of books grew, thanks to his first grade teacher who read to him. Yet he credits becoming a teacher to Mr. Rogers, a journalism teacher who pushed, encouraged, and was responsible for the young student's college scholarship. College would have been impossible otherwise. Although Mr. Rogers is no longer around to push him, Dr. Orci still receives encouragement today. In the summer of 1991, Dr. Orci was one of 30 superintendents selected out of the 16,000 school districts in the nation to attend a summer institute of technology with his wife Louise in Israel, all expenses paid by the Israeli government! There, the couple toured the cities and countryside, a collective farm, and Hebrew University. From his camel ride to his meeting with the Jerusalem City Council which governs the schools, Dr. Orci describes the experience as "fabulous!"

Impressed with Israel's ideas about multicultural education, he says, "they're not killing the languages. When I grew up, people were trying to kill Spanish. It's turning around. They're allowing the Arabs in Jerusalem's Arab section to teach their language and so forth. You can't separate people from their culture."

In Arizona, where rejection of Martin Luther King Day by the voters was called prejudice, Dr. Orci has introduced multicultural education to the schools.

"I have seen Dr. Orci's eyes snap with anger if he even gets a hint that a child's cultural diversity is not being honored," says Mrs. Sharon Bryant, former principal of Tempe's Rover Elementary School. "Under his direction, the Tempe District has developed a strategic plan that has, as a main component, the appreciation of all students."

In Dr. Orci's eyes, he's doing what comes naturally. "I like to be where the kids and teachers are," he says of his visibility. "If you really want to know what's going on, you've got to be around people who are doing the tasks. To me, that's the only way you can effectively run an organization of this size."

Every large organization has people who disagree with those at the top. Not threatened by critics, Dr. Orci has no problem surrounding himself "with good people who won't be yes people."

"I can't deny that the attacks don't hurt sometimes," he says. When he refereed football games, he learned not to have "rabbit ears"—reacting to outside criticism. "Sometimes people take cheap shots or criticize without any information. If you get down on their level, then you're like them. You can't respond to people in kind. Sometimes you just can't win them all," he says.

Dr. Orci, standing just 5-feet 6-inches, towers over most men. If he could change one thing in the world, he says, "I'd like to see politicians really service not only the education, but the social welfare of children. If we could accomplish that, everything else would take care of itself."

Dr. Orci feels frustrated by everyday life's inequities—a child without food or clothing or one who has a medical or psychological problem. He says, "America can go to war in the Persian Gulf and deliver a missile through the front door of a bunker, but we can't make sure that kids in poor areas have what they need to be successful. To me, that's a terrible injustice."

He points out admirable qualities of famous people and of those close to him and says, "I'm a person who views the world of people and tries to replicate the good things, whether it's a project in the school district or a characteristic that a person I admire has—Hispanics who have come up out of adversity, colleagues who have educated themselves. They did it. I like that."

But Dr. Augie Orci himself is someone to look up to because he's been making a difference in multicultural education and in the ways in which non-Hispanics view Hispanics. And while he's been making those changes, he has remained a truly humble man.

While we try to integrate our personal need for roots with our lives in the world around us, sometimes we're successful; sometimes we're not.

In 1989, Michelle Young's *In Celebration of America* first appeared in a now-defunct newspaper. On February 6, 1991, she presented the "America the Beautiful" portion added to the end of a prayer she wrote at the request of the Phoenix Board of Rabbis for a reading to an audience of 500 people. The prayer has since appeared in publications across the nation. She has never accepted remuneration for either piece. Here, the prayer appears at the end of *In Celebration of America*.

In Celebration of America, 1989, and Prayer for a Nation, 1991

Morning breaks the black blanket of night around five a.m. on July 4 on the Pine Ridge Indian Reservation in South Dakota.

A wide expanse of the plains allows you to savor its beauty bathed in the rising sun's reflection. Magical in [their] effect, those early morning hours raise the curtain [on] a stage set for planned festivities.

Here, on one of the nation's most densely populated Indian reservations, the Oglala Sioux mark Independence Day with powwows of ceremonial dancing, great food, fireworks, and traditional beaded buckskins.

Yet the reservation holds historical and painful memories of Wounded Knee where over 200 Indians were massacred in 1890, and of that village's seizure in 1973 by the same number of Sioux, a protest that resulted in over 300 arrests and the deaths of two FBI agents.

As much as we might not care to admit it, all historical moments create great nations in the same way as they do great families. The vivid traditions and culture of our original native Americans strengthen the Great Indian Nation and the Union itself with a richer heritage.

But this great nation thrives on much more than the uniting of settlers and native Americans.

Today America, the melting pot, blooms with tradition and culture from every corner of the world.

Our Lady of Liberty in New York Harbor continues to provide a ray of hope for refuge to all who are oppressed and persecuted.

Still, there are those in this nation who, like past exploiters of liberty, feel threatened by differences in people. Terrified [by] an unknown future world where all might live in harmony, these are the insecure exploiters of the nation who fear—just as small children fear nighttime and dark rooms. In their organization into parasitic groups like the KKK and skinheads, these individual cowards feed on each other's insecurities and, like a cancer, attempt to pervade the body of the nation.

They don't seem to understand that true superiority is born out of humility and love.

We've survived other cancers: the semi-slavery and slavery of indentured service, the sweat shops, McCarthyism in the 50s. The cancer of prejudice, too, can be beat.

Our great nation, replete with heritage, is an exquisite tapestry woven with threads of red, ebony, brown, cream, and ivory.

This is America.

Remove one thread, and the beauty is destroyed, the tapestry becomes worthless. Use the same color and the same texture throughout, and the tapestry—again—is worthless.

We celebrate another double birthday this year [1989] in this, the 200th anniversary of the first Presidential inauguration.

As we marvel at fireworks exploding in the night skies, say a prayer for those who can't celebrate with us this year—the Russian Jews still trapped in a nation that neither wants nor is willing to relinquish them, the students in Beijing's Tiananmen Square, and all others who long for the freedom we live.

And while you say that prayer, add a special thanks that you are an American.

My name is Maria, Suzette, Natasha, Lien, Michiko...Miguel, Pierre, Mikhail, Ly, Shinya...

Oh beautiful for spacious skies...

I am brown, white, black, yellow, red or a mixture of some or all of them...

for amber waves of grain...

I'm Christian or Jewish, Buddhist, Hindu, or one of the many other religions in the world...

for purple mountains' majesties...

I live in Phoenix or New York, Atlanta or Seattle, Kansas City or Honolulu...

above the fruited plain...

I speak Spanish, French, Russian, Vietnamese, Japanese, English...

America.

I'm a doctor, a janitor, a teacher, a factory worker, a housekeeper, a computer engineer. If I don't work, I go to school...

America.

If I don't work, someone refuses to hire me because of the color of my skin, the slant of my eyes, my accent, or my still unrefined use of the English language.

God shed His grace on thee...

I serve in the United States Armed Forces...

And crown thy good...

I pay taxes...

With brotherhood...

I am an American...

From sea to shining sea.

Lord, You have created a world for us, surely with the intention that we could live together in peace and in harmony, a world of babbling brooks and rolling hills, fertile and lush green land, and miles of sand dunes punctuated with a palm or two. But we are mortal and like children in the face of greed, fear, and insecurity. We don't learn well from past mistakes, and again we need Your help.

Help us, Lord, to remember harmony and to return to peaceful times. Guide us in uniting with our world neighbors against more important wars to save our planet, guarding against famine, water and air pollution, the loss of forests through abuse or fire. Protect us from our shortcomings, especially now in this critical time of war.

Forgive us for the foolish mistakes everyone involved has made that brought all of us to this state of war. Extend Your blessings [over] our world for peace and tolerance among all peoples of the world. And please, Lord, bring all now fighting in the Mideast back to their countries, back home—safely and alive. Amen.

Many extremely interesting, important, and controversial viewpoints have been presented in this chapter on the Americans. But merely having an interest in or seeing something as interesting is not a point at which we, as individuals, should stop thinking. We need to focus on the importance of the topics, concepts, and issues, now and in the future.

Whether we call the Western hemisphere North, South, and Central America, the New World, the Americas, or the United States of America, the name won't always reflect the underlying attitudes, motivations, or feelings. Yet names leave impressions just as they do when two people are introduced. Rather than looking at the area's names from a mono-viewpoint or perspective, we need to consider all represented cultural groups and peoples, past and present, comprising the Western world.

Before the exploration of the New World, several hundred tribes of Native Peoples lived in the wide expanse of geographical regions throughout the Americas. Vast differences in land and climate influenced the great variety of cultural customs that developed.

In American history classes, students learn the events leading to the birth of the United States of America and the more than 200 years that followed. But controversies have risen about the period before the nation's birth and the fulfillment of "Manifest Destiny."

"The New World was discovered," say the history books. But how can a land inhabited by thousands of people be discovered?

From Columbus' perspective and those of other Old World explorers, the East could be reached by sailing West. But much to their surprise, the Americas stood in the way of their journey to the East. Imagine their shock at finding such a large land mass in the middle of what they'd believed to be the entire world! But this land mass opened European explorers' eyes to new surroundings they'd never dreamed existed. Therefore, people living in the eastern hemisphere commonly used terms like "Old World," "New World," and "discovery."

To the Native Peoples, on the other hand, little or no attempt appears to have been made to examine the history behind Columbus' and others' arrivals on the shores of the Americas, much less the Native Peoples' discovery of the European explorers! Perhaps to the Native Peoples, the explorers had come from the New World. With an emphasis on multicultural education, we're now beginning to develop an overall multicultural perspective, rather than one of monoculturalism.

Spain's exploration of the New World made a dominant impact throughout the region. Bringing both horses and new diseases with them, Spanish explorers—or exploiters, if you prefer—swept into the Americas, especially in the area now known as the southern United States, the Caribbean, Mexico, Central America, and South America. Many Spaniards, apparently motivated to acquire wealth while furthering Old World goals and ambitions, stayed in the Americas and married Native Peoples, producing the encompassing cultures generally called "Hispanic."

The term *Hispanic* creates a misleading umbrella under which a myriad of cultures and nations are expected to fit. Many people are offended by this label because it lumps together several cultures and national origins. People with Cuban, Mexican, or Puerto Rican heritage possess unique and individual cultures inherent to their geographical roots.

For the most part, many groups or tribes of Native Peoples throughout the Americas remained monocultural or intermarried with other Native Peoples. Yet a wide range of cultural differences among Native American Peoples prevailed throughout history, making our development of a multicultural perspective especially important in our perceptions.

Until recently, Hollywood's depiction of Native Peoples and several other cultural groups influenced many of the attitudes lingering in some people's thinking today. Early American history books, news stories, folk tales, and even those passed by word of mouth through individual families equally reinforced a broad spectrum of activities and attitudes. We cannot continue using the same approach.

But American society alone cannot be held culpable for its patterns of negative perceptions that have developed through the educational system. The state and national governments of the United States established the reservation system for Native Americans in the mid-1800s, producing a series of isolated cultures within the many other cultures in the Americas.

Many people within the fifty states of the Union neither understand nor even try to understand the issues, problems, and challenges facing most Native Americans today. When outside pressures—rather than internal leadership choices—destroy or greatly alter a culture, the long-term effects are devastating.

When we address contemporary issues, problems, and opportunities, we court danger in clinging to falsely-based perceptions and subsequently acting—consciously or unconsciously—in negative ways. Rather than setting ourselves up for potentially negative situations, we need to revise our textbooks and resources. By instilling new materials with fairness, truthfulness, and sensitivity, our truth-based perceptions will reflect positively on our conscious and subconscious day-to-day and long-term interactions.

Both of us have lived and worked in a variety of cultures, frequently as individuals with a minority cultural heritage. Each of us was provided opportunities to understand people by their actions, what they did and how they did it. And we each had choices to perceive these differences as positive or negative, superior or inferior, when we compared each of our previous experiences to these new cultural environments.

Some people, experiencing this temporary anomaly of being a minority within another culture, choose to enhance their skills and gain additional perspectives. Others elect to impose their views and perspectives on others or withdraw and become extremely critical and destructive.

Regardless of our personal cultural backgrounds, we all need to develop more patience, understanding of, and respect for others and their cultural backgrounds. Why all of us? The land we call the Americas, a land of many things to many people, has changed and is in a continuous process of changing. We aren't groups of people thrown together by blanket collections of cultural labels—Hispanic, African, Asian or Pacific Islander, Native American, Anglo, or any other of the more than 100 racial ethnic identifiers we are given. Although we may identify with a particular group associated with our geographical, cultural, or racial roots, all of us need to be considered as individuals first.

Let's re-examine our thinking, attitudes, and actions in relation to terms like New World, the Americas, discovery, Indians, Mexicans, foreigners, and so on. In one sense of the word, we're all "foreigners" in a strange land, each contributing to the diverse cultures within the Americas.

We—as individuals and as a country within the world at large—need to be willing to develop and implement multicultural attitudes and approaches in all areas of our modern-day globalistic society, focusing our resources, talents, and skills on building a beneficial future for all.

The Americas and its peoples, called Americans, share a past and present in its history and composition. Now we need to honor our cultural diversities, relating to one another as individuals, each solely unique yet possessing so much in common.

Chapter 3

The Western Europeans

More than 100 years had passed since the Continental Congress adopted Thomas Jefferson's Declaration of Independence. Boats packed little better than cans of sardines entered American ports, bringing immigrants to the promise of the new land, offering hope to those who had endured religious or political persecution. And the nation grew every bit as well as her forefathers had expected and then some.

From Vienna, Bonn, Granada and Sicily, Paris, Copenhagen, Brussels and Amsterdam, people of every age, from every walk of life, stood on American soil and breathed free air. Tears flowed freely then, perhaps more freely than they do even today. They stood alone, in couples, and in families, carrying babies and toddlers, some old and infirm. Stuffed carpet bags might have been all they'd been allowed to bring. And few probably spoke this new tongue. But America had become a symbol of freedom, and these new citizens of the young nation had heard a silent invitation they couldn't resist. It's not hard to imagine what might have inspired one young woman who, particularly moved by the scene, sat down one day in 1883 and wrote a poem, *The New Colossus*, that ended:

> "Keep, ancient lands, your storied pomp!" cries she

With silent lips. "Give me your tired, your poor,
Your huddled masses yearning to be free.
The wretched refuse of your teaming shore.
Send these, the homeless, tempest-tossed to me.
I lift my lamp beside the golden door!"

The Statue of Liberty, a gift from France, came to New York Harbor three years after Emma Lazarus wrote those words, perhaps prophetically. Whether she imagined what the Lady of Liberty would look like, who knows? But she spoke with the heart of one who knew:

Not like the brazen giant of Greek fame,
With conquering limbs astride from land to land;
Here at our sea-washed sunset gates shall stand
A mighty woman with a torch, whose flame
Is the imprisoned lightning, and her name
Mother of Exiles. From her beacon-hand
Glows world-wide welcome; her mild eyes command
The air-bridged harbor that twin cities frame...

Emma Lazarus was still young when she wrote the words. Just thirty-four years old. She died the year after the Statue of Liberty's arrival in America, and another sixteen years went by before her words were inscribed on the bronze plaque in the base of the Lady with the Lamp.

The spirit of freedom kindled Lazarus' pen to write those words that expressed the symbol of a nation. In the same way, those who crossed the imaginary line from international waters into America, setting foot on Ellis Island became the concrete foundation that symbolized the nation for sixty-two years.

Whether their family name was Bass or Cohen, Fiorelli or Mastrogiaccomo, Ramirez, LeBlanc, or Heinz, Ellis Island became the symbol of hope as they entered to begin new lives in the foreign land they grew to love.

In 1992, *VFW Auxiliary Magazine* published *Coming to America: Immigrants Remember Ellis Island on Its Centennial*, a series of "family accounts of their part in the largest human migration in modern history." The magazine's editors granted us permission to reprint what we needed from the series, and we are grateful.

"In their search for economic opportunity and freedom of speech and religion, more than 12 million immigrants passed through Ellis Island between 1892 and 1954. Today, nearly half of all living Americans can trace their roots to ancestors who came through the country's major federal immigration facility."

Through these personal accounts of hardship in a strange land, we begin to understand the bonding of cultures through nationalism. And while each culture retained its individual ethnic flavor, each developed a passion for this new land where new customs, traditions, and holidays enticed them into a different way of life. Each culture began to learn from others, and what was called the melting pot chapter of American history was born.

People entering the United States in the years before the Depression had never tasted many of the foods we take for granted today. The newcomers tasted white bread, baked beans, bananas, and apples for the first time, often with surprising reactions.

"...how miserably seasick they were during the voyage; one woman would repeat the story of how she ate her first banana at Ellis Island—peel and all!" said VFW *Auxiliary Magazine* (November 1992) in its anecdote about Frankisck and Cecelie Sramek who left Vodice, Czechoslovakia, for the United States in 1920. "Another couple recalled their wedding dinner in a Chicago restaurant; they had no idea what they had ordered, but would never forget that special meal: pork and beans."

The magazine's July/August issue carried the immigration story of Peter and Julia Martino and their two daughters. But while Julia gave birth to a son on the day their ship docked at Ellis Island, the day was far from happy. The older of their two girls, four years old, had a scalp disease which would require a quarantine and six months of painful treatments, said authorities, and threatened the family with deportation.

Peter exhausted their savings to pay the legal fees to prevent them from being returned to Italy, and they were allowed to stay. A private doctor helped too, examining the child with the problem scalp and finding birthmarks, not the previously diagnosed ringworm. But the treatments she endured in the meantime caused her curly locks to fall out. When her hair grew back, it was thick and straight.

Some people, like Anna Heidrich, were creative in moving to America. Anna left her native Lithuania in 1911, paying for the voyage "by cooking and cleaning aboard ship." Ragnar Calab Johnson left Halmstad, Sweden, under similar circumstances. He paid "his fare by working on seven trips across the Atlantic".

And many of the newcomers didn't find life what they'd envisioned in this new country.

"I came to America because I heard the streets were paved with gold. When I got here, I found out three things: First, the streets weren't paved with gold; second, they weren't paved at all; and third, I was expected to pave them," goes an Italian saying in *VFW Auxiliary*, December 1992/January 1993. And perhaps that was true, but Mary Antin wasn't alone in her eagerness to live in America: "So at last I was going to America! Really, really going, at last! The boundaries burst. The arch of heaven soared. A million suns shone out for every star. The winds rushed in from outer space, roaring in my ears, 'America! America!'" she wrote.

Countless tales are told of newly-arrived immigrants being robbed or cheated and subsequently jailed, being considered illegal aliens and being terrified of the consequences of getting sick or injured on the job.

At seventeen, Anthony Thomas Kasunich left his home in Zagreb, Yugoslavia, to start a new life in America. Describing Ellis Island in 1913 "as a deplorable, terrible, and dirty place," he worked hard to establish himself in the new land, working in coal mines in West Virginia and in steel mills in Syracuse, New York, and Pittsburgh, Pennsylvania. And when he broke his elbow and hurt his legs on the job, he suffered through the pain, fearful that he'd lose his job.

"People don't realize what these immigrants went through. There were many prejudices against the foreign-born, and there shouldn't have been. These are the people who built our America, and without them we wouldn't have the blessings we do," said Anthony's daughter, Ruth, of North Syracuse.

Ellis Island has often been the source of wonderful and true although almost magical stories that somehow pass through families, friends, and neighbors. Such is the circumstance surrounding the following story, passed through Paul Christiansen.

<u>Goose Grease</u>
Danish Culture
Passed on by Gudrun (Rasmussen) Folkestad

In 1900, Sophus Rasmussen and Mathilda Nielson were with a group of other immigrants coming from the Island of Fyn in Denmark. The couple were engaged to be married as soon as they settled in America. As was the custom, these young people had dark rye bread, grease drippings, and other food with them to supplement the poor food that was served to the fourth class passengers on the ship.

After passing through Ellis Island, the groups boarded trains, having to depend on the conductor to alert them when they'd reached their destination.

The couple had made close friends with a Mr. Jensen who was headed for his sister's home in Iowa. In the middle of one of the group's supplement meals, the conductor told Mr. Jensen that his destination was the next stop. He gathered his belongings in a hurry and inadvertently grabbed a small white and blue crock containing Mathilda's grease drippings for spreading on their bread.

Sophus and Mathilda were married one year later, 1901, in Fremont, Nebraska, and eventually moved to Albert Lea, Minnesota, in about 1916. Sophus got a job harvesting ice on Fountain Lake. In the course of events, Sophus got into a conversation with a fellow worker and discovered that they indeed had been fellow passengers on the ship and the train.

Mr. Jensen asked Sophus if he had married Mathilda. When Sophus replied in the affirmative, Mr. Jensen said that the little grease crock belonging to Mathilda was still at the home of his sister in Iowa. He promised to bring it back from there on his next visit, which he did.

The little white and blue crock is still in the corner cupboard of Mrs. Don Christianson's home in Fort Atkinson, Wisconsin.

New generations of these Old World families were born in America, and many lost touch with their European heritage; others maintained at least some contact through oral or informally- or formally-written family histories. In general, all of us become curious about our family roots. They seem to provide a colorful yet psychological balance for our own lives as they weave powerful patterns of the lives of those before us.

The late Arthur Ashe traced his familial origins back ten generations to Africa. The late Alex Haley traced his family background to roughly the 1700s, and he wrote the best-selling novels *Roots* and *Queen* which later became successful made-for-TV movies.

Unrelated to the celebrity with the same name, but coincidentally related to actor Robert Taylor, Richard Harris asked his mother to send him a Harris family history. Following is her reply, tracing part of their family origins to the pre-revolutionary colonies in the early 1700s; she also wrote extensively about the family during the 1800s.

Richard Kennedy Harris
Scottish, Welsh, English and German Cultures
A Family History

Unfortunately, I do not have such specific information about a lot of your ancestors...I have picked the branch about which I do have the most knowledge.

It would be most interesting to know how the Brughs, who had been Baptists and Lutherans, became Dunkards, but I just don't know. I assume the Ives were originally United Brethren members since Grandpa came out to Kansas for his last two years of college at one of their schools. The Stines and Williams were Presbyterian. The Jewells and Kennedys were Baptists earlier but when they did not live where there was a Baptist church, they attended other churches. One thing I do know, they took their religion seriously, and, until my parents' generation, were prohibition advocates and did not believe in dancing or card playing. The Jewells did live in Holland for a time which might indicate religious reasons for leaving their home country. So far as we know, the Sharpes and Trowbridges were Episcopalian. They all helped establish churches as they moved west. For example, the Rev. Anthony Jacob Henckel, whose descendant married a Brugh, established the first Lutheran church in America in Germantown, Pennsylvania, after his arrival in 1717. I am sure that the Harrises helped start the Episcopal church in Ottawa [Kansas].

John Kennedy [not related to the presidential Kennedy family], of Scottish descent, came to this country from Ireland. [Settling in Hardy County, Virginia,] where he married Elizabeth Arnold, he engaged in farming in that area until about 1834. They moved to Franklin County, Ohio, so poor that almost their only possessions were a horse and wagon.

In the fall of 1836, [John and Elizabeth] moved to LaPorte County, Indiana, where—despite Indian problems—John managed to clear farmland and build a cabin. In 1836, he died, leaving his widow and seven children virtually destitute.

...A.J. Kennedy was about twelve...[when] Mrs. Kennedy broke her leg. Friends were kind enough to offer a place to stay while her leg mended. The two smallest girls stayed there, too, but there wasn't enough room for everyone. A.J. and a brother stayed alone in the family cabin. One night, [they heard] a sound outside [and] slammed the shutters closed just in time to forestall a bobcat [from] jumping into the room.

A.J. had as much formal education as the time and place allowed, but [he] had to do much of his learning through his own reading. One summer he worked for $4.00 a month...to buy [his] books... Later, he taught in the one-room schools of the time. Eventually, he married another teacher, Rebecca Morrell, daughter of Jacob and Mary (Bowman) Morrell.

A.J. and Rebecca moved to Mercer County, Missouri, near Ravanna, where he taught school, farmed, had a nursery business, and was very active in the Baptist church, apparently acting as a lay minister when the need arose. As such, they sometimes entertained travelers which must have been a little hard for his wife.

One man who chewed tobacco went to what he thought was an outside door to expectorate. It was, unfortunately, the door into the parlor.

A.J. served one term in the Missouri Legislature. Because of his hatred for slavery, he enlisted in the Missouri militia units. He was first elected second lieutenant and later commissioned a captain.

Rebecca was a charter member of the (Women's Christian Temperance Union) and her husband, a long-time Republican, eventually chose to vote for the Prohibitionist party candidates.

A.J. Kennedy's daughter, Elma, attended a girl's school in St. Joseph, Missouri. She studied music and gave lessons, [going] from farm to farm on horseback. In 1886, Elma married Elias Jewell, son of Daniel W. and Sarah Clapp Jewell. Elias had lived on a farm and [grew] up in the Ravanna area.

He could remember seeing the Jesse James gang riding into town. Like his father-in-law, Elias was very much self-taught, an avid reader and an energetic traveler. He moved to Greeley Township, Sedgwick County, Kansas, with his parents a few years before the town of Mount Hope was established.

Elias did not care for farming. [Doing] some other things first before his marriage, [he] purchased the local furniture [store and] had a mortuary. In 1886, he and Elma Kennedy were married and spent the rest of their lives in Mt. Hope.

Elias and Elma saw to it that their children had good educations. Several of them attended a Baptist-affiliated college in Ottawa, Kansas. There was no Baptist church in Mt. Hope, so the Jewells attended the Methodist church; but at least some of their children were baptized in a Baptist church in Wichita.

Several of Elias' and Elma's grandchildren also attended Ottawa University. Gladys Jewell [Elias' and Elma's daughter] married Walter Richard Ives, son of

James Richard and Minerva Brugh Ives. James had come to McPherson College, a United Brethren school, to finish his education. There, in the farm community of Galva, he met Minerva Brugh from a Dunkard family.

Those who passed through Ellis Island bonded, like a family, with others about to enter the United States. While not all of the bonds were positive ones founded on dreams of a great future, they were ties based on common experiences, fears, and—most of all—hopes. And once they arrived in the new promised land they called "Amerika," they discovered even more bonding through their perceptions of this country they now called home.

"In 1920, Anna Pollari Chirco and her 19-year-old daughter Carmela sailed from Palermo, Sicily aboard the French ship *Patria*. They traveled in the first-class section, enjoying such amenities as a dining room and recreation room during the twelve-day voyage. Still when the boat docked at Ellis Island, it was quarantined for another twelve days due to lice infestation," a writer for *VFW Auxiliary Magazine* wrote in the December 1992/January 1993 issue.

"Five years later, in New York, Carmela married a man with the same surname: Joseph Chirco. Their daughter, Ann Barlow, is a member of Auxiliary 399, Westport, Connecticut."

We tracked down Mrs. Barlow with the magazine's help, and she related her experience as a first-generation Italian American.

Ann Barlow
Italian Culture
VFW Auxiliary Member

I remember being brought up in a very strict environment where, in Italian tradition, the father and husband ruled. We [didn't] have the extras and luxuries that many others seemed to enjoy; but since my father owned his own grocery store, we always had plenty to eat (including sweets!) Of course when [you're] young, you don't realize how important food is unless you don't have enough.

I can remember in the first or second grade, standing in line to the water fountain (Fitch School, now a nursing home) after recess, nonchalantly eating one of those delicious 1¢ Hershey bars. All of a sudden, one of my classmates grabbed most of the candy from my hand and stuffed it into her mouth! I was surprised, to say the least, but not angry. [I] felt sorry for her, thinking she must not get any candy at home. I can still remember the girl's name. And it still bothers me that people do not have enough to eat in this world of plenty!

[Then there was] Valentine's Day. Since money was tight and Valentine cards [weren't] essential items to an Italian family that didn't quite understand all the U.S. customs, we seldom got new Valentines to send others. So one year, I neatly erased the penciled ones and re-sent them the following year.

One classmate immediately caught on to my scheme and accused me of this terrible act in the presence of others. I tried to deny it, but I knew from my total embarrassment, they all knew. I can still remember that girl's name also. Today, I probably would be applauded for recycling. How things change!

My father did not allow me to walk to or from school. I was constantly asked why. (I allowed my two children to walk to their heart's content if they wished, but I [wouldn't] do it today.) We were family-oriented, especially when my father's sister had a baby in her later years. I remember visiting them every Sunday afternoon. Today, I only see this "baby" first cousin maybe once a year at a party or special occasion. Both my husband and I like people and have acquired many friends over the years, but circumstances have changed so there is less time for visiting and talking.

Not all of us, however, live comfortably with our ethnic roots. Mark Kohan, editor of *Polonia's Voice: The Polish American Journal*, struggled with growing up Polish in America. Today, he prides himself on those roots.

Mark Kohan
Polish Culture
Editor

"You're not all American, and you're not all Polish. You're a *hybrid*—Polish American. If you're brought up in ethnic surroundings, you may hate it; but in the long run you realized you were better off for it. When I went out on my own, my friends and I went through the phase of experimenting with our heritage: we cooked *pierogi*, went polka dancing, and read [1905 Nobel prizewinning author of *Quo Vadis*, Henryk] Sienkiewicz and [Joseph] Conrad. It helped us to understand other people better; people who lived this way. You can understand other people's plights or scenarios.

"People don't realize the sacrifices their ancestors made to ensure good lives for their children and grandchildren. Two or three generations ago, people looked at their surroundings differently. They took things at face value. Today, you might gripe about K-Mart not being down the street, or you don't appreciate donuts as anything special. But two or three generations ago, people packed up everything they had and crossed the ocean to America.

"Look at the ways we cook. It's part of our culture to be closer to real ethnic basic things, which is why we like polka music. There's a move now to identify the culture we now have as Polish Americans. I play in a polka band and play polka music. It's a dance. A lot of the songs are Eastern European folk songs.

"I grew up in a real heavy Polish house. Like many second- and third-generation Americans of Polish descent, I [took the attitude that] I'm not Polish; I don't want to learn Polish. Our parents wanted us to learn Polish. Ironically, once we were out of the house, we were down to the Polish center to learn Polish. The grandson remembers what the father forgets. I do wood working in my basement now, like my grandfather did. Perhaps it's the generational thing. But as each generation goes on, there [are fewer] people who take interest in their ethnicity.

"I heard Poland called "God's Playground." For years, Poland was respected for many things—its power, culture, warriors and horsemen, artists, and thinkers."

He speaks of a tribute to Crazy Horse being created in South Dakota. Although the sculptor Korczak Ziolkowski died before its completion, he made his name at the World's Fair with a statue of Paderewski. The Crazy Horse monument is now being finished by the sculptor's wife and son. He mentions more famous Polish people whose abilities and marks on the world equal the contributions of Tennyson, Blake, Newton and others. "...Sienkiewicz, [Polish astronomer Nicolaus] Copernicus...

"When I was growing up, *opłatek*, the Christmas wafer, was part of the Christmas tradition to share. When you share this with someone, you take all of the bullshit you had with someone and throw it out the window to start again. This is really great. So now, my wife and I have *opłatek* out at Christmas. My wife went through a born-again Polish thing too.

"The image of ethnic groups has always been misaligned in America: Italians were considered macho because they're dark and strong; the French were great lovers; the Germans were cold and precise; and Poles—people who, in reality, knew a dollar's worth, mowed their lawns and washed their floors on their hands and knees—were considered slow, backward. There was nothing romantic about being Polish. That is all changing now. A good example is when Solidarity was hot and heavy. People—Poles and non-Poles alike—were wearing the union's buttons. Suddenly it was cool to be Polish because we were defiant to the communists, defiant to the oppressor. Everyone got in the act."

Like Mark Kohan, many children and grandchildren of those who passed through Ellis Island in search of their new lives struggled with their ethnic identities. Perhaps many of them were raised with ethnic customs without being given the opportunity to explore their heritage. Not really understanding why, many people living in the United States today experience the same feelings of separateness from their ethnic roots.

Mitch Rustad
Norwegian Culture
Freelance Writer

Revealing the traditions and history of my heritage is a tricky assignment. I wasn't brought up with a great deal of knowledge about my relatives and their lives. Many of them, in fact, I've never even met or heard of. Since my ancestors' history wasn't always a happy one, it was a non-subject in my house when I was a child. But as I thought back, images and memories at first trickled, then came flooding through. There's a lot of fascination and mystery about my heritage as a full-blooded, 100 percent Norwegian that I'd like to share.

My mother tells me that my Norwegian relatives were born into the school of hard knocks—exhibiting both toughness and resiliency to be able to survive each bone-chilling Minnesota winter. Both my grandmothers came to the Land of 10,000 Lakes from Norway in the late 1800s hoping to start a new life. My relatives endured below zero weather for months with only pot-bellied stoves stoked with firewood to heat their homes. To ease each other's burdens, neighbors would come over regularly to visit, often bringing loaves of bread and other goodies. Such was the simple struggle for survival in small town northern Minnesota at that time. And we think we've got it tough today?

But what was it actually like growing up one hundred percent Norwegian in the 1960s and 1970s in a small town densely populated with people of similar backgrounds? I have no quick, patented answer for a question like this, but I do know that many responses and personality traits have been formed as a direct result of my heritage.

Likely you've never been subjected to an "Ole and Lena" joke—very familiar to everyone in my circle of people growing up. The Norwegian stereotype goes as follows: They're not very bright folks, mundanely unemotional and slow-witted, with the men all too often getting drunk and their wives nagging and...well, check your neighborhood Norwegian joke-book store for more specifics here.

The reality of my ethnicity is a far cry from this, of course. To me, being Norwegian has always been a bit of a mystery. I had no real awareness of my roots as a child. Hearing my grandmother—the only grandparent I had who lived long enough for me to get to know—babble in Norwegian, seemed far removed from anything to do with my life. My family wasn't much on traditions either. My memories tend to revolve around the do's and don'ts I learned and followed, behaviors and belief systems handed down from generation to generation, rather than customs and traditions.

Open discussions of problems and feelings in my family were rare, if they existed at all. Free-flowing affection and happiness or sadness was even less likely to surface. I considered it a real weakness to show my feelings and simply shrugged off anything that bothered me as trivial. I didn't want to bother anyone, and every relative I knew was the same way. Say nice things; don't talk about anything bad, and always be nice so people will like you. That's how I remember my environment. It seemed like a simple enough way to live; but as I grew older, this mentality began to destroy me. The realities of parental disputes, financial problems, and growing up overwhelmed me. I needed to talk, express myself and have somebody listen without all this discomfort and denial.

Although I'm still far more comfortable keeping the stereotypical check on my emotions, I've noticed as I've allowed myself to evolve and grow as a person, the more emotional and comfortable with myself I've become. While I'm sure difficulty dealing with emotions isn't confined to any one blood line or nationality, it seemed pervasive and inescapable in mine.

I don't think the cold-blooded Swede (or Norwegian) thing—all stoicism and control—is as much in our blood as it is in our minds, our society, and our belief systems. I noticed so often the uncomfortable way people I knew dealt (or didn't deal) with their emotions. What other people thought of me was often more important than what I thought, and this melding of emotions certainly played a part in the development of my emotional life. An integral part!

It was as if our emotions were the enemy, to be avoided and controlled at all costs. My family was perhaps an extreme example of this trait—which they

68

still insist is "normal" for Norwegians, but I believe most families of my heritage can identify intimately with this idea.

Pouring your heart out to a family member or friend was virtually an impossibility. I would never have considered the idea of talking over a problem or uncomfortable feeling with anyone, and I never got the idea that anyone I knew would either. I know the same emotions bubbled up inside of everyone, but too often these feelings were stuffed, ignored or soothed by the bottle. The message that feelings are weak, embarrassing, and unacceptable seemed to be everywhere.

Thinking back, I felt many emotions as a child and teenager I wasn't able to convey. I felt different. I was dying to express myself, but the price seemed way too high. I felt the intensity of people's expectations and judgments that I be [a] normal and predictable [person]. The endless ridicule you'd receive if you were at all different was too terrifying to risk. I can't remember anyone who was unique and expressed it who wasn't labeled "weird" by everyone. Anything different seemed to make everyone uncomfortable.

Along with this, ironically, does come a flip side. People who are very concerned with other people's business and approval are often extremely warm, kind, and friendly. People needed people and that attitude was more pervasive than anything. They really cared about each other. It would be absolutely unthinkable and unacceptable not to know and protect the interests of the people on your block. Your neighbor was your ally, to be respected and welcomed, certainly a different attitude from many neighborhoods that exist today. I must admit I've lived in more than a few apartment complexes where I didn't know my next door neighbor.

As long as things were nice and acceptable, life could be very good and people were comfortable and very warm with each other. A day off from school because of a heavy snowfall led to a brilliant day making snow forts and sliding down a nearby hill. Innocence, trust, and goodness prevailed. Not a thought of being afraid to go somewhere or stay away from a certain neighborhood. This luxury was just a given, and at the time I couldn't imagine life being any other way. It's unfortunate—tragic, to be sure—that many children today will never experience this feeling.

But I think the mentality that leads to seeing only the best side often led people to ignore the truth of their lives as well. Denial was a way of life. It took a rare person [to] deal with a problem directly and admit it without humiliation. Problems were direct reflections of us, I learned, and were something to be ashamed of and hidden at all costs. Only bad people have problems, and they certainly don't talk about them!

As I look back on the development of my personality, I perceive myself as a combination of all these things. I have a genuine sense of caring, morals, [knowledge of] right and wrong, and responsibility for which I'm very grateful. Yet at the same time, I've been emotionally shackled, shut down, and too often out of touch with my true feelings. A people pleaser extraordinaire instead of a fully developed person. In my effort to please, individuality wasn't even a consideration for me. Going against the popular opinion, forget it! I wanted to be like everyone else. As a teenager, I didn't dare challenge anything I didn't agree with. The truth I didn't learn is that you can be an individual, be different and unique, and **still** belong.

Perhaps I've drifted from the subject a bit. Does any of this really have anything to do with [my] being Norwegian? Isn't much of our society, regardless of nationality, littered with these rules? Perhaps, perhaps not. But I feel it set the groundwork for my life. My environment as a whole (which certainly included more than Norwegians!) was my teacher. But I believe the belief systems, expectations, and genes I have are a direct link to my family tree.

Through much hard work, study, and introspection, I've been able to slowly come into my own as a person. Many of the ideas I grew up with, I've discovered, don't work for me at all. I've learned I can appreciate the best parts of my development and discard the rest. I have the right to embrace my individuality and feel free. And I can enjoy my memories while creating a new, exciting future that makes sense to me.

Now, my annual visits home for Christmas keep me in touch with my roots, my beginnings. I haven't forgotten about the distinctly Norwegian traditions of *lefse* (which I love) and *lutefiske* (which I hate!) which flood many Scandinavian homes over the holidays. I still find an occasional "uff-da" flying out of my mouth, the exclamation I heard my mother and many relatives use a million times a day over some unwelcome or gossipy bit of news.

My eyes are still blue, and my hair is still blond, although of course not every Norwegian falls into this category either. As often as someone creates a stereotype, there is always an exception to the rule. But I do know I feel more comfortable now with myself and my life than I ever have before.

I can laugh at those silly "Ole and Lena" jokes and feel true affection in the midst of my family's mix of hidden or unexpressed emotions. At times, I choose to keep my feelings inside, but I do feel them now. I'm making sure to say "hello" to my neighbors and make others feel good about themselves when I have the opportunity. I guess you could say I'm more and less Norwegian than I've ever been.

Many families integrated into the American way of life and lost apparent touch with their roots. Yet world events played a major role, not only in the ways in which they perceived their lives, but also in the ways in which they were perceived by others. For children, those roots may have been even less apparent—until something significant happened, and they became, by someone's actions or words, suddenly "different." To a child, "different" can be a four-letter word until they grow up and realize it's a blessing.

Karen Day
German Culture
Writer/Editor

The Penn Central Railroad tracks stretch along the northeastern border of my hometown, adjacent to Mr. Miller's cornfield. When we were young, my brother and I used to ride our bikes along the gravel road that led out of town. The trains that appeared on the horizon were silent as they sped along, almost as if they were floating on the tops of the yellow stalks. We wouldn't actually hear the trains until the late fall and winter. That was when the winds would change direction, bringing with them the stench from the casting factory north of town and, of course, the whistle from the train.

The railroad tracks run through the center of town, separating it in half. To the south are the main business district, the junior highs and high school, the YMCA, the library, and the old, three-story Victorian homes on Michigan and Indiana Avenues, or "the Avenues," as my grandmother says. To the north are such neighborhoods as Pole Town and Hungry Hollow, where the town's large influx of Polish and German immigrant families—and the town's half-dozen black families—live.

Located on the edge of the steel mill industry that rimmed the south shore of Lake Michigan, LaPorte was a factory town in its own right. American Can, American Rubber, and Allis Chalmers, with its sprawling factory on Clear Lake, were part of a large group of factories that employed nearly half the town. Many of the other town residents were small business owners or farmers.

Like so many small Indiana towns, LaPorte once had a thriving downtown. When my mother was young—and even my grandmother who also grew up in the town, she would walk by the different stores on Lincolnway, stopping in at the Boston Store, a two-level, fashionable clothing store, or the Roxy, the best place in the county to buy sheet music, both for piano and organ. People always went downtown to Zelden's Shore Store, Sporting Goods, and the A&P because there was no place else to shop.

All of that changed in the 1970s. As the factories began to lay off employees and finally close their doors, the town began to experience an unusual level of unemployment. And when the Boston Store relocated to the Maple Lane Mall on the far west side of town, the move was a precursor to what would happen in the rest of the decade. One by one, specialty stores either moved to one of the various mini-malls that sprouted up on the outskirts of town, or simply closed their doors because of lack of business. Today, the downtown struggles to stay alive with the several specialty stores that have remained. But for the most part, especially at night, the closed down storefronts and the empty lots where buildings once stood make LaPorte look like a dying town.

But LaPorte did not change completely. The old rules that dictated where certain families lived and who mingled with whom remained. No one knew this better than my grandfather.

Growing up, [my grandfather] lived with his family in a small wooden house in Pole Town, north of the railroad tracks. At the turn of the century, his parents had come to this country from Bavaria, Germany. They passed through Ellis Island and then traveled by train to LaPorte, where my great-grandfather took a job with the slicing machine factory in town.

They were poor, and as a young man, my grandfather took a job to help contribute to the family. He delivered milk to the wealthy houses along the Avenues. At one, a mansion turned into a private home for elderly women, he would stand at the back door and peer into the massive parlor. There, the women would be sitting in silk and linen, sipping tea and talking among themselves. He knew that he was poor and that these women had come from some of the wealthier homes in town, but he [didn't] feel any different from them.

Then one Sunday, just before the first World War, he and his family took their normal pew in the Catholic Church. His father was a simple and quiet man who minded his own business and who did not like to create scenes or attention for himself. But when the priest began blaming the German people—not those who still lived in Germany, but those who lived in this country—for the war, my great-grandfather stood up in the middle of the sermon and walked out. The next Sunday, the family began attending the Protestant Church down the street. And thus began my grandfather's education.

My great-grandfather never forgot the incident. Nor did he ever try to integrate himself into the town. But while my great-grandparents forever remained in their community north of the tracks, my grandfather stepped out. Although he spoke German at home, his English was uttered without an accent. He was a good athlete, good looking, and he was very smart. LaPorte opened its doors to him. After he went to college, he came back to town and later opened a very successful accounting business. And he moved south of the railroad tracks.

My mother felt none of the discrimination that my great-grandfather experienced. And growing up, I never realized that there was any either. Sure, the kids at school made the Polish people the butt of every joke. And as long as one of the black kids from Pole Town was a good athlete, he fit into the school environment just fine. To me, LaPorte was a sleepy, harmless little town. I lived south of the railroad tracks.

But now when I take the South Shore Railroad into town, I can't help but see things differently. After living in New York City, I think there is a side of my hometown that seems narrow-minded and dangerous.

[It's] the comments I hear that bother me so much: Did you know we have a Hispanic mayor now? His name is **Gonzales**. And did you know that Oprah, a **Black** woman, bought a house just outside of town, on Saugany Lake? And if you didn't vote for a Republican, who did you vote for? You're not a **Communist** are you?

Anything foreign, left-wing, or simply different is looked at with suspicion. I think this attitude is dangerous because [it's] so subtle. The discrimination is not as pronounced as it is in New York, and yet in small towns all across America, it is just as serious. Children grow up living and breathing it without even realizing what [they're] doing. Discrimination stems from ignorance, and ignorance is the root of all social problems.

When I go home, I love seeing my family, playing tennis on the high school courts, and visiting my grandparents. And at night, when I lay in my old bed, I can hear the train whistle. And I think [I'm] lucky that [I've] been able to take that train out of town and experience other cultures, other cities, and other countries.

Traveling has opened up my mind and made me more tolerant and more accepting. But what will open the minds of those who live in small-town America and never leave?

We have seen a cross-section of cultures represented in the experiences of a variety of people whose heritage is traced to the region of the world which we commonly call Europe. Tending to view Europeans stereotypically as white middle class people living in the United States of America, we interchangeably use identifying words, such as "the majority culture," "whites," "Westerners," "colonists," "immigrants," "Anglos," "explorers," and so on, especially in reference to a specific historical period.

Europe, from both historical and contemporary perspectives, is a tremendously culturally diverse region of the world. At first glance, Eastern and Western Europe's cultural differences seem to be the most apparent. Yet the old Yugoslavia, plagued with strife during the early 1990s, abounds with major cultural diversity within its small geographic region.

As stereotyping of people categorized as members of a minority group has occurred, similar stereotyping has happened with the Europeans. Gaining a more in-depth understanding of Europeans from a non-European perspective requires consideration of still other factors: Do all of the people in any particular country possess that nation's heritage and predominantly speak its language? A significant number of Bosnians live in Germany, for instance, and many people in southern Denmark speak German as their primary language. And just as differences in heritage and language exist, there are also differences in other components of culture.

We need to think of the specific similarities and differences within and between countries rather than lumping people into a group or groups. By looking at Europeans and the people of all other world cultures as individuals, we can free ourselves from the limited vision of stereotypes. No longer will anyone feel the need to condemn Europeans and their descendants, now living in the Americas, as exploiters, destroyers, racists, bigots, and so on. Just as we hope others can relate to us, now we can be free to accept others as individuals, regardless of their skin color or other identifying characteristics.

In the years following the original Europeans' emigration to the Americas, their descendants married people from other European heritages. Eventually, these intermarriages produced the largest number of people in our country, and the term "Americans" came into existence.

But to some people at least, becoming an American meant one had to attempt to acquire the attributes of the intermarried European group. And yet if a random number of people labeled "American" were asked their definition of the word, their answers would have varied as dramatically as the nation's topography. The majority of this group would most likely describe an American as one who spoke English, came from a European heritage, went to church, celebrated the Fourth of July by viewing a parade and fireworks, and so on. Depending on the person's place of residence in the United States of

America and whether their individual heritage was modified by ancestors' intermarriages, the answers would have tended to be more or less specific and limiting. The more exclusive one's background—whether through heritage or experience—the more narrow their definition of an American would be.

Yet we must keep the perspective that the term "Americans" includes all of the western hemisphere and not just the United States of America. While we attempt to view people as individuals, the countries of their cultural heritage still play an integral role in their personal relationship to this nation itself, and we need to consider what really makes a person an American from the United States.

If we expect to achieve unity between the variety of cultures in the United States of America, we must consider our common factors as well as respecting our cross-cultural differences.

A common language plays an integral part in unification, but that common language should not be the determining factor in the amount of respect someone has earned. Since English, for instance, has already been established as the major language of the United States of America, those who are fluent in that language should encourage and help others living in the nation to learn to speak, read, and write English. In the same vein, limited English speakers should be complimented and encouraged for their attempts to speak the language, regardless of errors.

Conversely, fluent English speakers can learn a few words in a limited or non-English speaker's primary language. This small gesture bridges the gaps in understanding between cultures. While limited or non-English speakers sense the respect and offer of friendship, the fluent English speaker can sense the frustration of trying to learn another language.

To those who have lived, grown up, gone to school, and worked in a community where one tongue was spoken, the concept of learning another language presents a potential difficulty. Imagine not speaking the language where you live. Picture your difficulties in finding housing. Do you know which of your customs might offend others in your new surroundings? What about your usual groceries that might be considered gourmet? Or what if you or a family member suddenly took very ill, could you communicate to the health professionals tending to you?

Search for an opportunity to immerse yourself in another language, even for just a few hours. No matter where you live, you probably live near many bilingual or multilingual people. Arrange to spend an evening with one or more of these people who speak a foreign language, and prepare for the adventure of entering the non-English-speaking world!

Similarly, as to who really discovered or rediscovered America... who cares? The discussion of America's discovery and other sources of heated historical debates should include several factual viewpoints. Many historians, for instance, credit Columbus with discovering America, but the Vikings and other groups appear to have preceded Columbus' arrival in the New World. And some historians believe the Native Americans may have migrated across the Bering Strait from the Gobi Desert region in Asia.

Spending time and energy in debates about "who's on first" makes us vulnerable to polarization over this issue, separating us and weakening the nation. But America's discovery discussions don't stand alone in arguments about historical accuracy. These situations hold true all over the world.

When multicultural issues become polarized, no one achieves anything positive. By applying the concept of unity in diversity to all areas of life, everyone—regardless of their cultural background—can be respected, and the individual differences in people's beliefs and actions can be viewed as positive. At the same time, all people in the country, community, school, and family can embrace the beliefs and actions held commonly with others from all walks of life.

Chapter 4

The Jewish Holocaust and Beyond

Throughout world history, both peace and war time stories have shaded and colored our perspectives of any particular historical period. Yet few have left the impact that those of World War II did. Millions upon millions died in the most inhumane and horrifying ways in the longest eleven-year period humankind had ever seen.

Perhaps World War II's atrocities overshadowed the tens of millions of casualties resulting from the ravages of World War I. But war does those things. Someone dies, becoming one more casualty, one more in a long list of names that soon becomes a blur of many names. How many of us remember one name—just one—on the list of casualties after the Crusades, even after World War I?

Yet counting the numbers of casualties from war neither lessens the numbers nor justifies the reasons for the existence of war. At its roots, greed, power, and desire for personal gain fester, serving as fodder for leaders or would-be leaders. These three components as parts of our individual personalities probably wouldn't be conducive to declarations of war. But by slightly modifying these factors to their particular nation's community needs, many national leaders have been able to achieve their personal goals—the same three components that have been responsible for many, if not all wars.

A year after the armistice agreement was signed ending World War I, the 1919 Treaty of Versailles sought to restore world peace by establishing the League of Nations. The Treaty also required Germany to disband much of its army and pay $15 billion to twenty-seven Allied nations in acceptance of its total responsibility for the war. The doomed Weimar Republic began to crumble.

By 1923, the Republic was on its last legs, necessities became cherished commodities, and butter and white bread were luxuries reserved for the very rich. Average citizens had lost their confidence in the government; their morale had sunk to a new low. That the economy was suffering all over the world was of no concern to German citizens. To them, no people could be suffering from the times more than they.

One particularly power-hungry politician saw the situation as his opportunity to seize control of the government. Late in that year, he made his move for a coup in Munich. His poorly planned takeover, however, was quickly nipped, and he received a prison sentence for his efforts.

But although the young man they called Adolf Hitler was sentenced to five years in prison, he only served less than a year. If anything, his trial and subsequent prison time worked to his advantage. He revised his political platform while reaping free publicity from the trial itself.

In prison, Hitler wrote *Mein Kampf*, his autobiography, in which he established his political and philosophical goals, sharing with the downtrodden German people his vision of a once-again strong German nation. The master race, he believed, offered Germany and its people the future.

Did the German people realize the diabolical steps Hitler planned to use in achieving these goals? If they did, perhaps their own fears precluded any thoughts that Hitler might be the messenger of an endless macabre nightmare. But analysis becomes nothing more than second guessing. The experience, on the other hand, becomes everything.

An 18-year-old Jewish pianist from the United States arrived in Germany on the *S.S. Reliance.* Her parents had given her the opportunity to pursue her dreams of studying to become a concert pianist at the Conservatory of Music in Berlin. She kept a journal, and what follows begins July 21, 1922, just over a year before the attempted Munich coup. These words make up the memoirs of a foreign Jewish girl in a nation filled with disheartened words and lost hopes.

Sonia Feinbloom Petitte
American-Born Russian and German Jewish Culture
Concert Piano Student

We arrived safely at Cuxhaven this morning and oh how I rushed madly around the boat, looking at Cuxhaven pier in order to make myself really understand that I am in Germany. Estelle was worried a great deal over our trunks and suitcases but I was much too excited and I had no time to worry about suitcases.

I said goodbye to all of my friends and they all wished us Goodluck, etc. In a way I felt sorry to leave the steamer because we had such a wonderful trip...I stood on deck watching the German children who were watching us from the pier.

But at last it was our time to get off and what a feeling we had while walking down the stairs to ground. As I reached the land I turned back and looked at the *Reliance*. What a large beautiful steamer it is. Then we hustled into the custom house and there I first received a telegram...

There was so much excitement in the Custom House, everyone was running around trying to find their baggage and to have the stamp put on...While Mrs. Erde and Estelle were attending to the trunks, I was watching the German children outside. But finally our trunks were checked and we went into the depot part which is like a large restaurant. Everybody sits at tables and could be seen having sandwiches and beer. We did not have time to order anything because then the train came to take us to Hamburg. What a funny looking train it was! It has little compartments for four or six people and the doors by each compartment for entering. We managed to crowd seven or eight in our box (that's what it is like) and I sat on top of my hatbox which was next to the windows. We're off! We're off! We are in Germany!!

...I don't believe the Prince of Wales could attract as much attention in New York as we attracted in the station. Everybody, man, woman and child, stopped and stared at us. I don't know their opinion of us but I know my first impression of the Germans in appearance.... They looked like poor farmers, all have such rosy red cheeks and such extremely funny clothes. They all had blond hair and the women seemed most amusing because they wear such ill fitting corsets...

July 22, 1922 In Berlin:
...The dollar was 500 marks and that was considered unusually high so the Nitkes advised us very foolishly to sell all of our dollars and we were fools enough to take their advice. At the time we felt like millionaires; it was later when we realized only too well our sad mistake...

The people here in Germany eat very little because they are so poor; they just barely afford necessities. They do not serve butter or white bread as that is too expensive. They eat black bread and not much of that either...

At this Pension there are quite a few Russian people from Riga, a beautiful Spanish woman and two children, Yanka and Carlos, from Central or South America besides German people and we who are from the good old U.S.A.

Tonight Lulu took Estelle and me for a short walk. It is quite dark on the streets because the city cannot afford the upkeep of sufficient electricity. They only have hot water here once every two weeks, so if you wish to take extra baths you must go to the bath house and pay 50 or 100 marks for a bath.

In Berlin the houses are locked outside at eight o'clock. Here, the people eat first breakfast at nine or nine thirty; second breakfast at eleven or twelve; *mittag essen* at two thirty and then everyone sleeps until five o'clock when they have tea. No practicing or voice is allowed in Berlin between the hours of 2 and 4 as then everyone sleeps and rests. Even the stores, most stores, are closed.

...They have funny telephones here also. They remind me of those of long ago.... The styles for women in Germany are ridiculous. They are terrible, so homely with no taste whatsoever. Everytime we go out we always ride in a taxi or *drushka* because it costs almost nothing for us.

July 24, 1922 Berlin, Germany:
...We walked around the ex-Kaiser's *Schloss*, the Crown Prince's *Schloss-Palacerati* (sic); the great palaces are now being used as art museums. In front of the ex-Kaiser's *Schloss* there is a wonderful statue representing the Might and Strength of Germany. Then we walked up *Unter der Linden* which is the Fifth Avenue of Berlin. It must have been a beautiful street formerly, but now they are not keeping the wide streets clean and the magnificent buildings are very old and lately they have not been repaired.

August 2, 1922 Berlin:
...The morale in Germany is much lower than that of America.

August 3, 1922 Berlin, Germany:
Regina...told me of their experiences in traveling. There is not much fun now in traveling through Europe; one has too much trouble and danger to

constantly watch out for.

August 11, 1922 Woltersdorfer:
This morning after first breakfast Gisela, Anne, and I went walking. Anne is also a Deutsch girl and she is staying here for a while. It was quite hard for us to talk quickly because the girls do not speak English very well and I, with my two words of Deutsch. But withstanding all we had just loads of fun and we managed to understand each other...

August 14, 1922 Woltersdorfer:
...The mark is beginning to fall and it is almost as bad for me as for some Germans here because I sold all of my dollars at 500 marks. Now it is almost 1000 marks to the dollar...

August 15, 1922 Woltersdorfer:
Gisela, Anne, Edith and I played checkers *(Damen)* quite a bit today. Tonight I played piano for a little while and later I played poker with some people here. I won 20 marks. While we were playing Frau Stein-Schneider rushed in quite excited, she had just arrived from Berlin and she said that there was some excitement now as the mark dropped to 1800 for the dollar. I felt sick when I heard the news because I sold all of my money, on Nitke's advice, at 500.

Sonia Feinbloom Petitte's journal ends there. In retrospect, she said she saw signs of anti-Semitism cropping up here and there and simply stopped writing. Word of the coup attempt had reached Berlin, and tension had begun to build. Sonia, however, did not return to the United States until 1924—after the attempted coup in Munich.

In the ten-year span after Sonia left Berlin, President Paul von Hindenburg appointed Hitler chancellor, and Hitler wielded his political power effectively. Within eighteen months after Hitler's appointment, his Nazi party dominated in the *Reichstag*. But dominating the *Reichstag* hadn't been a difficult feat to achieve. Hitler simply ordered the arrest of his opposition by making their parties illegal. Next, the Nazis maneuvered the Enabling Act into law, and Hitler swiftly moved from chancellor to dictator.

Hitler's party, too, continued to assume more and more power; by 1935, the Nuremberg Laws were passed, and Jews were no longer afforded the privilege of German citizenship. Back in the United States, Sonia married Bernard Petitte, an Italian shoemaker, in April of the same year.

Gerard, the second of Sonia's two sons, was born, eighteen months before what became known as *Kristallnacht*, the Night of Broken Glass. In 1959, Gerard was stationed with the United States Army in Bremerhaven, Germany, approximately 300 miles from Berlin. He saw the first barricades being constructed before the Berlin Wall was actually built on August 13, 1961, and he saw the Wall itself. Gerard, like Sonia, felt the pain of the Jewish experience as he talked with those who were there—the Holocaust survivors, former Nazi officials, and their children—almost fifteen years after World War II was over.

Gerard Petitte
American-Born Italian and Jewish Cultures
Junior College Instructor

When Germany was defeated in World War I, the spirit of the German people was extremely low. They had lost all self-esteem.

Dr. Wievelt, an elderly physician from Bremerhaven whom I had befriended in the early 1960s, was a young health officer working with the "occupied forces." He'd helped to set up milk pasteurization procedures and food inspection systems.

"The man in the street," said Wievelt, "was either totally lethargic or extremely hostile to all. He just lived for today and abandoned the process of planning for tomorrow. He deeply resented anyone who had more but held no pity for anyone with less."

My mother, Sonia Feinbloom, studied music at the Conservatory of Berlin from 1922 to 1924. As the daughter of rich American parents who could afford to pay for such an education, she was shielded from the realities of that man on the street.

"When Hitler made his *putsch* in Munich in 1923," Mother had said, "we in Berlin thought it was a lot of hob over nothing. Why couldn't these ne'er-do-well's who took part in his little uprising follow more useful pursuits like we were doing? We couldn't understand why some people resented us so. We'd had nothing to do with their situation."

I met Horst Durla in 1960. At that time, the elderly artist and his wife were living in an artist colony in Bremerhaven. During World War II, Herr Durla was a private in the German army. His job was to patrol the dike along the Weser River between the *Flugplatz* and "U" boat station on his bicycle.

"At the end of World War I, our whole society and economy had been destroyed," said Durla. "People who had worked hard all of their lives, suddenly discovered their life savings wouldn't even cover the cost of a loaf of bread because the rate of inflation had gone that high and the worth of their currency had fallen that low.

"When Hitler promised us food, clothing, cars, and so on, we wanted desperately to believe him. We had nothing and wanted for much. When Hitler blamed the Jews, we were willing to accept his charges since they seemed to have much of what we lacked," Herr Durla had, in essence, told me. "When you are in the bottom of the toilet, you'll do anything to climb out, and you don't care who has to pay what price for you to do so."

I also made the acquaintance of Hanon Roman, a high official of Jewish affairs under the allied forces and a member of the West Berlin Jewish Community in 1960. Hanon, a young resident of Berlin, fled to the Middle East with Hitler's rise to power. Joining the *Haganah*—I'd consider them to be the Jews' then-World War II answer to the Green Berets, later integrated into the Israeli army—Hanon fought against the Nazis in a British-commanded Jewish unit. With Hitler's fall from power, Hanon returned to Berlin and became involved in Berlin's Jewish community affairs.

"After Hitler became chancellor, we began to see flyers on walls, kiosks, and light poles, showing Jews as rats and pigs infecting other deprived members of society. Then the brown-shirted hoodlums began to appear. They would break windows, deface various buildings, and push people off the sidewalk into the street.

"With the passage of time, the situation became worse as Jewish men, women, and children were beaten in the streets. They were denied access to schools, libraries, and hospitals, either as professional providers of those services or as receivers of them," Hanon said.

Gerdt Von Brentz, the son of S.S. General Karl Von Brentz who was hanged by the Nuremberg Court, was my age—only eight years old—at the time World War II ended in 1945. When I first met him in Bremerhaven in 1960, he still retained much of the knowledge passed on to him by his father and "Uncle Josef" (Goebbels, Hitler's Chief of Propaganda).

"According to Uncle Josef," said the younger Von Brentz, "the Jew was like the rat in the food locker or the wolf in the goat herd. He was a parasite and a destroyer. He couldn't help what he was. That was his nature. But for the good of the true superior race, he had to be removed."

In the 1960s, Kaptain Haufman Friess was the conductor of the Panzer Division Band of Bremen. But during Hitler's regime, Friess conducted the

Weremacht's Premier Band, Hitler's private honor guard band. Recalling the "glamour and prosperity" during the Hitler era, Friess regarded Hitler as a hero. He also remembered the many so-called social undesirables—prostitutes, homosexuals, and so on—who were sent to labor camps and relocation centers.

Dr. Max Plaut, Chief Rabbi of Bremen, was a key witness in the Adolf Eichmann trial in Israel. He remembered *Kristallnacht* on November 9, 1938, when the windows of various Jewish establishments were smashed, the interiors of synagogues desecrated, and prayer books and holy scrolls were burned. He vividly recalled the screams of people as they were pulled from their homes and beaten in the streets during their round-up for transport to the death camps.

Herr Stein was the caretaker of the former main synagogue in East Berlin when I met him in 1960. This magnificent house of worship on the *Judengasse*, destroyed on *Kristallnacht*, was used by the Nazis as a mule stable and execution site. When I visited the synagogue, I could see the fire-scorched wall where the ark and scrolls had been. The floor was pitted from the shoes of the mules and horses stabled there. It was still stained from the animal droppings and the blood from those who'd died there. The walls still bore holes from the execution guns.

He told me the story of a young rabbi who rescued a small Torah and two prayer books from the fire in the synagogue, smuggling them out of Berlin into the countryside where he wrapped them in oil cloth and buried them under the feed trough in a pig sty to keep them from being destroyed by the Nazis before he, himself, was caught and executed.

Mr. Gruber was a former prisoner of the Nazis in a prison off the *Judengasse* from 1942 to the fall of Berlin in 1945. When I met him in Connecticut in 1963, he described some of the conditions he and others had to endure there:

> We had no sanitary facilities to speak of. We relieved ourselves in a makeshift bucket or in a hole in the floor. Cleaning consisted of everyone and everything in the cell being washed down once a week with a fire hose on an unannounced basis. The food we were given was putrid, but it was all we had to sustain us.
>
> The abuses we suffered were something else. Some people were executed "firing squad style" in the center courtyard. Others were used as "moving targets" for the amusement of the more sporting members of the prison cadre. Some people were hanged in the courtyard. Others died through more creative methods: the swinging "bat ball," "Gladiator versus the Hounds," and "Whale in the Pond."
>
> Some of the "pretty" young boys and girls were selected to be objects of sexual pleasure for various members of the cadre. Some of the "less pretty" young boys and girls were selected for more imaginative

games with dogs and mules for the amusement of lower members of the cadre.

I visited Herr Gruber's cell in that prison two years before I knew who he was or that he even existed. After that meeting, however, his whole situation came shockingly to life.

Dr. Jacobs, a former Auschwitz inmate whom I first met in New York in 1965, painted a similar picture. "We were transported to the camps in enclosed railroad box cars with no food or sanitation facilities. The air was stagnant and the light almost nonexistent. Many died along the way.

"When we arrived at the siding outside of the camp, those who survived were ordered out of the cars with their belongings onto the apron at the side of the tracks. We were then ordered to leave our belongings and line up in double columns of two in order to enter the camp. The sign above the gate as we marched in," said Dr. Jacobs, "will stay with me for all time: *Arbeicht Macht Frei*—The work will make you free."

Their words tug at me, and their experiences sear into my brain in one conversation—as if the voices blend into one:

"The *Kapos* would board the box cars after the new arrivals had marched into camp and pull the bodies of the dead together with their belongings out. These corpses were loaded into trucks and driven to the stripping section of the processing complex. All of the belongings were loaded into other trucks and driven to the merchandise section of the processing complex." —Herr Stein

"Newcomers to the camp were led to a large assembly room where they were ordered to strip completely and leave all their clothing on a chair. Then they lined up in double columns of two and were led into the examination room where they were examined by the doctors. After that, they were segregated into groups 1 and 2." —Dr. Plaut

"After the new arrivals were led from the assembly room to the examination room, the *Kapos* gathered up all the belongings, loaded them on a truck, and drove them to the merchandise section of the processing complex" —Herr Stein

"The people from group one were led across the compound to the cleaning portion of the processing complex. They were told that they would be given showers and deloused. They were led into the shower room in groups of one hundred. The doors were closed and locked.

"The Zyklone B gas was administered through the shower heads in the ceiling. After a while, fans cleared the air so it was safe to enter the chamber. The bodies were pulled out, loaded onto carts and rolled into the stripping section.

The *Kapos* would then wash out the shower room and eliminate the bad smell so the shower room was ready for the next group." —Dr. Jacobs

As I stood in the shower chamber in Dachau, I could almost hear those terrified screams of "GAS!!!" "MURDER!!!" I could almost feel the tight constricting in my throat and chest. In the crematorium, the ovens looked cold and ominous. The racks—sticking out of the huge open doors—looked like grotesque tongues. I could almost hear the crackle of the flames and smell the burning flesh.

"The people from group two were moved from the examination room into the dressing room where they were issued prison uniforms. They dressed and lined up in double columns of two. They moved from the dressing room into the interrogation room, where they were verbally examined by administrators who were seated at desks. At that point, the people were further divided into sub-groups." —Dr. Plaut

"One group consisted of health and medical professionals like doctors and nurses. Another group consisted of administrative people like accountants and secretaries. A third group was made up of trades people like carpenters, tailors, cobblers, artists, plumbers, electricians, painters, and so on. A fourth group was made up of strong unskilled laborers. Those remaining were split into two categories: the pretty young girls and boys were sent to brothels for the pleasure of soldiers and officers. The rest were kept apart and used in various medical and materials experiments." —Dr. Plaut

"When bodies were brought into the stripping section, they were stripped of any clothing they might have had on. The clothing was checked for hidden money or other valuables and then burned in an incinerator just outside. All moneys and valuables were placed into carts for transport to the merchandise section.

"The hair was cut off the heads of the corpses and put into a separate cart for the merchandise section. Jewelry and gold teeth were pulled from the bodies and put into the cart with the moneys and other valuables. Bodies with unusual tattoos had the skin cut away. The skin was tanned to make lampshades and other unique decorations." —Dr. Jacobs

When I visited Dachau, some of the tanned skin artifacts were on display. They were extremely beautiful in a macabre sort of way.

"The bodies were then placed on carts—like so much firewood—and rolled into the crematorium where they were burned in the ovens" —Dr. Jacobs

"The hair, gold, luggage, and other belongings were taken to the merchandise section—where they were segregated by item, counted, logged in, and stored. When orders were received for various items—canes and crutches for a military hospital, hair for a bomb site factory, or clothing for a civilian distribution center, they were processed and sent out." —Herr Stein

"The inmates were billeted in airless wooden barracks without sanitation facilities. They slept on bare wooden pallets without mattresses, sheets, pillows, or blankets. The inmates were awakened at the crack of dawn and assembled in the area in front of the barracks where they were accounted for. While the inmates remained in the assembly area, *Kapos* went into the barracks to check on those who'd failed to come out. After the accountability check, the inmates were moved to the kitchen area where they were fed foul-tasting, foul-smelling, watery slop." —Dr. Plaut

"After the able-bodied inmates had moved to the kitchen area, the *Kapos* went into the barracks and removed the bodies of those who had died during the night. Anyone who was alive but unable to get out of bed, was simply beaten to death with clubs and their bodies added to the rest." —Dr. Jacobs

"In the experimental unit, some inmates were tied into large tubs and their body temperatures lowered with ice and ice water until they eventually passed out and died. Each stage was recorded with the results noted so that medical personnel could establish at what cold levels consciousness could be maintained and at what cold levels life could be maintained." —Herr Stein

It's interesting to note that modern doctors use this same thermal technology in heart surgery and transplants.

"Other inmates were subjected to extreme heat conditions in a similar manner while other inmates were used to test various biological organisms and chemical agents." —Herr Stein

"Inmates in the labor section worked long and hard without mercy or consideration. If someone was working on a road or in a field and collapsed during the work activity, they were simply shot through the head and buried in that field or under that road. If someone was covering over an old latrine site and helping to relocate a new one, they—if weak enough—could end up being buried alive with the rest of the waste matter." —Dr. Plaut

"Many of the favored in the brothels went insane in a very short time from the abuses they'd suffered. They died in various horrible ways. Many were infected with diseases like syphilis and suffered likewise. Some of the young girls who became pregnant, were aborted by various chemical and physical means. Many of them died. Others were incapable of producing children as a result." —Dr. Jacobs

"During the time the *Führer*—Adolf Hitler—and his people, the Nazi Party, were in power, we lived far better than we had before. My wife and I were given a nice apartment with good furniture for a very low rent. We got very nice clothing at very low prices, and we even got two very fine bicycles of our own."
—Horst Durla

While the Durlas and others were enjoying such benefits, we now know what happened to those who provided them.

"When we were defeated by the Allies in 1945, we lost all we had gained."
—Horst Durla

In April 1962, I attended a Passover *Seder* in Berlin. There were Jews from all over the world there, representing the United States, Canada, Denmark, France, Israel, Norway, Holland, Austria, and so on.

We gathered for the *Seder* in a chateau which had been a former S.S. or Gestapo headquarters building on Joachimstler Strasse near the No Man's Land that divided East Berlin from the West. The lights were out. Only the candles on the table were flickering. We all stood in the magnificent ballroom of this former Nazi bastion, our wine glasses held high.

As we stared through the huge glass windows looking past the No Man's Land to the Wall and the guard towers on the other side, we all vowed that as we had seen the Nazi pillars fall, we would see that damned wall come down and look forward to a time of peace and tranquil understanding for all mankind.

The Holocaust extended far beyond the walls of Dachau, Auschwitz, and Bergen-Belsen. September 29-30, 1941, in Kiev, 33,771 Russian Jews were slaughtered by machine gun fire. German soldiers pulled the triggers.

Compassionate non-Jews, often Germans, risked their own lives to hide an entire Jewish family, even one person. Steven Spielberg's *Schindler's List*, released in 1993, told the story of one man who saved 1,000 Jews. In Hungary, Raoul Wallenberg, a Swedish diplomat, saved about 20,000 Jews. In Denmark, heroic Danes smuggled an entire Jewish community into Sweden.

About 2,000,000 Jews survived Hitler's horrors by the end of the war in 1945. But those who attempted to save the Jews and were caught, suffered similar fates to the victims of the German blood baths.

By 1942, some 500,000 Polish Jews were forced from their homes surrounding Warsaw, walking or riding to what was to become their new community. But on April 19, 1943, only 60,000 were left. Knowing they had nothing more to lose, they fought back. This time, the 60,000 Jews who died, died on their own terms—just as the Jews at Treblinka did four months later.

In the winter of 1993, Michelle Young met Maria Segal, one of the few survivors of the Warsaw Ghetto. A petite woman with short, bobbed, reddish hair, Maria tells of others whom she's met, others who have survived the horrors of the Holocaust.

She can only guess her age today. Her birth certificate was lost somewhere between the Ghetto's blazing inferno that April day in 1943 and the United States today. But birth certificates take second seat to losing your entire family. Maria is all that remains of her many brothers and sisters.

Maria spoke of her father, a shoemaker like Michelle Young's father. She mentioned a non-Jewish Polish woman who smuggled food and supplies into the ghetto for six-year-old Maria's family. Later, the woman would smuggle Maria out. Maria, said the woman, would help tend her cow. Maria believes she was chosen because she looked Polish rather than Jewish.

And when the child was finally smuggled out, the woman and the little girl returned until they could return no more, bringing food and supplies for her family—often from her father's grateful customers who remembered when he had been kind to them.

The day they stopped returning to the Warsaw Ghetto, the holes in the wall—Maria speaks of them in the following statement—were boarded up. That was the day Maria knew she wouldn't see her family again. Her tears in the silence of night always flowed.

War quickly erases a youngster's childhood, as it did for Maria. She eventually was moved to a Polish Catholic family in Warsaw, and she—for a life-saving time—lived as a Polish Catholic child. Finally, she was reunited with an uncle in Paris.

The memories are still fresh, as if they happened just yesterday. Unlike when she couldn't bear to talk about those days, today she speaks freely—not only for her own healing, but for each of us—so that we'll never forget.

Maria Segal
Polish Jewish Culture
A Warsaw Ghetto Survivor

It seems that I have been in hiding for fifty years. In the past, it was very difficult for me to speak about the Holocaust to my family and friends, let alone strangers. As I get older, I realize the importance of sharing my experiences of the Holocaust with others.

It is important to let the world know that the Holocaust should never happen again to humanity, be it Jew, Christian, Black, or White.

When Germany invaded Poland in September 1939, I was a very young child. At the time, I lived with my parents, brothers, and sisters. My family and I lived in a small village outside of Warsaw.

At the onset of the war, my father was still working, and we had food to eat. In 1940, Hitler built ghettos in Poland and Germany for the purpose of putting all the Jews together. Hitler had a master plan for the Jews.

One morning, the Germans decided to round up all the Jews in the village square of Okuniev. We were forced to leave our homes with clothes on our backs and little else.

The Gestapo got everyone out of the house early in the morning and forced us to march to the Warsaw Ghetto. The children were riding in small wagons. The elderly and feeble, who did not walk fast enough, were beaten, and thus some never reached the Warsaw Ghetto.

The Ghetto consisted of a small portion of the city, surrounded by a brick wall with barbed wire on top to prevent escape.

There were several openings in the walls, guarded by Germans on the outside and Jewish militia on the inside.

My family was fortunate to have relatives in the Ghetto; all nine of us lived in one room. Food was very scarce, and it was difficult to earn a living.

Starvation was a way of life. People were dying in the streets all the time. Their bodies, without proper burial, were covered with paper.

As time went on, the Germans began mass deportation from the Ghetto to concentration camps in Poland and Germany. The Jews were told by the Germans they were going to labor camps for work. Since the Ghetto conditions were so deplorable, a promise of a labor camp was more encouraging.

Later in the spring of 1943 word came that the Ghetto Jews were not going to work camps as promised; in reality, they were going to death camps, to the gas chambers, and no one was returning.

Thus, the Ghetto revolt started under the able leadership of Mordecai Anielowicz on April 19, 1943. A handful of Jews who were left in the Warsaw

Ghetto armed themselves with Molotov cocktails, homemade explosives, and whatever guns were smuggled in from the outside. The Jews decided to fight back [against] the Germans. [The Jews] were no longer willing to go to the concentration camps to die.

They fought fiercely and heroically, to the surprise of the Germans. In fact, it was necessary for the Germans to retreat a few times.

At this point, the Germans reinforced. They had to add more troops, brought in tanks and bombs, and burned the Ghetto, building by building.

This resistance lasted three weeks. The few brave Jews fought to the bitter end. They wanted to die with dignity and pride rather than going to the gas chambers.

A few ghetto fighters survived several weeks. After the ghetto liquidations, they were hiding in underground bunkers and sewers.

I was fortunate to escape the ghetto before the burning started. I watched the ghetto burn at a distance. That was the last time I saw my family.

It is important to know that the Warsaw Ghetto was the first civilian rebellion against the Germans in all of Europe. The Jews knew that they were going to die and that they would become the universal symbol of the human spirit.

I would like to quote from the brave, heroic leader Mordecai Anielowicz who said, "We will perish in the struggle, but we shall not surrender. A struggle for freedom. Long live freedom!"

I would like to see freedom for all nations. We can't dwell in the past. We must look to the future, a better future for all mankind.

Today, most Jews from the Baby Boomer era read *The Diary of Anne Frank*, usually before they reach their mid-teens. Most also know at least one person in their family, or in their family's larger circle of friends and acquaintances, with an unforgettable series of numbers seared into a forearm.

One doesn't forget having seen those numbers, numbers always reminding us that the Holocaust really happened. Those who don't believe have chosen to remain in a disbelieving state, not of ignorance, but rather denial. These disbelievers are to be pitied for their refusal to accept this historical nightmare, for they will always be in danger of having history repeat itself, with a series of numbers burned into their forearms.

We must never forget. We can't afford to forget.

Whether we want to believe all, part, or none of the atrocities taking place during the rise and fall of the Third Reich, our study of these events should be guided not by our wanting to know, but rather by our needing to know and understand. We record and study history because understanding the present and preparing for the future depends on our knowledge and understanding of the past.

In this impelling perspective of the Jewish Holocaust, we need to look at the underlying issue involving all of us, whether or not we like what we see: Hitler was not the first, nor will he be the last, to foster a system capable of destroying and living off the remains and endeavors of others for the advantage of a select few.

Throughout the world, there are seeds, organizations, and people who, in one degree or another, are caught up in increasing shades from dislike to hatred of people by some form of categorization. The category may be as broad and inclusive as race, ethnicity, religion, or socioeconomic strata, or as narrow and exclusive as health, mental ability, or even something as basic as how the dishes are washed, the house is kept, the money is spent, and so on.

All of us have experienced at some time a rush of negative feelings toward another person or people. This is a universal experience which, left to itself and unchecked, may grow as any cancer cell tends to grow. Few better analogies than cancer exist. When we dislike others, especially when we join forces with people who possess the same or similar dislikes, our dislike quickly turns into hatred which frequently continues to expand until we take overt action.

Although we've focused on the Jewish Holocaust in this chapter, holocausts have occurred throughout world history. We can't deny the strong relationship between the Ku Klux Klan movement, Nazism, neo-Nazism in Germany, and neo-Communism in Russia. And what about the former Yugoslavia and its cultural wars? What about our schools, neighborhoods, and places of work—not to mention our homes? We merely need to think about the news events in our individual communities, across the United States, around the world.

A common message of warning for all of us—regardless of who we are, where we live, or what we think—lies in the words of many survivors of the Jewish holocaust. These words and what they represent must not be separated. **History can and will repeat itself.** We must commit ourselves to take preventative measures—not someday, but now!

Starting with each of us examining our individual present views, feelings, and actions, we need to reach out, helping each other to move in a direction that focuses on mutual respect even when we don't agree and believe as others do.

We need to create a positive resistance to society's destructive forces—drug abuse, murder, rape, theft, lies, greed, and so on. More than likely, pride, envy, and selfishness form the underlying factors leading to negative behaviors. We often see these traits manifesting themselves in extremely destructive degrees among children; but when the same factors are played out in the adult arena, the consequences are far-reaching and affect many innocent people.

We must overcome the fear and insecurity inhibiting us from openly discussing our feelings. Whatever blocks our way in respecting others must be dealt with before the cancer conducive to hatred grabs a foothold, bringing destruction to our lives and those around us. In Part II, Chapter 10, we discuss in-depth ways of overcoming prejudice.

We hope you've identified in some way with one or more of the people in this incredible story spanning several decades. If you weren't able to identify with, or begin to feel the impact of their words, read the chapter again.

We tend to pass our mental impressions on to our children. As those images move from one generation to another, we interpret the related pictures through present-life circumstances. No matter what your individual life experience has been, your interpretation of the holocaust events or of any other episodes in world history, your reaction to those periods will be colored by your current experience.

If you were a descendant of a Nazi leader who had been tried, convicted, and sentenced to life in prison or executed, your images of the holocaust will not be the same as those of descendants of survivors or even of those who had no direct connection with the holocaust. In this case, your personal relationship to an executed Nazi leader may overpower the facts leading up to the actual commutation of the sentence itself, laying the groundwork to avenge that relative's death in another holocaust.

If, on the other hand, Holocaust survivors passed on only the images of those who initiated or followed the orders directly or indirectly spawning the holocaust, the same outcome might occur.

Whether the motives for revenge emanated from Nazi descendants or those of the holocaust survivors themselves, the atrocities would continue from one generation to another.

Today, we see similar circumstances in the Middle East and Northern Ireland, where revenge has bound the generations, where families—consciously or unconsciously—program future generations to dislike people they've probably never met.

Certainly we shouldn't view negative events as positive. We need to accept the situation fully and truthfully, refusing to deny any portion of the episode itself. Only after accepting that the circumstances exist can we begin to acknowledge the truth and learn to unconditionally forgive the individuals involved—**not** the situation.

When we refuse to forgive the situation but still reach out to touch the offenders in a positive way, healing can take place, over time. At that point, we can build a new foundation, developing that base through a greater level of understanding while not allowing the great losses suffered by everyone involved to go unnoticed and in vain.

While forgiveness is simple in concept but far from easy to achieve, it is not impossible. In fact, there are many examples where positive outcomes have taken place on an individual level, and similar outcomes can be achieved on the national level as well.

During the Iraq-Iran War, for instance, an Iraqi pilot fired on a U.S. ship in the Persian Gulf, killing several Americans. The wife of one of the dead Americans sent a Bible to the pilot, saying she forgave him for killing her husband. If people, regardless of their background and identification with the holocaust, the Iraq-Iran War, or any other tragedy, can overcome their hatred and not desire to take revenge, we too should strive to achieve the same regardless of our personal circumstances.

We must distinguish the difference between forgiving the individual(s) and accepting the act which led to the opportunity to forgive. We need to dislike, even hate, the acts taking place during the holocaust. At the same time, we need to reject our hatred of those who committed the acts themselves. Over time—and some of us do need more time than others, just as some events need more time than others—forgiveness and healing can occur. By distinguishing that difference, our words and actions can remain tall and strong, guiding the way for our future and that of future generations.

Significant numbers of people throughout the world have experienced or are descendants of those who have experienced a holocaust—an attempted genocide of a group of people—for one express reason or another. Whether or not that reason was valid becomes secondary. The primary factor, the foundation of the holocaust itself, is always the same: one group has something another wants.

But what about the many people in the world who are neither descendant nor survivor, the many who haven't been on either side of a holocaust? Are these people free from becoming victims or creators of a holocaust? We deceive ourselves when we think that our lack of experience lessens the likelihood of our being drawn into the situation. Like trying ignore a lump or slow-healing ulcer, pretending that lump, ulcer, or circumstance resulting in a holocaust never existed makes us more vulnerable to its painful conclusion.

All of us have, at one time or another, fallen victim to our own naive behavior. As children, we might have lied to protect a sibling or a close friend, only to find ourselves inextricably drawn into a web of deception that somehow made us sorry later. Perhaps you once naively took the blame for a friend, hoping to help in some way. Maybe someone asked you to drive to the bank and wait in front with the motor running because they were short on time. It sounded reasonable to you, and you did—only to discover you were suddenly an accomplice to a bank robbery and perhaps an accessory to murder.

While some of these situations may seem far-fetched in discussion, we cannot lose sight of the possibilities that they could happen. The Ku Klux Klan, for instance, is not and never has been merely localized in the Deep South. Former and present Klansmen live throughout the United States, and although not all believe in violence and murder, the organization was founded for that purpose—to rid society of specific groups of people whose heritage, religion, or degrees of skin pigmentation don't fit into their preconceived notions of American society.

Our individual perceptions are conducive to our preconceived notions of the world around us. In many areas, Gypsies and Bedouins have been stereotyped as nomadic, untrustworthy, unclean people. Native Americans have been plagued with generalizations. As a result, these groups and others have often been subjected to discrimination and genocide. Sadly, their misunderstood lifestyles have led to the stereotyping of these people.

Does someone get up one morning and decide to harm another person? More than likely not. A deeply-rooted feeling of failure, worthlessness, or unimportance often lends itself to the motive or reason behind a premeditated act against a specific target. Thinking, planning, and learning to dislike, disrespect, and hate can rule out all likelihood of the spontaneous decision to harm another person.

On the other hand, unpremeditated hostility—like liquid nitroglycerin—can be even more dangerous because of its spontaneous and highly volatile qualities. This kind of hostility takes place without warning.

Consider the following statement: **All people are capable of performing acts of hostility they never knew they were capable of performing.** Do you agree? Some people may find those words difficult to accept or believe. Take driving on a freeway, for example. Would you shoot someone just because they looked at you or maybe passed your vehicle?

Generally speaking, you probably wouldn't react with such hostility. But what if other negative events had happened or were taking place at the moment? What if you realized your spouse, parents, siblings, children—or someone else especially close to you—were in mortal danger? Could you guarantee, then, that you wouldn't be capable of performing hostile acts? These attitudes and feelings frequently develop in this gray zone, the area on which we need to focus.

A holocaust, whether localized, national, or international, involving and affecting a few or many individuals between or within categories of people, has similar roots and stages. We must look directly at these roots and stages to gain an awareness and understanding. Only then can we expect to succeed in preventing future holocausts.

Within the developer and precipitator of any holocaust, we find the roots—feelings of inadequacies, lack of personal accomplishments, and so on, that lead to feelings of despair, hopelessness, and other negative emotions. The accompanying reactions—depending on other factors influencing the character and personality of the individual— will either be passive or aggressive, laying a base for a display of hostile behavior toward others. Both passive and aggressive individuals may be potentially dangerous to themselves as well as to others.

All of us have an intrinsic need to be accepted. Failing to sense acceptance leads to feelings establishing the first stage in developing a holocaust mentality—**rejection.** Rejection's counterpart sets up stage two—**despondence,** characterized by the I-don't-need-you/I'll-show-you attitude.

Several variations, the main motive of which is **acceptance**, are possible. The continuing search for acceptance encourages the individual to seek gangs or more established organizations working with the same or similar obstacles to overcome, or the precipitator may elect to work alone at first and just try harder. More and more disillusioned at this point, the individual may look for an external scapegoat, someone and/or something to blame for the lack of feeling accepted.

Still tired of feeling rejected, the individual moves to stage three, **preparation**, taking on a variety of behaviors or being played out in the mind alone. But the mind is powerful, and images can be extremely realistic.

In this stage, the individual links the issues encompassing stage one and develops feelings of being better than others. Some individuals find areas of perceived superiority easier, for example, over people who are categorically a type of minority. Yet if the developer's self-perception includes minority status based on race, ethnicity, religion, academic achievement, or another strongly measured societal category, then the situation can become more complex.

If each of the three stages—**rejection, despondence** and **preparation**—are left to their own devices, the individual is primed and ready to move into stage four—**revenge.** Now the holocaust becomes a reality.

Don't be misled into believing that hundreds or thousands of people launch holocausts. A single individual reaching stage four can act out hostility with specifically targeted revenge. While plenty of media coverage will motivate some, revenge may be localized at first; media coverage motivates others to move from stage three to stage four with little or no hesitation.

At this point, we have the issue of leader versus follower; although there are, more likely, more followers than leaders. Who knows how many people in today's society are at stage three, just waiting for the catapulting stimulus into stage four? Yet the real question we need to ask isn't how many there are at which stage, but rather, where am I in all of this?

All of us are somewhere in this series of stages. Perhaps we're even providing the foundation which leads others on this course of destruction.

If I am not part of the solution, then I am part of the problem. There is no other place to stand, and no fence to straddle.

Chapter 5

The Baltic Peoples, Easterners, & New Russians

In the 1950s, newspaper and television news reporters brought a woman into the public eye. Her voice had the hint of a not-easily-recognizable accent, and she carried herself with an air of elegance and mystery.

She spoke of an era of kings and queens, czars and czarinas, but no one could be certain whether the tales she told were truthful or woven in some fantastic chambers of her mind. Her name was Anastasia.

According to Anastasia, she was the daughter of Nicholas II, the last czar of Russia. Nicholas II had been czar for twenty-two years, and what should have been a well-established monarchy had become a nation of tension and terror.

World War I, in full swing, had made the already poor economy worse, and the Russian people grew restless. Perhaps by now Nicholas figured he had nothing more to lose, and he replaced qualified government officials with what might have been called mindless dolts. Educated Russians became irate, and the situation continued to grow worse.

In December 1916, Anastasia's parents' dear friend and adviser, Grigori Y. Rasputin, whom they believed had saved her hemophiliac brother's life, was murdered by a group of noblemen. Within three months, the people revolted. Violence accompanied bread and coal shortage strikes in Petrograd; troops sent to calm the situation joined the angry citizens. By mid-March, Nicholas—politically alone and unsupported—abdicated his throne.

Imprisonment of the royal family followed. During the interim, the provisional government led Russia towards an anarchy-type of rule. A Bolshevik leader, Vladimir I. Ulyanov—who would later be known as V.I. Lenin—declared "all power to the soviets" in April. But by July, Lenin and his followers fled to Finland after their coup failed.

Somewhere in the fracas, between that foiled coup attempt and the assumption of power by Alexander F. Kerensky, a socialist who became premier before the end of the month, Bolshevik revolutionaries murdered the royal family. Or did they? Remember Anastasia. Was she really a member of the royal Russian family—the one that got away? Medical science says DNA reports are accurate; according to DNA tests done on Anastasia's body after her death, those one-of-a-kind biological identification prints match those of the royal family precisely. Coincidentally, when the royal family's bodies were found, the body of Czar Nicholas II's little girl, Anastasia, could not be found.

Romance and mystery, pomp and circumstance and intrigue surround the hundreds of years of Russian history. Depending on the year, your mind's eye may bring forth visions of religious icons or Tartar conquests, exquisite Fabergé eggs or vigorous Cossack dancers. Perhaps you'll picture the 400-year-old churches whose architecture marked the landscapes with colorful patterns and onion-shaped domes.

But as history helped to sculpt the multitude of Russian cultures, politics helped to shape the works of Soviet art. Unfortunately, the political shaping of Soviet art was one of rigid control, emphasizing the use of politics in paintings rather than the expanded use of religious beauty. One painting, for instance, showed Lenin as the leader of the Russian people, a dramatic contrast to the soft, gentle tones of the icons.

Yet before Communism placed rigid demands on creative endeavors, replacing religious art and God with political perspectives, the masters of art enriched creative thought throughout the world. In return, the Western world influenced the richness of Russian art, thanks to Czar Peter I, also known as Peter the Great.

And from the roughly 6,000 miles of the Russian steppes, which became the Soviet Union, came many of those who would soon be recognized as the classical greats of music, literature, painting, and ballet. Tchaikovsky, Rachmaninoff, Stravinsky, Moussorgsky, Prokofiev, Rimsky-Korsakov, Shostakovich, Khachaturian. The names themselves remind us of the music: *Swan Lake, Prelude in C# Minor, Fire Bird Suite, Pictures at an Exhibition*, and so on.

Russian writers have been as prolific, with works by Dostoevsky, Tolstoy, Chekhov, Turgenev, Pushkin, Sholokhov, Pasternak, and Solzhenitsyn; and the art world would be devastatingly poorer without the works of Marc Chagall.

Imagine the Christmas season without the Bolshoi Ballet's interpretation of Tchaikovsky's *Nutcracker*. Try to picture a library shelf without Dostoevsky's *Crime and Punishment* or *The Brothers Karamazov*, Tolstoy's *War and Peace* or *Anna Karenina*, Chekhov's *The Cherry Orchard*. And what would the breathtaking Biblical art on the windows of churches and synagogues be like without Chagall's direct or indirect influence?

But for all of the consistent beauty Russia's creative geniuses have contributed to the world—whether through the now-classic works of the greats, or the emotionally expressive crafts, folk music, and dance of the working people today—the political flavor of the land has continued to be strife-filled.

In 1922, Russia became the Union of Soviet Socialist Republics, and people began to sense little difference between the oppression of czars and czarinas and the Soviet leaders. Catherine the Great was protected from seeing the abundantly rampant poverty as she toured the Russian countryside. Similarly, Bolshevik and Communist leaders lived like the capitalists they described in written and spoken propaganda while people in the street struggled to survive.

In 1946, Winston Churchill warned the world about the divisive feelings left in the wake of World War II and the division of Berlin. The physical war was over, but the devastation and anger extended far past the new boundaries of the peace treaties. An economic and political separation between Western democratic principles and the Communist bloc, preserved by an intuitively sensed philosophical, intangible Iron Curtain, had evolved into a Cold War. Communists seized control of Czechoslovakia in February 1948. Five years later,

Soviet tanks moved into East Berlin to squash an anti-Communist uprising, and the citizens of Eastern Europe got a very clear message of what life would be under the pervasive Communist thumb. With the 1955 establishment of a defense alliance under the Warsaw Pact, the Communists continued to amass power, adding Hungary, Bulgaria, Albania, Poland, and Romania to its list of nations.

For a while, the now-massive Union of Soviet Socialist Republics looked invincible. Then in November 1956, another anti-Communist rebellion broke out in Hungary, leaving Budapest virtually destroyed after the tanks and planes carrying Soviet troops had gone.

Censorship and restriction became a way of life. Writers and others who didn't create politically mandated masterpieces were sent to Siberia, mental institutions, or other places where their artistic genius could be physically stifled. No longer were people free to travel between nations. If the Bolshoi Ballet traveled on tour to the United States, they did so with escorts—often KGB agents who could police the dancers' activities and conversation.

But average Soviet citizens, rarely able to explore the world, resigned themselves to learning about other nations from that which the government chose to reveal. Never knowing when the KGB might move to arrest them for often innocent comments, their daily lives became bleak reminders of their lost freedom. Basic liberties granted to Mr. and Mrs. John Q. Public, living in Anytown, U.S.A., through the Declaration of Independence—life, liberty, and the pursuit of happiness—became secret fantasies of the oppressed Soviet populace in the cramped quarters of their homes. Parallel to what had occurred in World War II, children—taught that loyalty to the state must come before loyalty to Mom and Dad—revealed innocent, intimate family conversations from home, and parents were arrested.

The Black Market thrived, commanding exorbitant prices for products otherwise difficult to obtain. Levis brand blue jeans from the United States, for instance, often cost as much as $300. The cost of foods like beef, cheese, coffee, and salmon fetched, proportionately, equally astounding prices. In some areas, even soap for laundry and bathing became a dearly priced commodity.

Like criminals in prison who go stir crazy from four walls and a locked door, the Soviet people longed for the rewards and small pleasures from their hard work for the government. In 1968, cracks and chips began to appear in the intangible Iron Curtain—not enough for Kremlin officials to concern themselves more than sending troops again. Czechoslovakia's Communist Party leader, Alexander Dubcek, had taken liberty with his power and introduced democratic reforms to the country. Assisted by the other Warsaw Pact nations, the Soviets invaded the Czech countryside, forcing Dubcek to return to Soviet policies.

By the end of 1988, popular elections and the Supreme Soviet legislature in the Soviet Union had replaced the Communist Party power base with the 2,500-member Congress of People's Deputies Party. The following spring brought the first multicandidate elections to the Soviet Union, and Mikhail S. Gorbachev was elected president.

Change came rapidly after the election, and by late 1989, the Iron Curtain had fallen. On November 9, the Berlin Wall was opened for the first time in twenty-eight years, and people from every corner of the world gathered for the unforgettable all-night celebration. Three million East Germans visited the West within the following week, and by December 22, Berlin's Brandenburg Gate was opened for unrestricted travel between both sectors of Germany. Germany was reunited, the Cold War was over, and *glasnost*—openness—and *perestroika*—political and economic restructuring—had joined the dictionaries of nearly every language in the world.

By 1993, the satellite countries of the Union of Soviet Socialist Republics, attempting to provide a cushion for the now-collapsed USSR, had divided into two major groups: the Commonwealth of Independent States (CIS) and Eastern Europe with a united Germany.

Yet according to Antonija Petrulis, Western Region Vice President of the Lithuanian American Community Inc., the three Baltic States—Lithuania, Latvia and Estonia—had a separate identity and were not satellites of the USSR. Nor were they Eastern European. Josef Stalin and Adolf Hitler had secretly signed a series of illegal treaties during World War II, the most famous of which was the Molotov and Ribbentrop Treaty, resulting in the forceful annexation of the Baltic States to the USSR.

"The treaty was too important to both leaders, and while the rest of the world turned their heads away, Churchill opposed these secret agreements," says Petrulis.

For the most part, the crux of Russian-Soviet history pivoted around the Baltic States since the beginning of the 20th Century.

"When Gorbachev visited Vilnius, Lithuania, he begged the

people to stop fighting back, that he would lessen the rule. But the Lithuanians said no, that they wanted freedom. Gorbachev realized at that moment the USSR would fall. The Lithuanian Communist Party then left Moscow. From then on, it was the domino effect. Other nations gathered the courage to follow suit, leaving Gorbachev with egg on his face. Like the phoenix, Lithuania kept rising from the ashes," says Petrulis.

Today, people in the **Baltic States**—Estonia, Latvia and Lithuania; **Eastern European nations**—Albania, Bosnia-Herzegovina, Bulgaria, Croatia, Czech Republic, Macedonia, Poland, Romania, Serbia, Slovakia, and Yugoslavia; and the **Commonwealth of Independent States**—Armenia, Azerbaijan, Byelarus, Georgia, Kazakhstan, Kyrgyzstan, Moldova, Russia, Tajikistan, Turkmanistan, Ukraine, and Uzbekistan—tend to be extremely politically and regionally nationalistic according to the boundaries established prior to the end of World War II. Considering themselves neither new nor old Russians, the citizens of these new political boundaries cherish their individual cultural heritages. As a result, many people, regardless of the political boundaries created by the formation of the CIS, think of their particular state as a country, setting the stage for difficulties in holding this commonwealth together.

But political uncertainty has become a way of life in the 20th century, and undoubtedly this enormous land's changes are far from complete. The old Bolsheviks, communist leaders, and the new national leaders harbor resentments, adding to the tensions already created by resistance to and conflicts about nationalism and major economic problems.

A rich yet tragic history and an equally rich degree of cultural diversity surround the people of this region of the world, and we focus on these aspects of the area in this chapter.

When interviewed on a personal level, Antonija Petrulis expressed how difficult it was for her to discuss the most personal side of her feelings about these times. To her, discussion is equivalent to baring one's soul, something with which she's uncomfortable. When we asked her to go deeper, she replied, "But being official is what I do best and so much. It's easy to speak being official."

Yet she did speak—intimately and richly—about her own experiences, experiences that obviously helped her to develop a career as a compassionate and empathetic teacher of English as a Second Language.

Antonija Petrulis
Lithuanian Culture
Teacher

By the time I was five years of age, integrating my Lithuanian heritage with the American culture was very natural for me. I lived in Canada after we moved from Lithuania and the DP (Displaced Persons) camp. I knew I wanted to be, in the general sense, in America because it was free. That's synonymous. Everywhere in the world, America stands for freedom and democracy.

My parents wanted desperately for us to get into the American zone for the DP camp because you got everything there, and that was one step closer to coming to America. As luck would have it, we ended up in the British zone.

My father was enough of an entrepreneur that he got a job in the American zone, and it was like heaven. We went to Christmas parties for the workers, and that was the first time I saw an orange. My mother told me to get one, and I asked, "What's that?" The tropical fruits were completely foreign to me. We had only been familiar with apples and carrots and so on.

"Thank you" was very hard for me to pronounce because the "th" is difficult to say in foreign languages. My favorite word though was "Okay." All of the American soldiers, they were always fun, always laughing. As they were moving out, I heard them saying, "Okay, okay."

The [American] soldiers always had something for the kids, quite different from the British zone. Sometimes we got chocolate. Chocolate was a luxury, just as the tropical fruits were. Americans were associated with having a lot. Who else could have given you these exotic delicacies? Bananas, however, were peculiar, slimy to me. It took some time for me to grow accustomed to them.

I remember everybody crying as we left Europe. This was going to be the very last time we might have seen our homeland. Back then, I didn't understand. Of course today, I do.

Going from Halifax to Toronto, I remember going on the train and being astounded by the abundance of lights. In Lithuania, everything had to be darkened because of the potential for bombs.

I remember going into kindergarten and not speaking English. Then all of a sudden, I was able to speak English. No one made fun of my last name, Jakimavicius. Maybe it was because there were so many children arriving in America at the time. All Lithuanian names are short. Mine wasn't. We were always surrounded by many ethnic groups. I went to a Polish nursery school. Every nationality went there. But none of us ever felt poor or discriminated against because we were all on a multicultural boat, yet we could communicate in English.

My parents and teachers encouraged me to speak Lithuanian because of my heritage. With my own children today, I tell them to speak Lithuanian at home. That was the thread that kept us together all the time, even under political oppression. The only way we maintained any semblance of our heritage was through our native tongue, Lithuanian. Even under penalty of death, children were taught to read Lithuanian. If the conditions are tough, it's almost easier to maintain your identity. Lithuanian was a sense of pride. You had something to hold onto with Lithuanian as the oldest living language in the world. Lithuanian traces its roots back to Sanskrit.

DP was considered very degrading. But as immigrants, you always worked harder. I grew up in a very Anglo-Saxon environment, very waspy, very formal, true blue and orange. But the immigrants slowly changed Toronto into an international community. Evolution there was slow though. Native Americans are the only natives here. The rest of us are all DPs with seniority, as one writer put it.

Right from the very beginning, children were politically knowledgeable about the secret treaties between Stalin and Hitler giving away the three Baltic States. But most democracies did not recognize the forced and bloody annexation of Estonia, Latvia, and Lithuania. That's where the cattle cars were going to the *gulag*, to Siberia. I remember hearing about children whose fingers had been chewed to the bone because they were so undernourished that they sucked on their own blood for liquid. Today, I have a sense of responsibility to my roots.

How one maintains the seed, how one waters the plant and nurtures it, it will grow lopsided or completely die off. If you cut off the roots, the plant dies. You have the support group, the community, even the government. It has to be within the philosophy of the nation. We need to say we're going to work on it. It's a heavy responsibility; but if you want a rich, fulfilled life, you have to do it. I feel so at home when I'm with people who have roots. You don't even have to say anything. There's an acceptance, an empathy. You know they understand. We need to reach beyond tolerance to empathy. If you are a person who only lives in a glass house with *things*, no one will share feelings and history with you.

Food is the greatest way to share cultures. In Toronto, the International Caravan was established in the 1970s, and each ethnic group presents its culture, tradition, and culinary skills.

We always want to wear make-up, cover ourselves with cosmetics. It's hard to bare your soul. You feel so undressed and vulnerable. But it's the only way we can achieve understanding.

A nation's physical location and size often play a critical role in its vulnerability to outside forces. In general, the smaller the nation, the more vulnerable it is. If the nation also lies along a trade route or serves as a bridge between two crucial points, it becomes a prized possession to those who would capture the land.

Control of the small landlocked nation of Armenia has yoyoed between the Byzantine, Arab, Ottoman, Mongol, and Russian Empires since the early 13th century. The country's historical roots lie in ancient civilizations before the birth of Christ. Today, Armenia, about the size of the State of Maryland in the United States of America, is a mere wisp of its original size. Yet the nation's location—wedged between the Black and the Caspian Seas—continues to be a precious jewel coveted by many.

Sadly, although the conquering nations set out to capture this treasure of a land, they often abused the defeated country and its people. In the end, no one won. The process of conquering had destroyed the real jewel—the richness of the land and the people.

Like many cultures whose people give children biblical names, Armenians often name their daughters after the river where Noah's Ark landed near Mt. Ararat. Sadly, language barriers often cause the symbolic meaning of these names to be lost.

Anonymous
Armenian Culture
Retired Teacher

During the early massacres in [Armenia in] the 1890s, my father and his family came here [to America]. My father's family was all killed except for him and two nephews. He knew he'd never go back, no matter what happened.

He liked America, and I was fully ingrained into the American culture. College education was very important to Armenians. I became a school teacher. My brother became a doctor. One thing about Armenian families, they're very close.

I never suffered discrimination here. I was born in the midwest and moved to Chicago, Illinois, around 1917. There were no Armenian churches, although later there was one. I was in the Methodist Church, and I stayed in that church. We moved to Pittsburgh, Pennsylvania, in the 1960s.

We have the Armenian American Club, organized here in Pittsburgh shortly after I moved here. About five or six years ago, we built a replica of an Armenian library for the University of Pittsburgh nationality groups, as each of the other nationality groups have done here. There's a Lebanese room, Israeli room, Chinese room, African room. At least thirty rooms altogether.

I prepare the Armenian foods I had when I was growing up.

Stalin rose to power, and the people of the Ukraine were starved into submission in a wave of oppression. Yet that does not mean that earlier waves were any less oppressive. And the Ukrainian people did submit to authoritarian rule, but they remained strong and committed to their beliefs, to their cultural heritage, and to each other.

Many Ukrainians escaped from the area in the earliest parts of the 20th century, some crawling through trenches, under barbed wire fences, to freedom. Vera Carlson, the daughter of two escapees from the Ukraine, was born in the United States following this period.

Vera Carlson
Ukrainian Culture
Retired Housewife

I was fortunate to have an older sister whom I could turn to. Communication had been very difficult.

My father preceded my mother [to America] in 1903. They came because they were aware that Russia and Japan were going to war. My mother came in 1905 because male children weren't allowed to leave the country. She had a horrible trip on the ship to Ellis Island. She lived with me during most of my married life so we had a chance to discuss this.

My father died at an early age, so she had it kind of tough. My mother related many things. She was unable even through her Orthodox priest to keep in touch with her brothers and sisters because of the conditions over there. She felt badly. She never thought she'd hear from or see them again. Like all of us older ones, we drift into the past.

The Ukraine, they killed people left and right there. My niece's father came from White Russia, and his parents were killed. Ukraine was hit very badly. We don't even know if we have any relatives left over there. It's no different than what we have today. Look at what happened to the Jews.

For me, communication was difficult. My parents spoke and learned the English language, but if you told an amusing story, they couldn't translate well [enough] to appreciate it. My father was a furrier-tailor. I spoke kind of half-baked Ukrainian. I didn't speak it fluently. My older sister could. One brother and one sister had been born there.

My parents' devout religious training rubbed off on us. I retained a lot of that, and my younger brother did too. We also retained much of the cultural tradition, not only in foods but in holidays too. I had no problem with children in my childhood community. My parents wouldn't join the Roman Catholic Church. There are always problems among the adults. There was much more prejudice in the Eastern communities of the United States than I experienced. In the Orthodox churches, there were problems between them and the Roman Catholic churches.

Understanding and empathizing isn't always an easy process for people born in the United States of America. The Bill of Rights guarantees inalienable freedoms to all people living in the Union. But at one time or another, each of us is guilty of taking these rights for granted. Yet to those denied these freedoms, the feeling might be likened to drowning. You struggle to breathe freely, your lungs swelling to draw in air that never fully comes. And those who do escape, breathe, taking long, unlabored, deep breaths of freedom— as if they've suddenly found the surface of the water.

In one way or another, people are transformed through internal change on escape, as if they've experienced what some English Literature professors might call a baptism of water. Whether or not the change is visible to the naked eye, it's as tangible and real as that baptism of water or the original oppression had been.

To some, the symbolism of escape is analogous to birth

Alena Goldberg
Czech Culture
Art Historian

I left Czechoslovakia with a friend of mine, using some falsified documents. I didn't have a chance to get legal documents. My father had been persecuted in the 1950s when the communists took over the Czechoslovakian government. That was the main reason why the whole family was unable to travel to the West. We had to ask special permission for any travel abroad, and we had not been granted it.

I was in Prague, working and helping to distribute dissident press, like [1970 Nobel winner Alexander] Solzhenitsyn, coming from Canada illegally. I didn't have total knowledge of who I was working for. I just knew I was working for a good cause. It was a chain of people who distributed the literature. The major break in my life went with the antigovernment event—the signing of the Chart of 1977.

That year, the police searched many homes, including my apartment. One day, I was taken away from the street to the police station for an interrogation. Later on, I knew that some of my colleagues were arrested, and I had to plan to escape.

I left the country on April 4, 1978, with a friend. We left basically on a four-day trip to Vienna, each of us with one little bag. We couldn't take much foreign currency. $50.00 in hand. Both of us knew that we had to get to Traischirchen, a suburb of Vienna that was an Austrian refugee camp. We knew we could ask for political asylum there. My friend, a male colleague from my work, and I stopped at the Czech border. They refused to let us through because it was lunch time. We had to back up, and we noticed that we were watched so we went to the nearest Czech town.

Later, we decided to try a different border crossing. Going there, we were actually escaping back home! It was a feeling of going back home. We arrived at another crossing at the Czech-Austrian border, not very far away, a couple of kilometers. My friend was asked to stay in the car, and I was taken inside the customs offices where I was asked questions. Where we were going. For how long.

The male friend was not searched, but I was strip searched by a woman. No reason given. My vagina was actually searched. They only knew we went to the other crossing, and now we went to this one. They said it was routine. Not many people were going to Austria at the time. They let us go after an hour.

They let us cross, and we thought we were free. We believed that. Just seeing the grass very green on the side of Austria and very yellow on the Czech side made me feel it was real. We crossed the border about 4:20.

When my son was born, ten years after, it was the Fourth of April at 4:34. I started all the action with the border about 2:00 o'clock, exactly when I went into labor.

We got to Austria, and we became immigrants as everyone else was. Most of us were put in separate confinements because we asked for an asylum. My first experience with freedom was kind of like prison or so because I was alone in a bedroom with no bathroom, no toilet. The toilet was on the outside. That's what the Austrians called quarantine. Males usually get longer quarantine than the females. I stayed there about one-and-a-half days. Then I got my room which I shared with other immigrants—Polish, Hungarian—about six to a room, triple beds. I stayed there six months, but we were allowed to go out with special I.D. cards, and I was allowed to work inside the camp.

I spoke a little German, and I was also able to apply for a job in the camp in the supply office, where they distributed blankets and pillows, provisions, etc. I spoke a couple of other languages and that helped me to deal with immigrants who did not speak any German.

Immigrants took showers only once a week. Families couldn't shower together. Women of all sizes and shapes, little boys and girls showered together. [It was] not a divided area. Males went separately. The person who took care of [the bathrooms] was a male. This male checked the women when they took showers, and then he'd pick somebody to be his assistant in these bath areas, to clean the showers, to clean the floor, sweep around, and assist this man with I don't know what.

I didn't want to do this job because I liked the work in the office much better. But my female boss there said they had to fire me from the office but I could make the same money in the bathroom area. Having no papers and waiting for an interview with the US Embassy, I took the job.

It happened obviously that the man started to harass me, demanded some sexual favors which I refused, and after a week of trying to clean the place and just get rid of him—he really disturbed me every minute—the man always bothered me, I thought it was enough. I [wouldn't] go to bed with him, and I left and went to complain to the camp director. He told me that this sometimes happened to pretty Czechs. I thought that was supposed to be a compliment, but I didn't go back to my old job. Later, I found a job in an antique shop in Vienna.

My problem in the refugee camp was in [my] not being "obedient," I think.

111

I obviously asked for political asylum when I came to Austria. But after my complaints to the camp director, I was refused political asylum and received instead an economic asylum, apparently based on my social background: a working class background. At the same time, the Czech government said I was anti-working class because my grandparents had property before the communist takeover. On the other hand, my friend was given political asylum.

I understood that my freedom was disappearing in a way, but I knew this was a form of harassment that happened routinely to women in the camp. Everybody needed to try to just get out of there as soon as possible. What I questioned was how they distributed the asylum and how they treated people. In the camp, they have these racial hierarchies based on the assumption that the "German race" comes first. Most of the camp guards considered single women immigrants to be sex objects of their desires. But women supported each other, forming a powerful body to defend themselves against such "official abuses." Only a few gave up.

I had these camp showers constantly on my mind. My grandmother was in the concentration camp in Dachau for helping Jews. She also was scared of "showers."

I had questioned freedom, and I had decided to go to the United States to find it. I wanted to study. But in Austria, I just waited and constantly filed applications. Finally, I did get interviewed at the U.S. Embassy under President Carter's administration, and I was offered political asylum in the United States. I actually used an agency. They helped me to obtain interviews. Then I got to the United States.

There are many more stories. This one was the apex of my life. I don't know what happened to my friends in the chain. I consider my story emotional. I consider others very violent. They were treated the same way. Another friend escaped in a train with cows and had been pierced with sticks, bleeding, and arrived in Austria with blood in his pockets. A woman from Warsaw traveled in the trunk of a car. She was only sixteen. She was sent back to Poland because she was under age, where she was persecuted.

A man who was in compulsory Army service and who was a baker—I called him Baker—ran away, escaping from the Army with his friend. On the way, his friend with him was shot when they were crossing the border. The wounded friend was behind, and Baker got back and carried him on his back. They ran and crossed a little brook and a minefield they knew about. Baker's friend was shot, but [Baker] didn't leave him there. He carried him until they reached Austria. They both made it but his friend was dead. There were stories that seemed to be more terrifying than mine. Everybody I met had their own stories to tell. Everybody was kind of arrested, going through a kind of confinement, being checked. I ran away from one kind of confinement and came to another kind of confinement. That's when I realized there are always some kinds of unnecessary confinements. No matter where one is in the world, one must watch out for these kinds of confinements of freedom. I thought freedom was green because we said in Czech that in freedom, grass is green. The freedom is not green. The freedom is not blue or free either. The freedom has to be found.

In the late 1800s, anti-Semitism spread throughout the political systems of Europe and in the Russian portion of the continent of Asia. Political parties in Austria-Hungary and Germany adopted policies that espoused largely anti-Jewish pro-Aryan sentiments. Russia's official policies also discriminated against the Jews. About two million Jews fled their Russian homeland to new homes in the United States and what was then Palestine after hundreds of others were murdered in a series of *pogroms*.

This wasn't the first time Jews had been persecuted, nor, of course, would it be the last. Even during the Middle Ages, religious persecution was rampant against Jews and others who practiced what the Rome-based Church had called heresy. In the years to come, the Jewish Holocaust of World War II would adopt many anti-Semitic abuses of the Middle Ages—when Jews had been forced to wear ethnically identifiable clothes or badges, to live in the walled ghettos of Germany, Poland, and other areas, to work in specific occupations while being denied membership in work-related unions and craft guilds and being denied the right to own land.

And while Columbus was busy sailing to the New World, Spain expelled the Jews, who emigrated to Turkey. Many Jews were warmly welcomed to Russia at this time. Those who stayed behind for the tortuous onslaught of forced confessions in King Ferdinand's and Queen Isabella's Inquisition publicly converted to Rome-based Church teachings but continued to practice the Jewish religion secretly. They became what Jews today refer to as *marranos*.

But for all of the persecution Jews have endured throughout the centuries of Eastern and Western history, the Jewish people have not been alone. Virtually no group practicing their religious beliefs has been left untouched. Representatives of every religion suffered the horrors of being burned at the stake as Joan of Arc was during the Middle Ages. And many New World colonists had experienced religious persecution before they settled in what became the United States of America.

Like the Russian Jews emigrating to America to avoid the *pogroms*, the Old Believers of the Russian Orthodox religion also fled this late 19th Century persecution and looked forward to their newly acquired freedom of worship in the New World, according to their old ways.

Anonymous
Russian Culture
Russian Orthodox Priest

I come from a background of Russian people, people who came from the Russian Orthodox Church, those who were called the Old Believers, who refused to accept reforms in the Russian Orthodox Church in the 17th Century. These people became schismatics and were persecuted throughout two-and-a-half centuries of Russian history.

While a great deal of westernization of Russian culture took place after Peter the Great, it was never ascribed [to by the Russian Orthodox Church, whose followers] therefore remained the most traditional and conservative of Russian...people. Because of this, they were probably the least likely Russian people to emigrate here to the United States, especially in the turn of the [19th] century, when America was still a primarily European-dominated culture. [America] was a very foreign place for these old believers. While several million Russians of Orthodox Christian background emigrated to the United States in this century, a very small portion came for the reasons outlined earlier.

The Old Believers who formed the community [where] we lived in the United States came from an area that is now Poland. The people who made up our community came to the United States around the turn of the century. Especially at that time, there was a very strong feeling of what I describe as "America, love it or leave it."

My grandparents and the other members of our community, trying to retain their cultural, ethnic, and, most importantly, [their] religious practices, found it extremely difficult to do so in that American time. I suspect in some ways it would be a lot easier now, helping people to preserve their ethnicity.

I grew up in a community of second generation Russian Old Believers born in America. I guess a predominant memory I have—in the First Ward of Erie, [Pennsylvania], there was a combination of Irish and Russian American people who both shared the same geographical space, both trying to preserve many

114

of their ethnic customs. For the Old Believers, one of the most difficult challenges of this attempt to preserve ethnicity was the totally foreign culture that America provided.

Old Believers had come from the most conservative, traditional Christian background, and our lives are almost controlled by our religious practices. This meant we celebrated major Church holidays by the older Julian calendar. For example, this meant we were celebrating Christmas on a different date [than] almost everyone with whom we associated. A significant portion of the year was made up of fast days in which our dietary practices were very different than everyone else's. For Orthodox Christians, especially the Old Believers, the eves of the Lord's Day, Saturday evening, and the eves of all major Church feast days were to be spent in Church services that lasted for a number of hours. The result of this was where almost everyone else spent Saturday dating, at the movies, or at other entertainment, we were at least expected to spend these evenings in Church.

Long before the American Surgeon General deemed smoking to be harmful to health, Old Believers were taught that smoking was absolutely incompatible with being Christian. Where all this may not seem to cause any problems now, at least in the 1930s through the 1960s, [it was] very difficult to tell your friends that you were forbidden to smoke and that they were forbidden to smoke when they visited your house. It had a chilling effect on many social relationships.

Finally, just the fact that, again, Old Believers—trying to follow ancient Christian precepts, especially in many of the writings of St. Paul—were taught that vanity, especially in physical appearance, was antithetical to Christian life. This meant that men were supposed to abstain from shaving their beards, and many of the men in our community had their jobs threatened or even lost their jobs because of [their] refusal to shave. Again, in our time...so many men wear beards, [but earlier] there was a time when employers absolutely insisted their employees be clean shaven.

St. Paul had said that a woman's glory was her hair, and therefore women were expected to keep their hair long and simple. While some makeup may have been tolerated, any significant distortion of facial features was seen as being non-Christian. All of these factors made growing up as a Russian Old Believer a very difficult experience.

I think that all of the people in our community who immigrated to America were happy they had done so because of the political and economic climate in Europe through much of this century. But they also realized that American culture was a tremendous temptation to the preservation of ethnic customs, but more importantly, religious traditions.

And over the decades, the assimilation of our community into American society was constantly a source of consternation for Believers in the community. And to be honest, many of the expected practices outlined above were either lost or at least compromised along the way.

I often express to Russian people who immigrated to America after World War II, or to other more recent immigrants from other countries, that they must try to understand why, in our community, the loss of the "native language" in homes to the complete use of English was inevitable compared to today when we have a much greater emphasis on helping immigrants retain their ethnic characteristics. In our community, for the most part, we have been able to retain the religious traditions, but most of the ethnic customs have pretty much disappeared.

While that seems tragic, fortunately for Orthodox Christian people and especially Old Believers, the religious traditions are so strong and so prevalent that they still allow for the retention of communities even when the ethnic customs are gone.

Many other ethnic groups coming from Western European backgrounds probably are not able to stay the same. Let's say on Christmas morning, at the end of the fast we keep before Christmas, my grandparents and parents certainly would have broken the fast by having Russian dishes such as *kielbasa*, *piroshki,* and so on, whereas many of our young families might consider breaking fast with a pizza with pepperoni and cheese. While the food may be different, the religious tradition is the same and so different than the experience of most American society that the community is still preserved and intact. I really believe this, that the fear of most ethnic groups is once you lose the dance, the music, and other customs, you lose your identity. We work very hard on preserving that, not merely as an attempt to preserve ethnicity [but] because we believe it's part of the very fiber of who we are.

In the years following World War I, two definitive emotions spread among the people of many European nations. Downtrodden and disheartened, some hoped for strong political leaders who could guide them back into better economic times. Angered and determined to place the blame for bad times on someone, perhaps anyone, other people united into powerful forces that threatened what few positive feelings the people had left.

By the time World War II had begun, Europe had become a

continent of tumult. Political assassination and other forms of violence had turned world news into local events. Even after these two wars had ended, tension in this part of the globe had become the fertile ground for dictatorships and oppression of many people.

Not everyone escaped from the abuses that followed. But those who did either escaped through some kind of dramatic departure or through defection.

Sorin Balaianu
Romanian Culture
President, Tri-Soccer International

If this were six or seven years ago, or eighteen or fifteen years ago, I would be speaking about this in different terms. I started traveling out of Romania in about 1972 as a champion wrestler, and I realized that they think differently in the West than in the East. I was questioning my peers about the difference.

In 1973, I was here [United States of America] for the world championship, and I thought of defecting. I was here ten days, two weeks. I saw what was here in America—supermarkets and all of these malls. But my desire to go back and tell my friends about it was stronger than my desire to defect.

When I went back, knowing because of my ability to take trips with the Romanian wrestling team, I started thinking, "Why should I defect? I have my parents, my friends."

Then being manipulated by the regime on doing certain things—if I want to make the Olympic team, I have to join the military and become an officer. Me, as a champion, I had the ability to go to special stores and not have to wait two to five hours. Then I realized as things got a little worse each time, between 1962 [and] 1970, they had a flourishing type of culture—kind of like the Americans. When I came back from Sweden, I didn't have the courage to do it. I still wanted to research it even more. Right after the European championship, I made a decision that next time I got to the West, I would defect. Usually when I say things like that, I follow through.

December 25, the same day that 14 years later the Romanian president got killed, I defected. 1975. Here I am, defected to Turkey for five months, then from there I went to Italy where I took the Italian Championship for wrestling. I could have stayed there, but I wanted to come to America.

When I came to New York for the first time, my English was terrible. The Catholic Conference helped me to come here. They gave me three dollars a day to eat for a month, month-and-a-half, then I should find a job.

They sent me to New York to go to the Wrestling Club. I went there, and

I didn't have a tie and jacket to get in. I looked very Italian at the time. The porter and I got into an argument, and he was pushing me and I was pushing him. We were pushing each other. I went back to the hotel, and I didn't have a tie. I had a long brown sock, [and] I cut [it] to make a tie.

I wrestled there, and the same night I met a guy I had wrestled, and he gave me a dollar. He helped me get a job as a security guard at Saks Fifth Avenue and the Olympic Tower. Then I started meeting people and moved in with this gal on 34th and Park. While I was there, Hofstra University offered me a wrestling scholarship, and I ended up going to school there.

It was quite an experience going to school because I just barely passed in Romania. It was a lot more difficult in America because I was working, wrestling, and going to school, and I was not a good student. It was very hard.

While in college, I had some great relationships, like a beautiful time of my life, going to classes and experiencing different cultures. People from all over the world going to school there. Going to college here in America is almost like a fishbowl, like going to camp. Some people were interested in studying. They had people to help you there. Advisors. I think they tried advising me, but I was a good faker on knowing how to learn, when I should have studied more. If I was there for five years, I should have studied more. I didn't know what I wanted to do. I wrestled to go to school, and I went to school to wrestle. After five years, I should have learned more.

I want you to understand I have no complaints. Anything you do here in America, you do [because you want to]. But things were tough because I spent money—sending money to my parents—and traveling and getting to California. New York didn't do that much for me. I loved New York, but it was too much for me. I felt like I defected a second time.

I went to San Francisco, Lake Tahoe, [Nevada]. At Lake Tahoe, I worked with a company out of Canada that saw that I had a potential to set up some programs for them, a marketing program with Caesar's Tahoe. I would say it was the first marketing program done in the world with a casino and a time-share resort, and I was the first one. It just happened that I was there at the right time. Everything worked out right. I did that for about three years.

Then I became an American citizen the same day. Eight years later, I have become an American citizen. I arrived in America September 14, 1976, and became a citizen September 14, 1984. I was in Reno, Nevada, when I became an American citizen.

Right after that, I went back to Romania to visit my parents under the [Nicolae] Ceausescu regime. Everything seemed fine. Nothing was bad. Kind of like when I defected. A little depressing, but okay for Romanian standards.

Then I went back in 1987, the year before the revolution, and I came back about a month later. I was going to stay about six weeks. I went there, and the real story begins. I went to visit some of my friends. I'm up early, and I see people waiting in line at a butcher shop about 10:30 [a.m.]. I come back from visiting my friends about 8:30 that night, and the same people were there, waiting. That worked me up a little bit.

Then I wanted to take a shower. No hot water. I asked what was happening. I heard we only get hot water on Thursday and Sunday to save energy to build something.

Then I visit a friend of mine who is a doctor. He's not at home, so I visit him at work. He takes me around and says, "Sorin, we have no anesthetics, and sometimes we have to use the same needles."

He takes me to see the newborns, and he says, "We lose about 40 percent of them. They froze to death. The Red Cross won't take them till they're nine months old because of the death rate."

My friends don't have enough food. I cried at night by the end of the third day.

I'm not religious, but I went to the church and lit a candle and gave the priest the equivalent [of] about $250, and I prayed that God would help.

Seven days later, I woke up, set up my luggage and told my parents I had to leave because I couldn't take it. They didn't understand. I went to Italy and Switzerland to visit some other friends. This was not my plan.

So here I am in America. I kissed the ground in Chicago because I am so glad to be here. I met this girl, and we went out to lunch. It was snowing outside. People were laughing around me, and I started crying. I cried for twenty minutes straight. I was thinking about my friends, feeling guilty because I was doing so well. [I thought] about the kids.

I couldn't function for about three months. People here couldn't understand what I was talking about. I thought maybe we could do something. There was no one in this country to tell people how bad things were. I spoke to a friend and said maybe we could hire someone to kill the Romanian president [Ceausescu]. I thought, but my friend said about 20 million people were ahead of me. My friend said [I should] start talking to clubs that could put pressure on and do something that way.

I started working at a resort club. [I couldn't handle the job in Nevada anymore.] I couldn't do anything else because of the emotional stress. It was terrible.

I wish now [that] I would have gone to a doctor to get over this thing. It took four years when it could have taken three months.

I started speaking at high schools, conferences, colleges, and at the same time I started a federation. This country [America] is so beautiful. It has its faults, but you are still allowèd dreams and hopes that justice that will be done. Hopes that you can better yourself, no matter what. If I live in such a wonderful country,

I should be able to do something that I can build for this country. I need to do it because I like to. I heard if you do something you like, the money will follow. But sometimes you have to be realistic. You have to work at it and have patience and desire and the know-how. Nobody is smart enough to know everything.

So I became involved in soccer and doing something here in this country with soccer. I got involved in [these] soccer skills courts, which was a good decision because I ended up becoming involved with the World Cup [1994] soccer as a consultant with my soccer skills program. Now it has landed me in a solid partnership with a company that supplied some equipment to the World Cup soccer and is creating for me a light at the end of the tunnel, to follow the American dream, that I can see it through to reality, the way I see it.

I didn't come here to America to buy a big car and gold chains and a Rolex watch in my hand and flaunt all that. There's nothing wrong with that if it makes those people feel so good. I came here with freedom in mind, freedom of traveling, freedom of speech and opportunity that no other country can offer. That's what I came here for. Not only the opportunity, but also the thing that you can achieve your dreams. With the opportunity, you just have to take it, work hard, and it's there.

I'm very happy here. America has so many places. It's so big, beautiful, culturally wonderful. You travel eight hours by plane, and you see the same [American beauty]. It's continuity. Everybody speaks the same language, has the same money. That's why it's so great. I think when America decides to do something, they can really put on a party. Europeans thought America couldn't do the World Cup. We made more money. They sold two million tickets in Italy in 1990. In the USA, they sold three million. In one month in the United States, [the World Cup 1994 soccer] was as big as twenty-five Super Bowls. The most unbelievable experience. For me to have a part in it was wonderful.

Now I'm going home finally after seven years. I feel strong enough that I can go and see the country after the communist regime [has been replaced] with a new regime. I hope I'm not disappointed in the new regime. I've been helping them out a little bit at the California Economic Summit. It seems to me that Romania is coming about to be a player in the European Market. It looks like they're on the right path.

I'm different than I was six years ago. I'm different than I was ten years ago. But I'm sold on this country [America], no matter what.

If you've always thought of Russia and the Union of Soviet Socialist Republics (USSR) as synonymous, join the crowd. You're not alone. For the past fifty years, many people have placed several nations including Russia—and the millions and millions of people in those nations—categorically under the label of the "Union of Soviet Socialist Republics." Yet although the people of the Baltic States and Eastern Europe had once been incorporated into the former USSR, the vast majority of these people didn't go willingly. They were forcefully sucked into the union through one method or another.

But the Soviet Union began a transformation process in the late 1980s and early 1990s, and the earthquake effects of that transformation—the physical separation into various segments—and its after-shocks will continue to affect this area and the rest of the world for many years to come.

The former Czechoslovakia was divided into two nations—the Czech Republic and Slovakia—and the volcanic upheaval of civil war between the former Yugoslavia's Bosnians, Serbs, and Croatians erupted violently in 1994. Hostile rumblings continue in these former satellite nations once claimed to be among the USSR's pride. Attempts to bring peace into these areas included talks of dividing the former Yugoslavia into several independent nations, but little had been resolved as yet.

And who can forget global people's jubilance when the Berlin Wall came down after twenty-eight years of separating East and West Germany? People danced in the streets and dashed in both directions across the former borders of the now-reunited nation. Many ran into the arms of loved ones—families and friends—they hadn't seen or held in many years. But when the fireworks celebration had stopped and people had settled back into their daily business of living, the economic pressure of Germany's reunification hit people's pursestrings, and the honeymoon was over.

Similarly, when America's Vietnam Era prisoners of war were released and came home to their families, their initial joy often dissolved into disillusioned turmoil because their individual experiences during that period of separation had forced them to survive as independent people. Some families succeeded in starting their lives over together. Others weren't as fortunate.

Former East Germany, functioning for nearly three decades as a communist country, and former West Germany, a democracy, also encountered unexpected difficulties following the reunification. Although some philosophical perceptions had remained comparatively the same, difficulties arose between the lifestyles, technologies, and economies of the two once divided areas. Overall, the general welfare of former West Germany's citizens appeared substantially better than that of former East Germany. From the technological and economic perspective, the disparity was as obvious as night and day. Equalizing differences and healing the hurts that may appear from these differences takes years to accomplish. Unfortunately, people tend to be impatient, wanting yesterday what others have developed through long periods of time.

One consciously needs to avoid glossing over the important details of history, even when they appear minute. How many history students living in the United States, for instance, learned that Hitler had illegally given Stalin the Baltic States when neither man had even possessed that kind of right to give or receive? How does one give a gift of people to another? Few history books carried these details that resulted in millions of people's lives being destroyed through countless abuses that included genocide. It's easy at times to stand on the sidelines and watch—or even turn our backs—as hostile dictators of nations walk into neighboring lands and aggressively claim the lands and their people.

What will happen to the Baltic States, the Easterners, and the other citizens of this area of the world? That will depend on whether true democracy will be employed, where all people within any particular nation will develop and maintain their respect for one another, and whether neighboring nations will develop and also maintain that same spirit of mutual respect. Only in time, as history continues to unfold, will we know the outcome of these events.

Chapter 6

THE AFRICANS

All of us possess a common thread of experience in our humanness. We open our eyes and look outside in the morning, and we see a spectrum in nature. Plants are still green, the sky is blue, the earth is brown. And no matter our race, ethnic background, religious beliefs or the memories that have shaped our individual perceptions of life, our internal perception of nature's paintbrush is more or less the same.

Africa's gamut of land types, temperatures, and weather—dry and wet, hot and cold, low and high—forges versatile surroundings and continent-exclusive natural resources, including metals for high-tech industries. Although the people of Africa have too frequently been perceived as backward, uneducated, unprogressive, and savage, a highly diverse blend of cultures have populated this area that, perhaps foremost among the geographic areas around the globe, has been so misunderstood.

Egypt and Ethiopia had some of the greatest societies and cultures in history. In fact, many construction techniques of Egypt's pyramids are still not understood today.

Many histories have been woven into the story of the African people—the tales of the slaves and the traders, South African apartheid, international boycotts, student uprisings, and the multitude of cultures, all painting a picture of many nations in constant upheaval. But histories, perspectives of what happens to people during any particular event, are only as factual as the people who record them. Given opposing views, we must draw our own conclusions on the evidence presented. Not always knowing the real motives behind any event, one must remember that people are different whether or not they were raised in or experience identical geographic areas and cultures.

Geographically, Africa—a continent, not a country—has the Mediterranean Sea and Europe to the north, the Middle East, the Red Sea, and the Indian Ocean to the east, the Atlantic Ocean to the south and west, and the Americas further to the west. During the 15th and 16th centuries, many of the essential world trade routes skirted the northeast portion of Africa into the what is now called the Middle East while others traced south around the Cape of Good Hope on the tip of South Africa.

Europeans—predominantly British, Dutch, French, German, and Portuguese—had been involved in slave trading during the early 1500s, historically called the Colonial Period. But European merchants did not create the practice of slave trading. Before the Europeans arrived on the continent, African tribes enslaved other tribes. Along the west coast of Africa, slave trading was a common fact of life, just as it was part of daily living in many other areas of the world for thousands of years. It would be hard to identify any people that were not associated with some form of slavery at some point in their history.

Over 3,000 years ago, the Hebrews—ancestors of today's Jewish people—built many of the Egyptian store-cities during their 400 years of slavery. The Old Testament books of Genesis and Exodus recount centuries of bondage and the Hebrews' eventual release. And Hollywood filmmakers padded their pockets during the 1950s and 1960s with the profits from fans eager to see *The Ten Commandments* with Charlton Heston as Moses. Sadly, Hollywood was culturally inaccurate in casting without apparent consideration of characters who reflected the ancient Egyptian people.

But unlike Hollywood's hot multimillion dollar film hits, Jewish people customarily recall the exodus from Egypt to Palestine—now Israel and portions of the surrounding nations—at the traditional Passover seder meal and prayer service. In the years since the exodus, many Jews have migrated to Ethiopia and other African and Middle Eastern nations, even as far as what we now call China. Today, dark-skinned Jews live in areas of Ethiopia, and both Chinese Muslims and Jews can be found in and around the area of Kaifeng, China.

In ancient times, warfare contributed first to slave trading among northern African Arab traders, later to Portuguese and Spanish traders headed for the Caribbean and South America. Conquered people were commonly enslaved. By the 1600s, French, English, and Dutch colonists began to use black indentured servants and slaves—mostly from Western Sudan, transporting them to the North American colonies.

Yet not all indentured servants were black. Many people arriving in the American colonies often found wealthy benefactors who assumed the otherwise unaffordable cost of the trip from Europe. In return, the grateful travelers contracted to work for their sponsors without pay for periods lasting up to seven years. At the end of the period, many landowners gave their now freed indentured servants fifty acres of land with which they could start their new lives in the colonies.

White officials of the Dutch East India Company began to settle in South Africa in the mid-1600s. By the early 1700s, when slavery was rapidly increasing in the American colonies, the first Afrikaners—Dutch settlers' children—were born on African soil. Eventually, the term *Afrikaner* took on a new meaning of mixed blood natives, and that term held fast for nearly 200 years. Today, the definition has remained somewhat muddied. About three million white Afrikaners comprise more than half of South Africa's white population, where they held almost every top political and military post until the early 1990s.

In the United States today, black descendants of the Sudanese slaves from the 1600s hold political office, earn top military rank, and captivate fans as sports figures, show business entertainers, and film directing stars. But the road to this kind of freedom for black Africans has not been an easy one to hoe.

In 1947, Jackie Robinson broke the racial barriers of the all-white baseball teams and became the first black ball player in the major leagues as a Brooklyn Dodger—one-hundred years after Frederick Douglass, the most influential black leader of the 19th century, started the *North Star*, an abolitionist newspaper.

By 1863, President Abraham Lincoln had issued the Emancipation Proclamation, marking a turning point in United States history—the first stride toward civil rights. But even well into the 1900s, the black struggle for equality was just getting started. Many whites ignored contributions of people like George Washington Carver, who revolutionized agriculture in the South; Ralph J. Bunche, the U.S. diplomat who became the first black to win a Nobel Peace Prize; and Marian Anderson, who became the first black lead with New York's Metropolitan Opera. Booker T. Washington, a former slave and principal of Tuskegee Institute, called for racial harmony between whites and blacks in 1881. W.E.B. DuBois, a sociologist and historian, picked up where Booker T. Washington left off.

Langston Hughes, James Weldon Johnson, and Countee Cullen were among the great black writers of the 1920s. Bill "Bojangles" Robinson danced his way to fame, recognition that Sammy Davis, Jr. made sure didn't go unnoticed.

And many black notables were recognized because their talent was too great to waste—singer Paul Robeson, "Father of the Blues" bandleader W.C. Handy, Louis Armstrong, author James Baldwin, Duke Ellington, boxing champ Joe Louis, Olympic runner Jesse Owens, singing superstar Whitney Houston, Guion S. Bluford, Jr., who became the first black astronaut in space, tennis great Arthur Ashe who became the first black male to win the United States Open and Wimbledon...the list is endless. Those whom we've listed deserve recognition, as do those whom we've omitted.

From Harriet Tubman to Richard Wright, from United States Representative Jefferson Long of Georgia during the Reconstruction Era to United States Representative Shirley Chisholm of New York in 1969, black culture and history have become firmly ingrained into American culture and history. How do we ignore in American history books the integration of Little Rock Central High School in Arkansas in 1957, or Rosa Parks' refusal to move to the back of the bus in Montgomery, Alabama, two years earlier? Can we close our eyes to Sidney Poitier's Academy Award for his leading role in the 1963 film *Lilies of the Field* —exactly 100 years after Lincoln delivered that famous Emancipation Address? Not easily.

People with African roots and all shades of skin have contributed to world progress and humanity, and they need to be recognized and praised for their efforts—just as we all need recognition and praise. We need to avoid stereotyping this region's natives and descendants which included three Nobel Peace Prize winners, one Nobel Prize winner in the fields of physiology and medicine, and three Nobel Prize winners in the field of literature by 1991.

Not all ethnically African people are dark-skinned, nor do they reside in grass huts or belong to a tribe living off the land on a dark continent. Along the northern edges of Africa, the nations of Egypt, Libya, Tunisia, Algeria and Morocco appear to possess an Arab influence in their cultural bases. In *Casablanca*, Humphrey "Bogie" Bogart and Ingrid Bergman played on fantasizing film fans' senses about the mystery and intrigue of the Casbah, seducing us with exotic romance. Even fifty years after this film classic's premiere, television shows and advertising cashed in on Bogie's famous line, "Play it again, Sam," while the melody of *As Time Goes By* played in the background.

Understandably, it's easy to get confused about the location of these nations. Geographically, they're on the continent of Africa. But they retain a distinctly Arab flavor which tends to bring thoughts of the Middle East to mind. Nevertheless, the people of these nations— Arab or not—are African, and like Mohsen "Mo" Barakah of Egypt, not all are dark-skinned.

Prior to his interview, "Mo" translated his last name, Barakah. It means "blessing." A more appropriate word to describe this gentle, happy man would be hard to find. Michelle Young met "Mo" at his home a year or two before his interview. She and her husband had been invited to a party at his home, a gorgeous private retreat tastefully decorated with Egyptian influence. Michelle asked her husband, acquainted with Mo from the tennis courts, whether Kwong had mentioned her Jewish heritage to the host of the party.

"No," said Kwong, "and don't you mention it either."

In his interview, Mo revealed what Kwong didn't know—why Michelle's being Jewish wouldn't have mattered.

Mohsen "Mo" Barakah
Egyptian Culture
International Courier

I used to work for the Egyptian government, for the foreign ministry over-seer, as a security officer. They sent me here to work at the Egyptian consulate in San Francisco. I served with them two years. During this time, I got married to an American lady and stayed here since. I haven't been home in sixteen years.

After I finished working with the consulate, my time expired, but I didn't return to Egypt. When I finished working for the consulate, I tried to find a job here as a security officer, and I worked in restaurants as a host [and as] a busboy and then as an international courier for the last fourteen years.

...As a foreigner, I didn't have time to go to school here. I wanted to support my family, and I learned English from life. It's...very different...from the life and culture I had in Egypt. You can enjoy your life here. [If] you work hard, you can make money and buy anything you want. But life isn't easy anywhere.

I have everything I want here, and I appreciate everything here. I lived in California lots of time. (Mo discusses the international flavor of life in California, and that he didn't experience intercultural problems there.) But in Arizona, I had some problems, but I tried to do whatever I was doing without problems with everybody. Sometimes you feel prejudice. My accent will not change. It just is.

I'm an American citizen for over twelve years. I have family in Egypt. I have family in Saudi Arabia.

With the war with Israel, if you ask me my feeling about the war, it was wrong because they were our neighbors and we needed to live in peace. If you were in the Army, you kept your mouth shut because you were talking about your government. Sadat helped the situation with Israel. With Nasar (Nassar), you couldn't say anything. Sadat brought peace with Israel.

We waste a lot of time in war with each other because neither side was willing to listen to the other. War has destroyed the economy, and [the people] have suffered for years and years.

You have wise people and crazy people on both sides. From my heart and from that of the Egyptian people, they love peace. My dream is for Egypt and Israel to have everlasting peace.

We can do business together better than this. Both can work together to make the Middle East better. But in the Middle East, you still have stupid government, stupid thinking. The area needs peace now. Only God knows why this happened.

Thousands of years of history link the continent of Africa with what we call Europe, Asia, and the Middle East today. Once, people had been content with trading among themselves in their individual villages. Then they explored beyond their village boundaries, discovered new communities, and their concept of trade expanded to these new areas. Eventually, of course, their curiosity took them to far foreign shores which, in turn, encouraged intercultural trade between regions.

But not everyone learns or grows at the same pace, and philosophical differences about trade—and jealousy of others' possessions and land, that old cliché about the grass being greener—may have resulted in international tensions. Like small children plotting to take ownership of other children's toys, many people toyed with thoughts of territorial expansion and plowed forward.

The most elementary principles of intercultural trade, territorial expansion, and marriage operate identically: the relationship works if both sides practice sensitivity, respect, and encouragement of each other's growth. But although both sides want to develop the relationship, they don't always see a need for internal progress, and the process becomes a cyclical whirl of insensitivity, intolerance, and jealousy. This pattern frequently results in abuses of civil rights. But abuses will only last so long before a triggering event or person lights the fuse that finally explodes into civil or international war, or localized riots.

The 1960s became a time of turmoil throughout the United States. Antiwar protesters and pro-civil rights activists marched in Washington, D.C., and in other major cities, and the issues of war and civil rights became catalysts for violence in the streets. Perhaps not coincidentally, both issues involved civil rights. Both issues evolved into states of war.

In 1962, Federal marshals accompanied James Meredith to the University of Mississippi after troops quelled riots, and Meredith became the first black student at the school. In *The Fire Next Time*, James Baldwin predicted racial violence, and 200,000 demonstrators in Washington, D.C., demanded equal civil rights for blacks in 1963.

Three months later, John F. Kennedy, President of the United States, was assassinated in Dallas, Texas. For more than two decades, speculation focused on who actually fired the fatal shot and the motives for JFK's murder. Lee Harvey Oswald was blamed for the attack, but the details were as fuzzy as the possible motives. President Kennedy's diligent efforts for civil rights for blacks had often been mentioned as a motive.

Less than a year after JFK's death, the nation was getting involved in the crisis in Vietnam, compounding racial tensions stateside. Congress had passed the omnibus civil rights bills prohibiting discrimination in every facet of daily life including jobs, voting, public accommodations, and facilities, and so on, but tensions continued to heat up. Black nationalist leader Malcolm X was assassinated at a February 1965 rally in the Harlem district of New York City, and by summer, Baldwin's fears had borne fruit. Riots in the Watts area of Los Angeles, California, had left thirty-four dead, and enflamed emotions escalated into riots in other cities including Harlem in New York City. At the same time, U.S. combat soldiers left for Vietnam.

The riots continued across the nation even after Robert C. Weaver, the first black Cabinet member, assumed his post as secretary of housing and urban development in 1966 and Thurgood Marshall was appointed to the United States Supreme Court in 1967. On April 4, 1968, civil rights leader Martin Luther King, Jr., was assassinated in Memphis, Tennessee. Two months later, on June 5, 1968, U.S. Senator Robert F. Kennedy, JFK's brother, was shot in Los Angeles. He died the next day.

Nearly three hundred years of abused civil rights and broken promises led up to the pressures that erupted during the 1960s. Although slavery had been the bone of contention leading the United States into the Civil War between the North and the South, free blacks in the North had few rights. Northern schools and other public accommodations—hotels, restaurants, even houses of worship—were segregated, while in other instances black participation was banned altogether.

Free blacks weren't allowed to vote in most states, and in New England free blacks needed passes to visit other towns. Free northern blacks needed permission to visit privately with slaves, and most blacks were rigidly restricted from bearing arms. The few colleges and universities that allowed blacks to enroll severely limited the numbers admitted.

United States Representatives Henry Clay of Kentucky and John C. Calhoun of South Carolina teamed with other proponents of slavery in 1817 to establish the American Colonization Society. Planning to alleviate "the race problem" by taking free black volunteers back to Africa, the society established the colony of Liberia in 1822. In 1847, the colony became the first self-governing black republic on the African continent, but only 12,000 free blacks had volunteered to settle there over the next three years. To those still in North America, the United States was home.

Clay, now a senator, and Massachusetts Senator Daniel Webster collaborated to draft what became known as the Compromise of 1850, a law allowing newly acquired territories to decide about slavery in those areas. The law also prohibited slavery in Washington, D.C., assisted slaveowners in retrieval of runaway slaves, and admitted California to the Union as a free (non-slavery) state.

According to some historical reports, President Lincoln had intended to preserve the Union, not to abolish slavery. But his preelection debates with Stephen Douglas, a white supporter of slavery, revealed Lincoln's desire to rid the nation of slavery. Later research revealed that Lincoln had been politically advised to downplay his beliefs about slavery because advisers feared he'd lose the election.

Seven Southern states seceded and created the Confederate States of America before the Civil War broke out at Fort Sumter, South Carolina, on April 12, 1861. Shortly after the Fort Sumter attack, four more states joined the Confederate States. By July 1862, more than 200,000 blacks, now allowed in the Union Army, joined to fight on the side of the Union.

Despite discrimination in the army, the now-free blacks showed pride in their efforts. Robert Smalls, a South Carolina harbor pilot, hadn't even joined the armed forces when he sailed the *Planter*, a Confederate ship, from Charleston Harbor to the Union. After his legendary feat which brought him recognition as a black hero, he joined the Union Navy. In 1863, black troops attacked Port Hudson, Louisiana, a move that aided the Union in gaining control of the Mississippi River and earned twenty-three members of the black regiments the Medal of Honor for their heroism.

Black army regiments fought gallantly in the Indian Wars, but most of their efforts in creating the United States of America were ignored. On the other hand, the Native Americans—respecting the black troops and hating to fight them—nicknamed the black military "Buffalo Soldiers." "They fought like cornered Buffaloes," explained one member of the Buffalo Soldiers.

In April 1994, the United States Postal Service issued a commemorative stamp honoring the Buffalo Soldiers. Several speakers praised their achievements at the ceremonies held at Fort Huachuca, an Army base in Sierra Vista, Arizona, near Tombstone where the famed gunfight at the O.K. Corral occurred. The Buffalo Soldiers were stationed at Fort Huachuca and three other posts. At its entrance, the wood-burned letters on the polished sign read, "Last of old Army posts."

Elmore Leonard described places like this in some of his earlier novels. Surprisingly, Sierra Vista's population is much larger than the town looks—about 32,000, according to a listing in a 1994 atlas. On the day after the commemorative stamp ceremonies, the parade moved slowly down what appeared to be the main street, a wide road with buildings on either side. A tree here and there broke up the monotony of the predominantly yellow blanket of grasses on the flat thirsty land.

A military unit passed by the Sorry Gulch Saloon, but no one stopped to watch. Four black soldiers in dress uniform seemed to come out of nowhere to watch, just in time for the Buffalo Soldiers to pass by on horseback. As the riders drew close, each of the four men on the side of the road pulled his shoulders back, stood taller and prouder, and saluted with the kind of precision one gives with the deepest respect.

"Every African American soldier who has [served] or will serve the country is a Buffalo Soldier," said another speaker at the ceremony. "The Buffalo Soldiers demonstrated unflinching loyalty before having the right to vote or be citizens."

An almost completely white band played, perhaps a statement in itself. Too many years have passed without whites recognizing black achievements.

"The Buffalo Soldiers represented the heart of Black American history for more than fifty years from 1866," someone else said, adding that the white officers who commanded them volunteered for the post. "African Americans have enriched American life."

Buffalo Soldier Andrew Whitaker, 77 years old, spoke briefly about the Golden Rule, obeying orders, getting married, returning to work full time because he was "tired of being retired." He spoke with humor and love and, appropriately, received a standing ovation.

A black cowboy-poet recited a poem dedicated to the Buffalo Soldiers, and a military salute again honored their work.

But, says the local NAACP president, George Allen, "It's not enough to point out heroes and expect children to see their acts. We must emulate them."

At a Buffalo Soldiers convention in Las Cruces, New Mexico, three months later, still another speaker noted some of the little known highlights of black history and his opinion that Haitians "have a right to be in this country because they helped" the Union.

"The black army," he said, "broke down concentration camp gates—Buchenwald, Auschwitz..."

A white man in the audience stood and addressed the gathering. "In 1953 at Fort Hood, Texas, the 509th Tach Battalion became an integrated unit. It had been all-black. I signed the papers." But he never let on that President Harry Truman had issued the order to integrate the armed forces in 1948.

The black speaker highlighting those historical events faced the audience and summed up that which needs to happen in American schools: "If you know that I have a great history, you will respect me. If I know that I have a great history, I will respect myself. If you're waiting for somebody to drop this into your lap, you'll wait until the 21st century, and you still won't have it."

On July 24, 1994, *The Charlotte* (North Carolina) *Observer* wrote about "The Unsung Heroes of World War II." Included in the massive write-up developed by a team of reporters was the following story on the Buffalo Soldiers, circa 1944, 1945, reprinted here with permission of *The Charlotte Observer*.

"Protecting...when we didn't have freedom"
The Buffalo Soldiers
Black African Culture
by Jack Horan, reporter for The Charlotte Observer

They joined the 92nd Infantry Division, a unit that symbolically linked itself to the black "Buffalo Soldiers" of the Indian wars.

They became friends during World War II and, for more than forty years, have gathered each Wednesday night to play cards in a bridge club.

Their division fought in Italy against the Germans in 1944 and 1945, enduring combat, miserable winter weather, and racial segregation.

"This was one of the problems we black soldiers faced," retired school Principal Raymond Rorie, 74, said of segregation. "We were protecting our country when we didn't have freedom ourselves."

Another veteran and a former West Charlotte High School principal, Gerson Stroud, 74, agreed.

"It was very upsetting to realize you have given precious time of your life for supposed freedom (in a country) that was still segregated," he said.

(Eugene) Williams; Stroud; Henry Swift, 76; Raymond Rorie, 74; and Carl Hunt, 79, all became part of the 92nd when their regiments were united at Fort Huachuca, Arizona. Their uniforms carried a buffalo patch.

The division's 370th Combat Team was the first to land in Italy, said Swift, a retired plastering contractor who was in charge of an 81mm mortar.

Rorie, a medic in the 370th, entered combat near Pisa, where he took care of wounded soldiers at a first-aid station. "Medics worked all the time, twenty-four hours a day," he said.

The other regiments followed in the summer and fall of 1944.

Stroud, a supply sergeant in the 365th Regiment, provided ammunition for a company armed with six 105mm howitzers. "We would move from place to place in convoy, under the cover of darkness," Stroud said.

Williams went on active duty in 1941 and later joined the 366th Regiment, serving in North Africa and then in Italy in the winter of 1944-45.

"We were in the mountains with snow and ice for days without any heat," Williams said. He suffered frostbite on a patrol mission, left Italy and went to Camp Butner near Durham for treatment. The staff sergeant almost lost his toes to gangrene.

Two years ago, Williams wrote the Army for his service medals and discovered he had been awarded a Bronze Star in 1962 for "meritorious achievement in combat against the armed enemy." He doesn't know in which of two battles in Italy he earned the medal.

The only one who didn't get overseas was Hunt, who quickly moved up the ranks to staff sergeant. "I thought the Army's for me," said a disappointed Hunt, now a retired postal worker.

But Hunt injured his leg in training with the 370th Regiment at Fort Huachuca, cutting short his service in the war.

Slowly, surely, discrimination against blacks in the military has become less pronounced since the Civil War. Benjamin O. Davis earned the distinction of becoming the first black brigadier general of the Army in 1940, yet President Truman's 1948 order to integrate the military was never acted upon until 1952. Davis' son, Benjamin O. Davis, Jr., earned the rank of the first black lieutenant general in the Air Force.

Stateside, however, blacks continued to find discrimination in their daily lives. Housing, quality public education, and good jobs were still hard to come by.

After the series of riots that reverberated through the nation's ghettos in the 1960s, President Lyndon B. Johnson set the wheels in motion for a commission—the Kerner Commission, headed by Illinois Governor Otto Kerner—to study the causes of the fury. To many whites, it seemed that great strides for freedom had placed blacks in a better position than ever before.

Yet in the Kerner Commission's March 1968 report, the study indicated racial prejudice of white Americans as a major factor contributing to discrimination that included police brutality, and poor housing, pay, and education. The Kerner Commission also called for massive ghetto improvement programs and racial attitude changes in whites.

Martin Luther King, Jr., died within weeks of the report's release, and tensions of the black community seemed to totter on a vial of nitroglycerin. Many angry blacks had united into separatist militant groups, some of whom were violence-based. No more than one month had passed before the tension erupted into race riots in at least one hundred cities. In the riots that ripped through Newark, New Jersey, and Detroit, Michigan, sixty-six people—mostly blacks—lost their lives at the hands of white law officers.

But racial discrimination and violence can occur anywhere. In India, the highly structured **caste** system promotes racial discrimination at the formal level. In South Africa, until the first part of the 1990s, racial discrimination was called **apartheid**—separateness.

David Goldberg
White South African Culture
University Professor

I initially came from South Africa via Europe to New York as a graduate student. I was not intending to stay. I thought I'd go back to engage in the transformation of South Africa. But among other things, I met my wife, [who] is originally from Czechoslovakia, and stayed. We met in New York.

I came, not thinking I'd become an American, and yet although I became an American, I've never felt fully assimilated. I consider myself a dissident American. People here always ask me if I'm going to return home, to South Africa, where I grew up. But home is where I live now, not the same nostalgic place I last left some seventeen years ago. I love South Africa, what it has become—the land, the people who have overcome so much to establish their freedom. I'm **from** South Africa without **being** South African; I suppose I'm a citizen of the world. Some might say that I'm not really American, then, which I find extremely narrow-minded.

I have sometimes been called African American by my African American friends. My friends in America are predominantly African Americans.

I'm trained as a philosopher. My Ph.D is in philosophy, but I'm a professor of Justice Studies. A close friend and I made an avant-garde documentary on South Africa in 1980 and won a few awards. We also did the first rap video to be aired on MTV, Curtis Blow's "Basketball."

At that point in my life, at a crossroads between film and philosophy, I had to make a choice. Time and energy wouldn't let me pursue both careers. I was coming to the end of my Ph.D, very intimately involved in intellectual work. I wanted to write and found my film-making career intellectually unstimulating. So I removed myself from film making and music videos and began to write books and teach.

We moved to Philadelphia, and I became naturalized after my wife. I was asked to make an address at my naturalization ceremony. I considered it an honor. Had I not been asked, I wouldn't have thought anything more about it. But the address made me think about what I did to become an American citizen and reflect on the Bill of Rights and the meaning of it despite being crafted by white men. It led me to think about different social criteria historically for becoming an American.

From the 1880s, relating to the surge of immigration from Europe and Southeast Asia, assimilation to the dominant culture was assumed as the prevailing standard. That standard changed in the late 1950s and into the 1960s. Then there was a shift from melting pot assimilation to what I call pluralist integration. You now could hold on to your ethnic hyphenation at the margins, in private, while espousing the core American values in public. People were never fully absorbed by that melting pot assimilation. There was a fairly conscious attempt to exclude those who largely for racial and cultural reasons were seen as unable to assimilate. By the 1960s and in response to exclusionary experiences, people nevertheless saw the need to maintain their identity as a means of self-survival.

The standard of integration was set by the prevailing American values. You still had to know the Bill of Rights, the Constitution, the English language. A new standard emerged in the 1980s. What has emerged in the name of multi-culturalism is a critical transformation of the core values. What is under attack now is not just exclusion, but a transformation of what makes one an American, what counts in being an American. What began to emerge in the 1960s was not just black power, although there are still some remnants of that at one end. Black power was about asserting self-identity. Here the claim is that we're not going to let what being an American is be defined by those committed to exclusionary or marginalizing values.

There's a deep tension in American culture at the moment—the Christian right and conservatives generally trying to define morality for everyone. The kids however are once again saying: "Fuck it. We don't want this anymore." [They're] courting danger from bungee jumping to Lollapalooza, where people get thrown across a sea of hands.

Consider Cannery Row in Monterey, California. It has been transformed from hobos, bums, and grunge into a sterile environment like South Street seaport in New York. You have The Gap, Nike, the same restaurants—McDonald's. It's clean, sterile, and boring. That emerged in the 1980s. At the same time, the kids have bought big time into grunge and rap. Sterility on one hand, grunge on the other. Woodstock's anniversary was supposed to be sterile, but it turned into a mudbath. Alienation is sort of being undercut.

I was politically engaged in South Africa, and in some ways, watched by police although I was never arrested by police as some of my friends were. University politics in South Africa in the 1970s involved considerable activism. We were often chased by police dogs, tear gas, occasionally by bullets. I left South Africa, moved by thinking I needed to be at a good university—the excitement of a bigger broader world—and if I didn't leave, I would get myself into a lot of trouble soon.

The movie we made on South Africa was actually banned. I also edited a philosophy journal on apartheid that was banned, too. I left South Africa in 1977, and returned for a visit in 1981. I was quite nervous about how I'd be received. I was followed in London and New York by the South African Embassy. But one shouldn't make too much of this. Certainly black South Africans, and some white activists, have had many more harrowing experiences than I've had.

I think Nelson Mandela faces really deep problems. Mandela has to be very careful. He's very comfortable with middle of the road liberalism. If he's unable to deliver on his promises—jobs, housing, schools—things will unravel quickly. There are all kinds of political tensions that enter into South Africa [that] he's trying to reconcile. He's morally upstanding. He spent twenty-seven years in prison and walked out without condemning [those who put him there]. That's a remarkable person. He's really moved by a moral pragmatism, and he's calculated where interests lie. Were there no Mandela and no deKlerk, you wouldn't have had dramatic movement in this direction, though the two of them were pushed there by forces much larger than themselves.

Street crime in South Africa has been cut in half since the elections in April 1994. Think about this in the context of the current crime debate in the United States. In 1994, 90 percent of the eligible population voted in the elections. In America, it was less than 40 percent. Democracy on the way up, and democracy on the wane. In South Africa under apartheid, street crime was a venting of frustrations, a symbol or index of repression, as well as a form of economic survival. There's been a honeymoon period. But there are a lot of questions that need to be addressed.

There are some similarities between racial space in South Africa and the United States. One's more formalized than the other. Townships surrounded by barbed wire, urban ghettos divided by highways. [The abolition of apartheid] was like a renewed celebration of civil rights for black Americans watching what was happening in South Africa. A kind of rekindling of optimism that the investment of black America in South Africa in the 1970s and 1980s paid off. This movement was like the Civil Rights Act in the 1960s. Whether it will have a desirable effect down the road remains to be seen.

America will offer South Africa a central example, and South Africa can learn from the American experience. But equally important, America can learn from the South African experience, a transformation of attitudes that people really do have to live together. And values do have to change accordingly. There are things to be learned in America—with the police, for example. And the new South Africa may have something to offer America in return.

The media has been largely responsible for instilling in us a tendency to lump people into geographical races. But by buying into this pattern of clustering of people, we do ourselves and others an immense disservice.

The wide spectrum of shades spanning all geographical races make identification by color a pointless consideration. People of the white European geographical race possess light and dark degrees of various pigments ranging from fair to porcelain tones, cream, ruddy to reddish, peach to pale orange, medium beige and olive to yellowish. In the black geographical race, people's skin shades range from light easily mistaken for white to yellowish-brown, reddish-brown, and the darkest hues of mahogany.

You can select "White," "Black," "Yellow," and "Red" crayons, but none would represent the skin tones of the peoples of the world. "White" can best be described as the color of typing paper. Use the crayon on the paper, and you'll have trouble seeing the color. That's why one uses white liquid cover to eliminate typing errors. "Black" crayon could be used on a piece of onyx, but you'll have difficulty in finding the mark. Using a "Yellow" crayon on a lemon, you may only be able to find the mark if the lemon peel is unwaxed. With "Red" you could try to find a slash of color on a maple leaf, but your search still would be relatively hard.

People of every hue, speaking over 800 languages, live in Africa. About 300 miles east of Mozambique, a global stew of twelve million people live on the island of Madagascar. More than two million Malagasy people possess Malayo-Indonesian origins. The Cotiers represent a blend of mixed African, Malayo-Indonesian, and Arab cultures, and over 20,000 people have French, Indian, or Creole heritage. Descendants of East Indians live on the mainland. Pygmy and Khoisan people comprise about 75 percent of the indigenous population. Black Africans make up about 70 percent of all African peoples.

Timothy "T.A." Niles
Trinidad and Tobago Islands in the Caribbean
Black African Culture
Teacher-Ph.D Candidate

[I came] from an island made of predominantly East Indian and African descendants. The first thing that struck me at JFK Airport, I was shocked to see so many black people. I was twelve, and this was my first impression of the United States, what I thought had been a pristine, white country. It struck me, and I don't suppose I realized this till much later, there are many Africanisms within European Diaspora.

In interacting with African Americans versus Afro-Caribbean, they'd say, "He's not black. He's Jamaican," and I'd think, "How stupid." The attitude of the American blacks was that they were the only black people. They had pretty much identified themselves that way. The African descendants who have been transported into different locales see themselves as somehow separate, when, in fact, you look at different cultures, they retain much of their African roots. In Trinidad, you see it in much of the food, many of the words. They're very African.

Being transported from another place where we haven't had to deal with the oppression perpetrated through the media, I had a different perspective. African descendants ran the place I come from. You had an opportunity to develop a positive sense of self. The African Americans here [in the United States] see themselves in opposition to the white majority. I was able to approach people as people, not as enemies, just as other human beings.

With my experiences in the United States, then I too started developing some of that perspective, especially when I was in the military, during the late 1970s. There was still a sense of community among blacks. Racism was still pretty high, and we formed pretty close groups. Solidarity. The white soldiers started mocking us, pretending to dap, and there was some violence. The commander then told us "no more dapping." We didn't sit still for it, and we went around for petitions.

I found a lot of soldiers would talk about solidarity and togetherness, but when they were put in a position to be looked at [with] disfavor, they usually declined. The men in the lower ranks, however, did write. When I requested mass to speak with the higher ups, I met with a colonel as a spokesman for the group. He was highly upset we had the nerve to do this. I said we gave up a number of rights, but we didn't have to give up the right to greet each other in whichever way we chose, especially culturally.

In the end, they rescinded the order. But a week later, I ended up on charges for some silly incident with one of the corporals who had refused to write. For something along the lines of insubordination. [I] was held in custody for a week.

It didn't occur to me till much later that the racist behavior in the military had started from when I'd been recruited with the aptitude tests that qualified me for any job. They made me take the test again because I came from the inner city and therefore had to have cheated somehow. Again, I scored very high. I met with the military occupational coordinator who asked me what I wanted to do.

I said, "Computers."

He said, "Computers are all filled up right now. You could get into supplies."

I ended up a warehouseman, doing the most menial tasks. I was seventeen. It didn't occur to me that this was racism. I looked at the system in the warehouse and devised another system and took it to the lieutenant who liked it. I had to meet with the company commander and got spit-shined. He wanted to know why I did this.

He said, "God damn it, we don't pay you to think!"

I don't know for sure whether that was racially motivated, but I often wondered whether I would have been responded to in the same way if I'd been blond and blue-eyed.

In later times, I realized that the military—or at least the Marine Corps—was a microcosm of society at large because it wasn't utilizing its resources in the most logical manner. You have kids from inner cities relegated to nothing jobs because they come from the wrong place, the wrong culture. Luckily for me, I didn't spend the early formative years of my life in an oppositional environment, in opposition to white folks as it seems to me the African Americans have. In black culture in America, everything seems to revolve around this thought.

Despite the difficulties I endured in the military, where I had ended up very anti-white at the time, it helps me to understand the African American perspective better. I was in the military a very short while, but I started developing that same oppositional attitude. [I] ended up in Fort Leavenworth where I had the chance to reflect that I didn't have to let white problems stop me. Not all whites feel this way against blacks. Not all blacks feel this way against whites. Racism is always there. Those feelings need not color my perspective negatively to affect what I need to and want to do.

It helped me to see who I was, so to speak returning to my childhood where I didn't need to do more than realize I was black and go on with my life. In order to lift the entire society, you need to lift those at the bottom as well. I owe it to the general populace to help this group. Just because someone might be a different color, that they didn't look like me, doesn't mean I can't help another person.

Now I'm studying intercultural communication on a formal level. I'm applying the things I've learned in my life. I think a lot of the animosity and negativity between groups comes from different styles of communicating. When I originally started the idea for my masters thesis, I considered not doing it because I knew people wouldn't like this. The African method of communicating is very much from the heart. It reflects who you are. People are very much what they say.

From my perspective, the white culture doesn't appear to come from the heart. I thought a lot of it had to do with the ways in which the groups communicate, and I began feeling agitated because of oversolicitous communication between whites. I learned, however, that it has to do with cultural styles, not race.

People think [differences in communication are] inherent to race and so on, but it has to do with different values. We tend to lump people into categories and say "If you're this, then you're x, y, and z." While there will be some things coming from a particular culture even when people try to deny it, there are a lot of other things that won't be identifiable because people are a conglomeration of many things. People have cultural and individual styles, cultural and individual histories, and they all respond differently because of these factors and the ways in which they're treated. On one hand, I can talk about a certain culture on a macro level, but there's also a micro level in interactions. We can't ignore the group, nor can we ignore the individual. From the communication perspective, the context is all important. You have to look at so many things, or you do yourself and everyone else a disservice when you lump people together.

A few days ago, a white doctoral student around fifty years of age and I were discussing foods. He couldn't seem to get around the notion that Thai or Mexican or Japanese or whatever food, that it's all American because that's all part of America. American food is not just hamburgers and hotdogs and so on. He just couldn't understand. I didn't want to turn it into a cultural lesson, so I joked about it.

I argue with real radical anti-white folks that adopting the separatist-we-are-better-than-them perspective is the very same attitude whites had [in creating] this situation now. By maintaining this position, they are condoning the very situation they've protested. How can they justify having the very same mentality they've opposed?

Two days ago, I wrote how funny it was, that I pity the poor white folks who would come in contact with that mentality. It's all of our responsibility to remove ourselves from the oppositional mentality, to understand that cultural differences exist. Yes, they coincide with historical social development. Not anything necessarily innate or inherent to the human condition, [they coincide] because of our failure to develop individual identities. We look to groups to bolster ourselves and our personal identities, and in order to elevate ourselves, we need to denigrate others. Until we start teaching children—individuals—to develop a personal sense of self, of course maintaining a group membership in that overall self-concept, but not placing so much emphasis on that membership for the purpose of establishing identity. Until we do that, we'll continue to have group animosity.

142

If my group is better than your group, then I'm okay. We don't have the concept that I'm okay as an individual. It all stems from ego and identity. It starts with a sense of self and how that sense of self is developed.

In the late 1970s and early 1980s, a woman caught the attention of fashion magazines in the United States of America. The photogenic epitome of perfection with a flawless complexion, incredibly high cheekbones, enormous eyes, a full mouth, and an air of mystery, she was suddenly propelled from college into the glamorous world of modeling. The right chemistry at the right time, her discovery marked a fashion industry move to use multicultural or ethnic models. Her name was Iman.

Certainly gorgeous women hail from every culture, and after so many years of exclusively porcelain-skinned blondes—even brunettes were hard to find in this realm—the fashion industry needed to identify their switch of focus somehow. In reality, of course, everyone is multicultural. Everyone is ethnic!

Now an internationally famous model, Iman did make the world aware of Somalia, her birthplace and home to resistance fighter Mohamed Abdulla Hassan and internationally-acclaimed novelist Nuruddin Farah. Few folks know about Somalia and the Horn of Africa, its history or its people, yet this predominantly agricultural nation became the source of an intense international media focus in the 1990s after troops moved in to quell tensions.

Over 99 percent of the Somali population—roughly eight million—are Sunni Muslims. "Between ten [and] twelve million people speak the Somali Language, which belongs to the Hamitic-Cushitic original," a relative of the ancient Egyptian tongues, says Ahmed Ali, a Somali native. "The British and Italian Somalilands achieved freedom and reunited to form the Republic of Somalia," and the nation gained independence in 1960. Seizing power in 1969, a military junta ended the parliamentarian regime [and] became one [of] Africa's most oppressive dictatorships.

Major General Mohamed Siad Barre seized control after a

bloodless coup, replacing the government with a USSR-friendly socialist regime and "dragged the country into a civil war. In 1991, the people, led by various political opposition movements, defeated the dictatorship but...could not realize the nation's aspirations of democracy, peace, and justice because of power struggles between political factions."

By 1992, the combination of political chaos, warring armies, severe drought, and widespread starvation paralyzed the nation, as more than two million Somali refugees scrambled to escape the horrors of their homeland. "More than 500,000 fled the country seeking refuge in neighboring countries," writes Ali, who says Somalia is famous for its significance as the single country with the most camels in the world, its fine gold and silver jewelry, frankincense— used in religious ceremonies—and myrrh—"a gum resin used in perfume or medicine preparation."

Somalis drink the milk of their one-humped dromedaries, says Ali, who says Somalis also "eat its meat."

Ahmed Ali
Somali Culture
High School Mathematics Teacher

We in Africa learned English indirectly from the British, so we have this African British accent. I think Americans don't travel like other people so they don't have experience with different accents. [Americans] seem very provincial when they hear people speaking differently. They don't think it's all right to have an accent. Accents can be distracting, but many people are prejudiced against this accent. There's a kind of discrimination. You constantly need to show them. Some people think you are illiterate even if you speak four or even seven languages. People may make fun of you. It's kind of different with adults. Our African American brothers do not believe we're the same. They treat you like the whites do.

I started learning English...as a teenager. I was born with two African languages, Somalian and May, a dialect of two or three million Somali people. I also [learned to] speak Arabic and Italian. I was ten. I started French very late (in the 1980s). My French is disappearing because I can't access the language as frequently. Now I am learning Spanish. Mohammed said if somebody learns a language, it becomes a part of them. In our community, learning a language is rewarding.

144

We have educated people in our Somalian community. Refugees were never told to emigrate to the United States, and because of the civil war, they came, unprepared. The orientation they get is never enough to understand what this country is like. A Somalian lady almost killed her baby because she couldn't read the directions on the prescription [or] speak enough English to understand what the doctor was saying. Associations help these people. We encourage our community to work and overcome the obstacles.

The times were tense in the years preceding the Civil War between the North and the South in the United States. Family intimacy between brothers or fathers and sons shattered under the general umbrella of political differences. But here, where life, liberty, and the pursuit of happiness had formed the nucleus of the nation, the question of whether or not those founding principles included all men from all geographical cultures and races developed into the wedge between families and the seedling that bloomed into one of America's bloodiest battles. Both sides knew change was in the air. Yet what one side might have perceived as progress, the other side might have seen as an inevitable threat to the strength of the nation. Considering the economic impact on individual slaveowners, the abolition of slavery loomed over their financial assets like a storm cloud.

In New York State, where married women could own real estate as of 1848, Lucretia Mott and Elizabeth Cady Stanton had already made an impact for women's rights in the same year, formally organizing a convention to demand women's suffrage. Perhaps some slaveowners saw what women had begun to achieve as a threat to the very fiber of the nation, although the national fight for suffrage would take another seventy-two years.

Imagine the thoughts of a slaveowner who, until now, retained absolutely total control of his life and his possessions—from his wife and female children to his slaves! For years, he had been a godhead on his plantation. He may have seen himself as a generous and loving husband and father to his adoring family. To his slaves, he was lord and master who would meagerly dole out some minute favor—or lessened abuse—for work well done, often punishing with abandon for the most obscure slights. Perhaps he had encouraged the creation of public schools for poor families and had even been able to tolerate what some men called progress—more humane treatment of jail prisoners and patients in insane asylums and the admission of women to some universities. The abolitionist movement may simply have been more than he could bear. Even in his own family, he no longer knew whom he could trust.

Feelings were hot on both sides of the fence. The underground movements were thriving—with slavery supporters in the North and antislavery strongholds in the South. Harriet Beecher Stowe's novel *Uncle Tom's Cabin* exposed the abuses of slavery, inspiring more antislavery sentiment among the states, and southerners mentally began to divorce themselves from the rest of the Union.

By the mid-1850s, a secret system figuratively called an underground railroad was guiding fugitive slaves to freedom in the North. Thanks to Harriet Tubman, affectionately and appropriately called "Moses," more than 300 slaves escaped in a series of nineteen trips. Tubman, one of the most famous, was not the only so-called conductor of this well-organized pathway to freedom.

In the Kansas Territory, the New England Emigrant Aid Company and the Wyandotte Indians created an alliance of conductors and ports of refuge, providing the structure through which newspaper reporter and editor Clarina Nichols and many others operated in Quindaro, the first river port antislavery settlement. In Lawrence, west of Quindaro, Captain John E. Stewart, the entire Robert Miller family, and Joel and Emily Grover worked within the system. Abolitionist John Brown and a man named Adair used a cabin in Osawatomie, southeast of Lawrence, to hide runaways. Roughly three years later, late in 1859, federal troops captured Brown in Harpers Ferry, Virginia—now West Virginia—at a federal arsenal he and his band of followers had seized as the first step in a planned slave uprising. Brown was found guilty and subsequently hanged.

The underground railroad system provided an intricately devised access out of the South. Although the majority of eastern escape routes fell east of the Missouri River, a natural dividing line, western escape routes guided runaway slaves through forests, mountains, and back roads from one barn or cellar to another.

Meanwhile, a statehood debate brewed between free and proslavery activists in the Kansas Territory, sparking raids and massacres throughout the underground trails. Today, the state, often called "Bleeding Kansas," possesses a wealth of black history. Unfortunately, this great national resource still remains undiscovered among most people, even in the black communities across America.

Political tensions finally exploded into the Civil War on April 12, 1861, at South Carolina's Fort Sumter in Charleston Harbor. In contrast to *Glory,* Hollywood's brilliantly conceived version of what happened during the next four years, the United States Army's Fort Scott-based 1st Kansas Colored Infantry of slaves, fugitives, and freemen saw battle months before the 54th Massachusetts Regiment picked up their arms. Sadly, African Americans did not receive the Congressional honor of full military status for another five years.

The 9th and 10th U.S. Cavalries, the latter one formed and housed at Fort Leavenworth, Kansas, became two more all black military units of the blue-uniformed Buffalo Soldiers. Yet their possession of military status did not preclude the prejudices these soldiers endured, although they were instrumental in building forts, guarding railroad workers, laying telegraph lines, and fighting the Native Americans who had given them their nickname. Were they really named "Buffalo Soldiers" because of their tactics described earlier in the chapter as "cornered buffaloes," or was it because the Cheyenne Indians believed the Buffalo Soldiers' hair resembled that of a buffalo? The story behind the nickname varies, but that's often the case with legends.

How they received that legendary name isn't as important, however, as the recognition the Buffalo Soldiers have finally begun to receive since the early 1990s: General Colin Powell dedicated a fourteen-foot Buffalo Soldier Monument to the outstanding contributions and military records of the 10th U.S. Cavalry soldiers in 1992. No small feat in achieving this kind of praise, both the 9th and 10th U.S. Cavalries claim the most decorations of any regiments in United States Army history!

In the years following the Civil War, a former slave from Tennessee, Benjamin "Pap" Singleton, appeared to inspire the growth of several all African American towns throughout the South, in at least one area of Oklahoma, and in many areas of Kansas. Although the other communities seemed to disintegrate throughout the years, leaving little traceable history, the tiny town of Nicodemus, Kansas, established in 1878, was still very much alive by the mid-1990s. The site of the nation's oldest recorded African American-operated post office, Nicodemus—population sixty-five—also holds the record as the oldest and only completely black African American town west of the Mississippi River. Today, Nicodemus is home to many black retirees. According to Angela Bates, president of the Nicodemus Historical Society, people moved from there during the 1950s, then came back in their retirement years.

"The population has gotten older and older," says Bates. "It's not unusual to see an all-black community in the South; it is, west of the Mississippi."

As freely as many people from a wide variety of cultures shared their experiences with us, we were surprised to realize we had incredible difficulty in finding, specifically, American born and bred black females of the African culture who were willing to share their experiences. Where they were born and where they lived at the time they replied didn't matter, although each came from a different area of the United States. Most hesitated and seemed to be suspicious of the motivation behind the questions. Yet even a lack of willingness to share, or their desire for anonymity, speaks of the bridges to cross and the healing still needed among people from all of the world's cultures.

One woman, a media personality, briefly spoke—off the record—for a few moments. She originally agreed to share her story—anonymously. Later, she changed her mind, explaining her fear that someone would realize the story was hers, and she would be out of work.

Posed with the questions, another female media personality exploded, asking, "Don't you guys ever give up? I'm so sick of this stuff!" She later agreed to consider addressing the subject, only to change her mind again one final time.

In another incident, a magazine report on teaching methods in Mississippi schools—how the education of black children neglected to include more than nominal mention of civil rights leaders, especially beyond Martin Luther King, Jr., and how that education had not included activists like Medgar Evers and Malcolm X—led us to a casual conversation with a woman in Alabama who revealed an identical pattern in the schools she attended. Until she entered college, she had not known who Medgar Evers was or even "what the big deal was, and Malcolm X simply wasn't discussed at all because he was too radical." This woman too, also someone in the media field, declined further comment.

One needs to understand that identifying two specific states does not imply only these two. In fact, the situation existed in several other states and still exists today.

Still another woman who works in the public eye spoke about her children and her views of the white and black races. One of her daughters came home in tears after a planned visit to a swimming pool. When the youngster had entered the pool, the other children got out, convinced that her skin pigment would turn the water and therefore themselves black. Her son, a top-notch math student, began to receive low grades. When the woman questioned the teacher, the latter replied that she had known "he would be a poor student." The son, choosing not to disappoint the teacher, gave her exactly what she expected—nothing.

The mother also spoke freely about her perceptions of the differences between whites and blacks.

"Whites always talk about race," she said. "Why can't they talk about anything without race entering into it?"

She also perceived other African Americans as people who fear retribution for being themselves, for thinking they need to "talk white." She also senses a difference between being black in New York City's Harlem district and being black in other places where African Americans may hesitate to be themselves—at the movies, for instance. In Harlem, African Americans tend to get intensely involved in movies, passionately expressing "Get him! Didn't you see? He went that way!" Blacks in many other American cities tend to be less emotive, she says.

Angela Bates spoke freely.

Angela Bates
African American Culture
President, Nicodemus Historical Society

Where you live determines your exposure to the amount of black history you learn. I lived in Washington, D.C. for about thirteen years. When I was younger, I had assumed that all blacks were alike and we had the same perspective about our history and view of the white world. The minute I went to the east coast, I had the shock of my life. Blacks [there] were so drastically different than the blacks I knew back home in California. There was no closeness that I felt at home in California, just cliques. In Atlanta, I felt that the blacks were about twenty years behind times, they were just like I had seen in movies, subservient. They seemed like they were just right out of a book.

As black people, we have a tendency to not know black history. It's because we weren't formally taught it in school, [but] it's also because we were taught through slavery that we weren't important. Therefore, from that experience we have a leftover mentality that our history isn't important either. As a result, most don't want to know anything about our slave experience and/or other aspects of our history. The whole concept of Malcolm X during the time I was growing up was one of two perspectives: That you disassociated yourself from his thinking, or you embraced it. Many disassociated with his thinking because he was too radical, but he had many valid points about our history and our lives that we chose not to relate to because of his radical views. So many psychologically divorce themselves from him and his perspective.

We're ignorant about our history in general, and it's very sad. [But] like I said, partly because we haven't been formally given the history through the educational system and also because we've been brainwashed to believe that we and our history aren't important. If you ask the average black on the street about various historical figures or events in our history, most don't know who or what you're talking about.

My own experience is that I had to break free from the mentality that our history isn't important, and that was a major struggle on various levels. It was easy for me to identify with my pioneer black heritage experience because of Nicodemus and my connection to it, however, other aspects of our history— slavery especially—I stayed away from until I started to research my genealogy as it related to Nicodemus and the pioneers that settled there. Then I opened a new chapter in our American past that was so rich, I regret it took me so long to come to grips with it. You have to be brave enough to look slavery in the eye and really look at it with an open and receptive and non-judgmental mind. Our anger about it prevents us from looking closer at it and what happened not only in states where they grew cotton and had large plantations, but in states like Kentucky who had less than five percent of the white population owning slaves. Slavery takes on a different bent when the slave master ratio changes.

I was invited to speak at a conference about the African American experience in the West, and I've never been so shocked and disappointed in blacks as I was then. The entire conference was focused on the African perspective in education. I ask now, why was I even invited to speak, because all that was being promoted was the Africancentric perspective. I have problems with identifying with the motherland when I haven't come to grips with my most recent historical past here in America! Most children in urban areas have never even left their neighborhoods and have difficulty relating to what's going on across town, or in another state, let alone relating to another continent. Many children think Africa is a country in and unto itself. They don't even realize that when they relate to Egyptian history that Egypt is a country unto itself. I say let's start giving our children a firm and positive history lesson from the pages of American history before we negate the experiences of our forefathers right here. To negate slavery is to say that our ancestors here in America did not exist and their existence was...and is worthless to us today. I can look upon the faces in the photos of my great-great-great-grandparents and know that their lives weren't in vain and that I am here because of the pain and struggles they had to endure. I want to pay homage to them for experiences.

When I think about them, I think about how they were denied education and now we can pay our kids to go or stay in school. Many died learning to read and write, now our children are killing each other in schools over clothing items or even in response to the way someone has looked at them. Something is terribly wrong with this picture. We have a generation of complacent kids, and this is our future. We have to be responsible enough to know that if we don't give them something to be proud of and to live for that is worthy, then we don't really have a future.

I grew up in southern California, and my interest in Nicodemus was stimulated at an early age because we spent summer vacations there. There was no doubt in anyone's mind that home was where Nicodemus was. I had a perspective of the world and my place as it relates to Nicodemus. Nicodemus was a very special place for my family, for my relatives. We had our own town, and it was all black. I knew who I was when during the 1960s we were going through an identity crisis as a race. We still are going through an identity crisis. We are now referring to ourselves as African Americans.

In Nicodemus, we had the family, the extended family, and the town. We had Nicodemus in common with all who were from there. We had a real sense of who we were. I am a descendant from the black settlers of the West, and I'm very proud of my history as it relates to the western frontier.

If we take the time to educate our children with the rich American history that is ours and is real and not just the negative aspects of slavery, we can give our children a good foundation to stand on, psychologically as well as academically. There is finally a movement in the academic environment where our history is finally coming to surface. We must realize that what is important to us is in our own back yard.

As I started to do the research on my own family, I wanted to know about the faces of the people that I saw in many photos, and I tried to put the faces with the stories. As I started to do this, each bit of information I found pulled me further and further into the history. I've walked the same ground where my forefathers were enslaved in Kentucky, looked into the slave cabins where they

151

lived. With my interest and love of my history, I have truly touched their lives and I know that what they experienced was important and that their lives and history weren't, aren't, in vain. Now I am obsessed with our African American history and what a blessing!

A wide variety of terrains, languages, peoples, and cultures make up the fifty-four nations on the continent of Africa. Yet unless one views the thousands of years behind the overall picture, this global region can still be falsely represented and generally misunderstood. Centuries of interaction have passed between Africa's and other world cultures. Positive interactions have resulted in mutually productive relationships. Negative contacts produced difficulties between participants and their descendants.

Many immigrants to the New World who got homesick or simply didn't like what they found could earn their fares back home and leave. But to the majority of peoples arriving by boatloads from the west-central coast of Africa in the 1600s—neither indentured servants, adventurers, nor opportunists—their port of entry was an auction block where ownership of these once-free people was transferred from one owner-businessman to another.

Distinctions, however, must be made and placed in context without elevating one individual or culture above another. Not all people who might be categorized as Africans living in the United States of America are descendants of slaves. Unfortunately, stereotypes about the descendants of slaves have brought about a lessened sense of respect which has resulted in discrimination against these people.

Ironically, the ancestors of west-central African immigrants may have made it possible for the slave trade to expand as it did. Regardless of who was involved, the ancient practice of enslaving people—human bondage—is not African in nature. Individuals from many of the world's cultures sought and still seek slaves for personal gain.

Writers like *Roots* author Alex Haley have begun to return a sense of pride and dignity to descendants of the African slaves. Whether our cultural history makes us descendants of people living in bondage or in freedom, whether we have descended from the Ancient Egyptians or the Pharaoh-enslaved Jewish peoples, our knowledge of that history should not affect or determine who we are today. We need to take the first step—to stop listening to people who perpetuate such notions.

People are living under dictatorships today. Most of them, longing to be free, are just as enslaved as those who were bought and sold thousands of years ago. While this chapter was being developed, hundreds of Cubans fled their homeland, braving the seas to Miami, Florida. Praying they wouldn't be seen on their homemade rafts, they risked their lives to reach the land where they believe dreams could come true: America.

If we perceive ourselves as useless and hopeless, we enslave ourselves. Many people have spent their entire lives in physical bondage, remaining free deep in their souls.

In the United States of America, the African slaves created one of the first truly American styles of music, still popular today—jazz. Walk through the French Quarter of New Orleans, Louisiana, any night of the week, and you can still hear the memorable sounds of all-American jazz. No other place in the world can claim this great music of the nation. Created of the people, by the people, and for the people, jazz remains the music of the land—the reflection of the people who were only slaves on the outside. Inside, they remained forever free!

Chapter 7

THE MIDDLE
AND NEAR EASTERNERS

What if you were offered a terrific job in the Middle East and you'd never been there? Would you picture caravans moving slowly across undulating dunes? Would you expect to see sheiks and harems? Perhaps you imagine you'd need to dive every two feet to avoid the bombs of another Middle East war.

The double-edged sword of Hollywood's glittering, glitzy movie industry has inspired many of our mental images of the Middle East. Rudolph Valentino, for instance, brought passionate intensity to the silent screen, and female fans swooned over his 1921 portrayal of *The Sheik*. Yet while many of these flicks encouraged fans of both sexes to fantasize about romance and adventure in the desert sands, they also tended to promote lingering stereotypes about the people.

Not all Middle and Near Easterners are sheiks or veiled belly-dancing beauties in sheer sexy costume. Nor are all people living in the Middle East camel drivers or vengeance-seeking bombers. The majority of people from this region, in fact, are warm, loving, hospitable folks who often have large extended families and equally big hearts.

From Tel Aviv to Baghdad, a wide variety of phrases have described this region: Middle East, Mideast, Near East, Gulf States, Arab States, the Cradle (or Center) of Civilization, the Crossroads of the World. But labels can mislead and pave the way for the development and promotion of stereotypes. Reporters covering media-attracting events in this political hotbed seem to prefer the name "Middle East." For the sake of lending consistency to this discussion, not necessarily favoring this name over any other, we will use the same term.

Nightly world newscasts have covered a gamut of events in the Middle East—reports on Palestine's 1948 transformation into the State of Israel, the 1967 Six-Day War, and hundreds of other happenings that may or may not fill today's history books. At times we seem to be complacent about headlines of another skirmish in this region. Not that we don't care, but events in the Middle East frequently dominate the news.

Desert Storm was different. Desert Storm commanded the spotlight in 1991, and people wanted to know what was happening in the Middle East. The news filled our homes, reaching into our backyards and into the schools, stealing into every facet of our daily lives, and we listened because loved ones—family members, friends, or acquaintances—had been shipped out to that region of the world.

According to most world history books, the world's first people lived along the Tigris and Euphrates Rivers in what we now call Iraq, said to be the world's geographic center. But if the Middle East was the geographic center of the world based on its relationship to the world's first people, the term tends to be misleading.

Standard spherical division of the world customarily crossed the point where the fewest inhabitants and smallest land mass occurred. Find 0° longitude and 0° latitude on a current world map, not a globe, and you'll locate the exact division point somewhere in the Gulf of Guinea. The former Portuguese colony of Sao Tomé e Principe, now an independent island republic, lies nearest this point at 0°19N, 6°43E off Africa's west coastline—once called the Gold and Ivory Coast.

But by eliminating the oceans and studying the land and its intercontinental relationships, we find the Middle East wedged into a crossroads of the world's regions containing the vast majority of people between Africa, Asia, and Europe.

Most of Africa, Asia, and Europe dominates the area commonly referred to as the eastern hemisphere. This area's geographic center is located in the Indian Ocean at 90°E longitude and 0° latitude. The northern sector of the 90°E longitude line runs through Bangladesh, extreme eastern China, and the center of the former Soviet Union. Set apart from other eastern hemisphere land masses by the Red Sea, Arabian Sea, Persian Gulf, and the Mediterranean Sea, the Western World region geographically identified as the Middle East lies west of this line at the apparent crossroads of the eastern hemisphere, rather than at the global center.

Long before ships, railroads, highways, and air travel gave us the privilege of global jaunts, travelers depended on the camel, donkey, and their own human foot power. Transportation through the mountains and valleys of Europe and Asia lacked both drinking water and basic comfort. And what nature didn't impede, marauders—often lurking in narrow mountain passes—made dangerous. Even today, the rough terrain and unpaved roads along the way make Marco Polo's Silk Road and other routes as hazardous as they were back then. The Middle East offered simpler, less treacherous routes.

Although the oil fields of Kuwait, Iran, Iraq, and Saudi Arabia intrigue many people, the main thrust of world attention focuses on Jerusalem, Israel, for its significance to the three major monotheistic world religions—Judaism, Christianity, and Islam. Lacking economic or military value, Jerusalem plays an important role in past, present, and future world history. Orthodox Jews believe the coming of the Messiah will occur in Jerusalem. Literal Bible-believing Christians say the Messiah will return to Jerusalem. According to some interpretations of Biblical prophecies, several events will take place in Israel, affecting the entire future course of the world.

The Temple of Solomon and the Wailing Wall section of the rebuilt temple's ruins, symbolic of the Golden Age of Israel in old Jerusalem during King Solomon's reign, represent a particularly meaningful place for Jews visiting Israel. During the 2,000 years prior to 1948, when Israel was established as a country, the twelve homeless tribes of Israel—the Jewish people—were scattered throughout the world. Today, the majority of Jews, while living in a variety of cultural groups in many nations, still consider themselves bonded by the religious beliefs, traditions, and customs of their forefathers.

These cross-cultural bonds create a situation which might be called a culture within a culture. Like the Jews, other groups demonstrate similar cross-cultural patterns—among them, the Amish in certain areas of Pennsylvania, Ohio, and Iowa; the Ainu of Japan; Buddhist monks of Tibet; many Native American tribes, including the

Hopi, Navajo, and Yaqui Indians of the southwestern portion of the United States of America; descendants of the Incas living high in the Peruvian Andes Mountains; Basques of Spain and France; Sikhs of India; Laps of northern Finland; and the Tarahumara Indians of Mexico.

The birth of Jesus of Nazareth inspired the development of several solar calendars, including the most commonly used calendar in the United States of America today—the Gregorian. Generally accepted and easily understood, the Gregorian calendar uses a common, albeit Christian, thread between nations, noting BC as the years **Before Christ** and AD, **Anno Domini**, Latin for "In the Year of our Lord." In contrast, the Jewish and Islamic calendars—among several others—use the moon to divide the days. The Jewish calendar calls the years Before Christ, BCE, **Before the Common Era**, and After Christ, CE, the **Common Era**.

Jesus, a twelve-year-old Bar Mitzvah student, spent time in the rebuilt Temple of Solomon in Jerusalem at the peak of the Roman Empire. On what Christians call Palm Sunday, Jesus reentered Jerusalem at the age of thirty-three and was condemned by many Jewish leaders including King Herod the following week. Sentenced to be crucified on a cross outside of the city, Jesus, according to Christian belief, rose from the dead three days later, ascending into Heaven from the Mount of Olives—about ten kilometers from Jerusalem—about forty days later.

Muslim, also spelled Moslem, followers of Islam believe in the prophet Mohammed's teachings and writings. But unlike the roots of Judaism and Christianity, Jerusalem is not the cradle of Islam. Followers of Islam believe Jerusalem's Dome of the Rock Mosque, however, is where Mohammed (also spelled Muhammad) ascended to Heaven and returned to earth to continue his teaching.

Yet even King Solomon might not succeed in resolving the disputes between Jews who want to rebuild the Temple of Jerusalem and Muslims who worship at the mosque at the same spot. But all hope of resolution isn't lost yet. Some people now believe the actual site of the earlier Jewish temple was a short distance from the Dome of the Rock Mosque.

Born at a time when commerce was growing and thriving in Mecca, a center for commerce and religion, Mohammed was orphaned at an early age and was raised there by an uncle. As was the custom of the times, Mohammed, like other boys from the cities and villages, went to live with a Bedouin family to learn desert Arab frugality and self-reliance.

Mohammed, believing he'd received a revelation from Allah (God), taught the people of Mecca about what later became known as Islam. Meeting resistance and persecution there, he traveled about 280 miles north to another commerce center and a Jewish settlement in Yathrib, later called Medina, "the city of the Prophet," formally known as Madinat al-Nabi. There, the Jews—some of whom converted to Islam—welcomed Mohammed.

Persecution from Mecca's religious leaders strongly increased, and Mohammed encouraged his early followers to move across the Red Sea to Christian-dominated Abyssinia in Africa. There, the Christians displayed hospitality and tolerance to the Muslims who, in turn, developed respect for their hosts and their beliefs.

Encouraged by the large number of converts in Medina, Mohammed returned there some time later in a journey which became known as *The Year of Flight, Anno Hegira* or A.H. When he traveled again, Mohammed set out for Mecca.

Leading several battles against caravans passing through the area now called Saudi Arabia, Mohammed eventually reached Mecca. There, he destroyed the statues of the gods and proclaimed the Kaba—the large black stone in the center of a mosque there today—to be the central shrine of Islam.

Several of Mohammed's sons predeceased him, but his daughters and their families were still alive. With no heirs or named successors, disagreements began about who would succeed him, resulting in a predominantly political split and creating two main sects of Muslims, the **Shiites** (Shia)—followers of Ali ibn Abu Talib, Mohammed's only blood descendants—and the **Sunnis** (Sunna)—followers of his descendants by marriage through his daughters. Today, except for Shiite-controlled Iran, the Sunni majority controls most of the Middle Eastern countries.

Over time, many Middle Eastern place names have changed, often lending confusion to the already complex interweaving of events. For frustrated history students who struggle to grasp some understanding of specific time periods, linking ancient place names with those of the contemporary world is an experience that might be reminiscent of Abbott and Costello's "Who's on First?" episode!

With that in mind, let's look at the Middle East, base by base.

As biblical history tells it, before the first time Israel—then the Land of Canaan—became a nation thousands of years ago, a young Egyptian woman named Hagar worked for Abraham and his wife Sarah in their household. Sarah hadn't yet borne a child for Abraham, the claimed father of the nation of Israel, and he was already well up in years. At Sarah's urging, Abraham went to Hagar who bore Ishmael, Abraham's first son.

A few years later, Sarah conceived Abraham's son Isaac. But to Abraham's heartache, because he loved both children, jealous disputes welled up between the two women, and Hagar and Ishmael were sent away. Ishmael became the father of a great nation of twelve tribes, as did Isaac's son Jacob whose twelve sons created the foundation for the twelve tribes of Israel—establishing the bloodline bond between the Arabs, Hebrews (Jews), and Egyptians.

King Solomon's father, David, unified the Land of Canaan into the Kingdom of Israel. But after Solomon's death, the tribes separated. Ten of the twelve tribes of Jacob remained in the Northern Kingdom of Israel. The other two tribes formed the Southern Kingdom of the Hebrews, kept the capital—Jerusalem—and called this region Judah. The Southern Kingdom eventually became what we know as Israel today.

Conquering the Northern Kingdom of Israel, the Assyrians held Jacob's tribes captive around 722 B.C. But the Assyrians, influencing many world events from 960 to 626 B.C., and the more powerful Babylonians, met their match with the Medo-Persians who continued to hold the Hebrews captive until their releases in 538, 458, and 432 B.C. Today, Syria occupies this former Assyrian land, leading to the belief that at least some Syrians may have ancestral ties to the ancient Assyrians.

King Nebuchadnezzar ruled Judah and Jerusalem, its capital, from 605 to 562 B.C. In 586 B.C., the tribes of Judah and Benjamin were taken captive. The geographical center of Nebuchadnezzar's Neo-Babylonian Empire—the largest, most powerful, and socioeconomically well-developed kingdom of the period—was located in what is Iraq today. Although no one can be sure whether the ancient Babylonians were forefathers of the Iraqi people, it's conceivable that some Iraqis may be both Babylonian and Arab.

Around 539 B.C., the non-Arab Medo-Persian Empire defeated

the Babylonian Empire, continuing to dominate the Middle East until 330 B.C. Known for centuries as Persia, the area is now called Iran. The Iranian people—descendants of the Persians—are not Arabs. A target of the Iraqi Army during Desert Storm, the Kurds are believed to be descendants of the Medes.

The Phoenician influence made an impact throughout the Middle East region. Most of the land and sea trade routes passed through Phoenicia, the strong sea-faring nation now called Lebanon on the southeastern shores of the Mediterranean Sea. Although the Lebanese people are often thought of as Arab, many consider themselves descendants of the Phoenicians.

The Classical Greek Era was at its zenith during the Fifth Century, B.C. After its decline, Alexander the Great—a Macedonian—conquered many lands, including the Middle East and North Africa, between 336 and 323 B.C. After his death in 323 B.C., these lands were divided among Alexander's generals. Prior to the conquest of these territories, and during the Classical Greek civilization's decline, the Roman Republic emerged in approximately 500 B.C. and evolved into the dictatorial Roman Empire in 27 B.C.

Dominating many nations including the Southern Kingdom of the Hebrews (Judah), the Romans changed Judah's name to Judea, and later to Palestine based on the Philistine name Philistia. The Roman Empire divided into the Western and Eastern Empires in 395 AD.

The Western Empire lasted until Rome's fall in 476 AD, casting most of Europe into the feudal period and the Middle or Dark Ages. The Eastern Empire—including contemporary Greece, Western Turkey, and Cyprus—became the Byzantine Empire, which lasted until 1453 AD.

Around 700 AD, the Arabs, known as Moors then, gained control over most of the Middle East, including Palestine, and extending as far as North Africa, Spain, and the Central Asian steppes. The Moors brought great scientific advances and introduced Islam to these regions, yet their early forms of democracy enabled Jews and Christians to live, work, and worship as they wished. Moor domination over these areas lasted until 1400 AD.

The Turks began to move into the Middle East around 1300 AD, conquering more and more of the land for the Ottoman Empire. Then in 1918, a member of the British Army stationed in Egypt—the legendary Lawrence of Arabia—assisted in unifying the nomadic

Bedouin tribes. Led by Ibin Saud, the Bedouins drove the Turks from the Arabian Peninsula, what is now Saudi Arabia. Iraq, Kuwait, and other Gulf states were not in existence yet as we know them today.

Although the British influence could still be felt throughout the area, Saudi Arabia succeeded in gaining its independence from the Turks. Turkish-ruled Palestine's population was predominantly Arab by 1914, and the Arabs were demanding their independence. Offering to back Arab demands after World War I and asking Arab support during the War, Great Britain entered into the Sykes-Picot Agreement of 1916. But after an Arab revolt rose against the Turks in 1916, Great Britain denied promising postwar Palestine to the Arabs. The following year, Great Britain issued the Balfour Declaration, supporting the creation—without violating the rights of the non-Jewish population—of the Jewish homeland in Palestine. The postwar League of Nations' mandated territories were vague, however, and Palestine's Arab population became angry.

As World War II progressed, the Arabs rejected numerous compromises, including one dividing Palestine into two sectors, one Arab and one Jewish. Finally, Great Britain asked the United Nations to resolve the situation in 1947. The Arabs rejected the subsequent decision of the United Nations Special Commission on Palestine which was adopted by the General Assembly late in the year. Fighting between the Arabs and the Jews broke out, and when the dust had settled, nearly 700,000 Arabs had become refugees in nearby Egypt, Jordan, Syria, and Lebanon.

Throughout the decision-making process, England and other European nations decided the placement of the region's geographic boundaries without consulting the nomadic Bedouins, who were accustomed to moving across the region without concern for national boundary lines, and others who would live with the final result. Between the half-brother ancestry of the Arabs and Jews, the land's division into new nations by outsiders, and the re-establishment of the state of Israel, the Middle East was the setting for a great drama which would claim the world's attention for years to come.

Unfortunately, this drama has been a tragedy affecting the lives of many generations of people throughout the area. Without any intent of condoning violence, recognizing any political organization, or showing favoritism to any particular group over another, we examined the relationships between several peoples of the Middle

Eastern region.

The planned United Nations agreement giving Palestinians new citizenship and equal privileges in Egypt, Syria, Lebanon, or Jordan never materialized completely. When Jamal Abed Nasar was president of Egypt, Palestinians were allowed to live in Egypt, but they were denied citizenship. In Jordan, the Palestinians received passports and equal privileges. But their reception or their lack of being received in each of these countries tended to vary greatly. Every one of the nations involved probably has its own story to tell about what happened to the agreement; but no matter how the story is told, no one can deny that thousands of people were displaced, left without a country to call home, and seemed to be unwanted. Trying to make the best of an already difficult situation, many Palestinians went to Kuwait and other Gulf state countries and became an integral part of the workforce with people from Egypt, Jordan, Syria, Lebanon, and eventually the Philippines.

Claiming the tiny nation originally belonged to them, Iraq invaded Kuwait, and Desert Storm began. The United States, England, France, and other European countries joined forces with Saudi Arabia and the remaining Arab nations to liberate Kuwait, but most of the people still in Kuwait were Palestinian. After Desert Storm was over, many Palestinians were no longer welcome in Kuwait. Many went to Iraq, but there they weren't allowed to work or travel. Others traveled to Yemen and the Sudan. Since no other Middle Eastern countries wanted them either, many Palestinians were homeless again.

Post World War II boundary lines were drawn and decisions were made about the tiny land mass called Palestine—Israel today. Neither the Arabs nor the Jews really had a say in those decisions that resulted in people without a homeland. Today, the issue remains a source of conflict: Whose home is it really? But before we're too quick to reply, we might do well to ask: Does it really matter? Perhaps the answer lies in finding peace again, not between the Arabs and the Jews, but rather bringing the families of Ishmael and Isaac together again.

According to news media reports, some Middle East nations have begun to make attempts for peace. In 1979, Egypt signed a treaty with Israel. Jordan's King Hussein and Israel's Prime Minister Yitzhak Rabin took a first step toward peace and friendship in July 1994, ending a forty-six-year state of war and uneasy coexistence between the two nations, leaving just Syria and Lebanon without peace agreements with their Israeli neighbors.

Shortly before Hussein's and Rabin's historic handshake of peace, Iranian-backed guerrillas ambushed an Israeli-occupied area of south Lebanon, killing an Israeli soldier and wounding ten others. Israel's retaliatory air raids and a bombing attack on the Israeli Embassy in London followed Hussein's and Rabin's formal signing of an eleven-page document called the Washington Declaration, which began: "After generations of hostility, blood, and tears and in the wake of pain and wars, His Majesty King Hussein and Prime Minister Yitzhak Rabin are determined to end the bloodshed and sorrow." Both leaders denounced the attacks which Hussein said had "nothing to do with Islam, nothing with my religion." Hussein emphasized his wish for Arabs and Israelis to "live as members of one family."

The long-reaching impact of these peacemaking efforts may tend to become distorted through the eyes and camera lenses of television and newspaper reporters, leaving one with a feeling that perhaps nothing has really changed, that the move merely looks good on paper. Unfortunately, the media rarely mentions the positive side effects of these significant moments.

King Hussein and Prime Minister Rabin opened the door for peace, and some newspapers buried a small item illustrating a positive result of the event on the bottom half of a page. Other newspapers ignored the story. Yet the event's accompanying good will reverberated throughout the Middle East and in other parts of the world where Middle Easterners live, including in the United States.

On the same day as the historic signing of the Washington Declaration, the director of the Israel Museum proposed a loan exchange of ancient Hebrew relics to a museum in Amman, Jordan. In return for the Copper Scroll—one of the Dead Sea scrolls found in the spring of 1952—and a 2,800-year-old Balaam fresco, the national museum director offered to allow Jordan its choice of the Israeli collection. Since there was no existing postal service, the letter describing the proposal was hand-carried to its destination.

News reports also often fail to include the all-important human element—the perspective that events relate to living, breathing, thinking, warm-blooded human beings who don't always share beliefs with the reader. On the other hand, events affect people who share feelings and emotions with the rest of the human race.

One Iranian Story
Iranian Culture
Management

I was a translator for the American advisors when the Shah [Mohammad Reza Pahlavi] was in power in Iran and...a coordinator between the American advisors and the Shah's military ground force, Air Force, Navy. After the revolution came about, I was—[as]...a translator for the American advisors—prohibited to leave the country. [The government] would not give me the passport. That's why I decided to escape from Iran [and] rescue my family. I sent [them] to Italy. They [waited]...one year before I succeeded [in escaping]...going through the mountains on to Turkey. [I traveled] by car and walking...until we reached the border of Iran and Turkey. We were [at] the border about ten days [on] the Iran side [of] the mountain. We started walking, climbing the mountain until we got to the Turkish territory. There, I bought a passport, a forged passport, and had to pay the Turkish police to stamp entry to Turkey.

In Turkey, I was there about four months before I could exit...and join my wife and two children in Italy. You had to pay yourself out of Turkey. Every night, the Turkish police [came] with a van to the hotel, asking for the passport. They knew what they sold to Iranians at that time. They arrested us. ...From the hotel to the precinct [where] they were going to take us, we had to bribe them ten thousand, fifteen thousand Turkish *lira*, and they let us out. They would do this two times a week, sometimes one time a week, three times a week. Ten thousand, you're talking at that time about ten dollars, nine dollars. That was until I sent my passport to one of the people [who] had connections in Austria. They knew a lawyer and...issued me a visa under [a] false name...I had a visa going to Austria [which] was good for them after bribing the border patrol for the amount of 50 dollars. Also we had to pay to get a visa from Austria. I traveled by train through Bulgaria, Yugoslavia, into Austria [and stayed]...for two weeks until I got familiar with the border of Austria and Italy. A few days in fact, I went there and watched the borders because I did not have a visa into Italy. I went to the Italian Embassy, and they refused to give me [one]. One day after two weeks, there was a truck trailer...coming from Italy to Austria...the borderline was pretty busy. So I walked against the traffic, passed through the border, and from there, I called my wife.

I had to destroy my passport. If the police in Italy asked me, I would get arrested big time... At that time...lots of terrorists [hijacked]...planes and things like that. That's why I destroyed the passport and just walked in...a refugee from Iran [who] came there for refuge.

When I crossed the border to Turkey, the first thing I did, I called my wife in Italy and said, "I'm out of Iran." The next day, she [went] to the United Nations in Rome and [filed] for refugee [status]. [After] I joined her, the next day, I went to Rome [to] the United Nations. She filed for refugee, and she got accepted so I was automatically accepted as a refugee through the United Nations.

In Iran, it is a tradition that the wife does not lose her maiden name. In fact, when you get a passport and everything else, you [go by that name]. It helped us a lot.

When we were climbing...mostly...at night, we could hear the shooting from the Iran side... [Whoever] got caught going through the mountains, escaping the country, on the spot, they could kill them. Not the younger people. They used to take them back. At that time, we had a war with Iraq, and [Iran] would send them to the military. If they were eleven years up to the age of twenty-five, twenty-six, they would send them to the military. From there, they never came back. We had about over two, three million—they say only one million, but two, three million Iranians were killed during the war with Iraq. What Saddam did, they just poured the chemical into Iran. And they used to use those young people eleven years old. They used to brainwash them and say, "You go to heaven." And the Army used to send them ahead of time to neutralize the mines because Saddam [Hussein created many minefields.] They used to send those younger ones so the mines would go off and the division would go forward....[I left in] 1983.

It's the law here in America...they are not allowed to [help refugees escape]. [Wife says, "The day before the Americans left the country, we were at their house...partying...till two o'clock in the morning, and they could not tell us anything they're leaving....The next morning, they didn't show up at work. ...They boarded a plane and left the country. They couldn't say because their lives were in danger.] Most of them, they left in C-130 and C-140, those huge cargo [planes].

Once the United Nations accepted a person as a refugee, different countries had a quota. At that time, there were several—Canada, United States, a couple others, European countries... We said...we wanted to go to the United States. According to the 1945 Geneva Convention, by the laws of the United States and most of the European countries, Canada, once [the] United Nations accepts people as refugees, those countries must take [those people].

Iran was known as Persia. When the Arabs invaded Iran, it was actually

Mohammed, the Islamic prophet. We are Zoroastrian, the ancient Persian religion. ...[The Arabs] invaded [and] massacred all the Iranian people at that time...all Zoroastrians...because they were asked to become Muslim. Practically all of them refused....History repeats itself and the people [who] had the money, they escaped and...went to India where now...they're known as Parsi. The rest of them...married, but they did not give up the Zoroastrian religion, inside them, their beliefs. The Zoroastrian population...is about maybe...200,000 [including] the Parsis in India.

Kurdish, they were Zoroastrian to the fact that Mohammed invaded Iran. They said, "We are Muslim," but they are the Sunnis branch of Muslim, not Shiite. Kurdish are very close to the Zoroastrian in Iran, even when the Shah was in power. But at the end of his kingdom, it was getting very light.

In Iran, we had separate schools, separate drinking fountains. If we went to the fruit market, we could not pick the fruit. We had to ask the owner of the store to pick it for us.

[Wife: It was not in all the cities, it was just in the cities with Zoroastrians left.] ...was in Yazd, Kerman, and Teheran. Shiites [discriminated, believing Zoroastrians contaminated food and Muslim people]. You can kill so many people. After a while, it gets scary. I think one of the head men, in order to stop the killing, turned around and [said] "These people have been cursed. They are dirty, and if you touch them...something's going to happen to you, to scare, not to kill any more. Some other people say it was one of the Zoroastrian ideas, that this person became a Muslim and said [this religion] had been cursed. It was actually smart. It was passed to our grandfather and father, which makes sense because [the Muslims] were massacring.

We are the real Iranians. The majority [are] Muslim Shiites—that's why they rule the country. The Zoroastrians couldn't have been in office....When the Shah was in power at the end, he gave some authority to Zoroastrians, but other than that...

Anything to the Shiite Muslims, anything but Muslim, they call them atheists. An atheist is a person who doesn't believe in God, a person who doesn't belong to any religion. They think it's only the Muslims. They say the Koran said the lamb has to be butchered in such a way. They force them to drink the water, and blood has to come out. Zoroastrians eat all kinds of things. It wasn't prohibited.

[The Shah] was a Shiite Muslim. [There was such a conflict]. It's politics. He didn't listen. He lost himself under the power. He forgot what he was. He forgot who gave him that position.

My mother is here with my brother. But [my wife's family]—her mother, sisters and brother [are still there]. It was...difficult [to keep in touch] because [the Iranian government] censored. The mail was opened and resealed again.

167

They looked at the letters. If anything was said that was connected to the regime, they used to go instantly and kill that person [who received the letter] in Iran. Telephones, practically all of them were tapped. If the letter had a stamp on it, they'd take the stamp off, deliver the letter and they'd collect lots of money. "Okay, this is your letter. Do you want it or not?" The postman would stand there until you'd give them some money.

I love this country. I love America. And I believe, we all believe, my family...if there is a democracy, it's here in the United States. If there is freedom, it's here, and we can see it. It's not difficult. We pay taxes, we've got roads. We pay taxes, we've got facilities. In Iran, you pay taxes, but you have no roads, no facilities. In the United States, the people should go out of their homes and see other countries, and I'm sure they would appreciate what we have here. [From] our way of thinking because we came from abroad, and we [saw] some different countries, [it's] the truth. It's the number one country.

[Discrimination against Iranians], it's politics. [When] we saw the United States government [brainwash most of the people], once they say the terrorists are from Iran, the Middle East, they put it in such a way, that even [if] their own CIA agent [who] is Iranian wants to go in public and they ask him or her "Where you from?" [the CIA agent says] "I'm from Iran," [the American people] hate [the agent's] guts. It's people seeing one side of the story, people thinking one way. Look at it both ways. A good judge to me is the [one who] listens to both sides of the story and then pronounces sentence. I've faced [discrimination], I've faced it a lot. But I'm easy going. I have a good sense of humor. I laugh about it. So does my wife. That's how we taught and teach our children. [My children] are hurt. Maybe their child won't be.

There are people among those prejudiced people that talk to themselves or if you talk to them and explain to them, they understand and apologize and [maybe] will be your friend. Those who don't do that, don't open their minds, I don't want to be their friend.

The revolution, it wasn't actually a revolution; it was a coup d'etat by the United States because the Shah wasn't listening. He was the head of OPEC. He'd keep jacking up the price for oil, and here we are with Standard, Exxon, British Petroleum, Seven Sisters, Shell, Gulf...they don't like it....There's a limit. He couldn't get the chemical industry in Teheran. If he [did], he would have been the ruler in the Mideast. Nobody could touch him. That's why they eliminated him. They need Saddam, that's why they're keeping him.

After the Vietnam War, there were leftovers of weapons, the M-16s. They had to sell them in order to—I'm talking politics—make the money.... The Shah bought so much in ammunitions and weapons and vehicles...he had five military depot mothers...logistics, ordnance, quartermaster, engineering, and the mother...it was loaded. Americans were there as advisors...Nixon had contracted Shell during his first three years in office. Watergate came about in 1972. This was in 1970. So it was cargo, cargo and weapons and ammunitions that was to come to Iran. The money from the war was to go to pay for that. When it came about, all those weapons and things like that, all of the generals retired or they got executed. It was left with the major, colonel, and different ranks, and the soldiers who are still talking about [the] Shah's military. Many of the head honchos from the Western hemisphere were saying, "We want a war so we can get rid of those weapons and ammunition and vehicles—tanks and cannons and what have you."

So they go. They send a guy on the border who shoots one of the Iraqi and start a fight there. So the 16th Division goes, all was the Shah's military...they all go. Saddam pours the chemical weapon. None came back. 88th Division goes the same way. None of them came back, not even a single gun or bullet, nothing, not even a canvas or canteen came back. All was demolished. At the same time Saddam is using the chemical weapon, telling his boss, "Hey, man, that thing works. Or this part doesn't have as much an effect as this part does." Iran is losing people and the weapons. They are thinking ahead now. They're going to need all Yugoslavia, Bosnia, Russia. Brezhnev, Nixon tried to bribe Brezhnev, but he didn't accept it. But Gorbachev did. That's why I think, I don't know, that they bribed him so much. That's why he killed his country. Two, three years from now, it's going to be like the 1940s and 1950s in the United States [again], all the weapons.... They have to get rid of the chemical weapons, so the best place is other countries.

There is an old saying, wherever you are happy, that's your country. Wherever the heart of a person is happy, that's your country.

In the Persian Gulf, there [are] three islands where the inhabitants are Sunnis. They speak Farsi with an accent, and their ancestors [were] fishermen or merchants [who] went to India. They went there because it was all desert, and they started up a family. Those places are free port, no taxes. You go back to their history—Iraq, Kuwait, Saudi Arabia, all were under the Persian Empire.

[In Iran, my children would be studying history] from the viewpoint of what the government wants them to know. [There] if they talk what we told them, we would all be dead.

We visited with Louis Hasbany at Byblos, a Mediterranean restaurant in the southwestern region of the United States. A warm and friendly gentleman, his eyes become animated and twinkle as he relates happy stories surrounding his personal experiences with his people and his homeland. Yet his eyes tell all and become a bit darker and a lot sadder when he speaks of the sad tales.

"I'm not an Arab. I live in America. I am an American," he says. He was born over there, in Lebanon, but he's here now. In America.

We were especially impressed with his eagerness to share the interview limelight with his friends, restaurant chef Fouad Khoder and Fred Ackel, a former judge who says his cultural heritage combines the French, German, Mexican, and Lebanese cultures. An exceptionally tall man—or perhaps he just seems extraordinarily tall in comparison to Michelle Young who tops a mere inch or two over five feet—Ackel served in Korea with the United States Marines. Together, the three men tease each other, mercilessly yet lovingly.

The music softly swells in the melodic occidental Middle Eastern form that speaks of all Mediterranean cultures. It's fitting that we're sharing incredible Middle Eastern food with Hasbany in this environment. We talk, and we eat and we eat and we eat. Such is the way with these people, we learn.

There were cold green beans with tomatoes, olive oil, and heavy but not overpowering amounts of garlic, humus from garbanzo beans, and another kind of humus made from eggplant. The delicate flavors of marinated chicken blended perfectly with the pilaf, and the dessert—a custard-like almond pudding topped with crushed pistachios—reminded us of a well-loved Chinese almond pudding. The Turkish coffee, strong, sweet and thick, was served in an expresso cup.

But this is Louis' story—or is it? The three friends share experiences, similar memories, similar feelings. So perhaps Hasbany's story provides the Lebanese connection to that of so many Lebanese, so many Arabs, even so many of us.

Louis Hasbany
Lebanese Culture
Retired School Teacher

I came to the United States in 1956 [with] my grandmother. She couldn't speak English or Arabic right. She needed somebody to look after her. [She'd] get bread from the Salvation Army and [made] coffee. Bread and coffee! I was a young man, seventeen years old. I'm not used to this. Five o'clock in the afternoon, the sun was still [out. She expected me to be ready for bed.] Four months [later], I went to live with my aunt...

In 1959, I was drafted and [went to] France. My languages came in handy. I spoke French. I was treated like a special person. They put me in charge of fifty-eight French workers, Egyptians, and Algerians—French. They didn't know I spoke Arabic...

[I heard one guy:] "Look at that American jackass." [I said nothing]. The next day, they said a couple of bad words...

I said, "By the way, what is *hammar*?" Like I don't know.

He said, "You say very good!" (I said, "I said very good? Didn't you call me a jackass?")

"How do you know?"

I said, "I learned. Since yesterday, I learned Arabic. In other words, I'm not a son of a dog either." (He said, "You understand that too?") I said, "Let me tell you who I am. I'm in American uniform, but I am Lebanese." (He looked like he wanted to find a hole to crawl in!) "You've been taking an hour-and-a-half for lunch. Tomorrow you take a half an hour." ("But you're one of us!" he said.) I said, "You called me a son of a bitch, you called me a jackass and a lot of other names." News spread around. (They said, "Hasbany, that's a river in Lebanon.") I said, "Now you got the name. Now you associate my name with Lebanese." [Now I was] me "*Monsieur*," "*Capitain*," "*General*"—any names except the bad names.

In 1987, I went to Turkey with the Army. A Turk sees the American men—blonds and different colors—says, "You're not American."

I said, "Yes, I'm American. Don't you see my uniform?"

"No, you look different. You look like—Italian."

"No," I said. "What's this name look like?"

"Hasbany, Has-ba-any."

"Ah ha! You know how to say it. Arabic, right?"

He said, "You're an Arab?" [I said yes.] "What's your name?" [I told him.] "Oh, you're a Christian!"

They needed somebody who could speak Turkish and Arabic, [and I went] north, [to the Bulgarian-Turkish border with] the Turkish [and] American armies [for] a NATO maneuver.

[A] Turkish army officer asked my name. ("My name's Ahmed.") He stood back. "Ahmed? You? You're Muslim?" "Where you from?" [I said, "Lebanon."] "Oh, you're Lebanese?"

[He wanted me to meet his superior, a colonel, from Lebanon:

"Hasbany, you from Merjayoun? I'm from Merjayoun too, from [a nearby village], about two-and-a-half miles away. [You'll be my partner.] I need someone who [speaks] Turkish and Arabic. [Americans don't] speak Turkish and don't know our customs."

[Syrians and Lebanese], Muslims, had joined the Turkish Army. Their chef, from Lebanon, studied in Beirut.

Two guys—a sergeant and a black guy—watched the Turkish empty the water bladder, a big barrel, one day. The black guy was making fun, laughing with the sergeant. The Turks [didn't like blacks] making fun of the white people like that. [A Turk] got upset [and] yelled at the sergeant [who] asked me, "What's he talking about?" I went to [the Turk] and asked what's wrong.

"He, black guy, making fun of the white man? No, he can't do that. He was making fun of him, laughing at him."

I told [the black guy], "I'll pretend to kick you. Pretend I hurt your feelings. It'll make him feel better." I kicked him. He put his head down.

[The Turk] said, "Never do that again." The Turkish guy, happy, laughing, emptied the water. [He] came back the next day. "Black go?" (I said, "Oh yes. He's washing the dishes. He's cleaning the tent. He doesn't come out.")

You have to [watch people's] feelings toward others in different countries especially when you're going shopping. Black guys with us have to walk [alone]. They've never seen black people [and think of] them as slaves. [They're not accepted] as full human beings. This guy was really dark. They look at him and think he came from Sudan....

[A three-star general] knew I spoke Spanish, Arabic, and French. Commander of Europe, he was in his middle forties, used his rank to show off. He wanted me [to accompany him] everywhere. One day he said, "We're going to go to Egypt, to Cairo." He behaved in Cairo. He was invited to a village in Algeria, but the hospitality [is] different. He treated everyone the same, calling them names, joking around. It didn't work.

He called the chief a son-of-a-bitch. I [said], "You're a nice guy." Everytime the general [swore], I changed [it] around so the [Arabs] wouldn't feel bad that they were cussed at. I didn't tell him he was a son of a dog or [a] jackass. "You have a nice community, nice family, hope they all stay happy." I [smoothed out] things to [avoid] a problem. The general found out I wasn't translating right [and] got upset.

I said, "No, sir, you can't do that. [You'll] create a war [with] the villagers. [They're] very hospitable [and are] here to protect you. If you cross them, somebody will get hurt."

I don't think it was the colonel's American culture. [In] Spain, he behaved very well. Of course they understand English. He tried to be a bullshitter to see how far he could get....

[People] don't understand Arabs too well. [It's] an intelligent society. [But Arabs] ride camels in the desert, [so] people figure [Arabs] are backward.

Arabs have the greatest hospitality in the world. You never enter [an Arab] home and come back out hungry. [Even] if you say you just ate, you can eat. They force you to. They insist on it. You **have** to eat [or] you insult them. On the street, [if] you pass by somebody having a sandwich, the first thing they ask you, "Come join me." This is respect.

Before we left [the Algerian village], I told the chief, "Americans are wonderful people, but you have to understand their sense of humor." (He said, in English, "Yes, yes.") "We're Arab," I said in Arabic. "We know ourselves [and] how we do between each other."

We understand [but] we don't speak the same dialect. The language may vary from village to village. In Lebanon—from one village to another—they have different dialects altogether, but they're all together as one. It doesn't matter if you're Muslim or Christian. They're all the same. We have a common interest in ourselves [and] the same background in our culture. In Damascus, [people] stretch the words in Arabic so long.

If you don't live with Egyptians, you won't be able to understand them. [Every dialect is completely different from the others. I could understand Saddam Hussein's Iraqi dialect on TV] easier than I could understand the Jordanian dialect.

Iran and Syria are good friends. [They] were fighting Iraq. What's wrong with Iraq? [It's] an Arab nation. Where's their unity? The oil became very important. Kuwait, Saudi Arabia, [and] Bahrain became rich overnight. The Syrians have no oil [and] are jealous of [the Kuwaitis' wealth]. It's hard to stop. It's too deep and in their blood. Jealousy split the Arabs apart. That's what helped Israel. If Arabs [weren't] jealous of each other [and] united together, Israel would struggle for a long long time.

[Jews and Arabs aren't] fighting each other. The outside influence [created the] problem. [Arabs and Jews] lived with each other for thousands of years [and] never had problems until the [mid-1930s] and 1940s. We [had] 10,000 Jewish families in Beirut. Same thing in Damascus. Since the 1967, they escaped for their lives. They were threatened. It's not safe for them, so they felt [it was] best to migrate.

Zionist organizations started moving into Israel in the 1920s [and] didn't understand Arab culture [or] hospitality. The Arab invited you to their home. That's their hospitality. I think they misunderstood that. They say, "My house is your house." [The Zionists] took that for granted.

But even today, I don't think there's much problem with people in Israel and Palestine, Lebanon, or Syria. Just the outside influence. Pressure from the outside government. The more pressure, the more people are going to be against others.

They give Israel so many billion dollars a year. How much [is] Lebanon getting now? Twenty billion dollars a year? There's no balance. They want everybody treated equally. They don't want to have one nation that's stronger than another.

They couldn't even get together [and] turned against Christians in Lebanon. Publicly, [religions control the politics.] The Druze want more control, and the Maronites [not the majority, won't] give them [it]. The Maronites control the President; the Muslims control the Vice-President. [They] make decisions [and] control the Parliament. We are Christians—Orthodox. We didn't have control. [I can't have a job in high government] unless I turn Maronite. Even so, I'm a Christian. Again, jealousy.

Jews are a minority, just like the Armenians. They [both] have a seat in Parliament. [They're not] the majority [and] don't make decisions for everybody. [But privately,] if you come to my home, you don't come as a Jew. You come as a friend. You leave as a friend. Religion has nothing to do with it. I know you as a human. It doesn't matter who you are.

In the early days, they never mixed. One religion. That's it. Like the Melkites, the Maronites, and the Orthodox have their own churches, their own communities. The Armenians in Beirut stayed together [too]. When [they] came to the United States, they congregated in one area. The Arabs settled mostly in Dearborn, Michigan, the biggest Arab community in the United States. All Muslim community settled in Dearborn. Most of the Christians, my hometown [also], settled in Detroit [and branched out to] Lansing and Flint. They [looked] for industry, for factories, so they could work. They're [industrious] people.

They don't believe in [and you never see an Arab person] living on welfare. They take pride in their families. [If] you're ninety years old and you have children, they take care of you until you die. This is in their culture [and] belief.

This child [in my class lied] about everything. I gave her a D. The mother called the principal [who didn't] back me up. [In a conference, the mother called] me a foreigner with a weird accent. The principal didn't say a word. [Later] I told her, "You're supposed to back up your teachers, right or wrong." I was right in that case. I'm not [changing a] grade because her mother came down. The principal [disagreed, and] I filed a [three-step] grievance against her.

[When] the third step got lost in the shuffle, nobody found it before the time [limit] ran out. She was never reprimanded. I wrote a rebuttal to take her complaint out of my file. [She said I discriminated against and didn't like the blonde American child. I don't discriminate against anybody. I treat everybody the same. I [moved] to [another] school.

Lots of different people [live] in the Middle East—Arabs, Jews, and Christians, Armenians. Armenians, Christians, were persecuted in Armenia. [They wanted] a haven, a safe place to call home [and went] to Lebanon—then predominately Christian. Lebanon opened the door to them. They've been

174

there over a hundred years. They're warm, well-educated, [very productive] people—doctors, lawyers, all kinds....

Like the Lebanese Christians, lots of Armenians came [to the United States], migrating from that part of the world to seek a better life [and] freedom. They weren't persecuted, but they felt uncomfortable. They heard about the opportunity across the ocean, so they came here.

Just like us. We came, stayed, and made something of ourselves. We all worked. They're proud of their heritage, culture, language and families. Unity in their family is important.

[Some] Jewish families from Beirut wait here for peace so they [can return to their property and homes. Neither the government nor the Lebanese people deprive them of their deserted assets.] They don't tax you to death. You pay taxes if you own a business and make so many hundreds of thousands of dollars a year. Most taxes—import or export—go to the government for army, roads, schools and [so on]. It's a poor country, [but] you go to school free, all your medical free.

History doesn't give the Phoenicians—[Lebanese, 7,000 years ago]—enough credit. [These seafarers], the first on the sea, traveled along the Mediterranean [and] as far as Brazil. But they never kept records [except] in Tunisia.

(Fouad Khoder:) At the Temple of Solomon, they were famous for slave trading. Some books say [they] were famous for commerce. [It's true. They traveled.] Some say they discovered America. They came here [and] made a turn. Mostly, they'd get clients to travel with them, but [sold the clients] instead of [going] to their destinations. They were warriors [but never like] the big nations. Remember Alexander the Great? And Hannibal was Phoenician. They established Carthage. Tunisia. The Phoenician territory. They defeated the Romans the first time. The second time, [the Romans defeated them and] destroyed the whole city. They weren't the big force and power. We're mainly known for commerce. Phoenicians [got] the cedar woods from Lebanon for Solomon's temple in Jerusalem.

(Louis:) I'm sure [Jews] can go to Bahrain, Qatar, Abu Dhabi, Kuwait, Iraq, Syria, Lebanon, Jordan. [They can't] enter Arabia. Even Christians [can't] enter Mecca without permission. They're not allowed to go to the Kaba, the shrine. Jewish troops entered Saudi Arabia [during Desert Storm], but not under their religion. All Stars of David and all crosses had to be removed [before troops entered]. I speak the language, so they're not going to say anything. [They'll say,] "Well, he's an Arab." If somebody doesn't speak the language, [they'll] question that. Libya would be a question mark too. They don't like the Jews. I don't know why. Libya's always been [staunchly anti-Israel.]

[If you take] alcohol into Saudi Arabia, you're in trouble. It's forbidden. If you take vitamins, a doctor—theirs, not yours—[has] to analyze it. They say, "If you take it, fine. If you don't, sorry."

I remember back in 1983, we were up in Flagstaff [at] the ammo depot. It was nothing but stacks and stacks and stacks of ammunition—M-16s, grenades, and stuff like that... We loaded that stuff on trucks, and they were shipped down to the trains and were sent to Iran... All the stuff from World War II and from Vietnam, it was sent to Iran. I remember because we had to mark the boxes. We had to put "Iran" on it. You're talking about millions and millions of rounds of munitions...for the Shah. I don't think the United States ever got paid for it. Just in that warehouse alone, you're probably talking twenty million dollars in ammo. You see, they used to bring all the ammo from Vietnam over here to Arizona. And behind the backs [of the peacemakers], you're saying, "Hey, go fight." If you run out of ammo, you're not going to fight. You give up. The more you know you can have somebody to back you up, the stronger you're going to be.

Iran was more modern, more Western [then]. You were able to talk with them [and] deal with them. They were intelligent people to speak with. Saudi Arabia was a one-track mind, one goal. Outside of Israel, they don't want to talk with you. They would, but they're afraid to say: "We support Israel." [That's] like [Lebanon's not going] against Israel since 1947.

Lebanon didn't go [out] to stop Israel [when they invaded in 1983.] [Israel] didn't kill one Lebanese soldier. The shelling in Beirut, where [Lebanese were guiding the Israelis to the PLO hiding place], killed the only people.

We never had any problem with Israel. My hometown [has] been right there on the border with Israel thousands of years. [Israel provided] all our protection. [Lebanon never protected us] because Beirut was seventy-five miles away. And the Israeli border, only two miles. Less. Actually, eighty acres of our land was inside Israel. The mayor of an Israeli town was partners with my father before 1947. After the war, they [stopped doing] business with each other. Their lives would be on the line. They were still good friends [and] still [saw] each other.

If the outside influence leaves the Arabs and Jews to solve their own problems, they could live in peace forever. [Shimon] Perez wasn't given enough credit. [Without] Perez as prime minister, you wouldn't have had the Palestinians [or] Jordanians making peace with Israel. That man was born there. He knows the Arabs. [With] Menachim Begin, it wouldn't have worked. If Nasar were still around, you think we'd have peace with Egypt? Mubarek is a modern man. He understands his economy depends on having peace with Israel. If you have war all the time against Israel, you're not going to win [or] get anywhere. [You'll merely] build an army and destroy your country more and more.... Egypt is a very poor nation. It's not rich at all. The only oil they have is in the Sinai, and it's not that much. It's like Lebanon. Lebanon was based on tourism. Israel too.

Beirut was one of the busiest cities in the world. One of the most beautiful cities. Cleanest city too.

The interview is over, but the conversation continues perhaps another half hour. Among themselves, as in all cultures, they call each other names that would be considered ethnic slurs from any other groups. Among these friends, love surrounds the insulting words. Some of the conversation becomes almost intimate between them. But we're with them, and Louis' words ring in our ears, "My house is your house."

People from many cultures—at gut level, where the average citizen is—believe in and practice the "My house is your house" concept. You share conversation over a cup of coffee, perhaps a sandwich, with a friend behind the scenes, not caring whether that friend or you belong to the politically correct culture. But publicly, the politics—the political mandates of those in power—often overshadow that warmth, and tomorrow your private friend may become your public enemy.

Politics in the Middle East influence every aspect of daily life. The people seem more aware, more astute about the role politics play in their public and private lives. You live and work with citizens from a variety of cultures, developing friendships, creating memories together. Yet your friendships are fragile and easily broken in public view, and your first priority becomes survival.

In the Middle East, survival is easier for some. Not for the Palestinians. In many places, their greatest crime is their ethnic heritage.

A Palestinian Family's Story
Palestinian Culture
White Collar Workers

Wife: I left Palestine with my family. My father was a teacher in Kuwait. I moved to Kuwait [when] I was twelve years old. After the Gulf War, we had visas and came here [to the United States.]

Husband: When we came here, we applied for political asylum. Of course we couldn't go back to Kuwait, and we couldn't go back to Israel. This is after Desert Storm.

Wife: We've been here two years. After liberation of Kuwait.

Husband: After Kuwaiti people [came] back, I waited fourteen months to go back to my job. I worked in the state but the Kuwaiti people refused to get me back to my job. They said all Palestinians [weren't] desired in Kuwait. We must leave.

Wife: I was a teacher over there. They finished all the contracts for Palestinian teachers.

Husband: The Ministry, the government. They called us foreign. The United States knew everything about the treatment of the Palestinian people. They were treated like animals. Maybe animals were treated better. [Palestinians] were hit, and the electric was cut off. And [Kuwait] gave them hot water after midnight.

Wife: [Kuwait] killed more than 3,000 Palestinians after the liberation. Nobody knows. Families moved from Kuwait. They didn't know anything about their sons or husband or brother.

Husband: I know a woman speaking about her son. He worked in the Ministry, repairing cars. She came to me and asked me to speak with her about her son. I knew a Kuwaiti officer. I asked him. Every time, she cried. Her eyes had trouble from weeping. He promised [he would]. He was a neighbor. After four days, he said, "I looked everywhere, and I didn't find [him.] When [Kuwaitis] came back, they found some people and killed them, shot them."

Wife: They sometimes showed us on the television, film. It was dated March 26, 28, 1991. That's after the liberation. I don't remember exactly.

Husband: People were killed after the liberation. The news said Kuwaiti people killed by Iraqi people.

Wife: They were Palestinian people killed by Kuwaiti people.

Husband: And the government of Kuwait knew that.

Wife: Every house is full of guns and weapons.

Husband: I went to the undersecretary of the Ministry, and I said, "I want to go back to my job because I didn't do anything wrong to the Kuwaiti people." You know what he said to me? "Can you forget you are Palestinian?" My accusation, my problem is that I am Palestinian. This is my accusation! And he said to me, "The government doesn't like five nationalities: Palestinians, Jordanians, Sudanese, Yemenites, and Iraqis. These five nationalities, the government doesn't desire. I advise you to leave. We cannot hire any Palestinians for one of these positions. The government of Kuwait believes that these people support Iraq." Not individuals, because the government of these people support Iraq. Before the Gulf War, there were the same rights [between people of various nationalities in Iraq]. After the War, there were some difficulties. The government couldn't hire the people coming into Iraq. But people could do special work—drive cabs, can open for repair, open a small shop, but they couldn't go to work for the government.

Wife: We didn't prefer to go to Iraq. We were allowed to go when we were in Kuwait. But now we could not go. They started to kill the Palestinians. All the media every day, "The Palestinians support Saddam." But they could not work. They cannot come back to Iraq from any country. Only Kuwait. We couldn't go there because of the situation in Iraq.

Husband: We prefer to be here now.

Wife: We can teach our children. We can have our freedom. We can talk. Everybody leaves you alone. We don't feel discrimination. Maybe it is present, but I don't know. At [one] high school, they refused to register [my daughters]. [The school] wanted to change the visa to a study visa. At [another] school, they didn't ask about any visas. They accepted my daughters, and they started school from the first day. People told us [at the other school], they would make a problem for us. [At this school], everybody respects them. Sometimes they'd ask why they dress this way, is it religion or culture.

Husband: Some said, "My grandmother dresses like you."

Wife: I didn't feel we had religious discrimination. When I worked [at this school], no student asked why I dressed like this. [At graduation], one daughter dressed with a cap over her cover. The principal told her he was proud of her. Some students said, "You are a newcomer, and English is not your native language, and you wear the Honor Society sash. How come?" First maybe when we came, the idea about the Arabs, especially the women because they cover their hair—they are stupid, or they live in the desert—that's what they know. But the first time they're very good in school, everybody is surprised and it's okay. Sometimes a teacher calls her to talk about our culture, about our religion for the students.

Husband: The school has a multicultural club for students to talk about their cultures.

Wife: When we were in Kuwait, we needed a visa for [my youngest child]. I could not come to the United States when I was pregnant. The Ministry of Foreign [Affairs] told us we could not get a visa for the youngest, that they weren't allowed to take visas for any Palestinian. [But we already had visas for the other children and us.] My husband said, "This is very intelligent. I want to go to America with my wife and four children. What do I do with the fifth one? Throw him in the sea?" [The Ministry] told him, "These are our instructions and they got changed."

Husband: The American people are not complicated like Arab people. They give you visas at the airport. People understand.

Wife: Cultured people there.

Husband: Sometimes it happened when there was a shortage of jobs, it was easy for Palestinians to take visas to America. There is some instruction issued to facilitize the visa for Palestinians. I have one for five years.

Wife: When I was a teacher, and my husband was working also, and we lived in very high standards. When the situation changed, we changed our mind and we came.

Husband: The Kuwaiti people treated the people with what their president did. If I did wrong, take me to the court, and let the judge tell me. They said my problem is that I'm Palestinian. It depends on the political. This is the problem in the Arab countries. I graduated from Cairo University. My major was accounting. I moved to Kuwait and worked in the Ministry of Finance. Twenty years. Twenty years I worked in the government.

Wife: We have the same language, the same religion.

Husband: You find my salary maybe half [of] the Kuwaiti people with the same degree.

Wife: My father went to the Gaza Strip. He has Israeli I.D. But when he got his I.D., I was over sixteen and studying at the university. They only gave only for parents and those listed under sixteen. So my older sister and I did not get an I.D. My problem [now] is that I miss my family. My family cannot come to visit.

My brother signed a contract with a hospital in New York [to work in a pediatrics unit as a resident.] They sent the contract to him in Israel. They accepted him to train as a doctor in the children's [section], and he signed, and everything was complete. Before they gave him the opportunity to attend August 1. On July 28, he called them to get the visa, and I called them from here. They told us there is a problem. He must bring a certificate from the Ministry of Health that he will go back to Israel after he is done studying for his degree. He

180

sent for the paper from the Department of Health because the Gaza Strip is part in Israel, and Israel cannot give him as a citizen a letter that he will come back to Israel. Only the Department of Health in Gaza Strip, and they refused him, and then they told him there was no chance for him to come. It's very difficult.

The first man who helped us here is Kuwaiti nationality, but he's a Shiite originally from Iranian.

Husband: He knows what the government did wrong against the Palestinians because his brother married a Palestinian woman.

Wife: [Palestinian women] don't go out. Maybe we go to the park or to visit my cousin or to visit "Mr. Ball" (Christiansen). We don't go out to work or someplace else. That's why I [haven't] faced any [discrimination] here.

Husband: We go to college here. We are busy.

Wife: I wear the cover because of my religion, not my culture. When I went to the university to study English, especially the Japanese students want to know why I wear the cover because it's very hot. But I tell them I'm accustomed to it. It's religion. You cannot break tradition with religion.

Husband: The woman covers all her body except her face and hands. This is our religion.

Wife: Before foreign men, we cannot [uncover] our hair or body. But women, it's okay. [Americans don't always] know all the facts about us. When I applied for a substitute teaching position, the girl who took my application looked at me strangely. She asked me questions. I answered. Then she understood. First year, my sons took ESL. Last year, they were American people. Same thing with my daughters.

The Palestinians who arrived in the United States of America found new beginnings in the nation. Yet they've paid prices more dear than most of us could imagine being forced to do. Those who were treated brutally may have healed from physical wounds. But the emotional scars—of their own treatment, perhaps of loved ones' or friends' murders, and even of knowing they'll never again see the family they left behind—can never heal. Could we have fared as well in similar situations?

What specific Middle Eastern country was once their home serves little importance now—save for the memories—to those who can no longer return.

Shalom and Orly Shoer
Israeli Culture—Sabra
Lecturer at Cornell University
& Hebrew School Principal

Orly: When I came here—my husband was a student here, and we weren't married yet—the first day, he left me in the apartment and went to school. He tried to call me a few times and I was afraid to pick up the phone. I was so afraid to pick up the phone because I was afraid I wouldn't understand. I would smile at them, not understanding what people were saying. I could eventually manage in speaking with people. I was very lucky here in this small community. I felt people were very inviting. I worked at the pre-school when I got here. Maybe it was because of the Jewish community here. It's seven years since I came here. Now I feel so comfortable, I feel at home.

I learned English during my elementary school years and in high school. Here, the words started to come out. I tried to take a course but I learned my English was good enough. You learn. It's never perfect. It will never be perfect. If I would speak in Hebrew, it would be much better. You always feel your language is lower. There is a certain point where you just go. You learn words as you go along. I came on Passover, and we were invited to 12 different houses for *Rosh Hashanah*.

There was more fear than hatred when I was brought up. The reason there was fear was because of terrorist attacks. That was the main thing. Part of school, growing up, we went to visit Arab schools in other villages. There wasn't a lot of interaction, but here and there, there was.

Shalom: When I came here, I was a student. The first few months I was here, the only thing I ordered at a deli, I only ordered egg salad sandwiches because I was afraid to order anything else.

I signed up for basic math when I thought I was signing up for a more advanced course. After I left campus, the Jewish community was very eager to help. There's not the same sense of community in large cities. It was very easy to adapt to this community. We normally meet many people in the community.

Orly: We built a *sukkah* in our backyard, and neighbors wanted to know and showed interest. They ask questions about Israel.

182

Shalom: Four children came to our house today to help build our *sukkah.* What has been really interesting is that the child next door goes to Catholic school and he brought home the same workbook on Passover as we use.

We tend to overlook the rise and fall of previous civilizations, cultures, and regions of the world and nations. It's easy to do when one considers how much contemporary history and news has been focused on the geographic region known as the Middle East. In the news and in the stories woven into this chapter, several themes have been repeated over and over.

Is it unreasonable for people to want to live in peace? Is it primarily the ambitions of a few to scheme and deceive others to gain political and economic control over a nation or region of the world? We must relate to people who have lived among, between, and within war-torn nations in the distant and recent past with great empathy and understanding—just as we ideally think we should do with all people. Faced with many prejudice- and stereotype-oriented obstacles, all people of the Middle East should be included in our efforts to understand.

The misconception that Middle Easterners from oil-rich nations, especially the Arab people, are extremely wealthy is conducive to the idea that these people have caused many of the personal and national economic problems within the United States of America. In reality, the "Seven Sisters of the Western World"—the major American and European oil companies—had more to do with the formation of the Organization of Petroleum Exporting Countries (OPEC) and the increase in oil prices during the last quarter of the 20th Century. It was, at the most elementary level, simply big business.

Environmental concerns and the drilling depths themselves make oil production among most Western oil reserves difficult to produce in contrast to the Middle East, where much of the oil—under a degree of natural pressure—is closer to the earth's surface. As a result, the Middle East is usually able to outproduce Western oil at a significantly lower price, yet still pocketing a healthy profit.

The people whose stories have appeared in this chapter are no different than anyone else. People are people, and the Middle and Far Easterners are no exception. When we meet people whose heritage is bonded to the Middle East, we may have no idea of the stresses and strains they've encountered in their lives in the Middle East, in the United States of America, or anywhere else in the world, or the positive contributions they are still prepared to make to—and for—any country and its native and adopted cultures.

Late in 1995, Prime Minister Yitzhak Rabin of Israel, one of the key players in the region's goal for peace, was assassinated, leaving the question of peace still in the air. At this writing, the peacemaking process was continuing to unfold.

Chapter 8

THE FAR EASTERNERS
AND PACIFIC RIM

People born in the Western Hemisphere have long been fasci-nated with the Far East. One may picture pagodas, bonsai trees, and beautiful *geishas*, while someone else thinks of shrines to Buddha, girls clad in *cheongsams*, and junks in Hong Kong Harbor. But if one hundred people were surveyed about their impressions of the Far East, one hundred different replies might be given.

We tend to draw initial impressions about people and places ac-cording to our environmental and educational backgrounds. Yet that which we perceive versus the complete truth won't necessarily be the same.

The term *Far Easterners* encompasses much more than the descriptions above. The Far Easterners—the Asian people—come from the farthest reaches of the world: from the lowest area at the shores of the Dead Sea to the Nepal-Tibet border and the highest mountain peak at Mount Everest, from the torrid tropics at the Equator to the frigid frontiers at the Arctic. The continent of Asia covers nearly 33 percent of the world's land masses and is home to about 60 percent of the world's total population.

Over 5,000 years have intricately intertwined Middle and Far Eastern history. Yet history books generally separate the two, leaving many students with the impression that the Middle and Far East are not interrelated. As a result, one needs to make a conscious mental connection to remember: both the Middle East and the Far East belong to the Asian continent.

During the Middle Ages, a strong interest in spices from the Far East prompted sharp Italian businessmen to take advantage of the major trade routes. European traders traveled through the Middle East in search of tea, coffee, and spices from India, China, Malaysia, and Indonesia—the Spice Islands. But spices like pepper, cloves, cinnamon, nutmeg, and turmeric had become hot commodities in the world marketplace, and astute Genoans, Venetians, and people from other city-states began to monopolize Far Eastern imports and their distribution.

Of course the traders **could** always pay what the Italians were asking along the European-Middle East trade route; but that thought gave European traders little comfort. On the other hand, pirates on the Indian Ocean waited for travelers who somehow survived the treacherous navigation around South Africa's Cape of Good Hope. Frustrated by these monopolies and the minimum of choices left, Europeans began to consider alternative routes to the Far East—not an easy task.

Like other Europeans, Spain's Queen Isabella wanted those spices and precious goods from the Orient. Christopher Columbus had given her a great sales pitch: He'd hunt, sailing west through unknown territory, to open new Far Eastern trade routes; she—minus those headaches—could foot the bill for the ships, crews, and necessary provisions.

Since the Queen was obviously a good businesswoman who didn't mind a gamble now and then, she went for the idea. Columbus had the right idea, and he proved that the world was a sphere. On the other hand, he miscalculated a bit and discovered the Americas rather than another Asian region.

Who discovered the New World isn't really as important as the discovery itself. At some point, the New World would have been discovered—with or without Christopher Columbus or any of the other misguided travelers who might have arrived in the Americas before or after him.

Columbus' error in calculations also influenced the names of places in the New World, which changed the course of world history. As more trade doors opened, fresh opportunities for intercultural exchange became possible. What we know today as the West Indies stemmed from Columbus' thinking that he'd landed in the Far East islands, then called the Indies. What he'd thought were the Indians of India became known as the Indians of the Americas.

Intercultural exchange is the crux to understanding how external influences shape the future of any community—a collective body of many people or many groups of people living, working, and playing in a generally common area. Every culture within a community establishes a foundation for the development of social mores, codes, and laws which, in turn, shape internal and external politics. As the community's size increases, the influence of usually more than one culture will modify those mores, codes, and laws already in place.

In the United States of America, several levels of community operate to create the nation. Every state represents a regional community of counties or parishes which represent the smaller city, village, and town communities. Individual neighborhood communities influence the grassroots politics and behind-the-scenes workings of each city, village, and town.

Similarly, every nation influences the global community, and what occurs there—in the world community—ripples back downward. Naturally, from the global perspective, nations feel the impact of world events first. Downward or upward, every level feels the greatest impact of events at the next closest stage. Making this ripple effect even more complicated, often what occurs in one community laterally affects other communities when the influence ripples back in the other direction.

Two major forces have affected the Far East-Pacific Rim region over several centuries. Since the Far East-Pacific Rim and Europe belong to different communities within the broader global community, the expansion and exploration of European cultures and economics would be an external force. On the other hand, China represents a national community within the Far East-Pacific Rim sector, and the Chinese culture and economic influence operate internally within the region.

Australia, New Zealand, Papua New Guinea, Indonesia, and small island nations also belong to the Far East-Pacific Rim, and we have no intention of implying otherwise. But in the interest of doing justice to the individual stories from these nations, we've elected to highlight these nations, geographically known as Oceania, in chapter nine. We included the tremendously diverse former Soviet Union—also part of the Far East-Pacific Rim—in chapter five because of its enormous size.

The largest ocean in the world, the Pacific, links the coastal lands and islands in the Far East-Pacific Rim region. Vast and diverse in both cultures and resources, the area represents a massive blend of cultures and politics.

India, the seventh largest geographic nation and one of the world's oldest civilizations, is a land of diversities. Approximately 900 million people—roughly one-fourth of the world's population—make their homes in this geographically and culturally rich area extending from the Himalayan Mountains in the north to the Deccan Plateaus in the south. India's several independent states and nations include Pakistan, Nepal, Bangladesh, and Sri Lanka.

India holds one of the seven wonders of the world—the Taj Mahal—the exquisite white marble tomb of Indian ruler Shah Jahan and his wife. Twenty thousand workers built this mosque at Agra in the 17th century.

From its earliest beginnings around 500 years before the birth of Christ through the late 1700s, classical Indian society advanced in literature, the arts, and science. Culturally, the nation became a mixture of peoples from around the world. The Dravidians, India's indigenous people, merged with Aryans. The Biddojos, strong under King Asoka's reign in the third century, declined, making way for the golden age—the Gupta Kingdom—until the sixth century. Muslim Arabs, Turks, and Afghans provided the major influence from the eighth century until the Dutch and Portuguese influence of the late 1700s. When the English arrived, much of India became a British colony.

Rudyard Kipling, the English author of *Kim, The Jungle Books,* and many poems, was born in Bombay. Sent to England when he was five years old, he returned to India when he was seventeen and stayed until he was twenty-four. Among the nation's own literary geniuses, Indian poet Rabindranath Tagore received the Nobel Prize for literature in 1913. No Nobel Prizes were awarded Indian author Kamala Markandaya Taylor for her works, but her 1954 book, *Nectar in a Sieve,* made a dramatic impact on the study of Indian literature. In her story of a peasant woman's life in a poverty-stricken Indian village, Taylor's perspective refuses to color facts otherwise softened by the political scene.

Led by a Hindu leader, Mohandas Gandhi, India gained independence from British rule in 1947. But peace was difficult to achieve, and religious differences between Hindus and Muslims erupted into violence soon after. A member of a high Hindu class murdered Gandhi, a proponent of nonviolent disobedience, in 1948, and Pakistan—geographically divided to the northwest and northeast—became a Muslim state. Late in April 1971, East Pakistan declared its independence and became Bangladesh. India remained a republic within the British Commonwealth.

Rife with internal conflict between three major religious groups—the Muslims, the Hindus, and the Sikhs—India's political leaders have tried to foster cooperation among the nation's people. India's Kashmir and Punjab provinces have attempted to achieve independent religious status while Indira Gandhi's son Rajiv, Jawaharlal Nehru's grandson who succeeded his mother as prime minister after her assassination in 1984, struggled to improve the economy. To some degree, the office of prime minister became a family matter: Nehru, a close associate of Mohandas Gandhi, was India's first prime minister.

Today, India's own internal strife contradicts the important role the country has played in world history. In contrast to its significant contributions to parts of Africa, Europe, and the Middle East, the nation's centuries old **caste system,** a process of segregating the cultures and economic classes from each other, challenges its own need for change. Unfortunately, old habits are hard to break.

Every nation contributes special people to the world, people we wish everyone had the opportunity to meet. Joyotpaul Chaudhuri is one of those special people.

Joyotpaul "Joy" Chaudhuri
East Indian Culture
University Professor

Promise and Performance: An Asian American Journey

Now almost sixty years old around July 4, 1993, some shades and features of my own Asian American tiny little fragment of the American mosaic comes to mind. The fragment has its unique features and suggests its own hue to the American experience.

I was born in Calcutta, India, in 1933. I helped lower the British flag on my schoolground in India when India became free again in 1947. A little more than four years later, I was in America.

Pearl Harbor set off the first real world war and the aftermath of global vibrations that were to follow. Unknown to me, my journey was a tiny wave in the tremors of that period which pointed towards a more global economy and culture that was in the making.

My emigration to America together with my contemporaries constituted a sandwich between the smaller waves of Indians in the early 1900s and the larger waves from the late 1960s onwards, the later made possible by the final elimination of racial quotas in the immigration laws of 1965. I was acutely aware of the struggles of the Indians from 1900 to 1950 and their work for both Indian independence and justice in America, Canada, and even Mexico. Subsequently, my generation in America helped widen the understanding of the nature of justice and made a contribution to the changes in civil rights, racial justice, and immigration laws that were to follow.

In contrast with the poor Indian laborers at the turn of the century or the struggling students of the late 1940s and 1950s, the larger wave of post-1965 Indian emigrants had a different demographic profile. Many were doctors, engineers, and businessmen. The extent of their understanding of the contributions of the earlier waves of Indians in America, perhaps understandably, appears to be somewhat unclear or non-existent.

Each immigrant has their vision of the promise of America. While I too had the standard expectations of liberty, I had my own additional expectations of cultural diversity, of struggle, and [of] adventure. My marked interest in and expectations of American Indians was somewhat romantic—of relatively free peoples. My expectations of struggle was that it would be primarily economic—not racial. My expectation of adventure was individualistic. However, I was not quite prepared for the sharp edges of race and class which account for the acquired scar tissues in my journey. In the Old World that I left behind, there were hundreds of little parochialisms. But there were also protective communities as Alexis de Tocqueville understood in *Democracy in America*. However, in *The Lonely Crowd*, to use [David] Riesman's phrase of the American conceptions of self, one is directly confronted with the remaining forces of race and class. I am more reminded of my Asian ancestry by others than by myself. A brief sampling of these reminders may be illustrative if not instructive.

As a teenager, I ended up in Oklahoma where I expected to find insight into American Indian experiences. Instead, I found fast-eroding civilizations hastened by denials of civil rights and the continuing disappearance of American Indian lands and property. Being married to a full-blooded Creek as well as my social relationships with many other Indians provided first-hand experiences of the discomforts of the unassimilated.

The indignities I faced were shared by many American Indians and blacks as well. I was often denied service in a variety of styles in particular cafes, hotels, and taverns, between 1952 and my departure from Oklahoma in 1964. Sometimes I was mistaken for a black, for an American Indian, or [for] a Mexican American. At other times, I came under a general "minority" umbrella of discrimination.

In 1961, I was denied service at a motel restaurant in a community in Illinois. In 1965 I was denied a room rental in Ohio, [where] I was [also] involved in an attempt to help an African graduate student of mine whose rights were grossly violated. Because I did not know the system, the university where I taught paid me significantly less compared to my colleagues. I suffered more overt racial discrimination: sometimes because of mistaken identity, at other times because I was non-Caucasian.

My oldest son was denied admission to one school one year because he was not white, the next year again since he was not black—during implementation of desegregation. My apartment was broken into by police in Connecticut because I was misidentified as a Puerto Rican.

I began to strengthen my professional qualifications. I have now taught at eight different universities and have been a department head and a dean, among other things. My professional mobility was generally slower than that of many whites I have known with comparable records. While the overt discrimination of class diminished with mobility, the more subtle but nevertheless real encounters with discrimination remained.

Among other inequities, one department chairperson said that published research on India was "acceptable" provided it was in English. Another urged me to go back where I came from when I was engaged in advocacy on behalf of Asian Americans.

Mine has been a more difficult journey than that of comparable Anglos who I have known over the years. My America has changed so much for the better on issues of justice over the more than forty-one years that I have been here. But gaps between the promise and performance of America continue to exist. The promise makes the difference in the comparative ideals of countries. The improvement of performance continues to be an American agenda. For that I am thankful.

All of us recognize the most common threads among our personal lives: we're born, we live our lives, and we die. Those threads link us as human beings no matter where we live. But like contrasting threads in textiles, our human threads vary just enough to make each of us unique as individuals and as citizens of any nation. We're all the same, yet we're all different. Individual threads of people created the United States of America, and equally individual threads wove the United States into the nation it is today.

In the same vein, regardless of the global geographic area in which we live, the politics of our respective nations appear to affect our mood as citizens. At times, those politics change with such alacrity, the national mood seems to take on an almost schizophrenic air. Yet when the nation's political scene creates more subtle, less noticeable changes, the country's mood appears more balanced and less riddled with upheaval.

To people in the Western Hemisphere, the politics and boundary lines of many Eastern nations appear to change overnight. Especially since the early 1980s, old regimes gave way to coups and new leaders, and old borders of former nations on the continents of Europe, Africa, and Asia changed positions. Around the globe, people rejoiced as the Iron Curtain crumbled, and folks chipped away for bittersweet souvenirs of the Berlin Wall. Yet as old borders and old names changed with each news report, more and more maps became obsolete and everyone seemed confused about the whos, the whats and the wheres.

Border changes also tend to make a long-lasting impact on cultures. For years, Southeast Asia's people had been strongly influenced by apparently Chinese characteristics and customs. But the English, French, and Spanish explorers moved into the region, mingling and mixing with the people, and Southeast Asia's prominent Chinese cultural presence began to absorb the more global flavor.

Thousands of years of acculturated history have been woven into many Southeast Asian countries. As a result, characterizing people by birthplace or current residence becomes extremely difficult, especially in the triangular Southeast Asian land mass of Myanmar—Burma until 1989; Thailand—formerly Siam on the Malay peninsula; Laos; Cambodia—established, but not recognized by the United Nations and most non-Soviet-bloc nations—as the Kampuchean People's Republic in 1975; Vietnam; and the Philippines.

Which geographic culture applies to the Philippine-born child of a Chinese man and a woman with Polynesian and Spanish heritage? Asian? Hispanic? What if we complicate matters and move the family to the United States, where official forms often request ethnic and racial backgrounds? Is the offspring categorized as Asian/Pacific Islander, Black, Hispanic, Indian, White, or Other? The child actually represents a blend of at least three of those labels!

China dominated Vietnam until European explorers ventured into the area. But even into the late 1800s, several Vietnamese dynasties controlled the southern Chinese colony of Cochin, the central protectorates of Annam, and the northern Tonkin sector.

Ho Chi Minh and his army fought for independence from the French after Japan's occupation of the territory from the late 1930s to 1945. Following the 1954 Battle of Dien Bien Phu, the signing of the Geneva Accords marked Vietnam's division into two segments and planned national reunification elections to begin in 1956. After the then-Saigon government of President Ngo Dinh Diem cancelled the upcoming elections, a civil war broke out between the north and south.

About 2,000 American civilian advisors and military personnel were sent to South Vietnam in the Dwight D. Eisenhower and John F. Kennedy administrations of the late 1950s and early 1960s. During this same period, Tom Dooley, a civilian international health organization doctor, toured junior and senior schools across the United States, warning young people about atrocities being committed against communist code violators in Southeast Asia. Dooley had seen them. Those who spoke against their captors lost their tongues. Others, accused of vague offensive acts, came to Dooley with chopstick-pierced eardrums. His stories—none pretty, pleasant, or polite—were horrifying, but factual. Through his talks and sales of his books, Dooley raised funds for medical supplies and returned to his Southeast Asian patients even though cancer had captured his body as the communists had done to the region.

The civil war continued to escalate. The communist National Liberation Front had infiltrated South Vietnam, President Ngo Dinh Diem had been assassinated in a coup, and the number of U.S. military advisors in the country had risen to 15,000 by 1963.

In August 1964, two separate reported North Vietnamese attacks on U.S. destroyers heightened hostilities, and the United States Congress passed the Tonkin Gulf Resolution. But this was a presidential election year in the United States, and both major parties were focusing on Vietnam for political victories. Following the historic landslide re-election of incumbent Lyndon B. Johnson, who had inherited the Oval Office after the assassination of President Kennedy, the war escalated even more.

"I am not going to lose Vietnam. I am not going to be the president who saw Southeast Asia go the way China went," Johnson told the United States Ambassador to Saigon.

The Vietnam conflict, never officially declared a state of war by the United States government, spread into neighboring Laos and Cambodia. Perhaps what made the ugliness of the Vietnam War unique in comparison to other wars was the presence of guerrilla fighters who struck with a vengeance never before seen by the Western World. As in other wars, bombs and guns killed soldiers. But unlike other wars, communist guerrilla fighters devised intricate environmental weapons from bamboo and jungle vines. Not classically trained but vicious and brutal in approach, the guerrillas—men and women of every age, from every walk of Vietnamese life—hit ferociously and effectively. In the villages, identifying the vulnerable civilians from the guerrillas was nearly impossible.

From the perspective of American troops, guerrilla warfare had made its impact often in unexpected ways. Tragically, the results were equally horrifying on both sides. U.S. air attacks sent napalm bombs plummeting into suspected guerrilla strongholds below, killing thousands of innocent civilians. On the front pages of newspapers all over the world, the photo of a small child, her arms outstretched, her face contorted with pain, tore at the hearts of those reading the news. She survived a napalm attack. The use of Agent Orange, a herbicide employed to wipe out guerrilla-infested jungles, resulted in cases of cancer and other life-threatening health problems among the Vietnamese as well as American military and their families. In March 1968, a U.S. Army infantry unit, expecting to meet up with guerrillas at their former hiding place of My Lai, killed 300 civilians, most of whom were women, children, and old men.

A subsequent official inquiry was held, resulting in criminal charges against several members of Charley Company. Lieutenant William L. Calley, Jr., one of the unit's two commanding officers, was the sole member of Charley Company convicted in March 1971. Originally sentenced to life at hard labor for killing at least twenty-two civilians, his sentence was later reduced to twenty years, then finally ten years. But My Lai was not the only nightmarish response to guerrilla tactics. At the same time, members of Bravo Company committed more civilian slayings at My Khe. They were never prosecuted.

By March 1969, 543,000 U.S. troops were in Vietnam—more than twice the number of Washington's antiwar protesters later in the year. In the six years after Johnson's election, American protests, draft card burning, and draft evasion occurred almost daily. As the United States and South Vietnamese invaded Cambodia, the war seeped insidiously onto college campuses. Protest tension evolved into national tragedy at Ohio's Kent State University in May 1970, when National Guardsmen fired into a crowd of student protesters, leaving four dead and eight wounded.

No parades welcomed the aching soldiers home from Vietnam in March 1973. These veterans met with hostility from those who opposed this non-war in Vietnam. U.S. Marine Embassy guards and thousands of American civilians and South Vietnamese followed the troops home on April 30, 1975, fleeing Saigon in the final hours before the southern capital fell, and what remained in the wake of burning buildings and the dead became known as Ho Chi Minh City under the officially reunited nation now called the Socialist Republic of Vietnam. More than 140,000 Vietnamese refugees fled by air and in boats during the next five weeks.

Two decades passed before Vietnam War veterans received some semblance of gratitude from the American people. Some returned, crazed from torture and propaganda, plagued with flashbacks of North Vietnamese warfare. Some came back and entered politics with idealistic hopes that they could prevent this kind of tragic ending from occurring again. Still others came back in body bags, or flag-draped coffins.

More than 58,132 names of the dead and missing are now etched on The Wall, the Vietnam War Memorial in Washington, D.C. Across the nation, many families cling to their hopes that a loved one—one of more than 2,400 declared POW/MIA, Prisoner of War/Missing in Action—will come home again.

The Vietnam Era veterans, in the figurative sense of the word, have bonded into a tightly knit fraternity that appears steadfast to this day. In many ways, the bonds seem almost stronger than those of veterans from earlier wars. But then, veterans of those wars returned home loved, respected, and honored by the entire American nation. Vietnam Era veterans deserve that love, respect, and honor, too. Were it not for the men and women who served in the United States Armed Forces and in other nations' armed forces, the horrible moments of the Vietnam War and all wars might never have been brought to an end. Thousands of people from oppressed or formerly oppressed countries might not be free today.

De Tran
Vietnamese Culture
San Jose Mercury News Staff Writer

I came to the United States in April 1975 at the age of twelve. We left during the final hours of the Vietnam War, the day before the capital, Saigon, fell to communism.

I grew up in San Francisco in a blue-collar, working class neighborhood. When you're twelve, kids can be really cruel for your inability to speak English. That's when I realized I needed to learn English quickly to get along with people here.

People have asked me whether I identify with being Vietnamese or American. I tell them I still dream in Vietnamese but with English subtitles. In a way, it's true. You identify with both cultures, both countries.

The Irish writers used to have this thing where they refused to live in Ireland, but they also refused to write about anything but Ireland. Many Vietnamese American writers are the same about Vietnam.

My experience isn't unique at all. It happened on Ellis Island. It's happening in Miami with the Cubans, in California with Hispanics and Asians.

You always have the subtle prejudices. It's almost a given when you're a member of a minority. It happens in every country. The hill dwellers of Vietnam, the Hmong are some of them.

I used to live in Orange County, California, and I worked at the *Los Angeles Times*. My first night in Orange County, I was staying in a hotel for a few days. I went to a restaurant to eat, and this guy came up to me. He was drunk and said, "You know, you're lucky we let you into this country."

Children in Vietnam do not understand peace. I was born with the war, grew up with the war, and I left with the war. You don't think about it. It was always there. Because of the war, they had curfews at night. My first night out of a refugee camp in the United States, we were in San Diego. I was amazed at the cars traveling down the street at 2 or 3 a.m. This, to me, was the essence of peace.

I had English as a Second Language classes, and it showed me the diversity of the people here. One of my teachers was Cuban. Many of my classmates were from Central America. The controversy here is whether ESL is the best way to educate newcomers. I'm a product of ESL, and I think the school system did a good job on it. I learned English quickly with the help of television. When you're a kid, you love television. It can be a teacher.

History always becomes more tangible and real when one has the opportunity to speak with or read the words of someone outside of media earshot who experienced the events. Cambodia-born Jean Fernandez was a career soldier and administrator. Twenty years after escaping from Cambodia's fall, Fernandez is Board Chair of the Arizona Cambodian Association and president and Board Chair of the Arizona International Refugee Consortium, Inc.

"In leaving, the [North Vietnamese Vietminh] committed two premeditated crimes against Cambodia," he wrote in a history. "They left behind, their cadres intermingling with the Cambodian peasants. Then those cadres came out of the shadow, instigating their partisans known as the Khmer-Vietminh, with armed insurgencies in the Southern and Western provinces. Some of them were apprehended as far back as in 1961 and had confessed. Then without facing any trial, they were secretly conveyed to their embassies and representatives in Phnom-Penh, to be quietly flown back to Beijing and to Hanoi.

"They kidnapped and induced thousands of Cambodian children along their way back to North Vietnam. At the time, as the country had no accurate census control, no one seemed to take the circumstances seriously. Rather than believing what was really happening, there were just rumors about numbers of children mysteriously missing. And everyone thought children ought to be frightened that way so they will behave and listen to their parents. Only some twenty years later, during the 1970-1975 war when a number of those Khmer-Vietminh were captured during battles in the outskirts of Phnom-Penh, did all become apparent. Over 5,000 Cambodian children were abducted, from their villages, raised and brainwashed in North Vietnam to become perfect bilingual living robots that appeared as Cambodian in flesh, but rigorously programmed with an absolute mind of Revolutionary Communist Indoctrinated Vietnamese."

In 1969, Cambodia's relations with the United States were broken, wrote Fernandez. "Along the Eastern border with South Vietnam, many Cambodian peasants were killed or wounded by American air strikes. The Vietnamese communists, who schemed to inflame both sides (the Cambodians and the Americans), merely used their escape routes towards innocent Cambodian villages after their brief military incursions in Vietnam territory.

"Along the Northern border with Thailand, armed elements of the Khmer-Serei Movement, or Free-Khmers, supported by the CIA, airlifted from South Vietnam, repeatedly attacked Cambodian Army border posts leaving deaths and terror among the local population.

"For fear of the American Eagles but not as strongly as of the Russian Bears and the Giant Chinese Dragons, Prince Sihanouk managed to align his Kingdom more closely with Beijing and with those of the communist countries, allowing North Vietnamese Army (NVA) and National Liberation Front of South Vietnam troops (NLF), commonly named the Viet Cong (VC), to desecrate the Eastern border of Cambodia. In May 1969, becoming more and more entangled in the Vietnam conflict, Cambodia reestablished diplomatic relations with Washington to counterbalance the communist threat. The same year, President Nixon ordered the so-called 'Secret Bombing on Cambodia,' which was in reality the bombing on thousands of VC/NVA sanctuaries inside Cambodia's border, causing heavy casualties to the communist fighting forces and their logistics, as well as Cambodia villages....

"What the world was not aware of, or maybe too ashamed to mention, was that twenty years of war in Vietnam had nothing to compare to the devastation that wrecked Cambodia, only after the first year of the hostility. Imagine how much sweat and pain the Cambodian people had put forth to build with great pride that country since they obtained their independence from France!

"On April 12, 1975, the American Ambassador solemnly folded the Stars and Stripes, then precipitately took off in a U.S. Navy helicopter. Along with his staff, only the Cambodian personnel working at the American Embassy and their families were allowed to be part of this Historic Escape. One exception though was made: General Saukam Khoy, the interim Cambodian President who, a few days earlier, replaced Lon Nol, forced to leave for Hawaii, was unscrupulously counted among those privileged. Five days later, it was the turn of the new interim, General Sak Sutsakhan and his close associates to flee by helicopters in the wake of the night.... Without their leaders, the soldiers had already abandoned their defensive positions. The words were spreading fast as soon as the helicopters mentioned above had flown away. The Khmer-Rouge never captured the Capital by force as the world had believed. In fact, they were gestured by curious bystanders to walk through the city defense lines without encountering a major resistance. Ironically, yesterday's enemies had become instant heroes. With a big smile on each face, thousands of citizens went out on the street to greet and cheer the 'unknown liberators' in black pajamas. For a brief moment, it was a relief to breathe the ambiance of a fleeting peace.

"All of a sudden, the ecstasy turned into a dreadful nightmare for everyone. The entire population had been abruptly driven out of Phnom-Penh and all other cities to the countryside. Then, it was a blackout: a three-year-and-eight-month blackout where the world chose to turn a deaf ear to the outcries of the Cambodian people...where Cambodia was abandoned to the mercy of the two Cambodian communist antagonist factions—the infamous Khmer-Rouge, unscrupulously supported by China, and the Khmer-Vietminh, a by-product that North Vietnam had created and manipulated to simply conquer Cambodia, and...where the world resisted to call the Cambodian tragedy a holocaust. Over two million among the seven million of the entire population had perished through everyday's mass executions, purges, exhaustion, and starvation perpetrated by both Cambodian communist factions...

"My ambition ended abruptly on April 18, 1975, when I refused to capitulate to the enemy. I left at dawn, in a small boat with my wife Thaveth and four children (all under the age of six), and a six-year-old nephew, from Kompong Som...a sea-harbor province, where I was the Deputy Commander of Cambodia's 8th Military Region, besides my three other functions and responsibilities as Governor of Kampot Province, Commandant of the Kampot Military Subdivision, and Commanding Officer of the 20th Infantry Intervention Brigade.

"A day earlier, Phnom-Penh surrendered nonplus to the Khmer-Rouge as a result of the US disengagement from Cambodia.

"After weeks of an uncertain journey wandering through the Gulf of Thailand and along the Malaysian Peninsula, encountering numbers of unwelcoming harbors, we finally set sail across South China Sea to Subic Bay, a U.S. Navy Base in the Philippines, where we were flown out on June 26, 1975, to California's Camp Pendleton."

Fernandez went to school in 1972 at the U.S. Army Command and General Staff College at Fort Leavenworth, Kansas. As a result, when he was rescued and brought to the United States, he already had friends here, probably greatly easing his transition into his new American life. Certainly his ability to converse in Cambodian, English, French, Vietnamese, Thai, and Lao hasn't hurt him any!

Fernandez says he tries to understand others by putting himself in their shoes, believing that when people from different cultures come to another culture, they will encounter difficulties that will need to be solved between them while they learn English together. "For me," he says, "the keyword is acceptance. Two ways, always. I accept you. You accept me."

Jean Fernandez
Philippine, Spanish and Cambodian Cultures
Arizona International Refugee Consortium, Inc.

I have a confusing name...Jean Fernandez...Jean is a French name and I am from Cambodia. Fernandez is from my great-grandfather. The great-great-grandfather went to the Philippines from Spain with Magellan. From Spain, the great-great-grandfather came to Cambodia over a century ago. Fernandez started a new settlement in Cambodia last century. We are all Cambodian because my father was born in Cambodia as well as myself.

We belong to a family of seven people, and we worked all in the government. My father was a long time judge for a number of years, and he was a congressman for many governments of Cambodia, then finally he retired. I belong to a family of seven brothers and sisters. We are two sisters and five brothers, myself, I am the youngest in the family. And all of my brothers and sisters work for the government except one only, who was on his own. He was working in fashion *au couture*, and he went back and had his own business in Cambodia until the country collapsed in 1975. Myself, I spent over twenty years in the army. I started my career in 1955, and I ended my career in 1975 when the country collapsed. I was Governor of Kampot Province and Commandant of Kampot Military Subdivision. I was in direct command of the 20th Infantry Intervention Brigade. I was wounded twice and am lucky [to be] alive.

In 1975, the country collapsed. I preferred not to surrender. I escaped the next day, one day after the capital surrendered to the commander and before dawn the next day, on April 18, I escaped with my family, fortunately, in a small boat. I was picked up that same day by a group of three Cambodian ships who also refused to surrender. We recognized these ships were friendly because of the radio command contacts. At the same time, the enemy communists had bought our ships and all of our government ships. We had such a small army, we recognized each other by name, by face. We cannot go to Thailand, [because] less than twenty-four hours after the country collapsed, Thailand recognized the new regime. We were afraid that when and if we went to Thailand, we would be taken back to Cambodia.

We wished to go to the American base [at Subic Bay], or somewhere around there, but again it's a small area. It would also be very hazardous because of the Thai ships. We [knew] if we went to Singapore, they would imprison us because they have no refugee program. We knew everyone that landed there was put in prison. At the time, I was governor of the southern area, and we requested political asylum. We were waiting there. The Malaysian government had just decided that we could come closer, but they did not allow us to reboard the ships except women and children. Men were supposed to stay off the ship for security reasons. We were waiting there for about two weeks until Vietnam collapsed. Vietnam collapsed on April 30.

After Vietnam collapsed, the Congress [of the United States] decided to take the Vietnamese refugees, and we were included with them. The three countries included Laos, Cambodia, and Vietnam. So we were a part of the refugee program, and we were directed to the Philippines Subic Bay base. In the Philippines, we were put on an island for a period of time. I did not have the notion of time, but I did jot things [from] my memory. [From] there, we were flown to California. Camp Pendleton, California. We had a refugee camp there, a very large one.

In December 1978, Vietnamese troops invaded Cambodia in retaliation against Cambodia's repeated attacks on the southern regions of Vietnam. Millions of Cambodians were killed. But like a forest fire, war frequently gets out of hand even for the invading nations. Already angered over the treatment of ethnic Chinese in Vietnam, China unsuccessfully launched a counterattack on Vietnam two months later. Vietnam held its control of Cambodia until 1989, when Vietnamese troops honored an agreement to withdraw from the captive nation. Into the first half of the 1990s, Cambodia's political future and control remained uncertain.

Tensions spread easily in Southeast Asia, and Malaysia and the Republic of Singapore island nations southeast of Vietnam are no different in that respect. Here, one senses the influence of Portuguese, Dutch, and English who alternated their control of the area from the 1500s through the early 1900s. For the British, the region was economically hot. Here, the English developed the rubber industry with Chinese and Indian laborers.

Japan occupied Malaysia during World War II, and then Malaysians began to seek independence from all foreign domination. Malaysian guerrilla tactics won out in the two-year struggle that ended in 1959, and the land—including the Federation of Malaya, Singapore, Sarawak, and Borneo—was finally free. But tension developed in the new Malaysia between the Malay- and Chinese-dominated governments, and Singapore seceded, forming its own Chinese-dominated independent nation in 1965.

Racial tensions continued to build, flaring up in 1969 in Kuala Lumpur, Malaysia's capital, between the Malaysian-dominated government and the people of the Indian and Chinese cultures. Accusations of government favoritism of Malaysians over non-Malaysians heated the air. Although the Malaysian government has tried to bring peace and unity to the land, racial conflicts still occur.

One isolated event doesn't usually bring peace or start a war. A series of positive or negative events, motivated by intense human emotion, sets the stage for the trust or mistrust that eventually inspires peace or war. Yet human emotion goes full circle, just as history tends to replay those events.

Whether we're discussing peace and war, a chess match or a football game, if we're on the winning side, it feels good. Conversely, we struggle to win if we're losing, because otherwise it hurts.

The way in which an event plays itself out often depends on how the story has been reported. But in all fairness to the news media, one must empathize with the predicament of reporters whose emotions are also intense. Frequently injecting those emotions into stories with which they feel a personal connection, reporters often—intentionally or not—become puppeteers with historical events and political tides. How the story makes the front page or nightly news still depends on space or time available and editorial decisions. Like the rest of us, editors too are human. As a result, we don't hear or read all of the news.

Events are often ignored in not necessarily intentional preference to others. We won't always agree. In America in the summer of 1994, Asian newspapers covered an event overlooked by non-Asian newscasts and papers. The readers of Asian papers were outraged and accused editors of ethnic favoritism.

Michelle Young witnessed the event outside the White House in Washington, D.C., and watched for news coverage. Not intending to reflect favoritism of one Asian culture over another, she reported on the general lack of coverage by non-Asian news media and wrote a story involving three Asian cultures. All three cultures, as every culture does, deserve to be respected and honored—not always an easy task where emotions run deep.

White House Demonstration Ignored by Press

Mournful measured drumbeats accompanied Asian demonstrators outside the White House on June 12. Pacing their footsteps with the slow, precise pulse of the drums, hundreds of Koreans and Chinese marched quietly behind a black banner that read *United Against Japan for Justice and True History.*

The hot, muggy temperatures didn't seem to ruffle any of the sign-carrying marchers who wore summer sportswear, dresses, suits, or traditional Korean mourning clothes. But their signs told stories most World War II history books apparently failed to include.

Too young to understand, a child rode on his father's shoulders. His father had no hands left for signs. Just beyond, a businessman in his fifties who, during

World War II, might have been toted on his father's shoulders, held two: Neatly stenciled blue letters on a sign in his left hand read **Japanese War Criminals**; in his right, three black and white photographs told of unspeakable atrocities committed against China's and Korea's youth.

A beautiful young girl stopped to distribute information sheets to by-standers. As she glided through the crowd, her youthfulness gently reminded onlookers of the beauty, ages, and vitality of the dead young women in the photos.

Nearby, another young woman in Western dress carried the chilling words on a sign lettered in blood-red: **300,000 Chinese Slaughtered in Nanking**. Sign after sign wove the threads of untold history: **Japan Murderer of 30 Million People; Japan War Crime**. And still other signs made the demands: **Japan, Apologize for the Pearl Harbor Attack; Nuremberg Trials for the Pacific Front Holocaust; Japan War Criminals Repent!; Full Apology Yes! Token Apology No!**

Well into the march, a few news reporters arrived. Yet the story appeared to miss the focus of major newspapers across the United States.

In the crowd, a little girl in red held her mother's hand, walking in front of the stroller her father pushed. Elsewhere in the gathering, a slightly older boy of five or six carried a sign like his father's: **Japan Liars**.

Silently, police watched the orderly crowd filing past. Inside the White House, the President of the United States and the Emperor of Japan spoke of diplomacy and politics, leaving history to the demonstrators outside. At the White House gates, four-year-old Matthew Young, a Chinese American tourist from Arizona watched, not understanding. His sudden scream "to go potty" stole an on-duty security guard's heart, and he was quickly whisked inside for relief. In the streets, the demonstration went on, unnoticed by most Americans. The methodical thump, thump, thumping of the drums maintained their steady beat.

Author Pearl Buck's 1931 novel, *The Good Earth*, met with resistance from publishers who doubted the reading public's interest in China. But Buck had the last laugh on those who rejected the book: she won the Pulitzer Prize in 1932.

More than 60 years have passed since Buck's moment of publishing glory was transformed into Hollywood film, yet neither readers nor moviegoers tire of tales from the Orient. *Flower Drum Song* and *South Pacific* stole our hearts, haunting us with the mystery of Far Eastern places.

Bette Bao Lord's *Spring Moon, Eighth Moon,* and *Legacies* opened doors to China, giving us heartfelt views of people whose voices otherwise might never have been heard. *Spring Moon's* historical accuracy weaves reality into this novel of China before and after the communists seized control. In *Eighth Moon,* Lord tells about her sixteen-year-old sister's escape from Mainland China in 1962, prior to the Cultural Revolution. *Legacies* shares the voices of people still living in China, the result of Lord's official stay there with her husband, Ambassador Winston Lord. Mrs. Lord left Shanghai—her childhood home—for the Western World when she was eight years old. Her immigration experience became the seed that blossomed into her children's book, *In The Year of the Boar and Jackie Robinson.*

Writers like Amy Tan and award-winning movies like 1987's *The Last Emperor* offer more insights and answers to our questions about the mysteries of China and the people.

Historically, China made a significant impact in many sectors of the Far East-Pacific Rim region. Lying near the area's geographic center, this nation—one of the world's oldest continuous civilizations— has influenced many other cultures. But over 4,000 years of history can't easily be rolled into a thumbnail sketch of a nation like China, where several dynasties of native or nomadic peoples once ruled.

The famous Ming dynasty ruled the land nearly 300 years before the nomadic Qing dynasty took over in the mid-1600s. But in 1911, revolutionary nationalist Sun Yat-sen and his coalition of forces brought an end to the Qing dynasty, the last of China's imperial rulers. Territorial warlord feuds kept the new nation in turmoil until the early 1920s, when two political parties—the Nationalist Kuomintang (KMT) and the Chinese Communist Party (CCP)—began, hoping to unify China.

Following Sun Yat-sen's death in 1925, Chiang Kai-shek led the KMT, but the two parties no longer saw eye-to-eye. In 1936, Chiang Kai-shek was kidnapped and forced at gunpoint into agreeing to join the CCP against Japanese assaults on the nation. Internal conflicts continued another thirteen years until the United States helped to establish the free Chinese nation of Formosa, eventually renamed Taiwan. Chiang Kai-shek's plan to regroup and return to the Mainland, to fight for control of the nation, never materialized. Most of Taiwan's citizens are descendants of mainland China's immigrants.

On the mainland, Mao Zedong led the People's Republic of China from the 1949 split until his death in 1976. In 1950, the United States thwarted China's attempt to invade Taiwan. Chairman Mao, as he was often called, established two of the three major internal events affecting the country after 1949—the Great Leap Forward, from 1958 to 1961, and the Cultural Revolution, from 1966 to 1969.

In 1971, the People's Republic of China joined the United Nations and became a center for world trade and development. On June 3 and 4, 1989, a third major internal event affected both China's Mainland and the rest of the world, when troops opened fire in Beijing's Tienanmen Square, killing hundreds of dissident student demonstrators.

Many Chinese came to the United States and Canada between 1858 and 1885, recruited with promises of working a few years, then returning to China. But these newcomers were hired at lower pay to help build the U.S. and Canadian transcontinental railroads.

Many of those who worked on the railroads with these expatriates from China, because of barriers in communication and cultures, viewed people from Native American and other perceived non-American cultures as ignorant pagans who needed to learn western ways. Yet one—neither condemning nor condoning—must try to understand people's beliefs at this time. Perhaps national sentiment had—at least in some ways—perceived itself as a godlike, generous benefactor, relieving the ills of the hard-pressed peoples in the rest of the world.

In his 1873 book, *Travels Around the World*, Secretary of State William H. Seward advised Canada's and Mexico's "accession to the United States...that it is better to be an equal constituent member of a great, powerful, and free nation, than a small, feeble, and isolated state, even though equally free." His perception of China was, "Although China is far from being a barbarous state, yet every system and institution there is inferior to its corresponding one in the West. Whether it be the abstract sciences...the practical forms of natural science...or the concrete ideas of government and laws, morals, and manners...every thing in China is effete. Chinese education rejects science; Chinese industry proscribes invention; Chinese morals appeal not to conscience, but to convenience... If we ask how this inferiority has come about, among a people who have achieved so much in the past, and have capacities for greater achievement in the future, we must conclude that, owing to some error in their ancient social system, the faculty of invention has been arrested in its exercise and impaired."

The nation's newspapers echoed his beliefs, viewing the newcomers as "the beardless and immoral children of China...no sense whatever of any principle of morality...their brains were vacant of all thought which lift up and enable humanity...it is an established fact that dealings with the Chinese are attended with evil results."

Native Americans scaled treacherous mountain cliffs where other railroad workers were unable to succeed or even refused to try, and without the Chinese and other groups, railroad construction would have been delayed and much more costly. Yet Native Americans and other perceived non-Americans were ostracized, and America's discriminatory practices resulted in lower pay and higher company charges for supplies, preventing most Chinese and perhaps many other groups from paying their passage back home after the completion of the railroads.

As a result, many Chinese began to settle in what became the Chinatowns of the United States of America. Often, however, discrimination and persecution followed the Asians from the Far East, and the Chinese developed elaborate tunnel systems for a means of traveling through their communities without fear of being accosted in their day-to-day affairs. One such tunnel system was uncovered in the 1990s in Flagstaff, Arizona.

Who knows what the results of the North American railroads would have been, had the multicultural construction team been given equal respect and treatment? Unfortunately, many of these attitudes still exist today, leftovers from America's railroad days. Contemporary society might have been different....

Kwong Young
Cantonese Chinese Culture
USPTA Tennis Teaching Professional

As a youngster, I left Hong Kong at the age of six. What I do remember was how difficult it was for us to leave because there were so many others trying to do the same thing. I remember waiting countless hours for the immigration office, and we had to constantly go back.

Life was hectic, busy, noisy, congested. Hong Kong had a kind of garbage smell, like a stench in the air. I remember Mom taking me to the restaurant boat in Hong Kong Harbor while she mingled and played Mah Jong. I was just bored.

Dad wasn't around that much. He was addicted to the horsetrack. Upon arriving in the States, Mom remarried.

Growing up in New York, I lived in various places. Most of my upbringing was in Westchester County in New Rochelle, where we had a Chinese restaurant.

Different races came to the restaurant. Blacks made fun of the Chinese, from what I saw. They made fun of me, making Chinese slurs. That's who gave me the most hardships.

I lived in a town where one day I'd play with a black child, another day I'd play with a Jewish child. Still another day, I'd play with an Amerasian child of Black and Asian parentage, or perhaps I'd be with a WASP. That was basically through elementary school if I had any problems.

Maybe I was lucky because I was a people person. I got along with everyone. When I was in boarding school in Colebrook, New Hampshire, in a parochial school, I was the only non-English speaking [person] there since I was a new arrival from Hong Kong.

Kids would make fun of me. I had no friends except a dog that reminded me of Old Yeller. I played with him a lot. I remember crying quite a few times because I found it difficult to adapt. The nuns didn't have much patience with me. I remember getting disciplined by the ruler because I had a hard time keeping up with my work, because of the language barriers. I couldn't comprehend, and it was harsh discipline.

Growing up in the Bronx, I remember my parents told me to stay away from the blacks. My parents didn't trust them maybe due to the obvious skin difference. I remember they would always be the ones to give problems to the laundry business which my parents owned. I secretly played with them and made sure that my parents were not aware of this.

While I was attending college, I lived with my girlfriend, now my wife, in a WASP-like community in upstate New York. Our neighbor next door was your typical Archie Bunker, and he always had some remark. If you weren't one of his kind, "you're no damn good." You feel sorry for these types of people, but unfortunately they'll never change. They need to get a life, and you go on with yours.

The contemporary nations of North and South Korea have been Far Eastern hot spots for more than 1,300 years. By the late 19th Century, the Ti Dynasty's 500 years of rule had come to an end, attracting both China's and Japan's attention. Japan won out in 1910.

Yet had too many years of outside control inclined Korea's people to become overly dependent on external rule? Japan's World War II surrender had left Korea free, but the Soviet Union moved into the northern portion of the nation and the United States of America entered the south. By 1948, the Korean separation was official: The North belonged to the Kim Le-sung regime of the Democratic People's Republic of Korea; the Republic of Korea—led by the country's first president, Syngman Rhee, beginning in 1950—belonged to the free people of the South.

But simply dividing the nation in two solved nothing, and the North—supported by the Soviet Union and China—challenged the separation, igniting the Korean War between 1950 and 1953.

"Korea was a different type of war than the one fought in the jungles of Vietnam. They just kept coming and coming and coming, the North Koreans and Chinese just kept coming at you," said one Korean War veteran.

In the years since the war, South Korea has become an economic giant, competing with Japan as a key player in the global marketplace.

Jerry Yu
Korean Culture
Former Executive Director, Korean American Coalition

I came to the United States with my family when I was six years old. I remember that when we settled in San Diego, the first day of school I could not speak English. At lunchtime, I wanted to get a carton of milk and couldn't pronounce the word. The person [in the school cafeteria] couldn't understand me, and I was frustrated. Other kids were teasing me, mainly because I was different, timid, foreign.

There was one incident in the first grade. The teacher had this way of tracking our progress in reading by putting up one star next to each student's name for each book they read. During Open House, the teacher told my parents, "He hasn't read anything. Maybe he doesn't understand the assignment." My parents told me I was supposed to read, and they asked my older brother to help me, and we walked to the library every day. Soon, I read [and received the award for reading] the most number of books—a picture dictionary.

Teachers are always saying you should know better. That kind of reinforces certain stereotypes. Sometimes that makes you more responsible; other times you wonder, "Why am I being singled out?"

Fast-forwarding through college at [the University of California] Berkeley, I got a better sense of my identity as a Korean American mainly among whites. At Berkeley, it helped me to clarify my experience that I was who I was, brought here by my parents, and a racial minority from a distinct cultural background. In terms of my personal interests, I learned about the different kinds of systemic and institutional problems we have in terms of race and class. I decided somehow I wanted to make some of that change.

I went to graduate school in public administration. But during school, I got very active with different Asian American student groups, working very closely with African Americans, Latinos, and white students. I remember starting to participate in and marching in demonstrations in efforts to bring about changes in the educational system in California. One time we organized a statewide march and rally in Sacramento for more funding for public education and for improving multicultural curricula, [and for] more diversity in faculty and [in] student admissions. There were about 20,000 people who showed up at the state capitol. This whole effort was led by Asian, black, and Latino students mostly, led by Jesse Jackson, Delores Huerta, and others. I remember hearing that that was the largest demonstration since the Vietnam War.

Immediately afterwards, the governor said on the news that those people were just complainers and whiners, and there was no money for these things. A week later, the governor announced that there was a two billion dollar surplus available in the state budget and the state administration gave a tax refund to all the taxpayers in the state. I think what the governor did can be attributed in large part to our effort in the movement. Two years later, we had a second march that [inspired] different changes in the university and K-12 systems. I learned, as one person, I could contribute and could get empowered as an individual in a movement to bring about change. We strategized to get the permits for the march and so on.

After the rally, we drove back to Los Angeles. It was about two a.m., and I was feeling good. As I was driving home, I pulled up to a stop sign and I heard some noise. There were these three white teenagers making faces at me, yelling obscenities. Just by the fact that I was Asian. It struck a nerve in me at the time.

Here I was, involved in a movement for positive change in the state to benefit all people, and here [were] some people reacting to me without knowing anything about me except for the color of my skin. It enraged me.

I rolled down my window and yelled back at them, being really aggressive. Me alone! Whether it was what I said or the way I said it, they drove off.

If you think about people and affirmative action, there is not the kind of passivity in Korea or China as you would find as a stereotype among Asian Americans. It's the whole spectrum of those people taking up all the different roles in society. If [only] people were aware that Asians are not any particular way. They can be just as kind or brutal as anyone. That's when I began my activism and started working in the Korean American community for seven years.

It has kind of struck me that in America, we do have to speak up and be vocal, and that is the way this particular system functions. People have to speak up. Secondly, that we do have ongoing experiences in terms of the diversity of the people making up America, whether or not it's accepted by people. Myself, as a member of the Korean American community, we are just one example of that diversity. It's up to all of us that we have that responsibility to feel this is "my" country. And whenever we see something that's not right, it's up to us to do something about it. From my experience as an activist, one person can be empowered to change that thing and make this country better.

Our perceptions of history often develop through the events recorded in the succession of history books we're required to read in school. In the nation's elementary schools, for instance, many students acquired stereotypes about Native Americans because the required textbooks on westward expansion of the United States reported those events from a one-sided, white American viewpoint. But imagine how children with Native American backgrounds must have felt when they heard stories of "barbarian savages" and "unprovoked Indian attacks on poor and innocent white settlers"! By the time these students entered college, high school, or even junior high, their potentially molded stereotypes could have created mental images of certain categorically-grouped people.

In World War II, blanket generalizations about Japanese or German people led many American students to believe that all

Japanese and Germans were out to conquer the world and its people. Certainly one cannot diminish or ignore the events and their significant impact on the world. They happened, and they must be reported as accurately and nonjudgmentally as humanly possible.

Historical facts cannot be rewritten to minimize embarrassing or shameful acts of political leaders or nations. Neither can reports of moments in time be glossed over to alleviate political or national shame. History books and the concepts and events reported are only as accurate as the people who wrote them, but all facts must be included.

Only since the first few years of the 1990s have writers and textbook publishers begun to make some progress in unbiased reporting of history. But for many children who read horrifying accounts about people with whom they shared a cultural heritage, the pain is just as vivid and deep as that of their parents and grandparents. These children also have a right to learn that many people from their culture were positive forces from the past, role models who were often murdered or their lives otherwise destroyed in their attempts to sabotage the evils before and while they occurred. All children have a right to know that every person in every culture is a unique individual whose religious, philosophical, and political beliefs may not match with the prevailing mood of others in his culture.

In the mid-1980s, a young boy from then-West Germany enrolled in an American public school. Every day, the youngster returned home in tears because other students called him a Nazi. The child and other family members were crushed. "Just because we're German doesn't mean we're Nazis," said the mother.

With the help of two California-based newspapers, *Asian Week* and *Hokubei Mainichi*, we discovered the amazing World War II story of Chiune Sugihara. Reprinted here with permission of *Hokubei Mainichi* and each of the authors, the following four stories ran between April 14 and September 3, 1994

(Untitled Story on Chiune Sugihara)
Hokubei Mainichi, June 9, 1994

A wartime Japanese consul general who defied orders to save 6,000 Jews from the Nazi death camps will be honored in September by survivors of the camps and Japanese American veterans.

To celebrate the 50th anniversary of the liberation of Jewish victims from the Nazi concentration camps, some 100 Nisei veterans of the 522nd Field Artillery of the 442nd Regimental Combat Team and survivors of Dachau, which the 522nd liberated, will visit seven cities in Japan starting September 18.

The San Francisco-based Holocaust Oral History Project, in cooperation with the Military Intelligence Service, will sponsor the first traveling exhibit of photos and films honoring both Japanese and Japanese Americans who aided European Jews during World War II.

The main event will be a pilgrimage to a monument in Yao-tsu honoring Chiune Sugihara, who was Japan's consul general in Lithuania. In September 1939, he was so moved by the plight of thousands of doomed Jews who descended on his office seeking exit visas that he disobeyed direct orders from Tokyo and, with his wife Yukiko, stayed up for two days hand-writing visas.

His defiance of orders enabled some 6,000 Jews to leave the country and escape the advancing Nazi troops.

Sugihara has been called the Japanese counterpart of Oskar Schindler, the German businessman whose rescue of Jews is depicted in the film *Schindler's List.*

In April 1945, Japanese American troops of the 522nd came upon a place where they should not have been. While on a scouting mission near Munich, this advance unit of the highly decorated 442nd RCT stumbled upon the infamous Dachau concentration camp.

These battle-hardened soldiers could not believe what they saw beyond the main gate—corpses stacked like cords of firewood and a few emaciated prisoners who were barely able to stand.

Although well disciplined, these soldiers disobeyed orders from their superiors to not enter the camp or fraternize with survivors or displaced persons. They shot the lock off the gate, thus becoming among the first to liberate Dachau.

Other members of the 442nd came upon Jewish survivors of a hurried Nazi death march from Dachau and were the first Allied soldiers to give aid and comfort to these starved, half-dead people.

An appeal is being made for Jews who were saved by the Sugiharas, Dachau survivors, and veterans of the 522nd and other units of the 442nd to take part in the trip to Japan.

...Those interested in more information or in sharing their experiences are encouraged to contact the Holocaust Oral History Project at PO Box 77603, San Francisco 94107; (415) 882-7092.

Researcher Discovers "Sugihara's List" in Japan
Hokubei Mainichi, August 27, 1994

TOKYO (MDN)—Diplomat Chiune Sugihara, who has become known as "Japan's Oscar Schindler," saved up to 8,000 Jews in Lithuania during World War II, recently discovered visa records suggest.

The visa lists, found at the Foreign Ministry, gave 1,944 names of Jews. As it is assumed that in most cases Sugihara issued a single visa for an entire family, the number of Jews saved may exceed previous estimates of 6,000.

Hillel Levin, director of the Center for Judaic Studies at Boston University, found the list. He was quoted as saying that probably only one member of each family was named on the list, and that the number of Jews involved could be as many as 8,000.

Sugihara, who was based in Lithuania, issued visas to Jewish refugees fleeing Nazi persecution in Poland in 1940. Many were able to travel through the Soviet Union to Japan and later settle in other countries.

Levin has been meeting in the U.S. and Europe with Jews saved with Sugihara's visas. Most have told Levin that a single visa was issued for one family.

Levin found the 31-page "Sugihara's list" of visas issued from July 7 to Aug. 31, 1940 at the Foreign Ministry's diplomatic records office in Tokyo.

Yoshifusa Wakabayashi, an official at the office, confirmed Levin's visit. "The list was part of public records, but it wasn't well known to people," he said.

Sugihara issued the visas of his own volition and not because he was ordered to do so by Tokyo. In fact, he was reprimanded for his actions and demoted after his return to Japan.

Levin said Sugihara's humanitarian deed is different from that of the central character in Steven Spielberg's hit movie *Schindler's List*.

Sugihara risked his own life, while Schindler, a German, initially used Jews for his own profit, Levin said.

Schindler profited by employing Jews at low wages, but later became aware of the Nazi campaign to exterminate Jews and managed to save some 1,300 by employing them at his factory until the war ended.

Israel's Yad Vashem, a state organization that honors Holocaust martyrs and heroes, gave Sugihara the Righteous Among Nations award in January 1985, a year before his death.

The third story told of a very special event in San Francisco, California, when members of the Japanese and Jewish communities collaborated to celebrate and honor the bravery of both Chiune Sugihara and his wife Yukiko.

Chiune, Yukiko Sugihara Recognized for Saving Jews in 1940
by J.K. Yamamoto, Reporter, *Hokubei Mainichi,* September 3, 1994

The little-known story of "the Schindler of Japan" was told August 21 at an event that brought together members of the [San Francisco] Bay Area's Japanese and Jewish American communities.

Some 400 people attended *Liberators and Survivors: The Unknown Story,* held at the Japanese Cultural and Community Center of Northern California [JCCCNC] and presented by the San Francisco/Bay Area Nikkei Singles and the JCCCNC in cooperation with the Holocaust Oral History Project and the Military Intelligence Service Association of Northern California.

The focus of the program was on the late Chiune Sugihara, who was the Japanese consul in Kaunas, Lithuania, in 1940, and his wife, Yukiko. Their decision to issue transit visas to Jewish refugees from Poland and Lithuania is credited with saving thousands of lives. The refugees were able to escape the Holocaust by taking the trans-Siberian railroad to Vladivostok, then sailing to Japan.

Also recognized were the Nisei soldiers of the 522nd Field Artillery, part of the 442nd Regimental Combat Team, who liberated the Dachau concentration camp in Germany in 1945. It was noted that they were in the unusual position of being liberators abroad while their families were still interned in America.

Opening remarks were made by KPIX-TV reporter Wendy Hanamura, who is making a documentary about her father, a 442nd veteran. Stressing the importance of hearing stories of the World War II experience from those who lived it, she said, "Every day the window of opportunity closes. You may never hear these stories (first-hand) again."

Referring to *Schindler's List,* the Oscar-winning film about a German industrialist who saved his Jewish employees from the Holocaust, Hanamura said that if director Steven Spielberg had known about the Japanese consul in Lithuania, he might have made "Sugihara's List" instead.

San Francisco Supervisor Barbara Kaufman presented a proclamation from Mayor Frank Jordan, making August 21 Chiune and Yukiko Sugihara Day "for their dedication to mankind and for their selfless sense of compassion."

Actor/playwrights Lane Nishikawa and Victor Talmadge performed excerpts from their two-man play, *Gate of Heaven*, the fictional story of a fifty-year friendship between a 522nd veteran and a Holocaust survivor. The play ran earlier this year at the Osher Marin Jewish Community Center.

Eric Saul of the Holocaust Oral History Center introduced a traveling exhibit, which was on display during the program on Sugihara and the 522nd. A group of survivors and liberators will take the exhibit with them when they visit Japan from September 18 to 30. The group will also meet Yukiko Sugihara, who now lives near Tokyo (her husband died in 1986).

The exhibit, which contains 135 photos, will remain in Japan, where it will be viewed in four cities during a one-year tour.

Did Sugihara have to do it? The answer is no, said Saul. "He had sent three cables to his home office—'Can I issue the visas for these desperate Polish/Lithuanian Jews?'...Three times he was denied." Sugihara ended up disobeying direct orders from the Foreign Ministry.

Mrs. Sugihara, who was raising three children, "had to make that decision with her husband to issue those visas," said Saul, "knowing that he might be fired or punished or chastised by the Japanese government...

"Mr. Sugihara was fired, so the family did suffer. He became a salesman, worked for Army PXs. He was never able to work for the Japanese government again, never attained the status that he could have had he done the wrong thing."

Praising Sugihara as "a brave man" and a "hero," Saul said, "It's estimated that if the children and grandchildren of the people saved by the Sugiharas were counted, it would be in the tens of thousands of people worldwide. They truly owe their lives to the Sugiharas."

Saul also told the story of Holocaust survivor Solly Ganor, whose family had the opportunity to take one of Sugihara's visas but declined because they "didn't believe the Holocaust was as bad as they had heard." Except for Ganor, they all died in the ensuing years.

In an odd twist of fate, said Saul, "Ganor was on a death march in May 1945 when he again saw Japanese faces—this time those of American GIs who provided him with food." He said that they were the kindest thing that he had seen in nearly five years.

The highlight of the program was a long-distance telephone conversation with Yukiko Sugihara, which was amplified so that the audience could hear it. Translation was provided by Takako Hayakawa and Noboru Yoshimura.

Sugihara began by expressing her "sincerest admiration" to the organizers of the program. Yoshimura told her about the mayor's proclamation.

Jerry Milrod, one of the "Sugihara survivors," said, "It's a pleasure to talk to you.... You helped out many people and saved their lives."

He related how his family had tried to obtain visas from other diplomatic offices, including the American consulate, without success. Sugihara not only provided them with exit visas but also negotiated with his Russian and Dutch counterparts to ensure that the refugees had a destination. They were technically bound for Curaçao, a Dutch colony in the Caribbean, but many ended up in Kobe or in a Japanese-controlled section of Shanghai.

Another survivor, Berek Winter, said, "I want to say *arigato* to you, Mrs. Sugihara, for you and your husband giving me the visa."

Actor Talmadge, the son of a survivor, said, "I represent the next generation. Your husband and yourself managed to save my mother, my aunt, and my grandmother, and if it wasn't for you, they would not be alive and I would not be alive.... Thank you for all of your help."

Sugihara then responded to questions from Saul, Lani Silver of the Holocaust Oral History Project, and journalist Sam Chu Lin.

Asked to relate her memories of those days, she said, "I think my husband decided to go ahead and write the visas after he talked to five Jewish representatives who came to talk to him. He looked out the window and saw many Jewish people in line in front of the building."

Throughout August 1940, she recalled, "my husband started early in the morning writing the visas. The first two days he came down to have lunch with me, but after that he didn't even come down to eat. He continuously wrote from early morning to late at night, trying to write as many visas as possible."

Both she and her husband were "well aware of the risk," Sugihara said. "When my husband decided to write those visas, he knew that he could be fired or even be killed by the government."

Asked if they were worried about reprisals from Adolf Hitler when they moved to Berlin, she replied, "We didn't worry about Hitler finding out what we did. I think he was too busy attacking other places. I don't think he paid too much attention to what happened in Lithuania."

Reflecting on the events of fifty-four years ago, Sugihara said, "I didn't have any doubts about my husband signing the visas. To us, it was a natural action to do, and I'm so glad to hear the result that we saved so many people."

Given the same set of circumstances, she added, "My husband would agree with me on this point—we would do the same thing." That statement drew applause from the audience.

The traveling exhibit, she said, is "very important because the young generation these days doesn't know anything about war, and to have this exhibition in Japan will teach young Japanese that this should never happen again."

To this end, she has written a book, *Visas for Life*, which will be translated into English.

Commenting on conditions in the world today, Sugihara said, "I always get heartbroken when I find out that those miserable and desperate situations related to war are repeated again and again through these fifty years of our history. I feel that each one of us should think about...what we should do as part of this society."

Silver, noting that Winter's five children were in the audience, said, "It's the most beautiful thing because these people would not have been here without your courage. We are all...just in awe of what you've done."

Sugihara said, "I'd really like to see the survivors in person myself and see what we did."

George Oiye, a 522nd veteran who took part in the liberation of Dachau, said, "My first encounter with victims of the Holocaust were lumps of snow that turned out to be remains of human bodies, (people) that had starved to death, frozen to death...It was a frightening...and disgusting sight to witness."

While noting that "many survivors have thanked me for saving their lives...and have looked on me as a hero," he stressed that "there were no military heroes at Dachau. Those who survived the unspeakable atrocities inflicted upon them are the unsung heroes."

Oiye described Sugihara as "a real hero...who risked his life and career to save 6,000 Jews from the Nazi death camps."

Because the lessons of the Holocaust are so easily forgotten, he challenged those who have witnessed it "to come forward and tell your story.... Tell it to your children and let your children tell it to their children."

Ernie Hollander, a survivor of Auschwitz and Dachau, recalled the deaths of his parents and siblings at the hands of the Nazis and a death march in which anyone who couldn't keep up was shot on the spot.

The German soldiers suddenly ran away, and the prisoners encountered a group of Japanese American GIs. "We were afraid that Japan won the war with America and now they are coming here to kill us. They threw us bread and cookies, whatever they had, and everybody was scared to pick it up." But he later learned the soldiers' true identity.

Hollander emphasized "the responsibility of everybody who survived...to tell the stories of what happened to us" to young people. "If they do not know what happened, how can they prevent another Holocaust?"

Other speakers included Holocaust survivors Gloria Lyon and Bernard Offen, 522nd veteran Kiyoshi Okano, and redress activist and former internee Sox Kitashima.

Dachau survivor Paul Benko summed up the event by saying, "The reason we're honoring Mr. Sugihara and his wife is that we share a fundamental human value; we believe that life is more important than the rules of bureaucracy or the hostilities of governments. If we would remember that rule, I think we could solve a lot of problems today...

"We celebrate Mr. and Mrs. Sugihara for goodness.... We should not be ashamed of doing good; we should be proud of doing good, and we should tell that to our children and our children's children." Having spoken about the Holocaust at various schools, he said, "Our intentions are the same as those of the former internees of the U.S. concentration camps. I know they're not "the same intensity as the concentration camps we were in. But in essence, when you separate a people from others, you grease that slippery slope which ends in destruction.... Our efforts will bear fruit if we're consistent and reinforce each other's efforts."

Denis Kim and Arleen Honda spoke on behalf of the San Francisco/Bay Area Nikkei Singles. Certificates of appreciation were presented to Saul and MIS veterans Yoshimura and Harry Fukuhara for organizing the traveling exhibit.

The sushi and bagels served at the reception symbolized the unity of the two groups.

The final story reviews the April performance of the play, *The Gate of Heaven*, at the Osher Marin Jewish Community Center, prior to the celebration.

'Heaven' an Uplifting Story of Friendship
by Mark Nishimura, Reporter, *Hokubei Mainichi*, April 14, 1994

With nothing but a bare stage, two actors, and a few props, *The Gate of Heaven* provides a powerful examination of a fifty-year bond between two men—a survivor of the Dachau concentration camp and his rescuer, a soldier from the 442nd Regimental Combat Team.

Written and performed by Victor Talmadge and Lane Nishikawa, the play is currently running at the Hoytt Theater at the Osher Marin Jewish Community Center in San Rafael [California].

It opens with an exhausted Sam Yamamoto carrying a weak Leon Ehrlich outside Dachau at the end of World War II, while images of the Holocaust are projected on the backdrop.

"At first I thought the Japanese won the war," Leon later admits. "But then I realized that I was looking at an angel...with an Asian face."

After the war, the two go their separate ways. Leon moves to the U.S. to study psychology and talk about the Holocaust to anyone who will listen to him. Sam gets married, has children, and works for an oil company in the [San Francisco] Bay Area.

Then in 1959 at San Francisco's Presidio, Leon, after years of searching, finally encounters Sam. The reunion begins a long friendship.

From the assassination of President Kennedy to America's involvement in the Vietnam War to economic hard times in the 1980s, the two try to understand each other's culture and cope with racism in the U.S.

All by themselves, Talmadge and Nishikawa carry the bulk of the highly emotional play, gracefully balancing humor and pathos and delivering unforgettable performances.

Talmadge is brilliant as Leon, who has experienced all the horrors one person can tolerate. During one of his lectures, he is verbally attacked by a heckler. Without flinching, Leon keeps talking, louder and more angry, determined to tell the truth about the Holocaust.

Leon also acts like an innocent child fascinated with life. When he reunites with Sam, Leon is so delighted that he dances on top of his chair in a busy cafe, embarrassing his friend.

In another hilarious scene, the Jewish immigrant, awed by the multiculturalism of his new homeland, tries to coach Sam into going out to an ethnic restaurant on the Fourth of July.

"But I want good ol' American food," Sam complains.

"Then how about Italian food?" Leon replies. "The Italians founded America."

Nishikawa is a convincing Sam, a kind and helpful man who constantly denies that racism exists in America. Early in the play, he comments to his military superiors about the inhumanity he saw in Germany during the war, yet he does not feel any outrage about his own family being interned in the U.S. for their Japanese ancestry.

It is not until he befriends Leon that he comes to terms with the discrimination he endured during the war.

Frustrated with the anti-Asian comments he has encountered throughout his life, Sam asks Leon, "Do you think I fought (the war) for nothing?"

Leon answers, "It's better to suffer an injustice than to do an injustice."

With the help of sound designer Matthew Spiro, costume designer Susan Snowden, photographer Haruko, and consulting director Benny Sato Ambush, *The Gate of Heaven* becomes a dynamic look at friendship.

Japan's isolation from the rest of the world remained fairly constant until internal stresses and population growth brought the island nation to a decision to look beyond its shores in search of more land, more resources and food. The history of the Land of the Rising Sun dates back to 600 years before the birth of Christ, and Emperor Jimmu. Author James Clavell brought Japanese history alive in his novel, *Shogun*, providing the link to 500 years of Japanese culture and heritage with the power and passions of emperors, Shoguns, and feudal lords.

Before U.S. Navy Admiral Matthew Calbraith Perry's efforts encouraged Japan to open its ports to world trade in 1854, Japan's Shoguns had expelled all foreigners, believing these people were army spies of other nations. Perry's diplomatic achievements marked a significant turning point in world trading history. Japan's relations with the United States and Europe were dramatically altered, and Japan experienced internal changes that transformed the nation into a world power over the next fifty years. Coincidentally, in 1820, Perry served as a lieutenant and executive officer on the ship, the *Cyane*, which helped to establish a black American colony in Africa.

In the 1860s, years of yo-yoing power between emperors, Shoguns, and feudal lords finally returned to the emperors who continue to be the country's dominant authority today. Emperor Hirohito's *Showa*—Enlightened Peace—reign from 1926 to 1989, however, included Japan's involvement in World War II.

Following the war, U.S. Army General Douglas MacArthur, who respected Emperor Hirohito—was appointed to head Japan's return to self-rule. As Japan rebuilt its cities and the villages dotting the thickly populated land, the nation evolved into a successful, contemporary country that prides itself on industrial and economic growth and quality workmanship. The transformation that has continued to play a major role in 20th Century Japan has also brought a change within the country's political structure. Although modernization has given birth to an elected parliament and prime minister, Emperor Akihito, whose reign—*Heisei*—means Achievement of Universal

Peace, is still in power too.

Not all Japanese in the United States of America found themselves in camps during World War II. Some people from the Japanese culture believe "only those who posed a threat to the United States government" were segregated with barbed wire fences from other people living in America. Possession of a Japanese heritage often caused intercultural difficulties between Japanese and non-Japanese. But even worse, difficulties often rose between people within the culture, those who readily adapted to life in America and those who didn't.

Yoshiko Yamauchi
Japanese Culture
Elementary School Teacher

I don't speak Japanese because I wasn't given the opportunity to learn. When I started working at Hawaii's Plantation Village, older people spoke to me about their reservations about continuing to pass on the Japanese language, [caused] perhaps in part by Pearl Harbor. When I went to Japan, because I didn't speak the language, I needed an interpreter and felt like a foreigner.

My father left Okinawa in 1906, hoping to make a thousand dollars in three years—at the rate of two dollars a day. My mother, born and raised in Hawaii, married an Okinawan during a period when the Naichi looked down on Okinawans and frowned on Naichi-Okinawan relationships.

Pioneers in this relationship, not wholly accepted by the Okinawans nor the Naichis as children, we grew up as "half-breed" in a highly populated Okinawan area. The Naichis ignored us, and we were not included in their social activities. Because of our Okinawan surname, we were able to participate in Okinawan picnics and fun times.

We weren't really brought up in traditional Japanese culture, we were more western. The foods we ate were not Japanese Japanese. My mother, being one of the younger children [in her family], number eight of nine children, didn't practice the strict Japanese rituals of the earlier days. So at this point, the family became more [acculturated] to the local society, not only in the foods eaten, but in all other aspects—religious practices, medicines, what's accepted socially, and so on.

I can see where my mother was not as strongly aligned to the Japanese culture as her older sisters were, and I didn't find that out until I was much older and started questioning her. I always say we were brought up in the best of the cultures.

We enjoyed the Japanese festivities with my mother and her family, the Okinawan ones with my father. For Japanese New Year, we pounded sticky rice into rice cakes for a traditional new year food. The women prepared the rice and molded the pounded rice into rice cakes. The older dominant women made the special cakes for the customary offering for good luck. The men, on the other hand, cooked the rice on an open fire and pounded the rice. I didn't know the significance of the interaction until much later. It was just something we went to do and to eat and socialize together. But it was part of the celebration with my mother's family.

My father raised pigs. For new year, he killed a pig, and we would take a piece of raw pork to the friends and neighbors who helped us over the year.

I didn't realize until I was much older that I wasn't accepted. You sort of feel it without understanding. During this period (1940s and early 1950s), our teachers were predominately Western. They came from elsewhere. Our local teachers—locally trained Hawaiian and Portuguese—were called Normal School teachers. We had a lot of morals lessons, using folk tales as a basis of learning. Because I had a few Portuguese teachers, they really stressed the Catholic religion.

I think I knew my place. I didn't seek out the children who were predominantly Japanese or predominantly Hawaiian. You stayed within your clique to the homogeneous grouping.

Japanese with any connection with Japan, including church leaders, fishing fleet owners, teachers, newspaper connections, any hosts of Japanese government officials, were interned in the camps on the four major islands. From all the accounts we read, they were caught unaware. The U.S. government official would take the male figure, and the rest of the family was left alone until they were later taken to the camps. I only seemed to suffer repercussions from World War II from my Japanese name. I was the only child of Japanese ancestry in my class without an American first name. I was an unconscious child, flowing with the wind, oblivious to all around me. I guess it was my defense mechanism to eliminate more rejection and hurt.

Although pleasing my parents was important, my decision to become a teacher was based on my own painful experiences of class and ethnic bias in the classroom and my determination that I would become a teacher and be fair to all students—that I would strive to encourage and recognize the talents of all students, not only those with the advantages of class and social status. I wanted to become a teacher—maybe I did feel slighted, now that I think about it. The teachers gave awards, and I never got one although I could do the same things. A music teacher in high school gave me awards and rewards and gave me [back] so much of my self-confidence. The other teachers had not rewarded me, and I wanted to show them that I could be unlike them.

In my father's eyes, somehow ingrained in me, becoming a teacher and marrying an Okinawan was important. I wanted to please him. This job really fit in. And I certainly did marry an Okinawan, not that I said I would because he was Okinawan. It just turned out that way.

In my job, we need to share ethnicity and ethnic pride. We need to share with new people coming to Hawaii, that they shouldn't lose their cultural heritage, that they can live here and enrich this society.

In this morning's newspaper, the *Honolulu Star Bulletin* (September 4, 1994), my sister-in-law was quoted, and she said, "When I was younger, we were made to feel inferior to Japanese. But now we have pride. Now I'm proud to say I'm Okinawan." It goes on to say "she reaffirms her faith in her heritage every year when she returns to the Okinawan festival."

That's exactly the way most of us feel.

A majority of the world's people make the Far East-Pacific Rim region their home. Speaking approximately 1,200 different languages and dialects, the people of this area live within a variety of cultural traditions and possess the deeply rooted and rich history of prior civilizations—the nucleus of modern peoples' individual mosaics today.

The elliptically shaped Pacific Rim encompasses a wide range of languages and customs, but only two—Chinese and English—stand out as the primary or secondary languages spoken by the majority of its people. Although English is widely accepted and well represented as a universal language, Chinese is a universal tongue in the Far East region.

From San Francisco's Chinatown to Sydney's, from New York City's to the Chinatown in Lima, Peru, the Chinese language links a mind-boggling number of Chinatowns to cities and people in every corner of the world.

Yet although the Far East-Pacific Rim possesses the beauty, languages, and thousands of years of history, its people are refocusing and realigning into tomorrow's economic and political world geniuses and leaders. The Pacific Rim area has reshaped and expanded to include its midpoint region of the North Pacific's Hawaiian islands and the South Pacific's Marquesas Islands, and its outer reaches including North and South America's west coasts, Oceania, the southeast coasts of Asia, and a variety of cities—Vancouver, Los Angeles, Puerta Vallarta, Puntarenas, Panama City, Lima, Valparaiso, Wellington, Sydney, Jakarta, Singapore, Bangkok, Ho Chi Minh City, Shanghai, Seoul, Tokyo, and Vladivostok.

Oceania forms the southwestern arc's last cluster of countries along the ellipse of the Far East-Pacific Rim. The peoples and their homelands, from Indonesia to Australia—"The Land Down Under"—complete the beauties of our mosaic world.

Chapter 9

THE FOLKS DOWN UNDER

Remember elementary school, when you started to grasp the concept of the world as an enormous sphere of continents and nations? We progressed through school, learning about the larger nations of the seven continental regions. Visual aids even took us to many of those places—Paris' Eiffel Tower, the Taj Mahal in Agra, India; Egypt's great pyramids. Yet much of our education about the Pacific Island area of the world—often called Oceania—depended on our teachers' most basic knowledge.

Even in the early 1990s, which island nations actually fell into the Oceania zone appeared confusing. Some reference books said Australia's classification as a continent ruled out its inclusion in Oceania. Other references disagreed. We have elected to include Australia in this chapter to simplify the massive scope of the Far East-Pacific Rim area, allowing us to provide more continuity between the individual stories of this region.

But one cannot forget that divisions—man-made lines drawn on the map, for instance, separating politically conceived provinces, states, counties, and so on—and physical island groupings are arbitrary breakdowns, simply aiding one's identification of any particular area.

Since the late 1940s, Bloody Mary has enticed us to explore Bali's *South Pacific* magic through Liat's beautiful eyes and those of a young World War II U.S. Navy lieutenant; Crocodile Dundee has shown us the Australian rugged outback, and Roger Miller's *Tie Me Kangaroo Down* has paved the way for Olivia Newton-John's superhits.

Exactly how many islands dot the mosaic of the Pacific Islands region, nobody knows. Some experts estimate as many as 20,000; others believe the number exceeds 30,000.

The continent of Australia—commonly called "the Land Down Under"— and the countries of Indonesia, Papua New Guinea, New Zealand, and several South Pacific Island nations on both sides of the International Dateline form the body we'll call Oceania, the Pacific Islands region. Noted anthropologist Margaret Mead lived among the Samoan people for several years, providing the basis for her book, *Coming of Age in Samoa.*

One could spend a lifetime in learning about the history and cultures of the peoples in this immense, predominantly water-filled corner of the world. A myriad of islands and island chains link the waters of the Pacific from Indonesia, Australia, and Papua New Guinea, southwest to New Zealand and northwest to the Tuamotu Archipelago islands. Serving as a type of pivotal point for the region, the Tuamotu Archipelago islands lie 3,500 miles west of Peru and Chile, South America's coastal nations, and 3,500 miles southwest of Los Angeles, California.

The Southern Hemisphere's geographical nickname "Down Under" may have stemmed from its location compared to the rest of the world and the concept that "up" means north, and "down" is south. From the perception of the region's schoolchildren, perhaps we in the Northern Hemisphere are standing on our heads!

Malia Tina Weber
Samoan Culture
Accountant

If I go anywhere, they look at me and I kind of go straight to my point and say exactly what is in my mind. If you like it or not, sorry, that's the way I am. People sometimes judge you by your skin. I don't really [care because I know] what's right.... I'm part Samoan and Chinese, but I was [raised] Samoan.

My dad was Chinese. I don't know much about the Chinese culture. I live here now, and I understand American culture. At first, [I had a hard time with] the language, just like anybody else coming from different countries. When I came here, I already knew how to speak English, but I spoke with a very very heavy accent. The prejudice, of course, was also bad. But my personality...I feel I know you're white and I'm brown and have a heavy accent, they automatically put you down. To me, that was my biggest problem when I first moved here. I just look at people as the same. I came here for a better life.

The difference between Samoan culture and here, you get a lot of respect there. [Not that Samoa is perfect. In Samoa, too] there are good things and bad. There are no perfect people anywhere. [In Samoa,] they care for each other. We do not have homes for old people [in Samoa]. We do not feel it's right to put our parents or anyone in our family in that kind of place. [Samoans] respect the parents a lot. In our [Samoan] culture, you cannot talk back to your parents. Right or wrong, you just shut up and don't defend yourself.

They [Samoans] respect Sunday a lot. That's the only day they go to church, and they all wear white clothes. Sunday, we're not supposed to do anything else. No work. Over here, you can do what you want when you're eighteen. Over there, it's a **no no**. You can stay with your folks till you marry.

In school, they [Samoans] believe in discipline. I went to Catholic school, and those nuns would use anything.

The family is very very close. Our education is...important, at least in my family. Some Samoan families are just the opposite of my family. My dad was very strict.

Where we lived, there were no police. But there were ten kids in my family. My dad believed in self-defense. I learned it because I had to. Of course I will teach my son. I will also teach him both languages. In Samoa, when we were involved in a fight, my dad never asked more than who cried and who won. If you said you cried, he told you you would have to pick a fight with the person again. The reason why he was so strong in that, he saw a lot of Samoan kids be scared of somebody at school and not want to go to school. He believed if we were scared of somebody at school, that was no reason to stay at home. We were very strong on education there.

My dad was the only one to get up and fix us breakfast before we went to school. Not my mom. Every single day. He never missed. He woke up about four o'clock in the morning. Never missed. We didn't have a microwave or electric stove. Now we do in Samoa—not the microwave, just the electric stove. As soon as he finished making the breakfast, then he'd start waking us up. When he woke us up, he never believed in yelling. He stayed and called your name about a hundred times. As soon as we all sat down, he'd sit down too and start talking about how important education is and how tough life is. There were a few Samoans that worked for my dad. My dad would talk about not just going to school, but about learning something each day.

As soon as we got on the bus, he'd go back to bed. He had a big plantation, a lot of cattle. Those were his morning duties. But we never saw my mom do that. The youngest child always respects the eldest. The education is the strong part in my family, but in some Samoan families, they don't care.

Samoan women love to gossip. They're very creative with what they talk about. Not all, of course. But some people are very jealous of their success. They are not good sports. The jealousy is very strong over there...

If you work, you still give money to your folks. It's not like here, when you keep it all to yourself. You give to Momma. If someone related gets married, the whole family helps out. I like it but I don't really miss it because people talk about you. I feel what I'm doing, that's my business.

Over there [in Samoa], you feel they know more about you than you do. It's like a small town. But Samoa is a very good place to raise kids.

I am from Western Samoa, and there are not that many opportunities there. So you [have] to be very smart to get a job there. Competition is very high.

At dinner time, you always let the parents and grandparents eat first. It's very impolite to talk with your mouth full or stand up and eat. Before dinner, the family gets together to pray. Same thing in the morning. My family is a very strong Catholic family.

Columbus and other 15th Century explorers had sailed west to reach the east, the South Pacific, and landed on the shores of the Western Hemisphere's Caribbean Islands. But they failed to find Indonesia, a series of 13,500 islands dotting 3,000 miles of the Pacific Ocean southeast of Malaysia and Singapore, which supplied many of the spices the adventurous explorers sought.

Dutch, Indian, Middle, and Far Eastern cultures inhabited the Republic of Indonesia, a Japanese-occupied territory during World War II. Indonesia's accusation that the independent state of Papua New Guinea on the eastern half of New Guinea harbored an Irian Jaya liberation movement has led to strained political relations between Papua New Guinea and Indonesia, whose largest islands include Borneo, Celebes, Java, Sumatra, Timor, and the divided island of New Guinea.

Nearly every world religion, over 250 distinct languages, and more than 300 discrete ethnic clusters constitute Indonesia's integrated mix of Chinese, Malaysian, and other cultural groups in the predominantly Muslim populace. Indonesia's motto, "Unity in Diversity," sums up the nation's strength in its people.

One Indonesian Experience
Indonesian Culture
Student

Most of the time I think I get along with my Indonesian friends. That's for socializing. But in terms of schooling, I have to deal with other students, especially Americans—Caucasians—and my professors. I have some friends as well who are neither Americans nor Indonesians and don't necessarily belong to the majority of American society. My Indonesian friends, of course, I don't spend time with all of them. I try to be friends with everybody. But there are special friends who are part of my family. We play tennis, watch games on television. The other friends, we associate through meeting in the class room or related to my professors, or at a party, and we keep in touch.

I don't find things that always draw me with other people. No driving power.

I don't know whether I've experienced prejudice here. I'm more introspective here. I always think how people would react. I always wonder if it would offend someone.

I was driving in Des Moines at two in the morning, and I was tired and tried to find accommodations. I went to at least three places, and they said it was always full. So I slept in a rest area. I'm not saying it's prejudice. Maybe it was full.

Outside of campus, I don't think language is a major difficulty. On campus, because of the academic language, I must study again and again. Sometimes it's not the language, rather what's being talked about. For instance, when we're discussing a movie or a star from the 1950s, I have nothing to relate in my brain.

I have some difficulties but not major ones in finding foods. Sometimes I miss Indonesian tastes, there is no time to cook. I cannot find Indonesian and go to Chinese or Thai food. Sometimes close friends invite me, and that's always a big treat to be invited by Indonesian families.

I can't go out here at night. I really miss going out with my male friends in my home city. There are thousands and thousands of students so there are always vendors everywhere. I don't drink, so bars here are useless. At home, we can go talk about anything. If I go out with my American friends, where can we go? Pool? Bowling? Bars? I don't drink beer. I'm not really interested in that. There, I can go out in the night and feel safe.

I've been to Minnesota, Wisconsin, New York, Washington, D.C., and Georgia. I came here in 1988 and then home, and then [again in] 1991, then home again, then [here again in] 1992.

I was in New York, my friend was telling me, "Don't ever be in the subway after midnight."

Because my friend told me, and I was there at one in the morning, I was scared. These people would approach us and ask for money. I gave a dollar to one, and he became very nice. He didn't follow us down [the stairs] because there were two policemen there. Then the policemen ran after someone and handcuffed him. The man who gave us directions and I gave him the money, came to talk.

Linguistically diverse, mutually hostile tribes of Papuan and Melanesian people settled in New Guinea, where they lived in tribal cultures resembling those of the Stone Age period of world history. During the 19th Century, the Dutch, Germans, and British divided the island—the second largest in the world—among themselves. The territories became self-governing in 1973. Today, Papua New Guinea—independent since September 16, 1975—still struggles in its strained political relationship with Indonesia but maintains close ties with Australia.

One of the world's seven continents and the South Pacific's largest land mass, Australia tends to be the best known of the "down under" nation. A different array of animals, including kangaroos and koala bears, make their home exclusively in Australia. Most of the

Australian people tend to congregate in the urban Pacific coastal areas.

During World War II, American General Douglas MacArthur traveled to Australia from the Philippines and later led the liberation of much of the area including the Philippines, resulting in the defeat of Imperial Japan. But Australian troops played a key role in both world wars and in the Korean, Vietnam, and Persian Gulf Wars.

Most Polynesian islanders didn't venture to Australia before the Dutch and British reached its shores. But historical reports about Europeans' first sightings and the first Dutch landing on the continent vary. One book notes Australia's partial discovery in 1623. Another says the Dutch visited Australia in the 18th Century. Yet the land and the aborigines—indigenous people whose ancestors may have arrived from Southeast Asia thousands of years ago—were generally left undisturbed until Captain James Cook claimed the eastern coast for England in 1770. Australia's exploration, however, led to displacement and total annihilation of aborigine settlers in certain areas. Few minorities retained ownership of their original lands.

Many Europeans—often prisoners or members of the English army—settled in the British colonies that eventually developed into the cities of Sydney, Brisbane, and Hobart. But by 1851, the discovery of gold on the continent created a rapid increase in immigration. Europe's practice of shipping convicts to Australia finally ended in 1868.

In 1901, six colonies formed the federation called the Commonwealth of Australia. Today, the British culture predominates in daily life, but the Australian people vary as people do on the other world continents. Thanks to Crocodile Dundee, people all over the world are developing a new interest in the continent and its vast and varied terrains, including the great expanse of the outback.

The well-educated Australian people live in fairly upscale surroundings. For a while, Australia was the richest nation in the world. But like so many places where economic disparity exists, a great majority of the 150,000 Aboriginal Australians live in abject poverty and have become detribalized.

Australia's High Court, however, has passed laws to protect the nation's indigenous peoples from racial discrimination (1975) which led to *The Native Title Act 1993*, safeguarding traditional land rights of the Aboriginal and Torres Strait Islanders and rejecting earlier claims "that Australia was *terra nullius* (a land belonging to no-one at the time of European settlement)." According to a July 1994

Department of Foreign Affairs and Trade fact sheet, "Australian law should not, as one judge said, be 'frozen in an era of racial discrimination.' Its decision in the *Mabo* case ended the pernicious legal deceit of *terra nullius* for all of Australia—and for all time."

Torres Strait Islander Eddie Mabo, a member of the Murray Island Meriam people, and four other islanders sought "court action against the Queensland State Government seeking confirmation of their traditional land rights." The Mabo court decision led to Australia's efforts to right the wrongs against the indigenous peoples, politically and symbolically affecting the entire nation. "The 1992 High Court decision...and...The Native Title Act 1993 have had a major effect on indigenous land rights and the way Australians think about their nationhood in the context of 'native title.'"

In the years prior to 1973, extremely restrictive immigration to Australia left few doors open for people whose cultures may have varied from the people already present there. When these practices ceased, new waves of immigrants, especially from Asia, encouraged the development of a more global economy.

Judy Faulise
Australian Culture
Secretary in Government Offices

My attitudes have changed a lot. In Australia, I was brought up by an English mother, who told us "not to argue or have discussions with your father." Here in America, I enjoy talking. Previously, I had been told "keep quiet"; now, I'm told "talk up." Even here, you can brag a little, be proud, take part in your community rather than staying with our own class and not stepping out of line.

When I was working, there were about 75 percent blacks in the office. My boss was a black woman. I had never worked with blacks before. When I grew up, I never saw an aborigine.

I found I really admired my boss. She was a remarkable woman. She is now a county commissioner. I really admire her for what she's done. She hasn't forgotten her people.

While I was very friendly with some of the blacks, I found myself being too nice, patronizing, and there was some resentment because I was in a position of authority. Most of the problems were because of personality differences and a need for recognition of each person's ability and respect for each other. Mostly when we had problems, it was a lack of understanding for each other.

234

I also found I had a lot more personal opportunities for growth—courses I could take and other ways in which I could improve myself—here in America. Another thing I noticed, in Australia people tend to have no heroes. They're not people for bragging in any way. They go the other extreme. Here in America, I like to be able to be proud of something. Perhaps it's because many [Australians] started life in a new country as convicts. Australians are more laid back. They like a good time. They're not in a hurry. They're not high-pressure, high-powered at all. It's a different outlook.

As far as religion goes, I feel that it is a fact: there are more Americans attending churches than [people do] in Australia. My parents didn't go to church, but I had no choice. I went to the Anglican Church. Here, I chose to be Methodist, and I sing in the church choir. I didn't feel I was square because I chose to attend church. I noticed, when I went back this year, my sisters. One sister and I were able to talk about other experiences as children. The other sister felt it was disloyal to talk about these things.

We attended private schools because my mother was upper middle class English. She didn't want me to associate with [the] lower middle class. Private schools were all white. There was no such thing as integration. Aborigines—native Australians—lived on isolated reservations.

I came to America in 1964 as I was married to an American who lived in Florida. It was exciting. President Johnson had started Headstart, and a lot of things were going on. I became involved with activism here and wondered what my mother would have said. I wrote to her when I began working in an Emergency Preparedness office, and she wrote back, "Wouldn't that be bad for your allergies? Well, I guess someone has to do it." Her view of the life she wanted for me was far from the reality I was living.

My first husband was English. He was a U.S. citizen. In a way, it was history repeating itself. My mother left the security of England to marry an Australian. I am beginning to appreciate the adjustment she too had to make in a new country. My second husband was born here from Italian parentage. I have no regrets except wishing there were fewer miles between me and my sisters. I am proud of both my Australian and American heritage.

Judy Faulise stresses, however, that even among Australians, people's experiences differ in their native homelands and in the United States of America.

Alwynne Lamp
Australian Culture
Teacher

My father was in the Navy so we moved a lot in Australia. We moved to England when I was fifteen, when London was swinging. When we went back home, I returned to school, completed college, and got into teaching. I was interested in outdoor education.

When I left Australia, I wanted to go back to England and came to the United States where I did an outdoor program in Wyoming. It was the reverse of my image of the United States, where I expected pollution and crowding and desecration. Instead, I spent four-and-a-half heavenly months in the unspoiled land of Wyoming. I also went into canyon country in Utah, the wide open wilderness.

People here spoke quite openly about religion and spirituality. At first, I found that awkward and embarrassing because when I was growing up, that was real private and almost secretive unless you were a religious nut or wacko. That was one of the first surprises.

Then I spent another three years in Minnesota, working for an outward-bound school there. After [that], I met the man I later married, and I ended up staying in the United States.

Culturally, I found myself very compatible with Minnesotans, but when we moved to Florida about five years later, I really went into culture shock. Realizing the loss, that I would not be living at home [Australia] again, started to hit home. I felt here I was in this tropical paradise, but the values seemed out of step with mine. And the landscape was very different. I think I went through a real long grieving process which I'm just now emerging from. I'm now contemplating becoming an American citizen, and I feel for those people who give up their homelands.

I find the primarily financial barriers with maintaining contact with home very difficult. I've lived in West Palm Beach for almost seven years, and I finally feel I'm putting down roots in this community—although it's really the last place I would have chosen on the globe. It's my children's home, and gradually I'm part of the community. That's important.

Probably if I went back home, I'd be so unacculturated that I'd feel as foreign there as I do here. People are people. They have their worries and their griefs, their dreams.

I really admire this country for trying new ground. I know Australians sit back and watch what the United States does. This country sort of got the best and the worst, pioneering in so many different areas. My husband is a drug and alcohol counselor, and this country is doing so much. It's America's thing. We're not going to tolerate oppression as necessary.

That's what I'm grateful to this world for giving me, even though it's very imperfect. I've been in the United States about seventeen years. If I went back to Australia, it would probably be different too.

Sometime between the Ninth and 14th Centuries, the Maori people migrated to New Zealand's long narrow stretch of land from Polynesia. Although Dutch explorer Abel Tasman was credited with discovering New Zealand in 1642, the Dutch failed to return to Europe, and James Cook claimed New Zealand's two land masses—the North and South Islands—for England in 1769. In return for legal protection and rights of continued ownership of the Maori lands, the Maoris permitted settlers to colonize as a British sovereignty under the 1840 Treaty of Waitangi.

But all did not go smoothly following the 1841 development of the British colony. As British settlements continued to expand, the Maoris were displaced from their lands in bloody battles that spanned the next twenty-nine years.

Finally, in 1907, New Zealand's elevation to an independent nation within the British Commonwealth brought about the establishment of a parliament headed by a prime minister. Four Maoris are elected to Parliament from among the 250,000 Maori people. New Zealand, now predominantly populated by people from the English cultures, provides education to the Maori children.

New Zealand was one of the first nations in the world to establish a comprehensive welfare state with universal old-age pensions, public-sector medical care, and labor laws. In general, power plants, transportation, communication, mines, and forested lands are publicly owned. One may be inclined to picture New Zealand's masses of white sheep grazing in green, lush, undulating hills, and certainly sheep ranching plays a key role in this nation's economy. But one would be remiss in diminishing the importance of this island nation which administers foreign affairs and defense of several Pacific Island dependencies. Like its neighbor, Australia, New Zealand's troops provided invaluable contributions to the Allies in both world wars and to the United Nations forces in the Korean War.

To New Zealand's credit, this nation has been rigidly opposed to nuclear weapons and has held steadfastly to these ideals. In 1985, French secret service agents bombed and sank an antinuclear and environmental organization's ship in Auckland harbor. In 1986, New Zealand's refusal to allow U.S. ships carrying nuclear weapons port facilities brought about the dissolution of the ANZUS mutual-defense treaty of 1951 between New Zealand, Australia, and the United States. But if the United States government took personal affront at such a move, they shouldn't have: New Zealand also vehemently opposed French testing of nuclear weapons in the South Pacific.

Understandably, New Zealanders are cautious about people who would like to claim this nation as their home. New Zealand's people, for the most part, are content to remain here, peacefully living their lives without interference from those whose philosophies don't necessarily agree with their own.

Kirsten Broadfoot
New Zealand Culture
University Student

Most people my age in New Zealand, in their twenties and thirties, are not in New Zealand society because we are all overseas. Seventy to 80 percent travel. It's called the overseas experience, driven by a need to get out into the world because of our geographical location and because we are so far out in the world. I think it's because of a turn to the motherland experience.

When I told people I was coming to the United States, they thought I was crazy, and they still don't understand why I am here. I think it's because there are a lot of mixed feelings about the United States and New Zealand. A lot of that is historical, and not necessarily long ago historical, but even recently on the nuclear issue.

Our government took a no-nuclear stand and became part of an alliance

238

with Australia and the U.S., borne out of World War II, maybe a little later. ANZUS. When David Lange came into that policy with the United States, he said the United States couldn't tell New Zealand what to do. The United States said they would neither confirm nor deny policy, and there was a conflict of interest between the nations, and the alliance was broken over nuclear policies.

It seems really minor, but there was the America's Cup scandal, and we felt that the United States had cheated. There was a lot of anger and frustration. There's a general feeling in New Zealand that people from the United States cannot be trusted. It's based on things like these and the fact that a lot of Americans we see in New Zealand are generally older tourists who don't understand the accent and start yelling, speaking very slowly and childlike, and portray the ugly American. I was working in hotels in 1990, and that syndrome was still there. Because of that, I think it's a very different style of communication and why people don't understand why I'm here. They worry that I will be taken advantage of in the United States.

New Zealanders as a whole are very innocent people whose word is their bond. We come here, and the Americans are very good at making small talk, and they don't have much conversation on deeper issues and aren't willing to play the game. A lot of it comes out of the big cities. In the smaller cities in the midwest, it's very different. I think that's why many New Zealanders aren't here.

Life here is extremely more complex than it is in New Zealand. When I go to the supermarket in New Zealand, we don't have the same variety of choice. Here in the United States, you can stand before a certain item at the market, and you'll spend a great deal of time deciding which item [to select]. In terms of institutional things, I had a lot of trouble because I came here out of Japan. I went to the bank and was told I couldn't have a bank account because I had no social security number. I was furious. What was I supposed to do with my money then? I had to go to the social security office and get a number so I could get the bank account. They were very surprised that I didn't know my number and had to look at it. That's a key to American life. Without a social security number, you're not a person.

A lot of the time, they know I understand and speak English because I have a white face and don't look like your stereotypical foreign person. A lot of time, they think you're foreign if you have dark skin.

Two people who know me very well know I'm an international, and they gave me a questionnaire for American grad students. My friends assumed I was an American. A lot of time, people automatically assume I'm American and they think something's wrong with me because I don't know something that's clearly American. That situation is probably unusual for a lot of American people.

I've had some comments. Students ask whether we speak English there, whether we can drive there. They assume we wear grass skirts and live in huts.

People have told me New Zealand is very much like the United States was in the 1950s and 1960s in terms of society. When I return to New Zealand, I will have my family in New Zealand. I think that's what all of us do.

We explore the world, work overseas and experience what it's like in the world. And probably 90 percent of that group returns home to settle down. A lot of friends my age in England and in Europe talk about returning home within two years, before they turn thirty, to settle own. There is no way I would settle in the United States. I couldn't raise my family here. Fear on the day to day level rules my life here. It's a kind of irrational, illogical thinking that anyone can have a gun and value human life so little and blow you away.

I know a lot of Europeans, because of that thinking, will not return to the United States. It's crazy. I come from a country where we cannot have guns. Seeing the blood on your hands tends to deter people. For me, it's the total opposite. A lot of my life here is dominated by fear, and that makes my life more complicated.

New Zealand is a place where there's always someone watching out for you. We, with three million people, have a country where men still protect women. It's traditional. That's not to say there's no crime in New Zealand. At home, eleven o'clock, the pubs close and you, as a woman, don't walk after ten.

There is a lot of domestic violence there, and I think it's related to what we see as traditional roles for men and women becoming more blurred. Basically the same phenomenon as in the United States. Two-income families are starting to happen there. It's a very patriarchal society.

When I talk to women in the United States, I would like to have a career and family, there's no choice. I still want to raise my family, spending time at home. Either you don't work or you work at home. There's a big move in Australia and New Zealand toward working at home stations. It's an efficient way of managing the work force. For me, it will involve something that will not take me away from home.

Placing your kids in day care is something I can't come to grips with. The complexity of the society and both parents having to work to survive places stress on the children. A lot of work needs to be done on the inner selves of the children. For me, after living here for two years or so, that will be the end of my time in the United States. I came here to school, and when I'm done, I will leave and will return to Australia or New Zealand.

There's a very real need for me, as a person from down under, to live down under. There's a difference in the speed of life. I don't have the fear in New Zealand. That's the kind of life that I want for my children. I think there are a lot of people with those values in the United States, but I think they're in small towns.

People think New Zealand is exactly the same culture. It's not. We're getting a lot of bad U.S. sitcoms and other shows that portray untrue, incomplete images of the United States, and one has to wonder what kind of impressions that gives people in other countries.

Here, in the ethnic communities, these families seem to possess the same values. In my home, there's a lot of activity, and it gives you a sense of belonging to the group, the fact that I have two younger brothers and a sister. My youngest brother is legal, twenty, to go drinking. My sister and I share a room. All of our friends are part of the family.

Maori people, I think they are about ten percent of New Zealand's population. Contrary to belief in the United States, they're not like African Americans and they have more similarities with Native Americans. While they don't live on reservations, they share many of the same problems, alcoholism and so on. There are suburban Maori who have gone to school with us. They're very family-oriented people. I think the tribal mentality still exists. There has been a resurgence of establishing Maori identity because there are no full-blooded Maori left. The mentality is still where the elders lead the younger ones. But among the educated, the elders no longer know what's good for the people.

One controversial writer, Alan Duff, is a very honest assessor of the crisis facing the Maori. A lot of open-minded New Zealanders realize this is a large part of the population who have a lot of strength that we need as a country. There's been a struggle about land rights there. A lot of Maori have reclaimed their land which they consider sacred. Maybe the only key to saving us is Maori control of the land.

I think the Maori are facing an identity crisis. They're very open, honest. There has been a change in some quarters that we Pakeha, Europeans, white people, have a lot to learn from these people in the way of doing things. Social welfare system rule and design has deprived [the Maori] of mana, self-respect.

From the perspective of people living in the United States of America, conversations about native peoples might begin and finish with the indigenous people of North America, the Native Americans. But native peoples live in various countries around the world even on the northern island of Hokkaido, Japan.

A quick glance at Japan's Ainu people might trigger thoughts of the Native American tribes traditionally living in the northern forest regions of North America. Modern day Japanese, like most of the world, lack much awareness of the Ainus, who lost much of their culture after the 19th Century.

Prior to 1945, many Ainus were transplanted by the Japanese government which attempted to dissolve the Ainu culture, claiming the Ainus needed protection. The government, however, attempted to obtain the resources of the Ainu homeland for wartime use. Today, most of what's left of the Ainu population continues to live on Hokkaido. Since the late 1800s, the Japanese people have migrated to Hokkaido in large numbers, and the Japanese population there has risen from 20,000 to more than five million. Although many Japanese still cling to prejudices against the Ainu people, at least some of the Ainu culture remains intact. As for the Ainus, they've been denied their dignity, spiritually starved, and left to grope about in a Japanese-dominated culture.

Prejudice and discrimination are no more new than the centuries of global migration and immigration to lands occupied by others. Unfortunately, Americans in the United States tend to limit their focus on prejudice and discrimination to black and white relations. But the following thought bears repeating one more time: We need to view people as people and not as statistics entrenched in numbers according to one or more categories symbolizing the peoples of the world.

Visiting every island in the down-under South Pacific region and providing examples of the multitude of cultures represented becomes a nearly impossible feat. The easily navigable distances between the islands of the South Pacific encourage the theory that people have skipped from island to island for many centuries, leading to speculation that some islanders' ancestors might have been the first of the peoples down under.

Do the indigenous peoples of the Americas have their roots in the Pacific Rim? It's likely, according to geological theories. Perhaps a land bridge once spanned the Bering Sea from the route at the eastern Asian edge to the fiftieth State in the Union—Alaska. If that hypothesis is valid, it may well be that the Native Americans of the Americas and the Ainu people of the far northern reaches of Japan are related.

One tends to look at the segmented world map in such a way that the extreme eastern section of Asia appears on each end of the layout, leading one to develop a concept of an Atlantic Ocean relationship between the Americas, Europe, and Africa. But the Americas are equally related to the Far East and Down Under regions surrounded by a large portion of the Pacific Ocean, now known as the Pacific Rim.

242

The world and its peoples, as a result, seem so different, but we need to examine the picture more closely, keeping an open mind. Every one of us is interlinked with the globally crisscrossed pattern of peoples and their cultures, making our world a true mosaic. Our common bonds offer us the opportunity to provide ourselves and others an open door to think and believe as we choose, peacefully, side by side with people of the same or different cultural backgrounds, without fear of discrimination and persecution.

Political and economic realignments are making a great impact on the world now, especially among the Western World nations. As a result, we—through our businesses, communities, and schools—will need to address the cultural challenges ahead of us today and tomorrow. How these realignments with the emerging Pacific Rim phenomena are perceived and responded to will determine the future of most of the world. Within the Pacific Rim region itself, developing nations will most likely have much to gain and little to lose. But the Western industrialized nations of the world—those with relatively high standards of living—could lose more than they gain if we fail to take the awesome changes in the Pacific Rim seriously in all areas of our lives.

Magellan, we're taught, was the first to circumnavigate the globe. From navigation by sea to navigation through diversity, we can see the enormous mosaic through the eyes, ears, and feelings of the peoples of our multicultural world.

PART II

BUSINESS AFFAIRS

Chapter 10

CORPORATE CULTURAL CHALLENGE

According to the history books, most of the inhabitants of the pre-1492 Americas—the expanse of land from Alaska to Argentina—were what we refer to as Native Americans, Native Peoples, or Indians of the Americas, although cultural diversity among these people was as varied as the land itself.

People from Europe and Africa arrived in the Americas and settled in particular regions, and the demographic picture of those regions changed dramatically, resulting in an increase of cultural diversity. The subsequent mingling of cultures resulted in the creation of new regional cultures.

Demographic changes have been in constant flux since those early days of American history. While some may perceive the greatest variations occurring in contemporary times, this perception may not be entirely accurate. Our perspective of demographic evolution can make a great difference in our response or reaction to these changes. Which cultural group actually triggers these statistical changes in demographics doesn't really matter. What is and should be important—especially from the business perspective—is the change itself.

Adaptation to these changes may mean having the right product at the right time or preparing future graduates for the working world. Few people may perceive education as one of the nation's largest forms of business, especially in smaller communities—but its influence plays a critical part in this discussion.

The second major demographic movement, between 1890 and 1920, brought millions of people from Europe and lesser numbers from Asia to the Americas. Yet the most dramatic or perceived major change appeared to coincide with the third, or "new wave," of Asian and Middle Eastern peoples and the simultaneous relocation of American peoples within the United States of America in the 1990s. Because peoples with their respective cultures have lived in the Americas for several hundred years, we need to view these movements as shifts in demographics rather than as changes. These demographic trends demonstrate the major difference in population shifts of five major categories identified as *White, Black, Indian, Hispanic,* and *Asian/Pacific Islander.*

We may tend to falsely assume that people labeled as members of any of these groups, even for statistical purposes, may have very little in common. When peoples' attitudes within or between these groups were compared in research conducted by Christiansen (1975), no significant differences were detected. People are people, each one uniquely different. We need to consider all individuals and their preferences rather than making racial, ethnic, or even culturally-identified stereotypical assumptions.

Not a race, ethnic group, nor even a culture, the word *Hispanic* demonstrates the false-assumption concept. The term actually comes from a Latin word, *Hispania,* which refers to the Iberian peninsula of Spain and Portugal. Many of the world's people might be labeled Hispanic today because of intercultural marriages, but we must recognize the tremendous variation within the statistically labeled Hispanic people.

Now we must focus on the future skills which will be required by all who live within a particular society. In the United States of America, for example, the following comparative trends between new workers and future job availability have been forecast, based on September 19, 1988, projections by *Business Week:*

Type of Job	Ratio of Jobs to Workers
Unskilled/Manual	1:2
Old-style Assembly	more than 1:2
New-style Teams	more than 1:1
Technical/Professional	5:1
Professional	4:1

From the corporate world perspective, the above chart shows our need for all members of society to learn to work together successfully especially within the culturally diverse environment. Schools need to prepare students for this culturally diverse society, to develop their higher level thinking skills as well as higher performance in mathematics and science. Achieving higher standardized test scores is not the answer.

Entering the workplace where people need to work together successfully, students will need to possess highly developed social skills. If these social skills are only superficially achieved, working together will amount to nothing more than working apart. If we do not work together, we will work apart.

Corporate budgets will need to reflect the higher costs of training for entry level workers in many skill areas. Some skills—especially in the realm of cultural diversity—take a great period of time to develop and cannot be successfully mastered within a few hours, days or even months.

A multicultural approach to staff development and classroom sessions **must** be implemented in the schools. But the corporate world will also need to continue this focus in its future vision. Considering a shift in the company cafeteria's available food choices may fill the needs of smaller companies. Developing positive internal and external cross-cultural relationships, on the other hand, will play an integral role in the successes of corporations plunging into the world trade market.

Donald Utroska discussed the corporate need to develop positive cross-cultural views in "Diversity" with reporter Robin Tierney in *World Trade*'s December 1993 special issue "1994 Going Global Guide From A to Z":

> "We have a tendency to believe if it's good enough for America, it's good enough elsewhere," says Donald Utroska, VP/managing director at Paul R. Ray & Co., Inc., a Geneva-based consultant who has observed the degree to which cultural, economic and political differences influence the way people do their jobs. "You can't just set a U.S. template on another country," he says.

Profit is the reason why most non-academic corporations exist. Without delving into macro- and micro-economics, various factors affect profit and loss figures—among them, overall productivity and the cost of training workers. Workforce cultural diversity will affect profits even more in the future.

Corporations that successfully recruit and maintain a culturally diverse work force have a definite edge on competitors offering the same services or goods. The reason why lies in the numbers. The company with the larger pool of available workers meets and fulfills specific workers' needs more easily.

Two major factors determine the pool of available workers for available jobs: a larger student population in technical and professional job training, and corporations adhering to policies which consider all technically and professionally qualified workers regardless of cultural backgrounds.

But we must also consider the type of services and goods on demand from the now-rising culturally diverse population, marketing research methods, techniques, and findings, as well as management styles and procedures. Some people and corporations perceive demographic shifts as a challenge; others view shifts as an outright threat. Those who choose to move forward, challenged by demographic shifts, will be the real winners in our future international marketplace.

Many corporations and school districts, positively viewing cultural diversity, actively make lifelong commitments to encouraging, developing, training, and maintaining a culturally diverse workforce. This positive perception shifts away from old legislative quota requirements that perceived people as statistics or "tokens" to meet state and federal mandates. Sometimes legislation is needed to point out unfair hiring and promotional practices in the corporate and educational environments. The multicultural approach to hiring and promotion, on the other hand, considers individual qualifications relevant to the organization's need to move forward competitively and productively.

Companies of all sizes have begun to create management positions to deal with diversity in the workforce. Sadly, while some companies display total commitment to this concept, others seem to be motivated primarily by the benefits they'll receive from employing positive public relations.

We wrote to a number of major corporations, asking about their methods of addressing the increasingly diverse workforce. Some did not reply. Others replied by phone but refused to answer questions or even to submit a formal press release as a reply. Several corporations declined our invitation, but two were particularly delighted to share information about their efforts in cultural diversity/multiculturalism: Miller Brewing Company of Milwaukee, Wisconsin, and International Business Machines (IBM) of Purchase, New York.

According to an article in *High-Lites* (June 1991), a Miller company publication, "diversity includes all employees.... It's certainly not limited to ethnic groups or sex. We are also diverse based on age, marital and family status, where and how we grew up, physical attributes, personality, education and hobbies, to name just a few," said Shirley Harrison, Miller Brewing Company's director of training and compliance.

Warren Dunn, Miller's executive vice president, "cautioned against limited and short-sighted thinking that could allow stereotypes to cloud managers' judgments and perhaps lead them to pass over talented individuals."

The article discusses its support of ongoing multicultural training, but omitted any specific references to the methods Miller uses.

IBM Corporation's Director of Employee Relations and Planning Richard W. Hallock wrote "Accommodating an Increasingly Diverse Workforce" for the National Planning Association's July 1991 issue of *Looking Ahead*, a quarterly journal.

"Workforce Diversity in IBM is an 'umbrella' term encompassing equal opportunity, affirmative action, and work/life programs. Since the Hallock article appeared...IBM has made further enhancements to its work/life programs," J.A. Honeck, IBM Program Manager on Workforce Diversity, replied.

"It is important to understand that IBM approaches diversity as a by-product of its existing management philosophy," said Hallock, who described the company's relationship with employees as one in which it worked at perceiving its employees as "distinct individuals" rather than categorically broken down into generic groups. By doing so, he explains, the company has the opportunity to value and respect employees, fully appreciating and recognizing each of their attributes in the business world as well as in the global community.

IBM's theme in 1991, "Realizing the Diversity Advantage," was "designed to help managers first to recognize the diversity that already exists within IBM and their departments, then to develop leadership skills that will harness the potential of that diversity as a source of competitive advantage," wrote Hallock in *Looking Ahead*. "It is no simple task to achieve and sustain a productive, diverse workforce. The challenge is ongoing. IBM's success in this area is due in large part to its emphasis on the three key areas noted above—diversity as an asset, cultivation of a diverse workforce, and Work/Life support programs. For a global company striving to lead an innovative industry, there is no greater asset than a loyal and committed workforce."

In a telephone interview with Michelle Young, Hallock also addressed the intensified approach to employees sent to work in other nations:

> The employee [participates in an] orientation program in the United States before going to different nations. [They also have] access to video tapes for home viewing and information from the State Department. There's a variety of material [in addition to] an opportunity to visit the country, meet with others and have an orientation over there. When the person makes the decision and actually takes the job, a human resources individual assists the process.

Sadly, not every company operates with the same total commitment to multicultural education in the workforce. IBM's exemplary efforts deserve recognition.

From the non-academic corporate perspective, many companies attempt to address both employee and community needs. Positive reciprocal relationships between companies and communities generally result in increased local business and a healthy supply of personnel, both of which inevitably improve the local economy. By underwriting an ethnic play, US West Communications, for instance, reaches out to bridge racial gaps in certain communities. It is also possible that US West and other non-academic corporations funded this and similar projects in colleges and universities across the American nation as a means of allowing students—prospective employees—to familiarize themselves with corporate policies of their particular companies. But corporations, unlike public academic corporations, are entities within themselves.

Among public schools—from neighborhood grade schools to the nation's top public universities—responsibilities for these kinds of decisions follow a hierarchy of authority that link individual community schools and their school districts with county, state, and federal guidelines and mandates. All of these result in the composite academic corporation known as the public school system.

Federal guidelines and mandates affect all sectors within the academic corporation in every section of the nation. State guidelines and mandates, on the other hand, address those same areas from within the state, analogous to having a corporate subsidiary. Similarly, this same concept channels downward, through each subsequent level of this hierarchy, all the way back to the planes of higher education, secondary, and elementary schools.

Just as corporate personnel spans from the president and CEO to the maintenance and groundskeepers, school personnel ranges from certified—trained, accredited staff—to classified personnel who may not require training and accreditation at the higher education levels. But like all other corporate employees, people who work within the academic corporation need to work effectively with wide varieties of people from all cultural backgrounds.

Although the United States provides a common thread linking the multitude of the nation's school systems, complex factors distinguish any one state from another. Each state's individual geographic network possesses an intricate series of perspectives, policies, and methods through which each will achieve specific goals. As a result, making conclusive, blanket statements applicable to every single state within the Union as a whole becomes a next to impossible feat to achieve. Even if this task were made easier, one would need to question the sensibility of such a project since these perspectives, policies, and methods of achievement change almost daily.

In general, all state legislatures and departments of education—trying to address cultural diversity at all levels of education—may have reached beyond "should we do" and have begun to focus on "what will we do" and "how do we achieve." According to our research and that of James Boyer, Professor of Curriculum and American Ethnic Studies at Kansas State University, the state of Nebraska currently leads the nation in requiring cultural diversity training for certification at the higher education level as well as addressing cultural diversity/multiculturalism in every classroom among the local community school districts. Other state legislatures have mandated cultural diversity training for certification and are considering similar actions affecting the curriculum and its methods of delivery.

Nationally, teacher training institutions are addressing multicultural issues through various means, including new course development and/or existing course infusion. Approximately 700 students are enrolled at Dana College, a small liberal arts college in Blair, Nebraska. Yet the school has a multicultural coordinator on staff and offers specific courses on multiculturalism as well as multiculturally-infused courses.

Unfortunately, we did not succeed in identifying a specific elementary or secondary school district in any community where an effective multicultural model has been developed, implemented, and consistently maintained at all levels, including staff training and curriculum development.

A majority of the nation's elementary and secondary school districts appear to use what we call the Ethnic Holiday Celebration or Add-On Approach, a practice which **could** be conducive to mere tokenism, where activities and events of generally prominent minority classifications—African, Asian, Hispanic, and Native Americans—are represented. Using events like Black History Month in February or Native American Week in the third week of September, coinciding with a calendar of special emphasis at the national or state level, for instance, has some value if it is viewed as an initial step toward developing a true, multiculturally-infused curriculum. But when these events are used as the only approach to addressing cultural diversity, multiculturalism tends to be perceived as a shallow means of accommodating categorically-identified minority groups.

These ethnically-identifiable events should not be viewed as an opportunity for singular, plug-in, or add-on types of celebrations. Instead, these occasions can be used to highlight educational themes that are integrated in the academic curriculum, drawing attention to the event as an added emphasis of that which already exists and is studied throughout the school year.

Eating ethnic foods, listening to ethnic music, and so on, merely tends to make one aware of the many cultures in today's world. Although this initial step brings one closer to becoming a multicultural individual, one must still deal with the critical issues of prejudice and discrimination. The celebration of diversity included in Chapter 12 should take place as a culmination of the various points along the path to becoming a multicultural individual.

Certainly a number of school districts across the country are attempting to address multiculturalism. The best and most effective approach to multiculturalism in a school district appears to be through the development of an autonomous department that interacts with other departments. Ideally, in some school districts, the superintendent of schools directly oversees the multicultural specialist. But the size of school districts in many of the nation's largest cities might require that the multicultural specialist be an assistant superintendent.

Effective multiculturalism needs to be inclusive rather than exclusive, considering all people regardless of racial, religious, cultural, economic, or other differences within the community, state, or nation. It is important to avoid the pitfalls of incorporating the multicultural component into any department of the school district, including the district's desegregation or equal rights office, bilingual education, English as a Second Language (ESL), or any other similar efforts dealing specifically with minority issues.

Calling one's prejudices and subsequent discrimination by another name doesn't change the need for multicultural education. Prejudice and discrimination, behind the mask of another name, is still prejudice and discrimination. Whether people declare a situation to be bigotry based on socioeconomic status or they readily admit to prejudice against specific groups, exclusion based on differences can still exist and needs to be identified and effectively but respectfully eliminated.

Many areas of the community can and should be utilized to develop positive intercultural relationships. Over the last several years, there has been a strong trend in the direction of school and business partnerships. Although these partnerships have been developed primarily for working relationships between schools and some particular company, the participants can also promote intercultural understanding and enhance their self-esteem.

"In this country's culturally diverse climate, all levels of government, business, and industry are critically concerned with economic development," says Agustin A. Orci, Superintendent of the Northside Independent School District in San Antonio, Texas. Orci, an advocate and innovator of School-Business Partnerships, has successfully implemented this mutually beneficial project in Arizona and Texas schools.

"Schools are part of the infrastructure. A progressive, caring community will enhance its ability to improve its economy when schools are part of the picture," Orci says. "School and business leaders must work together for one key reason: employees, customers, and students are all the same people."

There are minor differences between schools and business, says Orci, "...the schools get these people sooner than business; therefore, there is tremendous mutual benefit in working together to improve learning opportunities for students who eventually become the workers and paying customers of the nation's commerce."

"How do these partnerships work?" we asked Orci.

"Business people act as mentors to individual students, working on special projects—for instance, architects working with kids to design a school, to make practical use of reading and mathematics—or, on a collective level, a business consortium contributing its offices for enhancement of high school business careers. Speakers can also visit classrooms to discuss the positive effects of applying knowledge learned in school to the workplace."

Making an effort isn't always easy, but the results are well worth it, Orci says. "Over the last few years, business has answered the call, and schools are no longer pretentious about accepting corporate help. School-Business Partnerships are alive and well because the stakes are high. Perhaps the nation's survival is dependent on the ability of its people to assist its youth, to be there for kids instead of leaving it up to the gangs, and certainly because it's the right thing to do."

In the work world—the realm of business, industry, and education—cultural diversity will more than likely determine the degree and extent to which people live and work successfully together regardless of any racial, religious, or cultural differences. But cultural diversity training needs to be implemented at every level within the working world, regardless of the organization's or institution's size. Those who plan, develop, and implement this training should be true multicultural individuals. Chapter 11 discusses in depth the definition of a multicultural person and the process by which one becomes one.

If laws are only considered and minimally met—just enough to stay within the boundaries of those laws—the resulting nondiscriminatory approach to training programs and practices will be accurately perceived as phoniness and tokenism. Tokenism produces Band-Aid politics and a feeling of legally enforced tolerance of others—a far cry from multiculturalism. The facility with tolerance-oriented goals in cultural diversity training, produces mediatory relationships at best.

"I'll put up with you if you'll put up with me" means we really don't care or have much use for others.

National and international mobility has led to the demographic shift—a higher degree of nationally- and globally-represented cultural diversity. But valuing diversity generates positive feelings that propel a company to become a creative force on the leading or cutting edge in an interdependent multicultural world. The pace has picked up considerably in the global marketplace, and change has become the most constant factor in the corporate world. Diversity in the workforce, therefore, can adapt more quickly to the essential evolution that may make the difference between success and failure.

PART III

BIAS AND PREJUDICE

Chapter 11

Understanding and Overcoming Prejudgment

Words like *globalism, multiculturalism, nationalism, unity* and *unification* spice today's newspaper headlines. But using the words doesn't ensure understanding the definitions or the implications behind their use, and *multiculturalism* stands in danger of becoming a dirty word.

The world, once clearly understood as a body of individual societies, is becoming what some may see as a homogenized global structure struggling to maintain the individuality within. But individuality does not have to be sacrificed for peace. Multicultural awareness gives each world culture the opportunity to diversify while appreciating other cultures for their unique qualities.

Some people tend to allow their egos to interfere with learning more about multiculturalism. With a little knowledge and a lot of vocabulary on the subject, these people pretend to understand fully, throw the words freely around, and establish personal or business approaches to multiculturalism based on their preconceived notions. Obviously, there's an inherent danger in this approach: Misinformation about a person or cultural group gets passed on to other people or cultural groups and—overriding originally good intentions—prompts the growth of more intolerance and misunderstandings.

Words themselves are also crucial factors in grasping the multi-cultural philosophy. In "A Semantic Tale of Two Cities," S.I. Hayakawa noted that some words can positively or negatively affect how we feel about ourselves and others. Using an example of one city calling unemployment *Welfare*, Hayakawa described another city where unemployment was called *Insurance*. The latter city prospered while the first city suffered from rising crime, divorce rates, and so on.

Positive thinking encourages growth; negative thinking stunts it. Negative, limited thinking may tend to foster antisocial responses, ranging from mental illness to criminal action. Collectively, the responses may promote the growth of gangs and other criminal element groups, increased problems in marital and family bonds, or—at the even larger collective level—war and anarchy.

Limited thinking about multiculturalism negates its intended positives, setting the stage for segregation and other forms of bigotry. Multiculturalism is not a mere offshoot of bilingualism, nor is it intended strictly for minorities. Positively used, multiculturalism promotes good feelings within and between individual cultures.

How any subject educates and promotes understanding most frequently depends on the media, its philosophies, and its policies. Old concepts are easy. They require little training for comprehension of new developments, and the process usually works smoothly as long as the basic premise, teaching, and end result remain the same. On the other hand, if any step confuses the issue—whatever that issue may be—disseminating that information becomes more difficult.

More often than not, the words *bias* and *prejudice* are used interchangeably to indicate an attitude of being against something or someone. Unfortunately, a quick check of your dictionary might reinforce the likelihood of your confusion about or your misuse of these two words.

But we need to gain an in-depth understanding of how bias and prejudice actually work in the real world, where people interact with other people. Consider the following definitions:

Bias: A preference for something or someone.
Prejudice: A preference against something or someone.

Although both definitions can result in identical ends, a bias can be far more hidden and dangerous on closer inspection:

A company's **bias toward Ivy League school graduates** results in virtual prejudice against non-Ivy League schools.

These biases may not look like prejudices. Many factors may influence the situation. A company's long-standing policy to hire only graduates of specific schools may not be borne out of any intent to discriminate. Perhaps no other schools have programs essential to the company. Still, we need to be aware of our personal motivations and actions, especially where people are concerned. In one sense, our acquisition and transmission of biases and prejudices stem from other people. But when we understand how we acquire these preconceived ideas, we will also understand their transmission to others.

According to Alfred J. Marrow in *Living Without Hate* (Harper & Bros., NY, 1951), "Racial prejudice also is a component of culture. Studies show that children under five years of age are rarely prejudiced, but rapidly become so." Yet Marrow does not mean to imply that children under the age of five haven't been exposed to prejudice. Children at this age have difficulty in developing complex concepts, a prerequisite for acquiring racial intolerance. But foods and other stimuli received through the senses and interpreted by the brain can be conducive to the formation of biases and prejudices prior to the age of five.

In comparison, biases and prejudices related to race, religion, sex or age are more complex. Several variables need to be in place, operating together within a short time period and being repeated over and over again. Repetition provides one of the most essential keys to acquiring these types of inclinations.

We have a strong drive for security. It's human nature. But the extent to which we need to be secure, or the means of obtaining that security, may vary between individuals and according to time considerations. Being safe from physical injury is generally more obvious and observable. Emotional security is not as easily identified.

At specific developmental periods, our inordinately strong basic drive to be accepted by others may increase in intensity—during adolescence, for example. Nevertheless, we never lose this need for acceptance; we have it throughout our lives.

Parallel to that need for acceptance, disliking whatever our identification group dislikes becomes easier than being rejected. Our fear of isolation and rejection frequently becomes so powerful that we accept others' biases and prejudices rather than rejecting them. Even if at first we only superficially accepted those jaundiced views, those feelings would gradually become embedded into our minds, into our hearts and eventually into our actions. Finally, we deceive ourselves into believing we can turn our feelings on and off, but we become entrapped in our self-deceit.

Consciously or not, we teach others when we interact with or are observed by other people. The most effective way to transmit information, ideas, concepts, and attitudes is through the eyes and ears of children. When children watch and listen to adults, the effect is generally greater. After children receive and process the information and so on, they take action through imitated behavior. As a result, negative attitudes toward people, based on their race, religion, and so on, are difficult to change.

On the other hand, positive biases and prejudices also exist. How we handle our preconceived notions makes the difference. We all discriminate every moment of every day. At the produce stand, we may reject certain fruits or vegetables because we dislike their colors, sizes, smells, and so on. If we reject a specific food on a regular basis, we will form a prejudice against that food. But if we seek out a specific fruit or vegetable based on its color, size, smell, or other consideration, and if we do so regularly, we will develop a bias toward that food. When we deal with people, we need to ask ourselves what limitations and discouragement we may be placing on others because of our acquired proclivities.

The earlier and longer our biases and prejudices have become part of ourselves, the more deeply imbedded they are rooted into our personality and character. People who believe they can "turn on and off" their use of negative words and non-behavioral initiation and/or response to others may succeed in doing so at first. But repetition of these biases or prejudices will plant seeds that eventually root and become part of the personality. Eventually, seemingly acceptable words we use around friends or in other intimate circles, will come flying out when we least expect. And although we may apologize profusely, the real message of what's inside us has been delivered. Numerous national figures, publicly and privately, have had to make such apologies and, in some cases, have been asked to resign their positions.

Heredity or environment also contributes to the acquisition and transmission of bias and prejudice. Today, society often enables people to avoid being held responsible for attitudes and behaviors, declaring heredity or environmental factors the extenuating circumstances for their negative behavior. But by taking responsibility for our behavior, we take an important step in understanding who we really are and that which we're capable of doing.

If we surround ourselves with people operating from negative biases and prejudices, we will gravitate to similar behaviors as our own attitudes change. Let's suppose our environment did have a negative effect on our attitude. Do we blame the environment, or do we change our environment and remove ourselves from people who possess and use negative biases and prejudices?

"The best of human institutions are capable of the worst perversion," says Robert Spear in *Race and Relations: A Christian View of Human Context* (Negro University Press, 1970). "It is with race as it is with sex. What God evidently intended for noble and enriching use has been often degraded to bareness and evil. Race prejudice and race strife have taken the place of race respect and race service and have poisoned the life of mankind."

But unity through diversity can be respected, appreciated, and admired. With sound multicultural approaches—from rearing children to working in a culturally diverse corporation—the picture can look very different. Tolerance is neither a goal nor a term which will achieve a mutually respectful environment between all people. Yet by employing specific strategies, techniques, methods, and activities, we will be able to live and work in a mutually respectful environment. The means through which we create that environment are the same as those required for becoming multicultural people.

Strategies to assist others in overcoming negative biases and prejudices need to be well-developed and tested, rather than focusing on building tolerance toward others as many multicultural strategies and programs have done. Overcoming these biases and prejudices does not mean simply changing our preference of foods, music, and so on; rather it means changing our negative attitudes, biases, and prejudices toward other people. Anyone can memorize the steps. That's easy. But a great deal more is involved—for instance, having the right leadership, time, commitment, and resources.

Becoming aware that we have biases and prejudices, then sharing that **awareness** with others in a safe environment is the first step. Next, we must accept by acquiring an understanding of the likenesses of all people. From there, we must begin to accept their differences through acquiring an understanding of why others are different. We must see others' differences as enriching and learn to **appreciate** them, accepting other people just as they are even if we don't accept their ideas, attitudes, and so on. Finally, we must begin to **apply** the attitudes and feelings that demonstrate our true respect for others.

Respect is the ultimate goal in becoming multicultural. But there are many ways of showing respect, and our perceptions of that which demonstrates a show of respect in one culture may be perceived as disrespectful in another culture. Still, many actions will be received by most people, regardless of their individual cultural backgrounds, as a sign of respect.

Consult a multicultural specialist when building a training program conducive to eliminating biases and prejudices associated with disrespect. The specialist will also make the critical silent factor—nonverbal behavior—easier to grasp.

Biases and prejudices—large or small, seen or unseen—can destroy the life within educational or company organizations of any size. People breathe life into an organization, and they must be able to sustain that life and make it flourish. In war, one man's prejudice in a military unit can mean the difference between life and death.

LuVerne Clausen
Danish Culture

Native Americans Who Served in World War II

When I arrived in Australia, I was assigned to the 41st Infantry Division...to B Company of the 163rd Regiment. The 41st Division was composed of Northwestern States National Guard units and was predominantly composed of National Guardsmen from Oregon, Idaho, Montana, and Washington, supplemented by Selective Service enrollees from every state in the Union. Our Indian comrades came from Montana's 163rd Infantry.

I soon learned to respect the American Indian, and I have often said, "If I ever had to fight another war, I would want to fight it with the American Indian."

The day before my twenty-first birthday, I was in New Guinea, and I had been bragging that "tomorrow I am going to be a man. Twenty-one years of age makes me a man."

The word got to a soldier...in charge of a reconnaissance patrol...leaving in the morning. I do not remember the name of this soldier, but he came to me [and] said, "I hear through the grapevine that tomorrow you are going to be a man, and I am going to give you a chance to prove it. Be ready in the morning to join the rest of my squad to go on a reconnaissance patrol. I want you to wear a fatigue hat and tennis shoes, as we do not want to make any more noise than is needed. Throw a bandoleer of ammo around [your] neck just in case you need it, but we will be only out there to gather information, and not to fight." This squad leader was [an] Indian from Montana. The assistant squad leader was also [an] Indian from Montana, and he brought up the rear of the squad.

We were quite a distance in Japanese territory, walking along this trail when our squad leader raised his hands to stop us, and he then motioned us to hide in the brush alongside this trail we were walking on. This we did, and while we were hiding, two Japanese soldiers came walking down the same trail we had been on, talking and laughing as they walked along. When they were far enough away from us, our Indian leader motioned us back on the trail to continue gathering information. I do not know how many miles we were in Japanese territory, but we had walked by old Japanese airplanes that were wrecked on the ground, crossed over small creeks, checked on a bridge to see if it would support one of our tanks, and we thought it would, but later on we found out that it did not support our tanks. When we were through gathering information, we asked our Indian squad leader how he knew that there was someone coming down the trail ahead of us, as we could not hear a thing. He smiled and said, "I can smell them."

I am seventy-one years of age now, and I will never forget how I celebrated my twenty-first birthday. Some of the best soldiers in my opinion were Indian, and they showed remarkable leadership to lead men in time of war.

The roots of multiculturalism are not new; but the true concept is new in the sense that "multi" includes all people. If asked to give their definition of the word "multicultural," everyone's responses would probably be different.

Academic and non-academic corporations use the following specifications in developing effective multicultural programs: **that all people, staff, students, employees, and community members respect their own culture as well as the cultures of others, that each student** or employee can identify positively with the training and working environment's various aspects, and that each individual in the corporation is successful.

Some individuals use multiculturalism as a forum for their views about other cultures, even if those ideas lack historical accuracy or are, at best, half-truths. Several issues have led to debates in multicultural circles—among them, the denigration of the Western World's ideals, activities, and peoples; the curriculum exclusion of some cultural groups' achievements, and the exposure of students and employees to a variety of religious beliefs and practices.

But rather than entering such pointless debates, one might better spend valuable time and resources in opening important avenues for learning with positive results. The greatest opportunities and challenges lie in the development of learning environments, activities and lessons through which every person can succeed and continue to grow. All people are capable of learning and possess the right to work and be taught in ways which will meet their needs as well as the needs of the corporation.

Multiculturalism is not an issue between *majority* and *minority* cultures. In every cultural group, one will find individuals who relate well to all people, regardless of any existing cultural differences. Conversely, one will also find people who cannot or choose not to relate well to others even those within their own cultural group.

One's willingness to learn about a variety of individual cultures must also include a receptivity to accepting the variations within each of those cultures. One generalizes about others, neither realizing the generalization nor the fact that a possible offense has occurred.

Portuguese is spoken in Brazil, for instance, and many Brazilians will be offended if someone addresses them in Spanish, the predominant language in most South American countries.

In the southwestern portion of the United States of America, *Anglo* appears to be an everyday word used to refer to all members of the Caucasian, or white, race. This same word will insult many whites who live in or come from the northeastern states. There, the word refers to people with British American/Protestant origins and the northeasterners more commonly call these people *WASPS*, usually in a derogatory manner.

And many people believe the Jewish American cultures originated in the Middle East or Europe, although thousands of years have created a rich, culturally diverse history of the Jewish people, resulting in Jews living in virtually every corner of the world. A visit to Kaifeng, China, for instance, will bring you to the Chinese community of Orthodox Jews there. You will also find Jews in African nations, South American nations, in the predominantly Catholic countries of Italy, Spain, Ireland, and many others.

In developing this book, we have attempted to avoid generalizing. But even a book this size has its limits. If our effort to broaden views has resulted in our inadvertent failure to communicate any major considerations of a particular culture, we sincerely apologize.

We need to have unity in order to achieve harmony. Unity can be achieved in diversity. Our individual cultural differences offer us avenues of creativity and richness in life. If all of us begin or continue to think in terms of *Unity In Diversity*, we will put this concept into action so every man, woman, and child will receive that which they need and deserve.

A Modern Fable

Once upon a time, way back in history when cavemen chose their mates with clubs, a certain bear decided the time had come for finding his mate. Searching high and low, he finally found the most beautiful female he'd ever seen, and he tried his best to woo her. Sadly, every time he sang that all-time classic hit, *Grizzly's Love Call*, she ran off, leaving him in her dust.

Now this bear had a minor problem, nothing unusual for a bruin his age. He was extremely myopic, a real Mr. Magoo of the animal kingdom. But he **knew** this was true love. His nose led him straight to her.

The harder he tried, the harder she fought, rebuffing his advances. Suddenly, he understood why cavemen clubbed their mates.

It's a long story how he managed a similar feat of clubbing her, but he did—just as he then refused to hear friends' admonishments as they tied her tail to his (while she was still knocked out, of course). When she awoke, she was livid. Such language he'd never heard from a lady before.

And he certainly didn't expect her to continue fighting to what appeared might be his or her death!

When he could take no more, he conceded she'd won, and once again, their tails were free. He had to let her go.

Moral: Even though the bear and the rhinoceros have been unified by having their tails tied together, that does not guarantee unity.

Many people use the terms *unity* and *unification* interchangeably, applying unification techniques to achieve unity. Comprehending the difference between the two words is as important as understanding how these two dissimilar approaches appear when dealing with people and their cultural differences in the real world.

Independent, interdependent—for instance, cooperative learning and working—and dependent relationships should be considered within the unity concept, including interactions ranging from those between two individuals to those between two nations or groups of nations. To achieve unity, we need to understand and apply the concept of interdependence as a foundation for positive relationship building.

The United States Constitution grants specific inalienable freedoms to people who live in America. Regardless of one's religious beliefs, cultural or ethnic background, all people living in the United States of America possess the right to worship, live, and work in a discrimination-free environment. But we also must consciously avoid imposing our beliefs on others through our positions in the workplace or community.

Certainly learning about any particular culture may be linked to developing some understanding of its religious beliefs and customs, but not all people from a given culture will share those beliefs and customs with the majority of that culture. Although one culture's celebration of a specific holiday may be religious, another culture may celebrate the same holiday from a secular perspective. One learns about significant religious customs related to the people of a culture without necessarily concentrating on that culture's predominant religion.

All religious groups deserve respect and consideration according to the following principles and guidelines:

◆ **Everyone believes in** something and/or someone which basically

could be called a religion;
◆ in the two-way process of learning, focus attention on religious beliefs or customs rather than religion;
◆ confirm that all information about religious beliefs or customs is truthful, and note the individual variations within religions rather than making gross generalizations;
◆ utilize community individuals as resources in studies of various religious beliefs and customs;
◆ integrate religious beliefs and customs in the study of a culture;
◆ be sensitive to the sacredness of religious beliefs and customs, being aware that certain songs, objects, and rituals are intended to be kept exclusively within the context of a religion;
◆ be sensitive to your own religious beliefs without compromising your principles during the two-way process of learning about contrasting cultures, beliefs and customs.

Establish a philosophy of cultural diversity, adopting a true and fair approach to cultural presentations, reflecting the cultures of the corporation as well as the local and broader communities even if various cultures are not represented in a specific corporate division.

The multicultural approach encourages everyone in the corporation and the community to be aware of the similarities and differences between and within cultures. Possession of this heightened awareness is conducive to an understanding which can evolve into an appreciation of cultural diversity. Someone who appears different may offer techniques or suggestions to ease the burden of accomplishing a particular task as effectively as if another method had been used. A cultural or physical difference is not intrinsically wrong or something to be feared. Every corporation and community can set goals to select activities from a multitude of cultures which invariably will effectively increase the learner's cognitive, social and personal skills.

The process of developing, implementing, and evaluating multicultural goals and objectives includes an integration of Bloom's "Domains of Learning" and Christiansen's "Stages of Becoming a Multicultural Individual." Figures 1 and 2 on the next page present these concepts.

Multiculturally-based goals and objectives are coded to facilitate the evaluation process by moving from Awareness to the Application Stage, from Lower to Higher Thinking Levels and from Cognitive to the Affective Domains of Learning (see Figure 2).

One would use Figure 2, for instance, to evaluate a teaching or

Figure 1
Correlating Bloom's Domains of Learning with Christiansen's 4 A's of Becoming A Multicultural Individual™

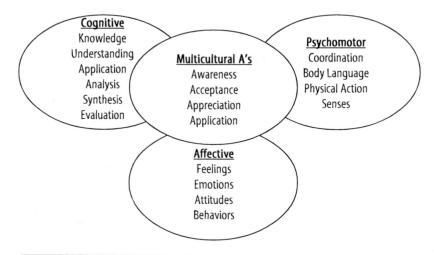

training session in which participants were encouraged to realize that all people possess common feelings. The coding would then read "MS 1" for Multicultural Stage 1, "CD 1" for Cognitive Domain, Level 1, and "AD 1" for Affective Domain, Level 1. The most effective lessons will incorporate one item from each of the major categories (in bold print) in the above chart.

Before a corporation implements staff development and training sessions, instructors leading these components must personally begin to incorporate the 4 A's of Becoming A Multicultural Individual™:

- **Awareness** for the need to work effectively with others, regardless of cultural backgrounds, addressing change as a prerequisite to the process—**seeing and recognizing** the need to change, **believing** one can change, **learning** how to change and **being open** to the opportunity for that change.
- **Acceptance** through acquisition of an understanding of the similarities and differences within and between cultural groups.
- **Appreciation** of people regardless of their individual and/or cultural differences.

Figure 2
Christiansen's Hierarchy
for Developing, Implementing,
and Evaluating Multicultural Goals and Objectives

Multicultural Stages (MS)	Cognitive Domain (CD)	Affective Domain (AD)	Psychomotor Domain (PD)
1. Awareness 2. Acceptance 3. Appreciation 4. Application	1. Knowledge 2. Understanding 3. Application 4. Analysis 5. Synthesis 6. Evaluation	1. Feelings (inner, outer) 2. Emotions (passive, aggressive) 3. Attitudes (likes, dislikes) 4. Behaviors (positive, negative, constructive, destructive)	1. Coordination (mind. body) 2. Body Language (non-verbal, gestures) 3. Physical Action (tactile) 4. Senses (hearing, seeing, touching, tasting, smelling)

● **Application** of the concept that unity in diversity, rather than conformity, can be achieved.

Cultural diversity training should utilize facilitators—selected from a cross-section of employees—rather than presenters or lecturers. This facilitator will interact with a participants, guiding and nurturing discussions but not becoming the limelight figure. Each prospective facilitator must be trained prior to implementing training sessions. If many of these sessions are needed, teams of four to six facilitators can be organized.

If the sponsoring organization doesn't sincerely strive to provide the sensitivity and quality essential to cultural diversity training, the participants will see it as a token gesture. A well-qualified multicultural specialist may be needed to assist in development and implementation in facilitator training and the sessions themselves. If a specialist who is truly a warm, caring multicultural individual is not available on staff, either outside consulting services should be used or a specialist hired.

An old Native American proverb says, "Never judge a man till you walk a mile in his shoes." American history books, generally written from one perspective, tend to encourage students to develop beliefs inconsistent with that particular admonition.

But every argument and every story has at least two sides, and one side isn't always more right than the other. A series of unrelated plays developed from various cultural historical perspectives are available for viewing around the nation and provide an excellent avenue into these perspectives.

Whether or not one has the opportunity to participate in structured cultural diversity training, these plays can also be utilized as a means to develop understanding of these perspectives. Participants in several of these shows have expressed a willingness to go on tour.

Writer/actor Jim Northrup, a member of the Fond du Lac Ojibway (also known as Anishinabeg or Chippewa) tribe, returned to his reservation in northern Minnesota after serving in the armed forces in Vietnam and living in Minneapolis and other large cities.

"My family and I live our lives with the seasons," says Northrup. "Right now, we're getting ready to harvest wild rice and turn it into food." Featured in the September 1994 issue of *Martha Stewart's Living*, Northrup describes his life with his family: "[In the fall] comes moose and deer hunting. Winter is the story telling time of the year. Spring is spear fishing, a hot potato around here. I do it as a treaty right. We also make maple syrup in the spring. In the summer, we make birchbark baskets. Like my parents and grandparents before me, I was born on the 'rez,' live on the 'rez,' and I'll probably die on the 'rez.'"

Northrup's book, a collection of short stories about life on the reservation, *Walking the Rez Road* (Voyageur Press), received the Minnesota and Northeast Minnesota Book Awards. His play, *On the Rez*, produced by the Minnesota Festival Theater, was underwritten by US West Communications. Developed from his newspaper column which appears in the Minneapolis, St. Paul, and Duluth areas, his short stories, and his poetry, Northrup's play tells about life on the reservation through the eyes of someone who lives there.

An equity actor seated in the audience heckles Northrup during the one-and-a-half hour monologue in which Northrup talks about racism, treaty rights, sports mascot issues, and the Gulf War. But Northup's perspective on life isn't always about the heavier issues.

"I'm finally at the age where it doesn't matter if my belly bulges a bit. No matter how many sit-ups I do, the bulge is still there. I did one just the other week. It didn't change a thing," he says in one part of the play.

"I also do commentaries for the Fresh Air Program. When I was young, we had no radio or television. So we told stories," he says about his natural writing talents.

He laughs when asked about prejudice. "It's a daily battle. [When] I leave my home and family, I have to deal with those problems." But he says the problems seem to increase closer to the reservation where he finds what he calls "a hate circle." On the other hand, he says the prejudice appears to lessen, and he's "treasured through contacts" as he gets farther away from the reservation. Northrup says he's interested in touring with the play, which has received excellent reviews.

Not all of these plays will be suitable for viewing by young children, but the Nicodemus Group in Bogue, Kansas, has developed age-appropriate educational presentations on *The Life and Times of the Buffalo Soldiers*. These dramatic performances portray buffalo soldiers from the post-Civil War period. In the K-6 format, a uniformed soldier from 1882 visits classes, speaking in first person about his life and times. Hands-on activities enrich children's learning experience.

The general format of the Nicodemus Group presentations takes the audience into the daily life of Congressional Medal of Honor Recipient Brent Woods, who describes the worm-infested hard tack and spoiled pork they ate, their military pay, guard duty at a railroad worksite and a subsequent encounter with a Sioux warrior, and the battle where he won his medal. A question and answer period follows the performance.

As of the mid-1990s, the production had toured school districts in Colorado, Kansas, Wisconsin, and Kentucky. Angela Bates, Nicodemus Group president, expressed the Group's willingness to travel anywhere they're invited in the United States of America.

Actors/playwrights Lane Nishikawa and Victor Talmadge wrote *Gate of Heaven*, the two-man story about a fifty-year friendship between a Holocaust survivor and a Japanese veteran of World War

II. The play, produced by a San Francisco theater company, has received rave reviews of audiences at the Japanese Cultural and Community Center, the Osher Marin Jewish Community Center, and the *Hokubei Mainichi* newspaper. Nishikawa said he and Talmadge are willing to go on tour with this outstanding play.

According to one newspaper columnist based in Raleigh, North Carolina is the first state in the nation that developed the concept of outdoor plays. *Pathway to Freedom*, performed in Snow Camp, southeast of Greensboro, is the only outdoor drama about the Underground Railroad. When describing North Carolina's unique places to visit, reporter Julie Ann Powers wrote in *The News And Observer* (September 4, 1994), "the actors, directors, and writers devote themselves to helping present generations make peace with a cheerless chapter in history: slavery." Powers calls the play "a moving one of healing and humanity." Although touring doesn't appear to be possible, visitors to North Carolina should make a concerted effort to see this outdoor drama. In the brochure promoting *Pathway to Freedom*, the Snow Camp Historical Drama Society says, "The play reinforces the thought that cooperative and sympathetic action to support human dignity is more important than violence and revenge in advancing civilization. It urges us to work for what ought to be, even against odds."

The Snow Camp Historical Drama Society's dramatic production *The Sword of Peace* focuses on the struggles of the peaceful, nonviolent Quakers during the American Revolution.

Even visits to museums provide a means of understanding various cultures.

◆ Dorothy Spruill Redford linked the enslaved blacks and antebellum plantation owners at a North Carolina historic site called Somerset Place. Redford simply wanted to answer her daughter's questions about their own family history. Ten years later, she had located thousands of descendants of the original 350 who had been enslaved at Somerset. Somerset Place, about three hours north of Raleigh, North Carolina, welcomes thousands of schoolchildren each year from both North Carolina and Virginia.

◆ Alabama's Birmingham Civil Rights Institute illustrates the post-World War I Civil Rights Movement through the 1980s, using multimedia presentations, music and storytelling.

◆ In Memphis, Tennessee, you'll find the $8.8 million National Civil Rights Museum, documenting the nation's painful growth.

◆ In the Northeast, a visit to Ellis Island should be a priority for everyone, whether or not their ancestors actually entered the United States of America through this particular door. Despite the usual noise spilling from tourist-filled halls, the haunting impact of seeing where thousands and thousands of immigrants waited to enter the United States or to return home is not soon forgotten.

◆ In Washington, D.C., the United States Holocaust Memorial Museum impresses visitors with a history one wishes never happened and prays will never be allowed to occur again.

◆ The New Echota State Historic Site near Calhoun, Georgia, retraces the Cherokee nation's history from 1819 to 1832.

◆ Carved in the round, the 641-foot long, 560-foot high sculpture of Crazy Horse will be completed at a site four miles north of Custer, South Dakota. Eventually, said museum officials of this nonprofit institution, the sculpture will overlook a university, museum, and medical training center. Sculptor Korczak Ziolkowski, who worked on Mount Rushmore in 1939, was asked by the Oglala Sioux Indians to carve Crazy Horse—the choice of Native Americans across the United States.

◆ A Danish museum retells the history of American Danes in Elkhorn, Iowa, along Interstate 80.

◆ The Spanish History Museum in Albuquerque, New Mexico, houses the little-known history of the Spanish people in the United States, including how the Spanish helped the colonies during the American Revolution.

◆ In Phoenix, Arizona, the Heard Museum contains the most extensive collection of Indian art in the Southwest. Also in Phoenix, one can explore a prehistoric Hohokam Indian archeology site at the Pueblo Grande Museum.

◆ The Whitman Mission National Historic Site in southeastern Washington, a landmark on the Oregon Trail, includes an Indian mission and school dating back to 1836.

◆ Colorado's Anasazi Heritage Center in Dolores and Mesa Verde Tours in Mancos provide tours back in time to a culture no longer in existence.

◆ Temple Mickve Israel in Savannah, Georgia, houses artifacts, including the Sephar Torah, of Spanish and German Jews who arrived in Savannah just five months after the city's founding.

◆ The Canterbury, New Hampshire, Shaker Village affords visitors the opportunity to see the self-contained Shaker lifestyle of the mid-1700s. Although this religious sect virtually disappeared in the early 1900s, many Shaker beliefs lived on even into the 1990s— among them, equal rights and shared work.

◆ Delaware's Winterthur Museum, Garden and Library in Wilmington offers the richest and largest collection of America's decorative arts made or used between 1640 and 1860. Two buildings—a composite of 175 period rooms and 3 galleries—house interactive displays and hands-on exhibits on the history and development of these arts which focus on social customs and artistic content.

But these places of interest for enhancing one's understanding of America's many cultural groups are meant to provide a starting point for your own search across the nation. If living history museums pique your curiosity even more, consider that simply one more avenue to explore.

◆ Massachusetts' abundance of living history museums will take you from Old Sturbridge, circa 1830, to Salem's Pioneer Village of 1630, to Plimouth Plantation (in Plymouth) of the same period.

◆ Virginia's living history includes, of course, Williamsburg, the Museum of American Frontier Culture at Staunton—giving the perspective of German, Northern Irish, and English settlers arriving in the United States from the 1600s through the 1800s—the Meadow Farm Museum in Richmond, and several others.

◆ The Fort Selden State Monument at Radium Springs, New Mexico, General Douglas MacArthur's boyhood home, features living history programs in the summer. During the rest of the year, appointments can be scheduled to see these productions.

◆ St. Mary's City, two hours south of Baltimore, Maryland, offers visitors a look at colonial life in the 1600s. In contrast, the Oliver H. Kelley Farm in Elk River, Minnesota, north of Minneapolis, portrays agricultural life in 1867.

◆ One can also tap into living history, although not in the structured form of a museum, with a visit to an Amish community. Several exist in the nation, including those in Northern Indiana, Eastern Pennsylvania, North Central Ohio, and Iowa.

◆ Just off US Highway 90 in Louisiana, a 22-acre living history museum at Vermilionville focuses on Cajun, Creole, and Chitimacha life, featuring Acadian crafts, an outdoor theater in the round with presentations about 19th Century pioneer daily life, social history, music, and so on.

◆ In Urbandale, Iowa, near Des Moines, one can tap into 350 years of American agricultural history at Living History Farms. Among the variety of farms and artisan demonstrations depicted are the 17th Century Prairie and Woodland cultures of the Ioway Indians.

◆ In Mississippi, Florewood River Plantation State Park recreates an 1850s working plantation. Located near Greenwood, the plantation features a blacksmith shop, plantation store, a school, and more.

◆ Twelve acres of more than eighty historic structures portray America's growth from an agrarian society into an industrial world leader at the Henry Ford Museum & Greenfield Village in Dearborn, Michigan. Although automotive giant Henry Ford founded this intensive historical complex in 1929, neither the Ford Motor Company nor the Ford Foundation have any affiliation with the nonprofit, educational institution. The Henry Ford Museum & Greenfield Village utilizes displays related to American mechanized and technological innovations, national landmarks, famous Americans and average citizens since the birth of the nation. Within this gigantic monument to the American people, the people at Firestone farm—circa 1880—never step out of character and transport visitors back to the 19th Century.

◆ At Mystic (Connecticut) Seaport, one can visit a coastal New England village and learn about maritime life and whaling in the 19th Century.

◆ The villagers at Conner Prairie in Noblesville, Indiana, bring the year 1836 back to life. Like many of the living history museums around the nation, Conner Prairie also offers visitors an opportunity to try hands-on activities.

◆ At the Billings Farm & Museum in Woodstock, Vermont, the daily life and culture of a 19th Century hill farm family are portrayed through hands-on activities, the changing roles of family members and folklore. One unique characteristic of this particular museum is its still present existence as a contemporary dairy farm.

◆ The Farmer's Museum in Cooperstown, New York, focuses on the American Industrial Age from the growth of American farms to life in rural communities during the 1800s.

◆ In Eagle, near Milwaukee, 19th Century Old World Wisconsin shows a rural village's growth through the efforts of 16 ethnic groups. Both the Farmer's Museum in Cooperstown and the 19th Century Old World Wisconsin pride themselves on cultivating the old varieties of farm products.

◆ In Bristol, Rhode Island, one can travel back to the 1790s at the Coggeshall Farm Museum.

Again, one should not consider this a comprehensive or conclusive list of historic places portraying various cultures in the United States. These merely represent the vast variety available for viewing across the nation.

During the summer of 1994, University of Washington education professor James Banks spoke at a retreat for principals in North Carolina. *The Charlotte Observer* quoted him:

> One of the myths of multicultural education is that it's for them, not us. For blacks and Hispanics, not all of us. Often, when I go into a school I ask what kinds of multicultural education they offer. And I get the answer: none. "We don't have any minorities," a principal will say. Then I ask what kinds of Medieval and Renaissance education they offer, and they say, "Oh, we have excellent units on Medieval times and the Renaissance." But you don't have any Medieval or Renaissance people in your school. It's not just for them. We're all in this together...
>
> A...misconception of multicultural education is that it will divide the nation. What's that assuming? It assumes the nation is united. But this nation is deeply divided along racial and other lines. Multicultural education is not about dividing a united nation, but about uniting a deeply divided nation.

There are two sides, two perceptions to every story, and we must never lose sight of that reality. To one person, home in the United States of America may be the place where that person's family comes from one race and one culture. To someone else, home may unite more than one race and culture in the immediate or even extended family.

At times, that structure becomes still more complex, with two people of different races linked through marriage and one partner's close relative married to someone from a third race. One person with the heritage of several ethnic cultures and one race, spoke about subsequently growing up in a biracial home.

A Monoracial Child Who Grew Up in a Biracial Home

Basically, it was different at first. It took time to adjust to it. There was a lot of communication difficulty. There still are. It takes a lot more working out. I'm my own person. My dad is his own person. I didn't look at it as a biracial thing. It was a new marriage.

Not all monoracial children from biracial homes respond well to their new lifestyles. Many bury the feelings and negative experiences that often accompany their growing up years. Their attempts to absorb new experiences in the home are often mocked by other children and are patronized by adults who have made stereotypical assumptions about the child's family.

When other children are born into the biracial union, the child may feel different and may long to possess the same genes as the new siblings. Even if the child belongs to the so-called majority culture in the world outside the family home, the child—at home—may feel like a minority.

The family home is the most important and often the only world the child knows. Lacking acceptance outside the home can be dealt with, if the child feels accepted and develops self-acceptance inside the home. Unfortunately, despite the family's efforts, achieving these ideals isn't always possible, which may result in the child's subsequent rejection—at least for a time—of all personal cultural identification.

But people are people, and our willingness to be sensitive to others—whether or not their perspectives agree with ours—can prevent arguments and even wars. Rigidly adhering to beliefs that promote insensitivity among people accomplishes nothing and inevitably harms everyone. As the cycle of insensitivity continues, its painful results eventually can spread until the final sequence of the chain ricochets back to us or our children. Stopping that cyclical chain is up to each one of us.

American servicemen stationed in Vietnam during the War often left pregnant Vietnamese sweethearts behind. Some American GIs knew; some didn't. Some were devastated at being forced to return to the United States without these women and their Vietnamese and American offspring.

The United States government and many nonprofit agencies subsequently brought these children and their Vietnamese parents to the United States. In Vietnam, many had been victims of discrimination, perhaps as a combination of their birthright blend of two cultures and geographical races and the reminder of a war no one really wanted.

Racial persecution often follows these children to America, where people generally call them Amerasians, separating them from other children with a similar birthright blend of cultures. Segregating these children from others with similar blended heritages appears to stem from both the American and Vietnamese communities. But Amerasian, broken into its root words, is the combined form of American and Asian, and the children of these two backgrounds share much in common. Both have one American parent. Both have one parent from an Asian nation.

Those children who have been the products of the Vietnam War, however, often receive federal benefits and scholarships or other educational considerations not bestowed on other Amerasian children. Between these groups of children, the native tongues, circumstances of birth and lifestyles may differ in America.

Some Amerasian children were born into two races and developed an understanding of both of their parents' cultures. Others were raised with one culture and remain uncertain about the process of integrating both into their lives. Some wish to identify with only one of their birthright cultures.

Kim Young
Amerasian: Jewish, Italian, and Chinese Cultures
Gifted Student, Age 10

When I was five, we lived in an apartment. I was playing [outside] with another boy my age. [My mother was supervising us. When it was time to go] inside, I told him I'd see him tomorrow. Simultaneously, my mother and he both said, "No, you won't." But he added, "because all white kids go to school."

At the time, I didn't really understand what prejudice was, so I had mixed feelings. I didn't even understand what he was talking about with colors. When my older brother went to junior high, I played with [kids from] many cultures, and that's why I didn't understand.

In elementary school, a teacher didn't help me with my math because she didn't know how to handle my age [difference from my other classmates], or maybe it was because of my difference in culture. Possibly both.

Any time there's discrimination, I feel like I'd like to knock somebody's lights out.

One boy, when he got mad at me or when he just wanted to get my attention, would call me "Chinese Kid" or "China Boy."

My mother is a big mouth about racism. She won't stand for it.

280

Also, all of my different cultures help me out. If I see someone who is discriminated against or who is prejudiced, I get very angry.

One of my teachers told us he felt that George Washington and Thomas Jefferson were two of the biggest racists in American history. He'd give us trivia questions and gave us candy when we answered "Washington and Jefferson" to his questions about who the two biggest racists were.

Many people, because of my tan, ask if I'm Hispanic. They tell jokes about different cultures. A lot of kids ask if I'm Chinese, why aren't I pure white.

In 1989, the European Jewish Scholars Conference was held in Berlin, Germany. Rabbi Albert Plotkin attended the conference and told us what happened.

Rabbi Albert Plotkin
Reform Jewish Rabbi

The Vice Mayor (of Berlin) was giving the official greeting at the international delegates' reception as part of an official celebration. Russian Jews couldn't come. It was before Gorbachev.

The Vice Mayor, a very astute, charming man who welcomed us said, "I know how difficult it is for you to come to this city where so many Jews were expelled, where so many Jews were sent to the concentration camps. I was born after the war.

"We cannot undo what our parents and grandparents did to your people. But we are a new generation and a new Germany. We want to start a new relationship with the Jewish community.

"The first Jew who came to Berlin was Moses Mendelssohn, and he was asked, 'Why do you want to come to Berlin?'

"He replied, 'I came to learn.'

"At one time, Berlin was a great Jewish center for learning, and we hope someday that can be reestablished, and Jewish academies can be recreated. They were an important part of our culture.

"So I ask you to give us, the new Germans, a chance to improve our relationship and to try to build bridges. We live with a wall, but there is no wall between us and the Jewish community.

"We welcome you Jewish scholars back to Berlin. We are trying to rebuild what was destroyed. Please bring back to your community this message of hope for our children and our children's children, to remind you that we are reopening today a new chapter of understanding between all minorities here in Germany. I know it is not going to be easy and how difficult it is for both sides. Let's give each other a chance.

"I'm sure we may look forward to a bright future."

Not word for word, that was the impact of his words. I told him that was the finest statement from any German I have ever heard.

We must recognize that we all have biases and prejudices. Yet we need to be accountable for our acceptance or rejection of people whose race, ethnicity, or culture differ from our own. This chapter seeks to make us aware of our ability to understand and overcome prejudice in all facets of our lives.

There are absolutes regardless of our awareness and/or acceptance of facts, some of which we call laws of nature. Prejudice breeds prejudice, and hatred inspires hatred. Society's survival depends on transmitting certain absolutes—among them, the respect for life and people. No society can function without strong common bonds passed between generations.

The **4 A's of Becoming A Multicultural Individual**™ can be successful in any corporation, academic or nonacademic. But those who implement the cultural diversity training **must** be true multicultural people who follow its specific directives. **We cannot take any responsibility for the misuse of this model.** With cultural diversity, having no training is better than providing a token and inadequate session.

In the schools, cultural diversity training has been successful, even where these institutions have historically experienced problems with discipline, low academic achievement, and teacher burnout. When used and made an integral component of a school's operation, students can become motivated to learn, and teacher morale can be dramatically improved.

The challenge of moving from monocultural to multicultural

thinking, attitudes, and behaviors can be achieved with a limited budget. One of the major keys lies in establishing a strategic plan statement with a mission honoring cultural diversity, a policy disavowing discrimination, and a belief that cultural diversity is enriching and vital to students and society, that all children can learn. Cultural diversity serves as a foundation strategy for the development of a multicultural curriculum and cultural diversity training, infusing quality multicultural instructional resources representative of cultural groups in the school or district population.

Once everyone has the same goals, the same mental picture of an anticipated productive learning environment and its accompanying academic and social results, modifying the classroom into a multicultural arena for growth becomes possible. People—not as statistics or with labels placed on specific groups of individuals according to their genetic and/or heritage variables—make the difference in our transitions to multicultural classrooms, schools, and districts. People need to relate to one another, not as groups, rather as individuals.

In becoming multicultural individuals, we achieve the objective of *Unity in Diversity*. Unity, in general, has often been perceived as conformity, but history has demonstrated, time and again, conformity cannot be achieved without force. Yet a successful transition to a multicultural classroom can be achieved by mutual respect and, within reason, seeing the differences between people, their methods of doing things, and their opportunities for growth as well as recognizing the similarities between people, regardless of their cultural backgrounds.

No one can force another into becoming multicultural. The changes must begin on the inside, gradually working their way to the outside through attitudinal and behavioral changes, by developing an awareness and acquiring an understanding of the differences and similarities between people. We must learn to appreciate others, no matter their cultural backgrounds, and we must begin to reflect positive attitudes in our classrooms, schools, and communities toward all people, regardless of their cultural backgrounds.

Multiculturalism needs to focus on the word **multi**, meaning **all**, rather than focusing on bi- or triculturalism. Multiculturally-based education works most effectively when multiculture is infused into every classroom's curriculum, not just in a single discipline. Rather than forcing multiculturalism on teachers, they must willingly accept the concept and be given time outside of regular hours to develop the multicultural curriculum.

A few minutes in regular staff meetings is not the time to deal with multiculturalism. Significant and meaningful staff development needs to be incorporated into the planned structure. Unlike other areas within the curriculum, the unique concept of multicultural education requires a change in attitudes, and that change can be deeply rooted and extremely personal.

Successful multicultural classrooms, no matter the school's location in relation to the rest of the country, start with a district level multicultural specialist who is a multicultural individual, not necessarily in looks, but in attitudes reflecting a respect for each individual and a strong background in curriculum and staff development and teaching. The multicultural specialist will be able to assist in developing quality resources for staff and community. And, of course, if the specialist sees a lack in a particular area of those resources, this individual should be able to develop additional materials.

Next, a community-school-based multiculturally-oriented strategic plan must be developed. New, not revised, multicultural and cultural diversity staff development sessions for all staff members need to be implemented. Teachers need to be empowered and encouraged to develop a school-level multiculturally-based curriculum, ensuring adherence to state and district concepts, skills, goals, objectives, and so on. Teachers and staff members must be given sensitivity and time in changing their own attitudes and behaviors, providing those attitudes and behaviors don't directly interfere with state and local level goals. The key to motivating multiculturalism among our students lies in working toward *Unity in Diversity*, not in conforming.

Had multicultural attitudes and behaviors been adopted throughout the United States of America years ago, the following epitaph might not have been written: Across the street from the Birmingham Civil Rights Institute sits the 16th Street Baptist Church, where a September 15, 1963, bombing killed four children at Sunday school. The memorial plaque reads, "*May Men Learn to Replace Bitterness and Violence with Love and Understanding.*"

It's time to do things right, recognizing that cultural diversity at its best is *Unity in Diversity*.

Part IV

Celebration

Chapter 12

CELEBRATING
OUR DIVERSITY

By the time you've reached this chapter, we hope your perception of *diversity*—its definition and the personal experiences of people from various cultural backgrounds—will be a positive one. Now we unite diversity and what may appear to be a contradiction in terms—*celebration*—as a conclusion to our focus on multiculturalism.

We've provided you with an opportunity to experience the common bonds among all of us, regardless of our own individual cultural backgrounds. By recognizing these ties, we've opened the door to eliminating personal prejudice and discrimination from our lives without regard to anyone's race, religion, gender, national origins, or culture.

From this point on, we'll explore a variety of themes where cultural groups are perceived through their celebrations of particular themes or events. Thousands of cultures from around the world celebrate, so mentioning each one among the following is a virtual impossibility. Celebrating allows us to overcome negative feelings about others whose heritage may differ from ours. We hope the themes we've chosen will serve as an example of the similarities between cultures, yet their origins and homelands may remain years and miles apart.

In Chapter 7, we touched on the differences between calendars as we travel around the globe. Historically, most calendars have been based on the earth/sun—solar—or the earth/moon—lunar—relationship. The lunar-based Chinese calendar represents the longest formalized system of recording time in world history.

The solar Christian Ecclesiastical calendar is based on specific events in Jesus' life. The lunar Islamic calendar is based on key events in Mohammed's life.

In 1582, Pope Gregory XIII reformed the Julian calendar into what became the Gregorian calendar. The Roman Catholic Church officially adopted this new system, which was eventually accepted by much of Europe and is used as a primary or secondary calendar throughout the world today. The Orthodox Christians use the Gregorian calendar as a whole, although the Julian calendar influences the Orthodox holy days.

While space limitations in this chapter force us to limit a potentially endless list of world celebrations and festivals, several excellent calendars are available through direct marketing and retail outlets to provide anyone with additional avenues of exploration.

World Calendars in History

I. Ancient

A. Babylonian
B. Era of Nebuchadnezzar
C. Macedonian
D. Hebrew
E. Seleucid
F. Olympiad Era
G. Era of Tyre
H. Roman
I. Era of Armenians
J. Islamic
K. Fasli (Soor San)
L. Zoroastrian
M. Yezdezred
N. Jelali

II. Western

A. Early Northern European
B. Julian
C. Gregorian
D. Christian
E. Calendar of Saints
F. French Revolutionary
G. Soviet Ecclesiastical
H. New Year's Day

II.Central America

A. Mayan   B. Aztec

IV. African

A. Egyptian   C. Ethiopian
B. Coptic

V. Modern Near East

A. Iranian   B. Afghanistanian

VI. Far East

A. Chinese   B. Tibetan

VII. Southeast Asia

A. Akbar   D. Burmese
B. Fasli   E. Arakanse
C. Parasuram

VIII. Indian

Anatole France said, "To know is nothing; to imagine is everything." We've provided a focus key to help you hone in on ways in which you can use these celebration themes. But be sure to use your imagination to modify these themes for your own needs. Many work interchangeably.

Focus Key
Travel—❋
Organized Group—◎
Home Use—❋

Expand your horizons, learn more about other cultures, and use your imagination to assist you in starting your own festivities from around the world!

National & International Holidays & Celebrations

United Nations Day, October 24, celebrates the UN's 1945 founding. Historically, the United States President proclaims this a day when everyone—from top government levels to individuals—honors the UN's efforts for world peace in scheduled programs. Modify other holiday celebrations, focusing on their themes—**World Children's Day,** April 24; **International Labor Day,** May 1; **World Communications Day,** May 17; **World Environment Day,** June 5; **International Literacy Day,** September 8; **International Day of Peace,** September 20; **World Gratitude Day,** September 21; **Universal Children's Day and World Habitat Day,** October 3; **International Day for the Elderly,** October 9; **Human Rights Day,** December 10.

* Tour the United Nations in New York City to learn about this organization's critical work. Next, appreciate many world cultures' artistic efforts at the Metropolitan Museum of Art. For dinner, taste a culture's food you've never tried before.

* Plan a world cultures celebration. Parents bring ethnic dishes to share at a school dinner. Class presentations about the classroom's, school's, community's, or nation's cultures. Participants may elect to wear ethnic clothing—their own, or that of a nation being studied. Art projects for use as decorations include making different nations' flags. Play authentic ethnic music during dinner. Encourage ethnic-based talent shows, combining amateur and professional talents if budget allows. For corporate celebrations, include an international dining room menu and special global programs on business techniques or customs of other nations. Companies and schools may join forces for a community-wide effort.

* At home, modify the festivities. Family members pick nations to represent, using library aids. Plan a simple global menu everyone helps to make. After dinner, play a game with an international focus—either one already in existence or one you've created about the UN and world nations.

New Year's Day celebrates the first day of the calendar year. Many holidays, including New Year's, seem to come with prepacked mythology and superstitions. Without buying into them, looking at how they've historically played a part in the development of celebrations can be fun too. Yet one should remember, calendars are human concepts, and the dates on which we celebrate any holiday are arbitrary decisions. Perhaps no better holiday than New Year's points this out.

The United States of America traditionally celebrates New Year's Day on January 1, although nearly everyone else around the world celebrates the birth of the new year according to their cultural or religious calendars.

In America, of course, one can head for the crunch of the crowds in New York City's Times Square, Chicago's State Street, Los Angeles or any other number of large cities across the nation. And certainly there's the glut of televised festivities from most of these places too.

On New Year's Day, many Americans attend religious services at their place of worship while others stay at home to nurse hangovers they already regret. Whether one leans toward the revelry or the reverent, both may be leftovers from similar celebrations in colonial New England. Yet in contemporary America, in nearly every household across the nation, television sets will—at some time on New Year's Day—tune in to one of the spectacular parades announcing the arrival of collegiate championship football games in the afternoon.

Julius Caesar actually established the first New Year's Day on January 1, 46 years before the birth of Christ. Caesar dedicated this first day of the first month to Janus, the Roman god of gates, doors, and beginnings. Like those who look to the past, regretting yesterday's mistakes, and those who look to the future, eager to start again, Romans believed Janus had two faces—one looking to the past, one looking to the future.

Many people generally view New Year's as a time to make resolutions, although not all actually keep their resolutions—much less committing them to paper! Symbolically, however, New Year's is a psychological time of new beginnings. If the past year has been less than productive, one looks forward to the promise of a bright new start in the coming year.

Several cultures' celebrations of the new year appear interwoven despite the miles, languages, and even thousands of years that might logically separate them. Often, one culture's customary new year's celebration will show in another's celebration of a different occasion.

In Belgium, children write New Year's messages to their parents. On New Year's Day, the children read these decorated paper messages to their parents. Perhaps this Belgian custom inspired the American tradition of making resolutions.

Until the 1800s, husbands in England gave money to their wives to buy pins. From the American and English perspective, this custom gave rise to the term "pin money." But giving money for the new year is far from being solely an English custom: At the new year, the Chinese give red envelopes with an even—lucky—number of coins inside!

To the ancient Persians, their gifts of eggs for the new year were thought to bring productiveness to the recipient. The practice of giving hard-boiled red eggs, announcing the birth of a baby, continued among Chinese traditionalists who maintained this custom well into the 1990s. The use of eggs for celebrating holidays or events appears to be a universal intercultural theme.

To the Scottish people, New Year's Eve is known as *Hogmanay*, when friends and family gather to sing *Auld Lang Syne*. According to superstitions, if a dark-haired man is the first person—first-footer—to enter one's home after the stroke of midnight, people inside the home will have good luck in the coming year.

Russian Orthodox New Year's starts on January 14. Iran's new year, *No Ruz*—New Day—coincides with the spring solstice. Followers of Islam begin the new year on the first day of Muharram, their first month.

The Jewish New Year, *Rosh Hashanah*—Head of the Year—on the first day of Tishri, the first month of the Jewish calendar, marks the start of the holiest period of the year for the Jewish people. Coming at the end of the summer or at the beginning of the fall season, *Rosh Hashanah* precedes the holiest day, *Yom Kippur*—the Day of Atonement. The tradition of dipping apples in honey during *Rosh Hashanah* symbolizes the wish for a sweet, fruitful, prosperous new year.

At the Kremlin Palace of Congresses in Moscow, Russia, the enormous New Year Tree welcomes visitors to a warm winter dramatization of a fairy tale. Russia's version of Santa Claus, Grandfather Frost, and the Snow Maiden, his helper, present gifts to the children.

In Japan, people pray at their places of worship and enjoy red snapper for luck in the new year. Sweet-smelling pine boughs and rice cakes adorn homes of Japanese people who traditionally believe one should begin the new year without debts.

Many European countries count on good luck for the new year with a roast pig. In Greece, however, the person who finds the good luck coin inside the *peta*, a New Year's cake, enjoys that luck for the entire coming year. In the southern portions of the United States, many people believe eating black-eyed peas brings good luck in the coming year. Boiled new rice brings luck to homes in the southern portions of India.

The superstition that evil spirits are frightened away by noise may have been the catalyst for noisy New Year's celebrations in China and other countries. Many Chinese traditionally celebrate the new year with festivities spanning a four-day period. On mainland China, however, the celebration which occurs on the first new moon— between mid-January and mid-February—has been put aside for a three-day Spring Festival, beginning January 1.

In the United States, many people from many cultures look forward to the feasting and festivities that accompany Chinese New Year's celebrations. From the dancing dragon to the gaily costumed participants, the bangs and pops of the colorful parade winding through the larger cities' Chinatowns delights young and old throughout the nation.

At one time or another during the year, dazzling displays light the night skies of cities around the world, thanks to the Chinese invention of fireworks. Gala pyrotechnic shows paint the skies over the majority of cities across the United States as part of a national July 4 birthday celebration.

✸ But the United States is far from alone in celebrating a national day of independence. Canada's **Canada Day**, for instance, the equivalent of **American Independence Day**, falls on July 1. As a result, around July 1, the party—with more than 100 free events, parades and performances—begins for the **International Freedom Festival**, honoring the long-lasting friendship between the United States of America and Canada. Halfway through this two-nation, two-week long monumental birthday party, more than 3500 fireworks fill the skies with the largest annual continental—and maybe the world's largest—display of color. More than 3,000,000 people have visited the festival each year since its 1959 inception. Held on the Detroit River, between Detroit, Michigan, and Windsor, Ontario, Canada, the event was first created to honor Queen Elizabeth II on her historic visit to Windsor. Promoters say this is the world's most extensive trans-border festival.

⊛ Plan joint picnics for two organizations, corporations, or communities. Be creative in developing the day's fun events, planning two events into games wherever realistically possible—for instance, a baseball game **and** a soccer game. Remember, America's soccer is internationally called football! Make efforts to establish relationships with Canadian organizations, corporations or communities of similar size and composition. Ideally, both sides should strive to share successful and positive methods and ideas.

⋇ Modify and use the organizational concept with two families or neighborhoods. Establish a relationship and share ideas. Research to learn more about the cultures and lifestyles of other nations. Then adapt similar Independence Day plans with organizations and communities in other nations.

The following nations' or leaders' birthdays fall between June 14 and July 14: **Iceland**, June 17; **Egypt**, June 18 (National Day, July 23); **Luxembourg** (Grand Duke's Birthday), June 23; **Mozambique**, June 25; **Madagascar**, June 26; **Djibouti**, June 27; **Zaire**, June 30; **Burundi & Rwanda**, July 1; **Cape Verde & Venezuela**, July 5; **Comoros & Malawi**, July 6; **Solomon Islands**, July 7; **Bahamas**, July 10; **Sao Tomé e Principe**, July 12; **France** (Bastille Day), July 14.

Celebrate Mexico's **Cinco de Mayo (May 5)** holiday in Texas, New Mexico, Arizona, and California. Especially in the larger cities, Mexico's sights, sounds and flavors come alive in the fabulous fiestas celebrating Mexico's independence from France.

❤ Visit Cinco de Mayo celebrations in one of the larger cities in the Southwest—especially in San Antonio or El Paso, Texas; Santa Fe, New Mexico; Phoenix, Arizona; Los Angeles, California. Look for the best celebrations in southwestern communities with the largest Mexican population bases. El Paso, Texas, truly honors Cinco de Mayo festivities with drama, song and dance at the Chamizal National Memorial.

Mexicans in the Southwest enjoy the **Celebracion de la Independencia de España (September 15-16)** festivities, commemorating Mexico's independence from Spain. Mexico City's holiday hoopla far surpasses similar holiday fun in the United States. Historically, the "Father of Mexican Independence," Father Hidalgo, had urged the people of a little town, Dolores, to rebel against Spain's rule. His sermon became known as the *Grito de Dolores*, the Cry of Dolores. In Mexico's festivities today, the President of Mexico repeats the *Grito*. In the United

States, small celebrations include the *Grito*, which has become a symbol of the strength of the Mexican people. The heroes of the movement—Miguel Hidalgo y Costilla, Father Hidalgo, and Josefa Ortiz de Dominguez—are remembered in the words provided by the San Antonio, Texas, Northside Independent School District bilingual teachers:

Grito de Dolores
Leader: *Viva Miguel Hidalgo y Costilla.*
Response: *¡Viva!*
Leader: *Viva Josefa Ortiz de Dominguez.*
Response: *¡Viva!*
Leader: *¡Viva la Independencia!*
Response: *¡Viva!*
Leader: *¡Viva Mexico!*
Response: *¡Viva!*

❋ Festivities for the *Celebracion de la Independencia de España* tend to be more compact in the United States of America; these too are well worth visiting. Look especially in the heavier Mexican population-based cities mentioned earlier. El Paso, Texas, joins forces with their neighbors in Juarez, Mexico, for a fabulous fiesta of fireworks, song, and dance.

"Viva El Paso" (July-August), held in an outdoor canyon amphitheater, captures the city's history in a two-country blend of drama, dance and song. In **March**, a classical Spanish dramatic competition, *Siglo de Oro* (Century of Gold), presents melodrama dating to the early 1500s at the Chamizal National Memorial in El Paso. At the same stadium, the **International Festival** *de la Zarzuela,* a celebration of Spanish operettas from Latin America, takes place from **July** to **August,** and the **International Mariachi Fiesta** in El Paso, features talent from both sides of the border. A multitude of celebrities and mariachi groups and the coronation of the festival queen help to celebrate El Paso's *Fiesta de Las Flores* (Festival of Flowers) during **Labor Day Weekend's** three days of song, dance, and food.

◉ Adapt United Nations Day celebrations to a Mexican-oriented focus. Menus and dishes can be structured with a Mexican theme, reflecting the fiesta mood. Decorations can include colorful paper cut-outs. Continue efforts to reach into the international community. Corporations can find similar corporations in Mexico with whom positive relationships can be established. Corporations can also make an effort to adopt a community, to develop interpersonal relationships with less fortunate citizens in individual communities. The Mexican consulate may be able to assist interested companies in these goals. If your community hasn't already done so, encourage officials to initiate steps to get involved with foreign exchange programs bringing international students to participating high schools across the nation. **Sister Cities International**—120 S. Tayne St., Alexandria, Virginia 22314—established in 1971, pairs almost 800 American cities with more than 1,100 foreign cities in eighty-seven countries. One facet of this wonderful project is its selection of high school student teams to serve as community ambassadors to sister cities overseas. Schools can also look into **Hands Across the Border**, a program encouraging intercultural understanding between American and Mexican schoolchildren.

꙳ In creative homes, try to decorate your eating area in a Mexican motif. Plan a fiesta party menu with fun foods, and, if possible, get into the mood with gay mariachi music. If you have children, are any of them taking Spanish at school? Encourage them to work with you to make this celebration an especially meaningful one. To round out the day, involve the family in a discussion about some facet of life in Mexico. If your family is more hands-on-oriented, consider making a Mexican handicraft as a family working together, or let each family member create their own. One note of caution: Southwest and Tex-Mex cuisine is not the same as authentic Mexican cooking. If you would like to try the recipes of any particular culture, consider asking a person from that culture to suggest a favorite cookbook collection of authentic recipes from their culture. Next, of course, check the shelves at the public library.

Our inclusion of Canadian and Mexican celebrations in the United States of America is intended to give examples of the wonderful wealth of festivities from a variety of cultures across the nation. But one's attendance at a Mexican fiesta is not and should not be construed to be the same as festivals emanating from the many other Spanish-speaking territories and countries.

Puerto Rico Day (July 25) in the United States is called **Commonwealth Day** in Puerto Rico. Miami's and New York City's celebrations are among the best known in the Union, but these festivities liven other American cities' streets too.

The Cuban festival of **Calle Ocho** in Miami, Florida, claims to be one of the nation's largest celebrations. Over one million people from many Latin cultures enjoy great food, dancing, music, and fantastic big name entertainers at this March event.

At Hart Plaza in Detroit, Michigan, the annual **African World Festival** (third weekend in August) represents Detroit's largest cultural celebration. African crafts from around the world, the cuisine of more than twenty countries, activities, and free concerts—from reggae and jazz to pop, rhythm & blues, and gospel—allow one to explore and experience the cultures of Senegal, Uganda, Great Britain, the West Indies, or one of the several other cultures of the African people.

Mary Babin Duet
Cajun Culture
Secretary

You can ask about five different people in the South the difference between Creoles and Cajuns, and they'll all have different ideas. Cajun is short for Acadian, [from] most of the people of French descent who came down to Louisiana after their exile from Nova Scotia. They pretty much settled along the bayous, where I'm from. A lot of their economic strength came from farming—sugar cane and corn—and fishing. I call myself a true Cajun, but my blood line is mixed. A lot of us have Spanish, Indian, Irish. You name it, we have it all. I look at the Creoles as a mix with the blacks. The food seems to be spicier. Cajun French, too, is a mixture of French with Cajun slang. We were taught to speak in English at school. Now I think Cajuns are reclaiming [their] culture.

On Fat Tuesday, **Mardi Gras Day,** our parades are basically spin-offs of New Orleans' Mardi Gras parades. I'm to a generation where they changed what was once considered Mardi Gras. Everyone pitched in to a gigantic gumbo. This is not done today. And I've heard of Cajun Bastille Day, but I've never celebrated it. Perhaps my parents did. I never thought to ask. There are so many different versions and so many different perceptions based on where you live in Louisiana.

We have celebrations in the bayou for fishing season. Throughout the parishes, there are celebrations for everything. A lot of the Cajun men are storytellers. My dad was among the best of them. People think of Cajuns like people who just like to celebrate all the time. But while we're a lot of fun, we're hard-working people. I went through the black-white segregation through most of my schooling. When I was in tenth grade, we integrated. We had to change our way of doing things. They had to change theirs. Some of the black kids didn't like integration because our football teams weren't as good as theirs. But we adjusted.

We weren't racists, but we were prejudiced because of the way things were. Blacks and whites simply didn't mix. When we did [mix], we learned to get along. My father always taught us that it wasn't the color of your skin; it was who you were, inside, as a person. There were good and bad whites, and there were good and bad blacks. The person is what makes it. That's just the way it was.

Even in gangs, you have ethnic gangs, and you have white supremacists and the KKK. They're all gangs.

I'm proud of my heritage. I'm proud I was raised there. I credit a lot of that to my mom and dad who taught us to value life and people.

Like many of us, the Cajuns enjoy warm get-togethers with friends and family, and they do it well. At the festivals, there's plenty of great Cajun cooking—including Gumbo and Jambalaya. Informal gatherings offer small talk, music and dancing called two-stepping. Saturday morning jam sessions at a Eunice, Louisiana, accordian factory are a tradition.

Of the formal celebrations, those from the Louisiana Cajun culture seem to be in abundance: The **Mamou Cajun Music Festival** in June coincides with the **Jambalaya Festival** in Gonzales. The **Cajun Riviera Festival** in Holly Beach (August) starts another run of festivities. In September, Morgan City has its **Shrimp and Petroleum Festival,** and soon after, Lafayette's **Festivals Acadiens** begins. Bridge City's **Gumbo Festival** comes in October.

But every state has its celebrations, the formal and informal kinds. Some states share festive occasions. Prior to vacations or day trips, one can always contact the states or even specific cities to visit. Every state and many of those cities have visitors' bureaus or tourism centers which can provide current events of interest. A variety of regionalized magazines—among them, for example, *Mid-Atlantic Country, Southern Living, Phoenix, New Yorker*—also provide a column of current events. In the following list of celebrations across the nation, we've tried to present a sampling of some of these special events.

50-State Celebration Sampler

Alabama

Sweet Potato Festival (October)—*Tuskegee*
National Peanut Festival (November)—*Dothan*
Honoring former slave and leading American scientist George Washington Carver's sweet potato and peanut experiments. The Carver Museum, at Tuskegee Institute, houses his artifacts and papers.
Indian Heritage Festival (October)—*Huntsville*
Celebrates the southeastern Native American cultures.

Alaska

Kodiak Crab Festival (May)—*Kodiak*
Fishing is linked to this island community's roots. A Russian Orthodox priest blesses the fleet, and the celebration and athletic competition begins!
Midnight Sun Festival (June)—*Nome*
From the parade to the midnight softball tournament, festivities welcome the summer solstice.
Alaska Day Festival (October)—*Sitka*
Celebrates US Army 9th Infantry's 1867 raising of Alaska's first American flag. Parade, costume ball.
World Eskimo-Indian Olympics (July)—*Fairbanks*
Traditional competitions, dances and crafts of Native people from Alaska, Canada, and Russia.

Arizona

Navajo Nation Fair (September)—*Window Rock*
World's largest Native American fair, featuring intertribal powwow, rodeo, food, and folk arts.
Apache Jii (October)—*Globe*
Highlights include Crown Dancers, crafts, foods.
Frontier Days (around July 4 weekend)—*Prescott*
Arizona territorial capital celebrates the world's oldest rodeo, donkey softball, and more.

Arkansas

Tontitown Grape Festival (August)—*Tontitown*
Carnival, talent, crafts, fried chicken, and **homemade** pasta honor Italian priests' first grape harvest.

299

Ozark Trail Festival (October)—*Heber Springs*
Old-time fun: country fiddle-dancing, 19th Century costume contest, horseshoe pitching, down home food.

California
Philippine Fiesta Islands Fair & Expo (June)—*San Francisco*
Festival of Filipino talent, crafts, and food.
Calaveras County Fair and Jumping Frog Jubilee (May)—*Angels Camp*
Traditional fireworks, carnival, and rodeo...and more than 3,000 frogs in that world-famous contest.
San Francisco Fair (September)—*San Francisco*
From African drummers to a melange of international foods—Asian, Creole, Cajun...celebration of people.

Colorado
Durango Cowboy Gathering (September/October)—*Durango*
Cowboys' creative, artistic, leisure time talents.
Vinotok Celebration: Old European & Slavic Fall Festival (September)—
Crested Butte
Polka dancing, wine tasting, and old country stories.

Connecticut
Irish Festival (June)—*North Haven*
Folk music and dancing, sports competition, sheepshearing, and delicacies.
Brass Valley Traditional Music Festival (June)—*Waterbury*
Ethnic music—from Brazilian *capoeira* to polkas, gospel, and a folk song exchange.

Delaware
Great Delaware Kite Festival (March/April)—*Lewes*
Annual Good Friday international attraction to Lewes, the first town in the first state in America.
Nanticoke Indian Powwow (September)—*Millsboro*
Annual tribal gathering, featuring Native American storytelling, arts and crafts, dancing, and food.

District of Columbia
Greek Spring Festival (May)
Celebrates Greek culture in crafts, music, dance, and food.
Latin-American Festival (July)
A musical, cultural, and culinary celebration.

Florida

Miami/Bahamas Goombay Festival (June)—*Miami*
Features Bahamian steel drum, jazz, calypso music. Native junkanoos play cowbell and seashell music!

Billy Bowlegs Festival (June)—*Ft. Walton Beach*
Pirate parades, cannons, fireworks, and Florida's Emerald Coast gets captured by 18th Century pirates!

Georgia

Mountain Fair (August)—*Hiawassee*
Mountain crafts, cider, log-splitting, and quilting at a pioneer village.

Andersonville Historic Fair (October)—Andersonville
Two days of the War Between the North and South. Civil War music and a parade add to the event.

Hawaii

Kauai Taro Festival (October)—*Hanalei*
Crafts, leis, hula dancing, the largest taro, and poi—from cooking to eating competitions.

King Kamehameha Celebration (June)—*Honolulu*
Commemoration of King Kamehameha. Parade, lots of tropical native flowers.

Molokai Ka Hula Piko (May)—*Pu'u Nana Ka'ana*
Birth of the hula celebration.

Idaho

International Folk Dance Festival (July/August)—*Rexburg*
Dancers and foods from around the world.

Clearwater County Fair & Lumberjack Days (September)—*Orofino*
Logrolling, ax throwing, and tree climbing festival.

Shoshone-Bannock Indian Festival (August)—*Fort Hall/Blackfoot*
All-Indian Old Timers Rodeo, dancing, arts and crafts, and musical celebration.

Illinois

Swedish Days (June)—*Geneva*
Celebration of the Swedish culture, featuring the foods and crafts of Sweden—among them, *rosemaling*.

Trail of Tears Wagon Train (October)—*four counties*
Path follows Illinois' portion of the 1838-1839 Cherokee Trail of Tears. Begun in sorrow for what was, this one-week journey ends with stories and a powwow. Observe this event with reverence.

Taste of Polonia (September)—*Chicago*
An "Old World Polish Village" from *karczma* (Polish bar) to *pierogi* and polkas. Chicago's Polish population is only second to that of Warsaw, Poland.

A Gathering on the Theatiki (July)—*Bourbonnais*
The Kankakee River returns to French settlers' days in the 1700s. In canoes, the French sail down the Theatiki with crafts, stories, and foods to share.

Indiana

Columbus Scottish Festival (August)—*Columbus*
A Scottish celebration of bagpipe competitions, sheepdog herding, Scottish singers, and storytelling.

Feast of the Hunter's Moon (October)—*Lafayette*
French and Native Americans return to a fur trading outpost swap meet. Blankets, apple-head dolls, crafts, 18th Century buffalo stew, and fry bread.

Iowa

Pufferbilly Days (September)—*Boone*
Celebrates the Iron Horse, the American train.

Houby Days (May)—*Cedar Rapids*
Czech food festival, a polka mass, *kolache* eating contest, and dancing by Czechs, Moravians, and Slovaks.

Kansas

Pony Express Festival (August)—*Hanover*
Celebration of the Pony Express around 1860. Church services with a circuit rider, entertainment, food.

Dodge City Days (July/August)—*Dodge City*
The great train robbery, a treasure hunt for a $500 gold medallion, a cowboy poet gathering, **and** a five-day rodeo.

Indian Peace Treaty Pageant (September)—*Medicine Lodge*
History revisited—from Coronado's arrival in 1541 to the U.S. Federal government's 1867 treaty with Apache, Arapaho, Cheyenne, Comanche, and Kiowa tribes.

Kentucky

Fall on the Farm (October)—*Pleasant Hill*
Living history 19th Century farm demonstrations at Shaker Village in Mercer County.

Strassenfest (August)—*Louisville*
Festivities include a 10K *volks*-march, beer tasting, stone sculpting demonstrations, marionette shows, yodeling, schnitzel, and strudel!

Louisiana

Malaki Festival (June)—*Opelousas*
Celebrates African cultures with **egoongoon** (complex dance with costume), folk art, gospel, *juré* and *zydeco* music.

302

Carnaval Latino (June)—*New Orleans*
A parade, lots of food, Latino music, and arts from around the world celebrate the Latin cultures.

Maine
Windjammer Days (June)—*Boothbay Harbor*
Fireworks, seafood, sails, and a jazz band set the stage for this festival of schooners.
Common Ground Country Fair (September)—*Windsor*
An environmentally-oriented celebration of agriculture—locally-grown foods, demonstrations of sheep shearing, and weaving the wool into shawls.

Maryland
Honey Harvest Festival (September)—*Westminster*
A festival to beekeeping skills from fresh honey to sweets—even ice cream.
Banana Boat Festival (May)—*Silver Spring*
Caribbean celebration of calypso music, dance, crafts, and Trinidadian treats.

Massachusetts
Bells of New England Festival (November)—*Boston*
New England's handbell ringers bring holiday sounds to Faneuil Hall's Marketplace in merry old English spirit. One historical sidenote: When he wasn't warning colonists about unexpected visits from the British, silversmith Paul Revere crafted handbells.
Cape Heritage Week (June)—*Cape Cod*
A 15-community celebration of Cape Cod's history. Pilgrims and even visitors get involved.

Michigan
St. Ignace Powwow (September)—*St. Ignace*
Traditional dances, crafts, and new perspectives of Native American dishes are highlighted.
Norwegian Pumpkin Rolling Festival (October)—*Williamsburg*
This celebration features a one-shove pumpkin pushing competition, apple cider, Veiled Peasant Girls (fresh whipped cream and applesauce), and **blue** Chilean chicken eggs!
Emancipation Celebration (June)—*Dearborn*
Celebrates the emancipation of African slaves through drama, dance, music, and stories.

Minnesota
Big Island Rendezvous & Festival (October)—*Albert Lea*
Fur trading history relived, thanks to nearly 1,000 people from across the nation. Old-time food, candle and canoe crafts, puppeteers, and frontier souvenirs.

Scandinavian Days (June)—*Fergus Falls*
Summer Finnish Festival (June)—*Embarrass*
Spelmansstamma **(August)**—*Scandia*
   Three celebrations of each or all of the cultures of Scandinavia. Crafts, foods, music, and dance.
Viking Fest (July)—*Duluth*
   The Viking Age Players bring a historic Norse village to life.

Mississippi

Delta Blues Festival (September)—*Greenville*
   Celebrates the birth of blues music. Lots of food!
International Red Bean & Rice Festival (October)—*Jackson*
   Celebrates—what else?—Southern home cooking!
Dancing Rabbit Festival (October)—*Macon*
   Remembers the legend of rabbits that danced at the 1830 signing of a Native American peace treaty.

Missouri

Autumn Historic Folklife Festival (October)—*Hannibal*
   Mark Twain's hometown brings back 19th Century days of kettle corn, music, arts, and great stories.
Maifest (May)—*Herman*
   A celebration of German history, featuring music, dancing, a carnival, and fabulous food and drink.

Montana

North American Indian Days (July)—*Browning*
   Over 100 tribal ceremonies, parades, and dances.
Bannack Days (July)—*Bannack State Park*
   Ghost town's Gold Rush, shootouts, mock hangings, and panning for gold (dust).

Nebraska

Homestead Days (June)—*Beatrice*
   Pioneer skills, old-time fiddlers, horseshoe pitching, and square dancing celebrate 1862 Homestead Act.
Nebraska Czech Festival (August)—*Wilber*
   Accordian music, National Miss Czech-Slovak Pageant (contestants—at least 40 percent Czech—create costumes and speak in-depth about their family tree and ethnic roots) and a still-life narrative honor ancestry.

Nevada

National Basque Festival (July)—*Elko*
   Celebrates the Basque culture with native dance, wood-chopping, Basque

war whoop contest, and food.

Cowboy Music Gathering (June)—Elko
Known cowboy singers, two-steps, cowboy skill demonstrations.

New Hampshire

La Celebration Franco-Americaine (August)—*Durham*
Folk singers and dancers from Quebec, tracing family roots, crepe making, wine tasting, and Cajun music honor French Canadian heritage.

Fall Llama Fest (August)—*Durham*
Llama-shaped cookies, felt made from llama fleece, and an obstacle course for llamas!

New Jersey

Hungarian Festival (June)—*New Brunswick*
Celebrates the Hungarian culture in a street festival of music and great food.

Heritage Days Festival (June)—*Trenton*
Historical and modern-day celebration of Trenton's ethnic diversity, featuring food and music.

New Mexico

Intertribal Indian Ceremonial (August)—*Gallup*
A parade, powwow, and enormous rodeo with thousands of members of over 200 Native American tribes.

Lincoln County Cowboy Symposium (October)—*Glen Coe*
Trail rides, calf roping, stories, poetry, dancing.

New York

9th Ave International Food Festival (May)—*Manhattan*
Cajun, Greek, New Zealand, Philippine...tantalizing, tempting tastes of multicultural stew in **20** blocks!

Old Songs Festival (June)—*Altamont*
Cultural diversity in folk songs, dancing, and food.

West Indian American Carnival (September)—*Brooklyn*
Costumes, calypso, reggae, and steel drum bands, parade, and lots of food in this Caribbean festival.

Legend of Sleepy Hollow Weekend (October)—*Tarrytown*
The Headless Horseman, ghosts, a werewolf, stories, and tours of the Old Dutch Church graveyard!

North Carolina

Lost Colony Outdoor Drama (June-August)—*Mantee*
The story of the 117 English colonists who vanished from Roanoke Island between 1587 and 1590.

Curing Barn Party (July)—*Durham*
Return to 19th Century farming, folk songs, contests, tobacco harvesting and curing.

North Dakota

Norsk Hostfest (October)—*Minot*
Celebrates the largest Scandinavian population in the U.S. with Norwegian food, crafts, and music.

Potato Bowl USA (September)—*Grand Forks*
Festival features Potato Bowl football, pep rally, fireworks, and "French Friday" free fries.

Ohio

Tecumseh! Outdoor Drama (June-September)—*Chillicothe*
Sixty-five actors honor this great Shawnee leader's life.

Coshocton Canal Festival (August)—*Coshocton*
Living history tribute to the Ohio and Erie Canal.

Christmas in the American Tradition (November-December)—*Columbus*
Pennsylvania Dutch Santa, Belsnickel, and other cultures' 19th Century Christmas traditions.

Oklahoma

Will Rogers Days (November)—*Claremore*
Pioneer breakfast, parade, and birthday party.

International Brick and Rolling Pin Festival (July)—*Stroud*
Oklahoma's, England's, Australia's, and Canada's brick factories in towns named Stroud led to this brick and rolling pin tossing world championship!

Oregon

Miners Jubilee (July)—*Baker City*
Features state mining championship competition—jackleg drilling and hand mucking.

World Championship Timber Carnival (July)—*Albany*
Carnival, country music, logging crafts, and contests for log climbing, ax throwing, and wood-chopping.

Pennsylvania

Kutztown Folk Festival (July)—*Kutztown*
Celebrates Amish weddings, hex signs, *frantur*, music, and folk art.

Ligonier Highland Games (Sept)—*Ligonier*
Scottish dogs, dances, music, crafts, and men in tartan kilts.

Rhode Island

Black Ships Festival (July)—*Newport*
Honors 1854 U.S.-Japan trade Treaty of Kanagawa. Sumo-wrestling, kite-flying, sushi-making.

Heritage Day Festival (September)—*Providence*
Thirty ethnic groups celebrate their cultures with food, arts, and entertainment.

South Carolina

Juneteenth Festival (June)—*Greenville*
Celebrates the 1865 emancipation of slaves with African drumming, parade, picnic, and gospel music.

Autumnfest (September)—*Columbia*
A carnival, live catfish race, music, wine tasting, gourmet foods on the lawns of two historic mansions.

South Dakota

Fort Sisseton Historical Festival (June)—*Lake City*
Mountain men, Native Americans, and the U.S. Cavalry, 19th Century melodramas, military ball, and drills.

Sioux River Folk Festival (August)—*Canton*
A myriad of ethnic groups travel from world over to sing all types of music. Carnival and food.

Tennessee

Trade Days Festival (June)—*Trade*
From shoe cobbling and bread baking to moonshine, music dancing, powwow, and stories, they celebrate!

Memphis in May International Festival (May)—*Memphis*
One thousand artists from around the world in this bash!

Texas

Texas Folklife Festival (August)—*San Antonio*
A celebration of forty-three cultural groups who share their music, stories, food, and costumes.

CaymanFest (September)—*Port Arthur*
Celebrates the Caribbean heritage, featuring fire eating, reggae, and limbo.

Utah

Slavic Festival (June)—*Salt Lake City*
Eastern European tribute through songs, foods, and crafts—including decorated Ukrainian eggs.

Belly Dance Festival (August)—*Salt Lake City*
Learn or watch this 3,000-4,000-year-old Middle Eastern and Egyptian dance. Music, food.

Vermont

Scottish Festival (August)—*Quechee*
Try some *haggis* or one of the sheepdog trials, dancing, or game contests in this celebration.

Hildene Harvest & Craft Festival (October)—*Manchester*
Country fiddling and dancing, crafts, animals, and more in this old-fashioned fall fair.

Virginia

Celtic Festival (June)—*Leesburg*
A tribute to Celtic culture with Scottish games, bagpipes, and fiddlers, Celtic languages and crafts, Welsh choirs.

International Children's Festival (September)—*Vienna*
Cultural performances of children from around the world.

Afrikan-American Festival (June)—*Hampton*
Foods, music, material, and masks from the world's African cultures.

Washington

Viking Fest (May)—*Poulsbo*
Parade and three days of activities honor the town's Scandinavian seafarers.

Oyster Stampede (May)—*South Bend*
Blessing of the fleet, oysters any way you like 'em, and an oyster-shucking contest.

West Virginia

Dulcimer Weekend (August)—*Salem*
Dulcimer music, crafts, and food at Fort New Salem, a 19th Century Appalachian frontier settlement.

Italian Heritage Festival (September)—*Clarksburg*
Celebration of Italian culture with traditional dance, crafts, name entertainment, and great food.

Wisconsin

German Fest (July)—*Milwaukee*
Bavarian feasting and traditional music in this tribute to German heritage.

Milwaukee Irish Fest (August)—*Milwaukee*
The world's largest celebration to Irish culture and music!

Wyoming

Cheyenne Frontier Days (July)—*Cheyenne*
Celebrates the pioneers with four parades, three pancake breakfasts (free!), wild horse and chuck wagon races, military air show, Indian village and still more.

Fort Bridger Mountain Man Rendezvous (September)—*Fort Bridger*
Tribute to the days of the mountain men, traders, and Native Americans in the Old West. Similar festival at Mountain Days in June in Alpine.

Put into proper perspective, celebrations allow us the opportunity to learn about historical events and people, including ourselves and others. Under the right conditions, festive occasions can even benefit us psychologically.

Although children don't usually perceive celebrations as learning experiences, they've probably generally had fun celebrating and have been eager for more. On the other hand, as adults, many of us tend to put aside those joyful childhood events. We simultaneously learned and had fun, and then we grew up.

Every occasion—even the most minute—can and should be a reason to celebrate if for nothing else than the temporal release of daily pressures. Shared happiness with family or friends creates strong bonds that may withstand rough times. If the daily whirl of activity seems to gravitate to you, even an hour alone can be a celebration.

Depending on your personal or group needs, how much research time you're willing or able to invest, your free time in comparison to the event and, of course, your imagination, you can celebrate a lifetime of multicultural stew and never run out of new people, places and events to celebrate! Celebrations are as much or as little as you make them.

For every known person, place or event you've already celebrated, you'll discover one you never knew existed. Honor 61-year-old Annie Smith Peck who, in 1850, scaled the 21,250-foot top of Mount Coropona in Peru, or Robert Smalls, the slave who smuggled his family out of Charleston aboard one of the fastest and most valuable Confederate ships, turned the ship over to the Union and—after the Civil War—went on to serve three terms in the U.S. House of Representatives, become a major general in the South Carolina state militia, and helped to create the Parris Island Marine Base. Celebrate Peterborough, New Hampshire, home of the nation's first free public library, or Hoboken, New Jersey, home of the nation's first organized and recorded baseball game. Commemorate July 20, 1969, when Neil A. Armstrong took that first step on the moon and said, "That's one small step for a man, one giant leap for mankind," or Global Understanding Day on March 25.

A wealth of great reasons to celebrate are out there, waiting to be discovered! In the United States of America, even wacky and wonderful festivals, like the National Skillet Throw in June in Macksburg, Iowa; the International Cherry Pit Spitting Championship in July in Eau Clair, Michigan; and Crazy Day in August in Magee, Mississippi, are easy to find. If you're more creative and want a fun celebration at home, consider having a Windshield Wiper Celebration in tribute to Mary Anderson's invention, patented on November 10, 1903; celebrate Gutzon Borglum's birthday (March 25, 1871), the American-born sculptor of Danish heritage whose bust of Lincoln graces the rotunda of the U.S. Capitol Building and whose most famous work was South Dakota's Mount Rushmore Memorial; or commemorate Superman's first appearance in Action Comics on June 1, 1938.

But having fun must not preclude the use of good judgment, common sense, and heightened sensitivity to cultural and religious festivals. Know where to draw the line in your celebrations.

Religious fasts, including the Islamic, Jewish, and certain Christian denominational practices, are always observed with reverence. During *Ramadhan*, the most notable Islamic fasting period, Muslims abstain, from dawn to sunset, from food and drink every day for a month. *Eid Al-Fitr* marks the end of *Ramadhan*. After *El-Hajj*, the feast of *El-Eid-El-Kabeer*—or *Eid Al-Adha*—is celebrated during the month of *Dhu al-Hijjah*. Again, the Islamic calendar is based on lunar cycles, and religious events will vary.

In the United States of America, one's celebrations of Christmas and Easter/Resurrection Day appear to be determined by the depth of religious beliefs. Christians whose religious tenets guide their lifestyles consider the celebration of Christmas on the Gregorian calendar date of December 25 and on the Julian calendar date of January 7, or on varying calendar celebrations of Good Friday and Easter/Resurrection Day each spring, to be the most significant of the Christian holy days. Although these Christians may also recognize and participate in the commercialized aspects of Christmas and Easter, they do not lose sight of the intended reverence of these occasions.

According to the El Paso (Texas) Hispanic Chamber of Commerce, "an Hispanic version of Christmas caroling," **Las Posadas** (A Christmas Pageant) dramatizes Joseph and Mary's search for room at the inn. Participants sing and pray in a house-to-house search in this famous celebration which takes place before Christmas eve.

Not necessarily with the intention of showing disrespect for the religious significance of Christmas and Easter as Christian holy days, non-religious Christians—and even non-Christians at times—often participate in the commercialized Christmas and Easter holidays. Across the United States, exchanging Christmas gifts and visiting with the Christmas legend of Santa Claus, the legendary Easter Bunny, or their counterparts from a variety of other cultures, have become ingrained in the non-religious celebrations of these holidays and have frequently been responsible for the outgrowth of similar practices in non-Christian holidays.

Similarly, although St. Patrick's Day—universally celebrated on March 17 in the Gregorian calendar—is nationally and traditionally celebrated in Catholic Churches throughout Ireland, festivities surrounding this holiday in the United States have been substantially less holy. St. Patrick's Day parades and the "wearing of the green," corned beef and cabbage, and green beer have given a new interpretation to this originally holy occasion.

The Catholic Church honors the saints who died for their faith on All Saints Day—November 1; All Hallows Eve occurs the night before. Eventually, the name "All Hallows Eve" evolved into what is now called Halloween, a festival which grew out of Celtic and Roman festivals. Coincidentally, Martin Luther nailed his ninety-five theses to the door of the Wittenburg Church in Germany on November 1, marking the beginning of the Protestant Reformation. Today, Halloween bears little or no resemblance to its former ties to the Catholic Church, although the custom of bobbing for apples has survived many centuries of changes connected to one of the original Roman festivals.

In contrast, on the springtime Jewish holiday of *Purim*, children dress for religious services like four historical figures described in an Old Testament Bible story.

Chanukah, a minor Jewish religious winter holiday, and Passover, a major religious springtime holiday for Jews, are completely unrelated to the respective Christian holidays of Christmas and Easter, although the New Testament reference to Christ's Last Supper refers to the Passover meal, known as the *seder*. *Rosh Hashanah* and *Yom Kippur* are the holiest days of the lunar Jewish calendar.

In general, the Spanish-speaking peoples of the world tend to adhere to Roman Catholic religious beliefs. *Dia de Todos Los Santos* correlates to All Saints Day. The November 2 Mexican holiday of *Dia de Los Muertos*—Day of the Dead—celebrates the reuniting of loved ones' souls. But like Halloween, this celebration appears to be linked to combined non-Christian and Christian traditions.

The Feast of St. John the Baptist, Puerto Rico's patron saint, takes place in late June. Across the Union, people from a variety of cultures celebrate this holiday—also known as Midsummer's Day—with a combination of non-Christian and Christian themes, stories and traditions. People with Puerto Rican heritage honor their homeland's patron saint on this day which they call San Juan Bautista Day.

A number of Italian communities in the nation hold religious ceremonies and street festivals to patron saints. In cities like Boston and New York, these Catholic Church-related holidays bring song, dance, music, and plenty of food to the streets, where people from all cultures can appreciate the Italian fruits of labor and love. Many other cultures hold similar festivals rooted in their respective churches.

Listing the multitude of religious holidays throughout the world, or even across the United States of America, is a nearly impossible task, better left to theologians with a vast knowledge of every religion. With that in mind, one should avoid developing any preconceived notions about and display respect for others' religious beliefs. Tactfully asked, questions about others' beliefs, holidays, or religious practices generally won't be considered offensive if good judgment, common sense, and heightened sensitivity are used.

Although not every fifteen-year-old girl in the United States of America is fortunate enough to have a Sweet Sixteen party for her next birthday, most girls this age generally know such events exist. Perhaps the saying "Sweet Sixteen and never been kissed" led to this custom, but the Mexican tradition of the *quinceañera* may have also encouraged the rise of Sweet Sixteen parties in non-Mexican homes.

The *quinceañera* celebration of the attainment of fifteen years of age dates back to the Mayas and Toltecas; it is the age when a young woman prepares to enter adulthood. Today, a male and female court of honor—

fourteen of each sex, representing the first fourteen years of the young woman's life—accompanies the young Catholic Mexican woman to a mass held in her honor. The young woman's father presents her to guests invited to her birthday party following the Catholic mass.

Similarly, the coming of age is recognized in a religious ceremony called the *Bar* or *Bat Mitzvah* at the Jewish temple. The thirteen-year-old boy (*Bar*—son) or the thirteen- or fourteen-year-old girl (*Bat*—daughter) reads the *Torah (Mitzvah*—deed), signifying one's willingness to accept responsibilities of Jewish adulthood. Following the ceremony, a party is given in the celebrant's honor. The *Bar* or *Bat Mitzvah* can become quite costly if the family chooses to celebrate like many others do, and—like the other customs related to the coming of age—not every family elects to maintain these traditions and religious ceremonies individually.

Most cultures generally celebrate one or more harvests. In the United States of America, a traditional Thanksgiving meal—turkey, stuffing or dressing, gravy, potatoes, cranberry sauce, rolls or biscuits, a vegetable or two, and, of course, pumpkin pie—graces the table. During the 1950s, in the typical American home, the mother cooked and served the meal, and the father carved a picture-perfect turkey—at least that's what television shows back then often portrayed! But not stereotypically, in many Italian homes, for instance, lasagna or another pasta dish might have accompanied the turkey, and in many Scandinavian homes, *lefse* might have accompanied the Thanksgiving bird, just as an ethnic dish may have accompanied or replaced the turkey in other homes.

Neither rightly or wrongly, typically portrayed cultural traditions and customs vary according to individual homes, and the unique qualities of these individual celebrations create very meaningful festivities to be appreciated.

Many living history museums in the nation have Thanksgiving celebrations as well. In Plymouth, Massachusetts, for instance, visitors join the Pilgrims and Wampanoag Natives for the annual celebration on Thanksgiving Day. At the Jamestown Settlement Museum in Williamsburg, Virginia, 17th Century Pilgrims, sailors, and Native Americans share the food of that period.

Still, a number of cultures continue to share the traditions of their heritage whether or not they observe the American Thanksgiving Day. The fall harvest celebration of *Sukkot* and the spring harvest observation of *Shavuot* are considered minor in comparison to the Jewish High Holy Days, but Jewish people especially enjoy the warmth and camaraderie of these two special occasions.

The original *Oktoberfest*, spanning a 16-day period from mid-September until the first Sunday in October, celebrated the 1810 wedding of the son of the king of Bavaria. But this holiday, too, has evolved into a series of individually-inspired events coinciding with the harvest season throughout much of the United States. A fun festival of oompah bands, polkas, Strauss waltzes, knockwurst, and German beer, *Oktoberfest*, or a variation of the name and date, has stolen hearts across the nation from Helen, Georgia, to Milwaukee, Wisconsin (July), Hot Springs, Arkansas (latter part of October), to Herman, Missouri (May), to Tempe, Arizona, and to *Stiftungsfest* in Young America, Minnesota, in August.

Kwanzaa, from the East African Swahili word *kwanza*, meaning "first fruits," has taken a foothold in the black African community across the nation, often as an alternative to Christmas observances. Celebrated from December 26 through January 1, *Kwanzaa* encourages Africans to celebrate the harvest, their heritage, and family unity and to reestablish community ties. *Kwanzaa* also celebrates the fruits of African talent in a display of the people's finest song, dance, literature, and more. Uplifting words focus all eyes on the coming year. In the United States of America, many Africans have also found *Kwanzaa* an avenue of roots to their past. At the end of the week-long celebration, a *Karamu*—community-wide thanksgiving feast—is held. One who is not a member of the black African community should consider an invitation to experience this celebration as a great honor.

But many harvest celebrations assume a narrower focus and celebrate the cranberry (Harwich, Massachusetts, Cranberry Harvest Festival in September), the potato (Shelley, Idaho Annual Spud Day in September), the apple (Apple Harvest Festival in Southington, Connecticut, and Apple Butter Festival in Berkeley Springs, West Virginia, both in October) are among many of the crops, including corn and dates, honoring the harvest. One finds deep historical roots in these celebrations, roots that also return one to a closer respect for the common cultural bonds of humanity.

Cranberries, blueberries, and Concord grapes are the only major fruits native to North America. The Pilgrims called cranberries "Crane Berries" because the pink blossoms in the bogs in late spring resembled the heads of cranes. Thanks to the Native Americans who were familiar with these fruits, the Pilgrims learned how to use cranberries for food, medicine, and dye. Today, growers—in southeastern Massachusetts, including Cape Cod and Nantucket; Washington State, along the Pacific coastal region; Coos and Curry counties in Oregon; the Pinelands near Pemberton, Cassville and New Lisbon in southern New Jersey; eighteen central and northwestern areas of Wisconsin, including Eau Claire, Wood, Juneau, Waushara, Portage, Douglas, Rusk and Oneida counties; and parts of Canada, including Richmond, British Columbia, Quebec, Nova Scotia, Ontario, and New Brunswick—wet harvest this ruby gem professionally. Only four of the more than one hundred varieties of autumn's red-gold go into tasty winter holiday treats, but all create breathtaking views as they move into harvest stage. Shortly after Labor Day, fall's blazing colors surround the plush crimson-cloaked patches in the bogs, signaling the arrival of the harvest—a celebration of nature's best talents!

In Indio, California, the National Date Festival in February celebrates the culmination of the year's harvest sequence with a growing contest, variety display, beauty contest and camel rides. A possible 8,000-year-old history distinguishes dates as one of the world's oldest cultivated plants. Once grown predominantly in the Mideast, with the most varieties produced in the southern portions of Iraq, this valuable food crop has played an important role in commerce throughout the regions of the Middle East, especially in Egypt, Israel, Saudi Arabia, Iran, and Morocco.

Today, the United States also grows dates, thanks to the efforts of Catholic missionaries who brought them back to the country on their return from these hot areas. The date palms, accustomed to very hot weather, very low humidity, ample irrigation, but very low rainfall, struggled to survive in Florida. After a time, however, growers in the low desert areas of Arizona and California became successful in producing good fruits and have become active in the world marketplace, an important factor after the Desert Storm bombing devastated growing areas in parts of the Middle East.

Because dates are resistant to seeding or transplanting, the role Arizona State University (ASU) played in continuing research and production of these fruits in the southwestern United States became critically important for the future of this historical plant whose new plants and true-to-variety generational dates depend heavily on offshoots from the mother plants. ASU's arboretum has become an especially valuable resource to date production through their demonstration gardens which will protect these plants from extinction.

◎   Smaller-scale regional harvest festivals can be developed into celebrations by communities, schools, corporations and organizations. Using dates and cranberries as examples, these groups can obtain varieties, using flags to identify their respective countries or states of origin, giving the Arabic names and meanings of dates or the tribal dialect names and meanings of the cranberries. A variety of products can be obtained to display the myriad of uses for these or any other fruits highlighted in this kind of festival. Date syrup for topping ice cream can be purchased, and the Ocean Spray Grower Cooperative produces equally unique products, including cranberry honey and packaged dried and sweetened cranberries. And of course, a harvest-specific festival cookbook and bake sale can highlight the event as a fundraiser for nonprofit organizations too. Cultural groups who strive to heal historical wounds that created friction, may also consider celebrating a common harvest and shared fruits—a date tasting coffee or tea party, for instance as part of the peace-making efforts. A successfully integrated curriculum might include a focus on agricultural products through a variety of agriculturally-focused activities: creative reading, writing, and thinking skills (literature or developing compositions and short stories about specific agricultural products, country or state of origin), foreign language skills (development of vocabulary centered on some aspect of the marketplace—the products, shopping techniques, shopkeeper-consumer relationships), art mediums, geography, government, and so on. Lifestyles can also be pursued through classroom visits with people from the respective agricultural areas.

✳   At home, still smaller-scale, personalized festivals can be developed.

Even an ordinary product like bread can be celebrated in a festival. Just a few hundred years after the birth of Christ, one could have already created a list of at least seventy-two historical varieties of breads. Humankind's love affair with bread began years before, but the Greeks perfected the art.

In the years that followed the continuing development of new bread-making techniques, the finished results became more reliable, and by the late 20th Century one might have been able to count as many bread types as the cultural groups in existence. Here, too, an avenue for appreciation of the cultures can be established in a festival of breads—white, wheat, rye, pumpernickel, and black, the Eucharistic Host, Scandinavian flat bread, Irish soda bread, Jewish matzo and *challah*, French, Italian, Middle Eastern *pita*, Hawaiian, fruit breads, *stollen*, vegetable-based breads, herb breads, sweet breads, egg breads...

Eggs too can be another common ground for festivals. In the United States of America, many folks may consider them a simple and inexpensive foodsource for breakfast or lunch or, in pastel shades, as the source of a non-religious Easter egg hunt. Yet in other parts of the world, exquisite and priceless creative arts focus on the simplicity of the egg.

Fabergé, Russia's imperial court goldsmith, created works of art still coveted by collectors today. People who knew their pursestrings would never be large enough to buy a magnificent Fabergé egg considered adding marble, onyx, or other eggs to their collections. Perhaps not intentionally, the Chinese tea egg, hard-boiled and later shell-crushed, simmers several hours in a tea leaf blend of ingredients and emerges—still edible and incredibly delicious—with a well-marbled design. The Chinese 1,000-year eggs possess deeper and richer color, but they maintain an equally delectable flavor.

Many gift stores in the United States of America carry hand-painted, blown eggs that possess their own unique beauty. In the Ukraine and in several other countries, the custom of decorating eggs has become a treasured craft. Various tools, dyes, and beeswax are used to design elaborate art on blown or hard-boiled eggs.

Symbolically, in Europe, the King of France normally received baskets of eggs painted with exquisite miniature copies of artworks. But he was also given the largest egg—laid during Easter Holy Week—decorated with a red ribbon. In Europe, red symbolizes a wish for good luck. The color red in China carries a similar meaning. In fact, the predominant color in Chinese weddings is traditionally red. White, in China, symbolizes a state of mourning.

Additional common resources can be used to develop festivals and an integrated curriculum in similar ways, with apples or other varieties of fruits, maple by-products (syrup, sugar, and so on), various noodles, vegetables, wines, cheeses, coffees, or teas, herbs, spices, or oils as the event's major focus.

Thanks to people like Alex Haley, whose book and movie about his family heritage touched a vital chord in history, folks now recognize the wealth of facts one can access on the most personal level. Without implying a need for anyone to live in the past, we believe one can benefit from knowledge of that past. Hereditary disease might be prevented, and a wonderful history can be learned.

In your own family, decide which of the following categories you may want to know more about: date and place of birth; gender; hair and eye color; general adult height and weight; marriage(s); divorce(s); education; occupation; religion; major diseases, and date and cause of death.

Next, create a chart with the categories you've selected. You may want to purchase one of the available computer programs on the market to assist you with the formation of a family tree. A number of books on genealogy are also available.

Determine the horizontal scope of the search for your relatives. Will you limit your search to parents, grandparents, great grandparents and so on, or will sisters, brothers, aunts, uncles, and each of those respective families be included? Decide how many generations you'd like to research or whether you're interested in hunting as far back as you can.

Enlist the help of your living family members, and ask their help in filling out the chart. Are any family members willing to lend you available baby, scrap, or wedding books; diaries; letters; photos; certificates of achievement, birth, marriage, death, adoption, baptism, christening, confirmation; report cards and yearbooks; transcripts; pension or social security statements; proof of membership in organizations; deeds, titles; wills; loans; contracts; taxes; leases; mortgages; land rights; uniforms; badges; medals, ribbons or discharge papers; disability statements; indoctrination; Bible; written histories; traditions; reunions; naturalization papers; deportation papers; passports and visas; medical records; refugee information; newspaper clippings; licenses; family newsletters and heirloom items; obituaries and cemeteries.

When you discover essential information in any of the above sources, photocopy that which you need and return it to the family member who lent it to you. Fill in the information on your chart, if it answers one of your questions. If the information is merely a lead, slip the photocopy into a binder for easy access later. In some cases, an agency may also provide you with the information.

Although most of your immediate family and relatives may

applaud your interest and efforts in developing a family tree and history, remember that others may view your interest as a threat or invasion of privacy. Perhaps there were past events they wish to forget, even if those who had been directly involved have long since passed away. You may discover adoptions, divorces, incest, murder, and so on. As a result, you need to inform—with sensitivity, of course—your immediate and extended family about your intentions.

The Hatfields and McCoys weren't the first, nor will they be the last families to be involved in family feuds. In reality, that which occurs between nations—in the Middle East, for instance—is often nothing more than a family feud. But handled with tact, consideration, and respect, we can open the door for positive results, bringing the family closer together.

Paul Christiansen's maternal grandfather's stepmother—got that?—was a Danish immigrant with a number of children, nineteen, to be exact. An extended Brady Bunch family consisting of his, hers, and theirs. This particular side of the family established a family organization with officers who planned a reunion, various other events, and participated in the on-going development of a family tree and history.

"A few years ago," says Paul, "I was attending one of these reunions, and two new faces appeared. No one knew them, although many people were attending this reunion.

"At first, it seemed as if these men, twin brothers, were lost. But when they asked whether this was the Kristofferson reunion, people were surprised. The family lineage had a strong Scandinavian heritage, and the two men appeared to be of African descent. They were invited to join the reunion. A closer examination of the family tree revealed that they were indeed part of the Kristofferson family. In fact, these two men were more part of this branch of the family than I, since these two fellows were direct descendants of the patriarch for whom the reunion had been named."

Investigate the differences between cultural groups in your family, how records were kept, and how the last name was derived. Several generations ago, the Scandinavian cultures used the first name of the father and added "son" to form the male children's surname. In China, the last name generally goes first, and the mother often retains her name.

One should **never** conduct a search with the preconceived notion that one's self-worth is somehow connected to the results of the search. We are who we are, and our family history does not reflect any superior or inferior status on ourselves. Each of us remains our own person, accountable for our individual actions and praiseworthy for our positive deeds.

Once you begin your search, you can develop a network, and little by little, the pieces and finely-woven threads of your family history and branches of your family tree will come together. The adventure is contagious, however: Don't be surprised if other family members decide to join in on the excitement!

There are many avenues through which we can explore this multicultural world and celebrate its abundance of cultures. Classes might form teams through which they can develop world perspectives, for example, each team representing a culture. Integrated studies can be used throughout the day. Visitors from other nations can be invited to discuss their feelings about coming to a new country as well as the differences between their homelands and America, giving students an emotional understanding of others' feelings as they arrive in a new nation.

The key to any successful celebration lies in its authenticity and its regional and individual people's variations. Be sensitive to the knowledge that what is sacred to some may be secular to others, and be equally sensitive to the awareness that people outside a particular cultural group should not always celebrate events. Some celebrations are culturally exclusive.

During the early 1990s, a misunderstanding developed in a school over the use of eggs, sending a rippling effect throughout the school district and eventually the community. What had been intended as a springtime cultural activity during an art class had been offensive to a culture that viewed the project as a religious celebration. But the spring represents the continuing life cycle, when new animal babies greet the world. In many areas of the world, spring brings rebirth of the land after the long and severe winter. Animals wake from hibernation, and people celebrate by decorating eggs.

The controversy over the use of the eggs at school illustrates the complexity within and between celebrations. When we merely assume, the ground becomes fertile for disaster. Yet seasonal celebrations can and should provide an avenue for sharing intercultural traditions.

People have flocked to Sapporo, the capitol of Hokkaido, Japan, to participate in or watch annual winter snow sculpting festivities at the Japan Snow Festival. Here, those simple wintry creations many folks around the world made as children—graceful angels, roly poly snowmen, and occasional igloos—have advanced into adult-sized sparkling ice castles and more! But one doesn't have to travel to Japan for this snowy celebration.

Ice Carving and Snow Sculpting Competitions, one of approximately eighty indoor and outdoor events, fill the first weekend's fun at Minnesota's annual ten- to twelve-day Saint Paul Winter Carnival, which always begins the fourth weekend in January and ends on the first Sunday in February. Named "The Largest Event Ever Held in the State of Minnesota" in 1992, the dazzling display of ice palaces and other crystal creations has been said to rival other sculpting festivals.

Although the Carnival began in 1886, organizers did not succeed in making it an annual event until after World War II. Working with the City of Montreal, where a winter carnival had already been in place, the St. Paul organizers brought back the concept and the legend of the Canadian event. At the St. Paul Winter Carnival, the mythological magic of the Ice King, Borealis, who became Boreas Rex, and Queen Aurora, who evolved into the Queen of the Snows, unfolds at the King Boreas Grande Day Parade on the first Saturday afternoon, one of **three** parades highlighted in this phenomenal festival. Before the final night's fireworks, more than one million visitors will have attended the festivities, including golf in the snow; softball on ice; concerts, dances, and an international weekend with ethnic foods.

The very nature of the seasonal festival paves the way for cooperation and understanding. By practicing Chapter 11's proven concepts, we can avoid misunderstandings. Then, and only then, can an event or a simple school activity become a true celebration. If it's not a celebration for everyone involved, the event may become a celebration for none.

Positive learning experiences are possible when we're willing to reach out to others. A French child who spoke and understood little or no English enabled a third grade class to grow:

"The other children soon realized the boy's difficulty in communicating with the rest of us," said the classroom teacher. "Many of the students asked me if they might become his special friend. We all took turns helping even though none of us spoke his primary language. We searched the building for other French-speaking students or staff who might assist us. We could not find one person on-site who could help.

"We made it through the first day quite well. The next day, I had at least ten students come to class with French words they had learned overnight and were anxious to use these words to communicate with [him]. One student's mother had been on a mission in France and had sent several pages of French words and phrases. [His] smile that day helped to bridge the language barriers."

Another student who had only been in the United States of America for two months wanted to sit on the floor and use his hands when eating. After students discussed customs and feelings, various lessons were presented, using the child's language and symbols. Students discovered that the child was an excellent math student and may have experienced the same feelings many of them had in starting school before they'd learned to understand the language and customs.

The *4 A's of Becoming A Multicultural Individual*™ are our first step in establishing *Unity in Diversity: Awareness, Acceptance, Appreciation,* and **Application of** those principles in the world around us. Yesterday is behind us, and Today is here. Let's pave the path for Tomorrow—together!

EPILOGUE

Except for the index, we thought we had completed the book at the end of Chapter 12. But an article about Jeanie Greene appeared in a National Federation of Press Women publication, *Agenda*, sparking Paul Christiansen's and Michelle Young's interest in developing this Epilogue. Armed with the national roster, Michelle dialed the listed number for member Greene, whose singular efforts had begun to travel across the nation and even around the world. But finding her wasn't that easy: the number wasn't in service!

Undaunted, Michelle placed seven telephone calls to other members of the Alaska chapter, hunting for Greene. Finally, the two women connected, and Jeanie faxed to Michelle a story from the *Television Quarterly*, the official journal of the National Academy of Television Arts and Sciences, and the phone number for the author.

This second story, a global melange, received cover exposure in *Television Quarterly*. But ironically, below Jeanie's cover story heading were two more headings, bringing this book full circle back to multicultural stew. The lowest teaser read: Poland to Peru. The one in the middle? *"The Two Schindlers"*! Thanks to author Bert Briller for reprint permission of the *Television Quarterly* article and to Jeanie

Greene for being who she is in this world, we'd like to tie every chapter together here.

For the Forty Ninth State, A New Kind of Television

"Jeanie Greene's Heartbeat Alaska *is not a sitcom, but the exposure is really Northern and authentic. From a storefront studio with second-hand equipment she broadcasts her popular program to Indians, Aleuts, Eskimos and other Native Americans in remote villages with names like Shishmaref, Koyakok, Arctic Village and Mary's Igloo. Her amateur correspondents use their own* camcorders.*"*

by Bert Briller

ANCHORAGE—In a world where ethnic conflict is raging—where issues of "blood" have produced appalling rivers of blood—can television project an ethnic group's image without stirring up hate, can it build a people's pride without increasing prejudice? A unique, Native American-owned-and-staffed program, *Heartbeat Alaska*, is making a big impact not only in the 49th State with its very diverse population, but also in the Lower Forty-Eight, Canada, Greenland, and across ten time zones. Its success provides valuable input for evaluating television's treatment of Native Americans—and other minorities—at a time when some Americans advocate "the salad bowl not the melting pot" principle.

At the heart of *Heartbeat* is Jeanie Greene, a forty-three-year-old Inupiat Native Alaskan, who created the show, produces, directs, edits, and anchors it. For Native Alaskans, the half-hour Sunday night program is an absolute must-see. If it is cancelled, the phones ring in an angry chorus. As one viewer complained, "I waited all week for a program with our kind of people in it, and instead I got baseball."

I found Jeanie Greene in the storefront shop she's turned into a TV studio, next to a hairdresser's shop a couple of miles from downtown Anchorage. First, I asked why *Northern Exposure*, which is such a solid hit in the rest of the United States, doesn't cut much ice with Native Alaskans.

"*Exposure* is a joke," Greene says, "I zapped it when it showed tacos as part of native diet." *Heartbeat's* exposure is definitely Northern, but it's authentic—dedicated to showing the real Alaska through the eyes, ears and voices of the many ethnic groups whose ancestors crossed the Bering Straits thousands of years ago.

Greene, trained at the University of Alaska as an actress with a minor in anthropology, is articulate, dynamic, intense. Apologetically, she warns, "Don't let me bulldoze you, but I've got so much to say." And much of her energy comes from resentment at how Native Alaskans have been and are being mistreated. "In order to understand where I come from, you've got to understand what I've gone through." And that includes hearing television executives call her "that aboriginal" and other racial epithets.

But, she says, "I don't have any hatred. They did me a favor. They made me tough-skinned. I'm half white and I'm as proud of that half as I am of my Inupiat heritage."

The roots of *Heartbeat*, she relates, grew from the failure of Alaskan television to show Native Alaskans, except in negative situations. With her anthropology background, she tried to get a story on the air about Native Americans in Bethel, singing in their Russian Orthodox Church hymns lost in the Soviet Union. It was turned down "because natives are unintelligible." So she started a campaign to get native news on a local station. Armed with letters from the elders of several native villages, she got a deal to do three-to-five-minute segments of native news twice weekly on ABC's Anchorage affiliate, KIMO (from Eskimo), whose six p.m. newscasts used to be picked up by the Rural Alaska Television Network.

RATNet, as it's called, takes a selection of shows from Anchorage commercial and public stations and cable and beams them by satellite, microwave, and minitransmitters to over 240 communities in the vast wilderness (but not urban Anchorage, Juneau, and Fairbanks). The fourteen-member RAT council, which represents the audience and chooses the programs, loved Greene's segments.

To compress the story of her struggle against resistance to airing native news on commercial channels—although 17,000 of Anchorage's 250,000 population are Native—Greene finally decided to package a weekly half-hour native TV magazine program on her own. Managerial types gloomily forecast failure, but Greene says, "Telling me **no** is giving me permission to succeed."

Alaska—"The Last Frontier"—thrives on a Can-Do philosophy, relishes tackling formidable challenges, and Greene in 1992 began producing *Heartbeat* by herself in her cramped Anchorage apartment, moving out the dining room table to make space for her second-hand equipment. It was a "Mom and pep" operation. But she was soon joined by John Dimmick, an Inupiat cousin, a young sometime oil worker who serves as cameraman and keeps the vintage equipment working.

After surviving a full year in her apartment, the show finally was firm enough to set up her storefront studio on Fairbanks Street. The location allows her to get closer to some of her audience. Enthusiastic viewers often wander in asking how they can help the show.

Today *Heartbeat* has broad, if patchwork, distribution blanketing Alaska on RATNet, cable and tape; aired by Television Northern Canada across the continent; by KNR-TV Greenland; the Navajo Nation channel in Window Rock, Arizona; and picked up by various PBS stations via Tel-Star. Still, Greene worries about paying the rent.

She dreams of upgrading her equipment—two studio cameras, two field cameras and three-fourth-inch videotape and editing machines. Nevertheless, this self-taught do-it-all does complicated dissolves and moving inserts, without aiming for glitz and glamour. *Heartbeat's* strong features include videotape footage sent in by vidicam amateurs from the Arctic wastes, the tundra, the isolated outposts which get mail (weather permitting) twice a year.

The "home movies" come from remote places with names like Shishmaref and Koyakok, Coldfoot, and Kwigillingok, Arctic Village, and Mary's Igloo, but they're authentic. Gary Fife, reporter for KSKA, Public Radio in Anchorage, who does a five-minute segment of Native American news on each *Heartbeat*, says, "If Jeanie came to a tribal event with a professional crew, people would all straighten up and behave or show off. The amateurs' tapes give a natural, honest, refreshing picture of their lives."

Fife sees the program as giving natives a hand in gaining control of their own lives. His news segment surveys what is happening with native groups all over North and South America—and even Siberia.

"We're trying to tie things all together," he adds. "Natives have many common problems. If one group is solving a problem, others may learn from it. We're sharing views and showing many different sets of values—what works for the Sioux on the plains of South Dakota may not work for the Cherokee in the hills of Oklahoma. We're trying to give a picture of a reality television never showed before. We have to have our own vehicle, because nobody knows the complexities of our situation as we do."

Greene is convinced the program can reach beyond the Americas: "There's no reason our global village can't expand to include the Maoris of New Zealand." Because natives and Russians in Siberia were tuning in to *Heartbeat's* satellite transmission, a Russian journalist, Alex Lubosh, recently came here to interview Greene. Their discussions, which included a report on U.S.-Russian cooperation in counting the bowhead whale population, were carried on *Heartbeat* in both languages.

Her core concept is that natives should own their own lives and culture. She is very sensitive to what she feels is "the bootlegging of native culture."

"People from the outside are writing books, imitating native arts and crafts, telling our stories," she says. "In the name of documentation they are even robbing graves. It's all done with the best of intentions, by people who are not devious, but who are nevertheless making money from it. It's vital for us to own our own story."

She recognizes the complexity of the issues, especially in terms of each artist's right to interpret the world in his own way. Handing me a two-inch-thick scrapbook, she points out that she has played women of other races, Shakespeare's Cleopatra, Jonson's Duchess of Malfi. "Much depends on the artist's intentions and the individual situation," she says. Clippings show she also ran a dinner theater, did TV commercials, was the presenter on a local real estate program.

Natives object to being made "pets," even by social scientists. Greene tells me of an anthropologist who, true to type, grew possessive of the group she studied, the Yupiks. She'd cross her arms over her bosom and glowingly exclaim, "My Yupiks, my Yupiks." Amused, one native asked, "Why does she call her breasts '*yupiks*'?" Greene comments, "Native humor."

Fife, of Muscogee Creek and Cherokee parentage and a member of the Wolf clan, hails from Tulsa, Oklahoma. He says, "We natives are Americans' pet minority. But mostly we're dealt with in terms of 'The Poor Indian,' the Indian as Victim, the tragedies of the Trail of Tears and Wounded Knee. We're not shown as contemporary U.S. citizens. We're presented as happy dancers or dysfunctional drunks. An NBC documentary turned a whole tribe of Indians into a bunch of drunks—and won a Peabody Award for it!"

Prejudice against Native Americans stems from ignorance of history, Fife declares. "*Heartbeat* doesn't do the Sucker Story: a crying native child, a beautiful landscape, barbed wire, and a dead sheep," he says. "Broadcasters occasionally cover colorful ceremonies, but they ignore the bread-and-butter issues, the economic matters that are so important.

"Jeanie seeks out positive events. When *Heartbeat* shows a graduation ceremony, with kindergartners and high schoolers getting diplomas," Fife continues, "it touches everybody, as you were touched, and the scenes of natives' academic progress have an uplifting impact."

Natives are resentful of people from outside who think they know the land and its people. Michael Crichton recently told of a writer who visited an Eskimo village in the bush and was asked how long he'd stay. Before he could reply, another Eskimo answered for him: "One day, newspaper story. Two days, magazine story. Five days, book."

In the immense expanse of Alaska, twice the size of Texas, there are three native groups: Indians who speak some five different languages, Eskimos with four languages, and Aleuts with their own. Although one might not understand the other's language, they are interested in each other. Greene points out that she is very careful to call each group, not by the name used by anthropologists or journalists, but by the name the group calls itself: "Checking names for authenticity is one reason I have a $1,000-a-month phone bill."

"I am **not** the authority on native life," Greene stresses. "The authority is the person who lives in the bush, who has to walk on the ground of the village. We air their stories, but they are **their** stories. I use my skill as an editor, but with great respect for the people and their culture. They teach me constantly."

She emphasizes that *Heartbeat* is not the "Jeanie Greene Show." Now that it is attracting national attention, friends warn her about competition. Her answer: "If God wants to develop twenty more shows, am I going to tell Him no? The day this becomes the 'Jeanie Greene Show' is the day I lose it."

A typical show, one of six I watched, opened with shots of natives, a spirit mask, spectacular Alaskan scenery, backed by a rock song speaking of a heartbeat "loud as thunder" and proclaiming that "revolution is in the air." Greene showed clips of a local parade, with herself on a float, then introduced Fife's native news report.

This segment included stories on proposals for improving Alaska's native health care system; a meeting in Virginia of indigenous women setting up an international network; negotiations between the Mexican government and the Zapatista rebels; the Pequot Indians of Connecticut giving a $2,000,000 grant to the Special Olympics to be held at Yale next year; expansion of a Native Americans academic honor society; legal wrangling between the state of Nebraska and natives on repatriation of tribal skeletal remains and artifacts; and a Minnesota law barring the use of Indians' names on beer labels.

The programs are all broadcast in English, although occasionally there are passages in one of the native languages.

A major trend in the news Fife covers is economic growth under native self-determination. "We're calling our own shots more," he points out, "with native governments and corporations exercising more muscle under the treaties that give us sovereignty. Locally tribes are paving roads, building clinics, providing scholarships. On our lands, whether it's gaming, hunting, or access, if outsiders do business with us we have the right to tax them just as we'd be taxed in their jurisdiction."

On the same broadcast, Greene introduced a segment on how natives hunt and fish for subsistence on the North Slope. She followed with tapes of a fish-cutting contest (with the half-moon *ulu* knife) and a beaver-skinning contest in another village where the elders demonstrated traditional techniques to youngsters.

This program like many of her others boldly tackled the thorny issue of alcoholism. Although natives make up only sixteen percent of Alaska's population, they are thirty-five percent of prison inmates—most incarcerated for drinking or drug-related crimes. To fight alcoholism, Sobriety Potlatches were held in nine of the state's eleven prisons, linking sobriety to traditional rituals and family, community, and spiritual values. Greene presented tape clips from several prisons, including a "stake dance" in which the staked enemy is alcohol.

Even before that telecast Greene received warm responses from prisoners. The Native Culture Club of the Palmer Correctional facility wrote, "*Quyaanakpak* [Thanks, in Inupiat]... It really is a blessing for all of us in the institution to be touched and warmed by your program.... Many of the brothers would like a copy of the shows you have done on their home towns." Acknowledging the seriousness of natives' alcoholism, Greene's point of view is, "Don't blame others. Look in the mirror. Stop carrying the burden of the six-pack on your back. We're going to cure ourselves, heal ourselves, empower ourselves."

Another program reported on the torching of a one-room schoolhouse and other buildings in a remote community by a drunk discharged employee. The scenes of damage and the comments of villagers underlined the devastating effects of alcohol. One man said, compassionately, in jail the arsonist will get a chance to think about what he's done, to feel the sorrow of it, to learn that he did it under the influence of alcohol.

Greene tells me that as she edits the tape coming in, she's often moved to tears or to laughter. One example of native humor was a dance by an elder enacting rituals of the hunt, concluding with rubbing his stomach after the meal and finally fluttering his hand behind his backside in a gesture of relief. It was earthy humor that probably wouldn't have made it past network censors.

To outsiders, native stoicism seems to be passivity. I asked about a story in which teens were listening without visible reaction to a teacher stressing native self-respect.

Greene explains, "Their seeming dispirited, detached, [and] passive is a symptom of the oppression by Western culture. But you can't say the Tlingits, who battled the Russians, are passive. One of the strongest qualities of the Yupiks is their humbleness and ability to work together. Some hunting people trained their youths to sit straight-out in their kayaks for hours, to silently read the waves, to be master hunters. Along comes the shotgun. Pow! That defines displacement—technology taking away many aspects of the old life.

"Western culture is telling natives they're less than human," Greene stresses. "But natives have a fabulous ability to listen. They don't have to talk-talk-talk-talk. They allow others to be themselves. Have you ever been in a group of people who can handle silence without feeling awkward or having to fill the anxious moment of silence? Natives don't have the talking compulsion of Westerners."

In oversimplified terms, Native Americans have seen some of their old ways of life destroyed by the introduction of modern technology, but they have not been prepared for the new style of life, nor is there enough opportunity for them in an industrialized economy in recession. Moreover, cultural disruption is being played out in a society that segregated and debased natives.

Heartbeat gets into these sensitive areas. It covered the anniversary of Elizabeth Peratrovich, the Tlingit Indian woman who led the fight to pass an anti-discrimination law. Greene also devoted a special program to a film produced by the National Conference of Christians and Jews debunking myths and misunderstandings of Native Americans spread by the media. This presented testimony from eight Native Americans, including Fife and Wilma Mankiller, principal chief of the Cherokee nation.

Panelists called for a new study of history, an end to the vacuum of information about indigenous peoples, recognition that natives are not just a race but part of political entities having rights and treaty relations with the U.S. They stressed that the press should "take natives out of the shadows" and give them fuller coverage, because they've been on this land much longer than 500 years and can look at environmental and social problems from a more meaningful point of view—that we humans are part of this world, not dominating it.

The fight to counter media stereotypes, Fife tells me, is growing and minority journalists are joining hands. In July the Native American Journalists Association, on whose board Fife serves, met with three other associations, of Black, Hispanic, and Asian journalists.

In addition to the technology of industrial society invading the Arctic areas isolated by mountains, glaciers and enormous distances, a strong channel of contagion is television. Villagers are exposed to sitcoms and police dramas, CNN and MTV, commercials for Clairol and Nikes.

"People in the bush can't relate to the willowy blonde beside the Cadillac, nor can they afford the luxuries," Greene says. "Regular TV, which is so pervasive, is a foreign land to them. But they respond to *Heartbeat*. They see Indians and Eskimos and people like themselves. They see a different kind of beauty. The never-never-land of television, which seemed so impossible, is now attainable to them."

Yet the influence of pop culture is felt. Musically, rock has made headway. Frequently *Heartbeat* includes a music video. An Indian group, Red Thunder, features two sexy male singers who perform with passion and zeal. Their militant lyrics underline change and the consciousness of being native.

Many outsiders try to stereotype natives, want them to be their fantasy of "native," Greene says. "They think if we have a snowmobile or a telephone we're less 'native.' But my Inupiat ancestry is not diminished because I drive a car, have a fax, and call-forward."

She believes natives learn best by seeing demonstrations, and programs include reports that show the elders' skills, such as whale hunting or basket weaving. In this respect *Heartbeat* is becoming an archive of Native Alaskan culture. One program showed a native making an Eskimo drum. Some traditional materials were used, but new aluminum screws were incorporated, because they last longer. "That doesn't make the drums less authentic," Greene argues. "The sound and the song come from the heart and soul, not from the walrus skin."

The natives' warm relationship with their children is evident in segments on many *Heartbeat* programs. Two included cooking segments in which a father is helped by his six-year-old daughter. Eskimo halibut pie is not Julia Child's gourmet cuisine, and measurements are ignored, but as Greene says, "If you need exact quantities, you're in trouble" and the overall effect was charming.

Heartbeat gets some underwriting from Coca Cola, Alaska Trading Co., and Native Regional Corporations such as Cook Inlet Region, Chugash Alaska Corp. and the North Slope Borough, who are credited on the air with opening billboards. Spots can be bought on commercial stations that broadcast her show. These replace some of the public service announcements.

When prospective sponsors ask for Nielsen ratings, Greene replies, "Just get a map of Alaska. Pick any one of 240 villages out there. Put in a call and ask the operator to speak to anyone. The operator will ask for a name. Tell her, any name with an A or a B. When I get on the line, whoever answers will say, 'Hi, Jeanie Greene, we watch your show all the time.'"

Because they now have *Heartbeat* as a benchmark, natives are more critical of commercial television. When an Anchorage station did a slanted piece on drunk natives, a large number of angry viewers called Greene. She told them, "Don't complain to me; call the news director at that station. But I will try to do something to show the other side of the story."

Greene told me why she calls her production company One Sky. "I was being interviewed by a white journalist," she relates, "and as her fearful eyes looked into my fearful eyes, I felt she feared what she thought I knew. And I feared what I thought she did not know. Racial fear comes from ignorance. To be able to continue, I looked for some common ground—and thanked her for sharing her sky with me. And later I wrote a poem, 'One Sky.'

"Ultimately, we all share the earth as human beings, with all our differences and colors, different needs and ways. We need each other and need to share. Bottom line."

We'll see more of Jeanie Greene. Alaska's Governor Walter J. Hickel recently wrote her, "Your show fills a tremendous need in broadcasting not only for Alaska's Native residents but for many other Native American groups, as well as for others around the globe.

"Your dream for a Native American cable channel is a reachable goal and we want to encourage you in making it happen.... Just keep your positive focus, and we know you'll succeed."

After showing me a tape of a Native bowhead whale hunt, Greene led me to the set area where a hunter's spirit mask hangs as part of the backdrop. "The inner circle represents the earth, the outer, the heavens," she explains. "Around it are harpoons, whale flippers, seal slippers, feathers, walrus hide. The hunter's mouth is open, calling and thanking the animals and the environment with which he lives in one-ness and communication. It's a strong symbol—and I hope a symbol of its ties between native peoples and *Heartbeat Alaska*.

"I won't stop," she continues forcefully. "We've got a lot of myths to eradicate. We won't be the victims who are mired in a tragic past. Do I have hope for the natives? Absolutely. I think native peoples eventually are going to heal the world. I hope and pray that we can get to the rest of the world in time—if only by having people watch how we live and being inspired by how we work with nature."

Reprinted with permission. © Copyright 1994 by Bert R. Briller

AFTERWORD

This book has grown in length and depth in the years since we wrote the first words in November 1992. The information, concepts, and experiences presented in *Yesterday, Today & Tomorrow* represent a lifetime of learning, living, and researching for Paul Christiansen and a lifetime of learning, living, and writing for Michelle Young.

We hope each of you have discovered a part of yourself in these pages, whether you call home the United States of America or somewhere beyond—North, South, East, or West. Regardless of our individual cultural backgrounds, all of us belong to the multicultural mosaic of the world.

Each of us can make a positive difference. Read the following essay by Christiansen, and consider the importance of words as he sees them.

Much more important than one may realize, words can penetrate into the depth of one's inner being. Words can exhort, encourage, and provide hope to

333

live. Words of encouragement lead to understanding, appreciation, and trust.

Words can bring discouragement, grief, disillusionment, and even death. Words of discouragement lead to misunderstanding, prejudice, hatred, and distrust.

Not always selected by the sender, words may be a result of habits which reflect attitudes formed years before. Whether or not the receiver is aware of the motives or spirit of intent behind the words being said, the receiver will still feel their effects.

But if all meaningful and lasting change that takes place first occurs on the inside and works its way out, then the issue of negative words is two-fold: One can choose not to be affected by actual or perceived negative words, or one can choose to respond positively.

If we really hope to have a positive affect on negative words being said, we need to make our own response positive and realize that those who speak negatively usually reveal the state of their inner being.

As effective as air, water, and food in providing for life, words are not just words. Just as life—the positive interaction between people—should be far more than existence and survival, words should be well-chosen, delivered in a timely fashion, and intended to help others understand and appreciate who we really are and how we truly feel about them. Our verbal connection to people in our lives can lead to respect for ourselves and others.

It's easy to respect and love those we think respect and love us, but true respect and love shouldn't be contingent on how others treat us. Our actions and behaviors don't necessarily indicate who we are or the values we hold. Although one's behaviors are extensions of the individual, our focus needs to be on the individual, not [on] the behavior.

More than a series of properly placed letters and sounds, words are powerful. Maybe dictionaries should come with a warning label: "Caution! The contents of this book could be injurious to yours' and others' health." Let our words demonstrate respect, gratitude, encouragement, and empathy, so we can live and work together within our diversities.

A tremendous network of people, organizations, institutions, and corporations throughout the United States of America gave us access to our own surprising and exciting discoveries—among them, the stories about the Buffalo Soldiers, Chiune Sugihara, and Maria

Segal. These colorful and essential threads wove the exquisite tapestry which became *Yesterday, Today & Tomorrow: Meeting the Challenge of Our Multicultural America & Beyond.*

GLOSSARY

Absolutes: Universal truths upon which nations, societies, or cultures need to be developed to achieve stability, security, and productivity.

Acceptance: Action or behavior between individuals, providing a foundation for the establishment of positive relationships; second stage of the 4 A's of Becoming A Multicultural Individual™.

Accommodation: The fitting, or adjustment of any particular person, purpose, or thing to a situation. Booker T. Washington proposed a policy that urged education and success training for black African Americans when socioracial segregation was still accepted.

Acculturation: The process by which one culture is integrated into another culture. One cultural group tends to dominate and change the cultures of other groups in this process.

Add-On Approach: The creation of a facade of being multicultural by linking pre-existing programs and projects. Often, the methods used result in isolation.

Adopted Culture: The setting aside of all or most of one's birthright culture in favor of another culture, usually in response to outside pressures to conform.

Affirmative Action: Legislative mandates which attempt to create equal employment opportunities. Unfortunately, these mandates frequently create tokenism.

"Aimers": A nickname for the American Indian Movement.

Americanization: A theory of unilateral assimilation in which immigrants to the United States adopt the existing American culture, completely giving up their own cultures.

Anglo: Not representative of all members of the so-called white race, this usually negative term refers to the segment of society that possesses British American values and traditions.

Anti-Defamation League: This branch of the national organization of B'nai Brith is devoted to the equality of all people and the elimination of stereotypes.

Anti-Semitism: Most often related to anti-Jewish sentiment or actions, this term, literally defined, refers to hostility or discrimination against Semitic peoples.

Apartheid: Apartness or segregation. A situation in which members of a culture are forced to live separately from members of the dominant culture.

Application: Putting methods, strategies, or concepts to use; the fourth stage of the 4 A's of Becoming A Multicultural Individual™.

Appreciation: Valuing and enjoying cultural diversity; the third stage of the 4 A's of Becoming A Multicultural Individual™.

Aryan: Also called Indo-European or Nordic, this term refers to people with northwestern European roots. Adolf Hitler's goal to create "a master race" gave increased importance to this term during World War II.

Assimilation: The process through which people of different cultural groups become part of a larger community, often losing their original identity. This process may be multi- or unilateral.

Attitudes: Preconceived notions, beliefs, and values which are transmitted and displayed by various means, including verbal and nonverbal communication.

Awareness: Growing knowledge of the existence of a situation; the first stage of the 4 A's of Becoming A Multicultural Individual™.

Bias: Favoring certain ideas, values, things, or people.

Bicultural: A grouping in which two cultures are represented. One culture may be more dominant than the other. Having a bicultural setting is no guarantee of the two cultures intermingling or living compatibly with each other.

Bigotry: A state of intolerance. The act of stereotyping, which generally results in prejudicial acts against particular groups or individuals.

Bilingualism: The ability to communicate in two languages. Being bilingual, however, is not necessarily a sign of being a multicultural individual.

Biracial: The offspring of parents whose genetic heritage stems from two different races.

Birthright Cultures: The customs and traditions of one's roots.

Black Codes: Post-Civil War laws included in the constitutions of southern states to govern former slaves.

Blacks: A label often used to refer to African Americans.

Blend of Cultures: One or more of a culture's attributes being assimilated into another culture.

Blood Type: A genetic physical trait transmitted to offspring. The four human blood types are A, B, AB, and O.

Bootlegging of Native Culture: The marketing of a culture by someone from another culture.

Boycott: To combine against; the refusal to buy a certain product or any product in a particular store.

Caste System: A means of determining one's socioeconomic status. This determination results in benefits or restrictions according to one's birth.

Categorically-Identified: The systematic labeling of a person or group, often by ethnic or racial classification.

Caucasoid: Anthropological classification of the so-called white race.

Character: One's composite attributes formed as a result of the display of attitudes and behaviors.

Chattel Slavery: An item to be bought, sold, and used as an owner sees fit; in this case, a human being.

Chicanos: A name sometimes used to refer to Mexican Americans; a sporadically offensive term.

Civil Rights: Equal opportunities and benefits for all citizens in accordance with the United States Constitution's Bill of Rights.

Civil Rights Movement: Organized effort to gain equal rights for minority groups.

Colored: A label sometimes used to refer to all non-white people; since the 1960s, considered a highly offensive term.

Commonwealth: A state in which the people make the laws; a republic.

Concentration Camp: An enclosed guarded area where political enemies or aliens are held.

Controlling Ideas: Perspectives which direct people's actions. Each culture has its own set of controlling ideas, sometimes called cultural values.

Cross-Cultural: The interaction of cultures; generally related to an individual from one culture who lives and/or works in another culture.

Cultural Cleansing: An attempt to eliminate an entire group of people, usually based on cultural differences. Genocide, or holocaust.

Cultural Diversity: A multicultural setting in which a group of people, communities, or nations exist, where a variety of cultures are represented.

Cultural Group: A body of people sharing the same culture. Cultural grouping represents a portion of each ethnic group.

Cultural Heritage: The combination of one's racial/ethnic roots and the attitudes, beliefs, values, and behaviors transmitted by those who have reared the individual.

Cultural Identification: Classifying a person according to physical and/or behavioral characteristics. This classification may also include a culture to which one relates, whether or not that culture is one's birthright.

Cultural Pluralism: A condition in which people from different cultural groups live together in harmony and mutual respect, each retaining its cultural identity and many of its traditional ways. Some degree of assimilation or acculturation may occur.

Cultural Traditions: The common practices and lifestyles within a family, society, or nation.

Culturalization: The process of assimilating a culture.

Culturally Literate: An individual who is multicultural in knowledge as well as in action.

Culturally-Centered: Attentiveness to specific aspects of any particular culture.

Culture: The way of life, thought, traditions, and customs of a people.

Defacto Segregation: Habitual separation of any group of people by custom, rather than by law.

De Jure Segregation: Legally mandated separation of any group of people.

Desegregation: The process of removing separation of any group of people in order to achieve balance.

Dictator: A leader who exercises absolute authority—often oppressively or brutally—over a group of people.

Discrimination: The ability to make fine distinctions, or the treatment of or attitude toward an object, person, or group.

Emancipation Proclamation: President Abraham Lincoln's January

1, 1863, speech, freeing slaves in territories rebelling against the the Union (United States of America).

Emigrant: From one's homeland perspective, the person who has left the native country to live in another land.

Equal Rights: Identical opportunities for every person, regardless of cultural identification.

Ethnic Groups: Ethnicity. A body of people united by complex and common cultural traditions, such as nationality, language, religion, and customs.

Ethnic Role Models: Those people in a specific group who are recognized as worthy of emulation.

Ethnically-Identifiable: The categorization of an individual according to visual perception.

External Stimuli: Outside forces influencing any situation.

Extremism: A tendency toward immoderate or excessive policy or action, especially in relation to political matters.

False-Assumption Concept: The development of stereotypes.

Finessed Racism: Cloaked prejudice, where racism is attempted to be hidden through patronism and excessive gestures of acceptance.

First World: An implied but seldom used reference to world power and leadership as a result of highly advanced technology.

Freedom Rides: The active attempt of racially-mixed groups of people in the South to integrate buses and bus terminals during the late 1950s.

Genes: A protein molecule of the germ fluid DNA which transmits hereditary characteristics.

Gene Theory of Heredity: The concept of inherited physical trait determination passed from parents to offspring. This premise has sometimes been used by people who try to validate a case for racial superiority or inferiority.

Generalizations: The formulation of opinions or ideas whether or not they're accurately based; false assumption; stereotypes.

Genocide: The planned killing of a people and their culture.

Ghetto: A city sector where certain groups were once required to live. Since the end of World War II, the word has come to mean a city's inner, or lower, socioeconomic areas.

Global Community: A contemporary term for the earth or world; all peoples of the world.

Globalism: A synonym for worldwide perspective.

Heritage: An individual's inherited racial, ethnic, and cultural roots.

Holocaust: From a Greek word meaning "total destruction by fire"; an attempt to completely eliminate a group of people; genocide.

Homogenization: Melting pot; unification; conformity. The combining of a group's values without regard to cultural differences in order to achieve uniformity in expected behaviors.

Hyphenated Americans: People who have been simultaneously classified by their ethnic backgrounds and American roots.

Identification Group: A classification to which individuals relate and conform their values and behaviors.

Immigrant: From the new homeland perspective, one who enters the new country with the intent of calling this new land "home."

Infrastructure: The avenues through which cultures discover common ground and establish effective communication.

Infused Approach: An historically complete, inclusive, and accurate method of applying multicultural principles.

In-Group: A peer group's social mores, including common interests, attitudes, values, and so on.

Inherited Belief Systems: One generation's values passed to the next generation.

Integrated Curriculum: A learning program into which several subject areas have been infused.

Integrated Thematic Unit: More comprehensive than integrated curriculum, this program presents ideas based on a particular focus.

Intercultural: Between two or more groups of people whose roots may differ.

Interdependence: Multicultural mode. Cooperation; trading; the reliance on others to exchange goods and services.

International Mobility: The ability to move freely and effectively between cultures and world regions.

Isolationism: Separatism, rejection. Refusal to interact.

Jim Crow Laws: Once legally enforced segregation that took place in the United States.

Know-Nothing Movement: A political movement in the United States that strongly opposed open immigration from 1853-1856. The name "Know-Nothing" stemmed from participants who denied knowledge of the party's activities.

Legislative Quota: A country's laws establishing specific limits of people who will be allow to immigrate.

Mainstream: Acculturation; cultural assimilation. The integration of minority and majority cultures.

Melting Pot: A theory of multilateral assimilation consisting of a great intermingling of cultures in which all lose their individual identities to the pre-existing culture.

Melanin: The genetically-produced chemical that determines the degree of skin pigmentation one possesses.

Mongoloid: Anthropological label for the so-called "yellow race" when used as a proper noun.

Monocultural: Can be related to the melting pot theory in which all people are viewed as coming from one mold. A form of unification.

Monoracial: An individual possessing the genetic characteristics of one of three specific classifications of peoples: Caucasoid, Mongoloid, or Negroid.

Multicultural: A state of mind which, when applied on a continual and active basis, accepts all people as individuals whether or not all of their beliefs, attitudes, and behaviors are compatible with those of others.

Multicultural Curriculum: Culturally diverse, inclusive content designed to provide instruction/training of specific subjects/topics.

Multiculturalism: Culturally diverse, inclusive mission, purpose, or philosophy; the foundational beliefs upon which a corporation, organization, program, or curriculum is based.

Multiculturally-Based Education: Culturally diverse, inclusive foundation from which all instruction/training emanates.

Multiculturally-Infused: Culturally diverse, inclusiveness placed into an existing corporation or organization, or into a pre-existing program or curriculum. Multicultural infusion is the opposite of the Add-on Approach.

Multiculturally-Oriented Strategic Plan: Diversity-based set of specific guidelines from which an organization or corporation operates.

Multilateral Assimilation: The type of assimilation that takes place when the nondominant and dominant environments mingle and interact to produce a more or less new culture.

NAACP: National Association for the Advancement of Colored People.

Nationalism: Unity borne out of a strong sense of belief in a country.

Native Peoples: The indigenous people from any of the world's regions.

Nativist: Label for some advocates of prejudice and discrimination against immigrants to the United States of America.

Naturalized Citizen: One who has immigrated to another nation and has legally assumed permanent equal status with people of the adopted nation.

Nazi: A member of the National Socialist German Workers Party.

Negroid: Anthropological label for the so-called "black race," also referred to as "Negro," a Spanish word meaning black.

New Immigration: The 1881-1920 wave of migration to the United States from southern and eastern Europe including Poland, Russia, Italy, Baltic States, and Greece.

Niagara Movement: Organization founded by W.E.B. DuBois to promote civil rights through active protests against segregation.

Nisei: Label describing Americans with Japanese ancestry.

Of Color: A reference to minority classification based on skin pigmentation.

Old Immigration: The migration from northern European countries, especially from Ireland, to the United States from the 1840s to 1880.

Open Immigration: A policy allowing people to move freely from one country to another.

Out-Group: People whose interests, attitudes, values, and so on do not align with those of their peers' social mores. The peers often consider members of this group inferior.

Parochialism: Narrow in scope, exclusivism.

Pluralistic: Comprising more than one element; a type of society in which people of different cultures live side by side without dominance of any culture.

Pogrom: Organized massacre of a group, especially in relation to minorities.

Polarization: The result of a specific group's division by a particular issue which places the majority into one of two groups holding opposing views.

Prejudice: To be against certain ideas, values, things, or people. An unreasonable and hostile attitude toward a certain group. Judgment not based on fact. Prejudgment.

Quota System: A method of limiting numbers of immigrants allowed into a particular country from another country. United States immigration laws used a quota system from 1921 to 1965.

Race: Classification of people by specific anthropological definition. Because these labels are based on widely varying inherited physical characteristics, the resulting controversial categories are often vague, contrived, and difficult, and are used at times to isolate and disempower people.

Red: A label sometimes used to refer to Native American people.

Relocation Centers: Guarded camps where perceived enemies of the United States of America were forced to live during World War II.

Reservations: Tracts of land set aside by the United States government, once forcing Native American people to live there.

Scapegoat: A person or a group of people whose have been blamed for a situation. Originally, someone or something—a goat or a sheep—made to shoulder blame for mistakes or sins for another.

Second World: An implied, but seldom used term referring to countries in the midst of technological development.

Segregation: The situation in which people or objects are are separated.

Self-Esteem: One's mental vision of the kind of person they believe they are.

Self-Image: A mental vision of the kind of person one is or would like to be.

Social Codes: The unwritten set of common value standards through which a group or society interrelates.

Social Laws: The written set of common value standards through which a group or society interrelates.

Social Mores: Common values from which social codes and laws are established.

Social Undesirables: A group of people whose physical traits, attitudes, beliefs and/or behaviors have not been accepted by the majority.

Socioeconomic Backgrounds: The family history of an individual based on income and financial holdings.

Socioeconomic Bigotry/Prejudice: Acting on prejudicially held beliefs that one's value and quality are linked to the level of income and financial holdings.

Slave Codes: Laws enforced by harsh punishment as a method of controlling others.

Statistically-Labeled: The classification of groups based on predesignated, mathematical factors.

Stereotype: A generalized perspective of an entire group based on often isolated occurrences; for example, if a person buys a certain model of car that turns out to be a financial headache, the person may develop an aversion to purchasing that type of car again. One may also stereotype a specific group of people by certain dishes they eat, especially if these dishes are unfamiliar to the viewer's way of life.

Third World: A widely-used but misleading term referring to countries whose technological development may not be as advanced as that of other nations.

Token: Representing a particular group; often an official concession based on a demand.

Tolerance: A form of neutralizing or coping with differences between people. Forced tolerance can breed hostility.

Totalitarian State: Complete government control of the people.

Transition: The process of moving from one place, position, attitude, or behavior to another.

Transmission: The passing on of values, beliefs, attitudes, practices, or behaviors between individuals or groups of people.

Unacculturated: Not adapted to; living within a specific culture while remaining isolated by a failure to follow that culture's basic ways.

Unification: The result of bringing separate entities together—whether or not all of the people involved favor such a move.

Uniform Standards: Commonly held values, generally accepted codes providing the basis to which members of a specific culture conform.

Unilateral Assimilation: When a person or a group of people accept, or are forced to accept a dominant individual or idea.

Unity: The result of bringing separate entities together in harmony.

Unity In Diversity: A theme in which separate entities are brought together in harmony through the philosophy of this book.

Values: That which one considers good and essential to one's behavior and lifestyle, including ethics, knowledge, choices, and priorities.

WASP: White Anglo Saxon Protestant. A negative term referring to Caucasians; however, the term is a misnomer because not all Caucasians are Anglo Saxon, and not all Caucasians or Anglo Saxons are Protestant.

White: A label sometimes used to refer to Caucasians.

Women's Suffrage: Ratified on August 28, 1920, the 19th Amendment of the United States Constitution which gave women the right to vote.

Yellow: A label sometimes used to refer to Mongoloids.

INDEX

350

166, 267
Pisa, 134
Rome, 113, 166
Sicily, 57
Palermo, 64
Ives, James Richard, 64
Ives, Minerva Brugh, 64
Ives, Walter Richard, 63

J

Jackson, Jesse, 210
Jacob, 160
Jacobs, Dr., 85-87
Jahan, Shah, 188
Jamaican, 140
James, Jesse, 63
Japan, 108, 157, 193, 202, 204, 209, 213-218, 221, 223, 233, 239, 241-242, 292
Hokkaido, 241-242
Sapporo, 320
Honshu
Kobe, 217
Tokyo, 213-214, 216, 225
Yao-tsu, 213
Okinawa, 222
Japanese, 20, 52, 142, 181, 204-205, 211-213, 215-217, 219-224, 231, 241-242, 265, 273
Japanese American, 212-213, 218
Jefferson, Thomas, 33, 36, 57, 281
Jensen, Mr., 61
Jesus of Nazareth , 158
Christ, 107, 188, 221, 291, 311, 316
Jewell, Daniel, 63
Jewell, Elias, 63
Jewell, Gladys, 63
Jewell, Sarah Clapp, 63
Jewish, 6, 13, 17-20, 52, 79, 82-84, 88-90, 92, 113, 124, 127, 153, 157, 162, 173, 175, 182, 213, 215, 217, 220, 266-267, 280-282, 311, 313
Jew(s), 7, 28, 52, 81-83, 88-91, 109, 112-114, 124-125, 157-163, 173-176, 208, 212-214, 216, 218, 267, 281, 310-311
Marranos, 113
Jewish American, 215, 266
Jimmu, Emperor, 221
Joan of Arc, 114

Johnson, James Weldon, 126
Johnson, Lyndon B., 135, 194-195, 235
Johnson, Ragnar Calab, 60
Jonson, Ben, 327
Jordan, 162-164, 175
Amman, 164
Jordan and Israel peacemaking effort, 164, 184, 316
Jordan, Frank, 215
Jordanian, 173, 176, 179
Joseph, Chief, 15, 17
Judaism, 157-158

K

Kai-shek, Chiang, 205
Kamehameha, King, 301
Kansas, 62-63, 146-147, 273, 302
Bogue, 273
Dodge City, 302
Fort Leavenworth, 141, 147, 200
Fort Scott, 147
Galva, 64
Hanover, 302
Kansas City, 52
Lawrence, 146
Medicine Lodge, 302
Mt. Hope, 63
Nicodemus, 147-148, 150-151
Osawatomie, 146
Ottawa, 62-63
Quindaro, 146
Wichita, 63
Kapos, 85-87
Kasunich, Anthony Thomas, 60
Kasunich, Ruth, 60
Kaufman, Barbara, 215
Kazakhstan, 104
Kennedy, A.J., 63
Kennedy, Elma, 63
Kennedy, John, 62
Kennedy, John F. (JFK), 34, 130, 193-194, 220
Kennedy, Robert F., 130
Kentucky, 131, 150-151, 273, 302
Louisville, 302
Pleasant Hill, 302
Kerensky, Alexander F., 100
Kerner Commission March 1968 report, 135

Maldonado, Sergio, 15-17
Mandela, Nelson, 138
Mankiller, Wilma, 330
Maori, 237, 241, 326
Marconi, Guglielmo, 34
Maronites, 174
Marquesas Islands, 225
Marranos. See Jewish.
Marrow, Alfred J., 261
Marshall, Thurgood, 130
Martino, Julia, 59
Martino, Peter, 59
Maryland, 107, 303
  Baltimore, 276
  Silver Spring, 303
  St. Mary's City, 276
  Westminster, 303
Massachusetts, 40, 131, 276, 303, 312, 314
  Boston, 12, 33, 37, 303, 312
  Cape Cod, 303, 314
  Harwich, 314
  Nantucket, 314
  Plymouth, 276, 313
  Salem, 276
  Sturbridge, 276
Maya, 312
McBride, Mimi, 44-47
McCarthyism, 52
Mead, Margaret, 228
Medes, 28, 161
Medieval Period. See Middle Ages.
Medo-Persian, 160
Melanesian, 232
Melkites, 174
Mendelssohn, Moses, 281
Meredith, James, 129
Methodist, 63, 108, 235
Mexican, 2, 3, 15, 21, 23, 41-43, 47-48, 54, 56, 142, 170, 294-296, 312, 328
Mexican American, 191
Mexico, 40, 48, 54, 158, 190, 206, 294-296
  Acapulco, 13-14
  Dolores, 294
  Juarez, 295
  Mexico City, 294
  Puerta Vallarta, 225
Michigan, 40, 303
  Dearborn, 174, 277, 303
  Detroit, 135, 174, 297

Eau Clair, 310
Flint, 174
Lansing, 174
St. Ignace, 303
Williamsburg, 303
Middle Ages, 113-114, 161, 186, 278
Middle East, 83, 94, 124-125, 127-129, 155-157,159-164,168,170,174,177, 182-186, 189, 231, 248, 308, 315, 319
  Palestine, 113, 124, 156, 161-163, 173, 177, 266, 315
Middle Easterner, 155, 164, 183-184
Mideast, 53, 155, 168, 315
Military, 140-141, 166, 168, 176, 194-195, 198, 220, 264, 273
  1st Kansas Colored Infantry, 147
  8th Military Region (Cambodian Navy), 200
  9th & 10th U.S. Cavalries, 146-147
  20th Infantry Intervention Brigade, 200-201
  41st Infantry Division, 264
  54th Massachusetts Regiment, 147
  92nd Infantry Division, 133-134
  100 Nisei Veterans, 213, 215
  163rd Infantry (Montana), 264
  365th Regiment, 134
  366th Regiment, 134
  370th Combat Team, 134
  442nd Regimental Combat Team, 213, 215, 219
  509th Tach Battalion, 133
  522nd Field Artillery, 213, 215-216, 218
  Allied soldiers [Allies], 213, 238
  American GIs (soldiers), 105,140,216, 218, 265, 279
  American Troops in Vietnam, 193-195, 279
  Australian Navy, 236
  B Company of the 163rd Regiment, 264
  Bravo Company, 195
  British Army, 83, 161
  Buffalo Soldiers, 132-133, 147, 273, 335
  Cambodian Army, 198
  Charley Company, 195
  Egyptian Army, 128
  English Army, 233
  Green Berets, 83

Index

268
Genes, 70, 150, 279
Genetic, 26, 283
Genocide, 28, 95, 122
Global (-ism), 12, 34, 56, 121, 139, 152, 157, 187, 190, 192-193, 209, 234, 242-243, 251, 256, 259, 290, 323, 326
Heritage (Heredity), 2-3, 6, 17, 26, 29, 35-36, 39-42, 44, 47, 51-52, 55, 61, 66-69, 73-75, 95, 104-106, 108, 127, 139, 150, 170, 175, 177, 184, 212, 221-222, 224, 235, 278, 280, 283, 287, 298, 307-308, 310, 312-314, 317, 325
Hierarchy for Developing, Implementing, and Evaluating Multicultural Goals and Objectives [Paul D. Christiansen], 271
Holocaust, 82, 92-97, 199, 204
Homogeneous (-eity), 29, 223
Homogenize (-ation), 12, 19, 259
Ideas, 29, 261-262, 264, 294
Identity, 47, 67, 103, 106, 116, 137, 142-143, 151, 191, 218, 241
Ignorance, 14, 29, 73, 91, 150, 327, 331
Immigrant, 57, 59-61, 71, 73, 106, 111-112, 116, 152, 190, 220, 234, 275
Immigrate (-tion, -ting), 11, 13, 38, 59, 115-116, 136, 190, 208, 233-234, 242
Indentured servitude, 51-52, 125, 152
Integrate (-ting, -tion), 41, 50, 71-72, 83, 126, 133, 135, 137, 235, 269, 280, 298, 320
Intercultural, 8, 128-129, 141, 186-187, 222, 248, 255, 292, 296, 320
Intermarriage (-ied), 54, 74-75
Intolerant (-ance), 129, 259, 261
Isolate (-tion, -ting), 20, 26-27, 55, 221, 261
Issue, 40, 53, 55, 76, 92, 97, 129, 163, 192, 239, 253-254, 260, 266, 273, 324, 327
Joke, 47, 68, 70, 73, 172, 281
Label (-ed), 54, 56, 74, 121, 156, 248, 283
Language, 26, 39, 42, 44, 49, 52, 75-76, 103, 105, 107, 109, 111, 116, 128, 137, 139, 143-144, 152, 171, 173, 175, 179-182, 197, 208, 222, 224,

229, 231, 255, 266-267, 270-271, 291, 308, 316, 321-322, 326-328
Mainstream, 45, 47
Mandate, 102, 162, 177, 250, 252-253
Manifest Destiny, 54
Melting pot, 11, 30, 51, 59, 136-137, 324
Misconcept (-tion), 12, 16, 46, 183, 278
Mistrust, 28, 202
Misunderstanding, 28, 259, 321, 330, 334
Monoculture (-al), 54, 282
Monoracial, 278
Mosaic, 31, 190, 224-225, 228, 243, 333
Multicultural, 7-8, 11-12, 27-28, 44, 47-50, 54-56, 106, 179, 207, 210, 243, 249-256, 259-260, 263-265, 269, 271, 278, 282-284, 320, 333
Multicultural Stew, 6, 12, 305, 309, 323
Nationalism (-istic), 12, 59, 104, 130, 205, 259
Negative (-ism, -ity), 2-3, 7, 17, 28, 40, 48, 55, 92-94, 96, 141, 151-152, 202, 260, 262-263, 271, 279, 287, 325, 334
Notion, 95, 142, 262, 319
Partnership, 255
Perceive, 55, 69, 71, 97, 123, 145, 149, 153, 206-207, 243, 247-248, 250-251, 264, 283, 287, 309, 334
Perception, 17, 40, 47, 55, 64, 95, 97, 122-123, 149, 206, 211, 228, 247, 250, 264, 278, 287, 297
Persecute (-tion), 28, 51, 57, 110, 112-114, 159, 174-175, 207, 214, 243, 280
Perspective, 7, 28, 38, 40, 53-56, 74, 75, 77, 92, 100, 122, 124, 140-142, 149-151, 187-188, 241, 247, 249, 252-253, 268, 272-273, 279, 292, 303, 309, 320
Pigmentation, 26, 95, 139
Polarize (-ation), 28-29, 76
Prejudice, 6-8, 12, 16, 22, 29, 37, 43, 49, 52, 60, 93, 128, 135, 144, 147, 168, 183, 196, 229, 231, 242, 254-255, 260-264, 273, 280-282, 287, 298, 324, 334
Quota, 166, 190, 250
Race, 26, 28, 78, 92, 97, 112, 123, 131,

(YMCA), 71
Orient, 35
Oswald, Lee Harvey, 130
Ottoman Empire, 107, 161
Owens, Jesse, 126

P

Pacific Islands, 228, 237
Pacific Rim, 224, 242
Paderewski, Ignace Jan, 66
Pahlavi, Mohammad Reza, Shah, 165, 167-168, 176
Paine, Thomas, 33
Pakeha, 241
Pakistan, 188-189
Palestinian, 163, 176-181
Panama, Panama City, 225
Papua New Guinea, 187, 228, 231-232
Papuan, 232
Parks, Rosa, 34, 126
Parsi, 167
Pasternak, Boris, 101
Patria, 64
Peck, Annie Smith, 309
Pennsylvania, 157, 276, 306
   Erie, 114
   Germantown, 62
   Kutztown, 306
   Ligonier, 306
   Philadelphia, 34, 136
   Pittsburgh, 60, 108
Pennsylvania Dutch, 306
Pequot, 328
Peratrovich, Elizabeth, 330
Perestroika, 103
Perez, Shimon, 176
Peron, Juan, 39
Perry, Matthew Calbraith, 221
Persia. See Iran
Persian. See Iranian
Persian Empire, 28, 169
Persian Gulf, 50, 94, 169
Persian Gulf War, 177, 179, 233, 273
Peru, 228, 309, 323
   Lima, 224-225
Peter I, Czar, 101
Peter the Great, 101, 114
Petitte, Bernard "Polly," 18-19, 82
Petitte, Gerard "Jerry," 7, 82

Petitte, James B. "Jim," 19
Petitte, Sonia Feinbloom, 6-7, 19, 79, 81-82
Petrulis, Antonija, 103-105
Philippine, 200. See also Filipino.
Philippines, 163, 193, 200-201, 233, 305
Phoenician. See Lebanese.
Pilgrim, 303, 313-314
Planter, 131
Plaut, Max, 84-87
Plotkin, Albert, 281
Pogroms, 113-114
Poitier, Sidney, 126
Pol Pot, 28
Poland, 90, 102, 104, 112-114, 214-215, 301, 323
   "God's Playground," 66
   Okuniev, 90
   Warsaw, 89-90, 112, 301
Polish, 5, 65-66, 71, 73, 89-90, 106, 111, 216, 301
Poles, 28, 66-67
Polish American, 65-66
Polo, Marco, 35, 157
Polynesia, 237
Polynesian, 193, 233
Pony Express, 302
Poon Sai Kai "Dad," 208
Pope John Paul II, 23
Portugal, 248
Portuguese, 14, 124-125, 156, 188, 202, 223, 266
Powell, Colin, 147
Powers, Julie Ann, 274
Presbyterian, 62
Presley, Elvis, 37
Prince of Wales, 79
Prokofiev, Sergei Sergeyevich, 101
Protestant, 29, 72, 266
Protestant Reformation, 311
Publications Articles/Essays/Short Stories
   "Accommodating an Increasingly Diverse Workforce," 251
   "Cask of Amontillado (The)," 1
   "Celebration of America and Prayer (In)," 50-53
   "Coming to America..." series, 58
   "Diversity," 249
   "He's Cherishing the Old Ways," 41
   "Letter from an American Farmer," 34